Thinking Computers and Virtual Persons

Essays on the Intentionality of Machines

Thinking Computers and Virtual Persons

Essays on the Intentionality of Machines

Edited by

Eric Dietrich

Program in Philosophy and Computers & Cognitive Science
Department of Philosophy
State University of New York at Binghamton
Binghamton, New York

Academic Press
San Diego Boston New York London Sydney Tokyo Toronto

Copyright © 1994 by ACADEMIC PRESS, INC.

Academic Press, Inc.
A Division of Harcourt Brace & Company
525 B Street, Suite 1900, San Diego, California 92101-4495

United Kingdom Edition published by
Academic Press Limited
24-28 Oval Road, London NW1 7DX

Library of Congress Cataloging-in-Publication Data

Thinking computers and virtual persons : essays on the intentionality
    of machines / edited by Eric Dietrich.
            p.   cm.
        Includes bibliographical references and index.
        ISBN 0-12-215495-9
        1. Computer science.   2. Artificial intelligence.   I. Dietrich,
    Eric.
    QA76.T44   1994   94-9551
        006.3'1--dc20   CIP

PRINTED IN THE UNITED STATES OF AMERICA
94   95   96   97   98   99   EB   9   8   7   6   5   4   3   2   1

To my parents and sisters:
Stan, Jeanne, Lisa, and Lori.
Four great robots.

Contents

Contributors

Numbers in parentheses indicate the pages on which the authors' contributions begin.

Jack R. Adams-Webber (331), Department of Psychology, Brock University, St. Catharine's, Ontario, Canada L2S 3A1

Leonard Angel (277), Department of Arts and Humanities, Douglas College, P.O. Box 2503, New Westminster, British Columbia, Canada V3L 5B2

Patricia Churchland (157), Department of Philosophy, University of California at San Diego, La Jolla, California 92093

Paul Churchland (157), Department of Philosophy, University of California at San Diego, La Jolla, California 92093

David Cole (139), Philosophy Department, Universiy of Minnesota, Duluth, Minnesota 55812-2496

Daniel Dennett (91), Tufts University, Center for Cognitive Studies, 11 Miner Hall, Medford, Massachusetts 02155-7059

Eric Dietrich (3, 109), Program in Philosophy and Computers & Cognitive Science, Department of Philosophy, State University of New York-Binghamton, Binghamton, New York 13901

Michael G. Dyer (173), Department of Computer Science, University of California at Los Angeles, Los Angeles, California 90024

Chris Fields (71), 6708 Lakeridge Road, New Market, Maryland 21774

Kenneth M. Ford (331), Institute for Human and Machine Cognition, University of West Florida, Pensacola, Florida 32514

Patrick J. Hayes (331), Beckman Institute for Advanced Science and Technology, Urbana, Illinois 61801

Donald Perlis (197), Department of Computer Science and Institute for Advanced Computer Studies, University of Maryland, College Park, Maryland 20742

William J. Rapaport (225), Department of Computer Science and Center for Cognitive Science, State University of New York at Buffalo, Buffalo, New York 14260

Peter Resnick (37), Department of Philosophy, and the Beckman Institute for Advanced Science and Technology, University of Illinois at Urbana-Champaign, Urbana, Illinois 61801

Charles Wallis (307), Department of Philosophy, University of Rochester, Rochester, New York 14627

Preface

This book is dedicated to the view that cognition is computation. It presents a sustained and multifaceted defense of this view against a suite of arguments developed over the past several years designed to show that thinking—cognition—cannot be computation. The view being defended is called computationalism. It has two corollaries: computers can think, and the human mind is itself a kind of computer. Computationalism is the foundation of modern cognitive science, a broad field that includes everything from artificial intelligence to cognitive psychology to computational neuroscience.

The suite of arguments being attacked revolves around the notion of meaning or semantics. In one way or another, all these arguments seek to establish that a machine's computations are inherently meaningless. Computers are fancy tools, nothing more. Just as a hammer knows nothing about the nail it is used to pound, computers know nothing about the information they process. Computers do not *do* things; things are done with them by people. The antisemantic arguments tap into deeply held intuitions that computers are just not the sorts of things one can correctly view as cognitive agents, as persons.

The antisemantic arguments are attacked full force here. I believe they are refuted. Beyond that, positive theories explaining how computations are meaningful and how computers can be cognitive agents like you and me are advanced here. By the end of the book, I believe that a good case has been made for computationalism.

Making this case is the point of the book. This project started when I noticed that the case *against* computationalism seemed to be waxing in spite of the fact that there were several papers and results in the literature showing that computationalism was alive and well and doing the job it was supposed to do: supporting late-twentieth century research into the nature of the mind and brain. These papers and results were being overlooked and ignored. I thought that if the best of them were pulled together into a single collection, their mutual impact would be stronger. They would then be harder to ignore.

The real test of the thesis that cognition is computation lies in the day-to-day work of cognitive scientists and in whether we are eventually successful in explaining computationally how brains produce minds and in programming a machine to think. But as matters now stand, computation is the single most important notion in the foundation of cognitive science. Between this book and the daily victories of cognitive sciences, I think its role is secured.

This book is meant to be self-contained. Read the introduction first. I explain there, in nontechnical language, the major terms, concepts, and issues so that any person interested in the issues of minds and machines can follow the debates in the rest of the book.

I thank Thomas Lebhar, Michael Lindgren, and Mary Tressler of Academic Press and Kathleen Tibbetts (my first contact at Academic Press) for their help and encouragement. Thanks also to John Author for discussions about early versions of this book. Thanks to all my friends, colleagues, and graduate students in the Program in Philosophy and Computers & Cognitive Science who offered their encouragement. I also want to thank Yorick Wilks and the Computing Research Lab at New Mexico State University for providing me with a great, two-year post-doc during which some of the original work on this book occurred. The research atmosphere there was truly a joy to behold. Thanks also to Bill Roberts for being inspirational. And, I thank my friend Rob Ausich. He didn't have anything to do with the book, but he did save my life once. Finally, I'd like to thank Alan Strudler and Chris Fields for years of philosophy, biology, psychology, physics, computers, conversation, and John Waters movies—to you both, *Slainthe*.

Eric Dietrich

I

Introduction

◆ Thinking Computers and The Problem of Intentionality

Eric Dietrich

1. THE IMPORTANCE OF PHILOSOPHY

Among their duties in society, philosophers police the foundations of the sciences, trying to prevent or eliminate conceptual confusions. It's a difficult job. Sometimes philosophers miss a confusion: where were they during the tyranny of Galen? For approximately fifteen hundred years, until the late sixteenth century, instead of learning anatomy by dissecting human bodies, physicians read the works of Galen, an ancient Greek physician, thereby deforming medicine into philology (this wasn't Galen's fault, by the way; he would have been aghast). Sometimes philosophers are less than thorough in pursuing a conceptual profligate: Bishop Berkeley did point out the logical morass in the differential and integral calculus invented by Newton, but he didn't follow through, and few picked up the cause after him. And sometimes philosophers arrest the innocent. This book is about this last case. It is an attempt to clear the

Thinking Computers and Virtual Persons
edited by Eric Dietrich
ISBN 0-12-215495-9

names of artificial intelligence (AI) and computational cognitive science. These two related disciplines have been accused of a conceptual error so profound that their very existence is jeopardized.

Sometimes, however, philosophers successfully arrest and lock up the guilty. The best example of this, ironically, is in psychology. Trying to be as neutral as possible, we can define psychology simply as the science that seeks to explain why humans and other animals do some of the things they do. Before the current cognitive trend in psychology, psychologists couched their theories of behavior strictly in terms of an organism's publicly observable responses to various events and actions in the organism's environment. They eschewed as unscientific all mentalistic terms such as "thinking," "wants," "beliefs," "hopes," "desires," "understanding," "expectations," etc. This kind of psychology was called *behaviorism*. It lasted from the 1920's until the mid-1960's, roughly. It might seem paradoxical that any science worthy of the name "psychology" would disavow the mind, but that is exactly what behaviorism did, mainly because mentalistic terms referred to seemingly *un*observable properties and events. Behaviorists were among the first psychologists to want to make psychology into a robust science. In order to accomplish this, they knew they had to restrict themselves to objective, measurable phenomena. One cannot have a science if one persists in studying private phenomena, and behaviorists were convinced that mental events are private.

Though their heart was in the right place, by the late 1950's it was becoming clear that behaviorists were preventing rather than creating a scientific psychology. To everyone without a methodological ax to grind, it seemed obvious that there were minds and mental events, and both were involved in the causation of behavior. A new sentiment began to sweep the field: a scientific psychology should explain how minds are responsible for the behavior they cause. Philosophers were, in part, responsible for this new sentiment, and for the demise of behaviorism itself. (As just one classic text, I refer the interested reader to Jerry Fodor's excellent book, *Psychological Explanation*.)

My quick retelling of the history of behaviorism doesn't do it justice. Its story is rich and fascinating. I merely wanted to point out that philosophers have helped root out a conceptual confusion once before in the psychological sciences. Many philosophers think that they must do so again. This time the error is in *how* we conceive of the mind, in contrast to the last time where we didn't conceive of the mind at all as having any role in scientific, psychological explanation.

The error we cognitive scientists are accused of making is viewing the mind as a kind of computational device, a computer of some sort. Artificial intelligence and computational cognitive science are both committed to the claim that computers can think. The former is committed to the claim that human-made computers can think, while computational cognitive science is committed to the view that naturally occurring computers—brains—think. John Searle is the arresting philosopher of record, and one of AI and cognitive science's main philosophical antagonists. Without him, this book wouldn't be necessary (but without having to deal with his arguments over the years, we wouldn't have learned as much as we have about computational systems and cognition). In 1980, Searle published his famous "Chinese Room argument," which was designed to show that whatever computers are doing, they aren't thinking, nor can they be made to think. And, according to Searle, the human brain, whatever it is doing in detail, is not computing by any stretch of the imagination.

Briefly, Searle's position is this. Computers cannot literally be said to understand anything (and hence cannot think at all) because their computations are not *about* anything (they lack *intentionality*, to use the technical term). Computers are like books. The words in a book mean something to us, but not to the book itself. Hence the words in a book are not really about anything independent of readers interpreting the words as being about things and events in the world. Thoughts, on the other hand, are about events and things all by themselves, and do not need an interpreter to render them meaningful.

If Searle is correct, then once again psychology will have to change its foundational assumptions: brains aren't like computers, and minds are not the analog of software. But at least psychology would still be with us. AI would have no future if Searle is correct. AI would simply vanish, except for its engineering arm. This would remain, at least for a while, because some AI systems do useful things now and then, but only in the way a book or a hammer does useful things, according to Searle.

This book is a sustained refutation of this position. It argues that the computational foundation of AI and cognition science is intact and correct. In short, we are innocent.

In this introduction, I present needed background and definitions so that anyone interested in cognition, psychology, or computers can understand the controversy and its importance. First, I provide what are, I hope, controversy-free definitions of several key terms including "artificial intelligence," "cognitive science," "computation," and "computer." Then I define the term causing all the problems: "intentionality." I explain in detail the alleged error involving intentionality, the Chinese Room argument, and the importance of the argument, and I suggest how AI and cognitive science might be exonerated. The chapters in the rest of the book present the detailed defense and address other important, related issues.

2.   DEFINING OUR TERMS

The definitions of "artificial intelligence," "computation," "computer," and related notions are problematic—the latter two, especially so. In an important sense, the definition of these two forms the core of the debate about human and machine cognition. We do not want to get stalled on definitions, but we need some just to get started, so I will present those that I hope everyone can agree to.

Artificial intelligence (AI) is the field dedicated to building intelligent computers. The Holy Grail of AI is to build a computer that is as intelligent as you or I. Such a machine should be able to solve problems it hasn't seen before, learn from its mistakes, and survive in its environment. But of course a cockroach can do these (the last better than most), and some birds and mammals routinely and robustly perform cognitive tasks such as learning and problem solving. AI ultimately wants a machine that could solve very difficult, novel problems like proving Fermat's Last Theorem, correcting the greenhouse effect, or figuring out the fundamental structure of space–time. It should communicate in a natural language like Spanish or English or some medium even more robust. It should be able to learn art, biology, algebra, and how to drive a car in both Boston and London.

We are nowhere near building such machines. In fact, AI has not succeeded in building a machine even as intelligent as a cockroach, in this sense: no one has succeeded in building a robot that can survive in a natural, hostile environment. However, AI has also had its successes. To name just two: there are robots that inhabit relatively friendly environments (see, e.g. Brooks 1986), and expert systems routinely diagnose, design, and otherwise help us solve problems. I don't want to get sidetracked here, so I refer the interested reader to *The Handbook of Artificial Intelligence* (Barr et al. 1989) and *The Essential of Artificial Intelligence* (Ginsburg 1993), a recent, good textbook.

Historically, AI is associated with computer science, but the "compleat" AI researcher frequently knows a fair amount of psychology, linguistics, neuroscience, and mathematics, plus possibly some other discipline. These days "artificial intelligence" sometimes more narrowly denotes a dedication to a certain methodology taken when building intelligent computers: the *symbol level* or *knowledge level* methodology championed by, e.g., Allen Newell (1990). This methodology carries all kinds of commitments about what cognition is, what aspects of it are important, and how to implement it on a computer. There are many researchers trying to build intelligent machines that are opposed to this methodology—deeply opposed. Those exploring and developing artificial neural networks are a good example. These scientists have their own methodology, and their own commitments to what cognition is, what aspects of it are important, and how to implement it in a computer. Since the labels have not yet ossified, I believe I can still safely apply the term "artificial intelligence" to all attempts to build a thinking computer, regardless of the methodology.

"Computational cognitive science" (or just "cognitive science") is the term that covers most research into cognition, including AI research, and the work of some philosophers, linguists, and biologists, and of course cognitive, developmental and neuropsychologists. Unlike AI researchers, psychologists use the computational framework for explaining naturally occurring minds (human minds, mainly), rather than trying to build synthetic ones. This is a very important point. One of the reasons behaviorism got started was that psychologists couldn't devise a robust framework explaining how mental events could respond to stimuli and cause behavior. Without this framework, they thought they should just abandon mental events and focus on behavior—a very plausible and, indeed, responsible move, in my opinion. And, one of the reasons behaviorism failed is that behaviorists couldn't devise a robust framework explaining how various stimuli came to be associated with various behaviors, nor could they predict why certain stimuli caused certain behavior. Their theories never really amounted to more than compendiums of stimulus-behavior associations. Computation changed all that. Computation provided psychologists with the framework needed to link stimulus and response. Computation and computers provided them with notions like memory, control flow, and information processing. But more basically, it gave them both the idea of how internal states could mediate external stimuli and behavior, i.e., input and output, as well as some idea of just how complex those internal states could be.

AI researchers and cognitive psychologists frequently team up, and in so doing produce better models and better theoretical explanations. Everyone benefits. This is because all computational cognitive scientists share one deep assumption: we believe that thinking is computing. Here is this point put another way. Currently, psychologists do not have a robust theory of any entire mind, human or animal. But we all believe that when they finally develop one, we will be able to implement it on some sort of computer, or at least in principle, the theory will be implementable on some sort of computer (it might turn out that we humans lack the intelligence required to implement such a complex theory on any machine we can build). Alternatively, if AI researchers succeed first in building an intelligent machine, then though it might not work the way a human brain does, psychologists could mine the machine and its algorithms for clues that would help them develop a theory of human cognition. Again, what makes this sort of interdisciplinary exchange possible is that we are speaking the same "language": cognition is computation. I'll return to this point after I've explained computation and computers.

The term "computation" denotes a step-by-step, mechanical process with a definite beginning and a definite end where each step (called a state) and each transition from one state to the next is finitely and unambiguously describable and identifiable. This all means that the process is either at a certain state or it is not, it may either go to a certain next state from its current state or it may not, and any transition taken is finitely capable of completion.

We can fine-tune this definition by defining computation indirectly. Let's begin with the notion of an *effective procedure*. An *effective procedure* is an unambiguous, precise description of a set of operations applied mechanically and systematically to a set of tokens or objects (e.g., configurations of chess pieces, numbers, cake ingredients, and intermediate cake states such as batter, etc.). The operations correspond to the transitions described above, and the states are the states of the set of tokens—the configuration of which changes as operations are applied to them. It is important to note that the operations must be mechanically and finitely capable of completion. A tax form, a simple one anyway, is a relatively good example of an effective procedure because it is finite and the instructions for completing it are mechanically and finitely capable of completion. The recipe for cowboy chocolate cake (with two mugs of coffee) might be an effective procedure depending on whether or not its description is precise enough (how much is a mug of coffee?). Many workaday instructions for human tasks are only heuristic examples of effective procedures because they contain instructions that assume a lot of background information or are stated imprecisely (e.g., recipes say things like "mix ingredients"). Probably all such instructions can be turned into effective procedures. However, this is controversial because it is controversial whether humans are a type of computer or not. Of course, all computer programs are effective procedures. The terms "program" and "algorithm" are usually used interchangeably with "procedure." (The term "algorithm" is sometimes restricted to those procedures that never go into an infinite loop; we won't adhere to that restriction here.)

For any effective procedure, the initial state of the tokens is the input; the final state is the output. Almost everything in sight is assumed to be finite: the description is finite; the set of operations is finite; the input, output; and intermediate sets of tokens are finite; and though the set of all tokens need not be finite, each token is itself finite (or, more generally, a determinable element in some set). In the standard, digital definition of computation (see below), each token is either basic or decomposable into a finite set of basic elements or constituents. For example, though the set of all logically possible English language sentences is infinitely large, nevertheless each sentence is only finitely long and consists of strings of words drawn on an alphabet containing twenty-six letters. A natural language-processing program is usually defined over such an infinite set of sentences. Of course, in practice, the set of sentences actually operated on is also finite—computers as well as brains can hold and process only a finite amount of information. We can now sum all this up in a single phrase: a computation is the execution of an effective procedure.

Computations compute functions. There are two ways to define functions. Defined *extensionally*, a function is a *set*: a collection of pairs of inputs and outputs. Extensional definitions ignore how to compute the outputs from the inputs. Multiplication is a familiar function that pairs a product with two input numbers: <(2, 3), 6>, <(45, 52), 2340>, etc. (or 2 x 3 = 6 and 45 x 52 = 2340, in more familiar notation). No mention of *how* to compute these products is given; only the ordered pairs are specified. In general, for any extensionally defined function, there are an infinite number of *intensional* definitions for it—definitions of *how* the function is to be computed. An algorithm is an intensional definition of a function: it defines the function as a series of steps. So, for any extensionally defined function there are an infinite number of different algorithms for computing it (of course, we always know only a small number of them). Consider multiplication, again. One can compute 45 x 52 = 2340 either by repeated addition (not a good method if you are using pencil and paper) or by partial products (a better method). Also, note that any computation that associates 2 and 3 with 6 (and 45 and 52 with 2340, etc.) is a computation of multiplication regardless of how baroque the process is.

Like all basic, foundational definitions, our definition of computation crucially relies on intuition. What does it mean, really, to say that the operations must be applied mechanically? In a sense, we have merely gone around in circles: we have defined computation in terms of a mechanism, but if we were to try to define "mechanism" we would probably wind up using the notion of computation. So we're stuck; we must rely on our intuition of the notion of a mechanism. But we are quite confident in this intuition. Since the mid-1930's, mathematicians have invented several different formal, robust characterizations of the above intuitive definition of computation. There are all kinds of technicalities and subtleties involved in making such formalizations (there is an entire branch of mathematics devoted to studying them), but surprisingly, they are all equivalent—though they all look very different, they are provably just variations of each other. This discovery convinces many computer scientists and mathematicians that our intuitive notion of computation is robust and relatively stable, and furthermore, that the formalizations accurately capture the intuition in symbols and mathematics. The move from the intuitive definition of computation to a formal, mathematical characterization of computation is one of the great intellectual achievements of this century (see, e.g., Church 1936a,b, Turing 1936).

Finally, there are the distinctions between continuous and digital (discrete) computation, and between these two and analog processing. We will need these distinctions below. I will introduce three mathematical notions: discreteness, denseness, and continuity to help explain these notions. In the classical, mathematical theory of computation, computation is defined over *discrete* sets, i.e., sets with gaps between their members such that every element of the set has a nearest neighbor on all sides. Given a member of such a set, one can always find the *next* member of the set. The paradigmatic set with these properties, and the set over which computation is typically defined, is the set of natural numbers, $N = \{0, 1, 2, \ldots\}$ (sometimes the integers are used, $Z = \{\ldots -2, -1, 0, 1, 2, \ldots\}$). There are infinitely many natural numbers, but between any two of them there is *not* always another one (e.g., there is no natural number between 1 and 2), and given a natural number, one can find the next one (just add 1).

A *dense* set is a set where between any two elements, there is always another element. The rational numbers (Z together with all the negative and positive fractions) are dense. There is no notion of *the* next member for dense sets because no matter how small a quantity you add to one member to get a second, there will always be yet a third between the first and second. Though the rationals are dense, they still have gaps: π and $\sqrt{2}$, for example, are not rational numbers. In fact, the rationals leave out all nonterminating, nonrepeating decimals (these are called the irrational numbers). The decimal 0.1010010001. . . , where the number of zeros between successive ones increases by one each time, is an example of such a decimal; it is not a rational number, but it is clearly a number. So the rationals have gaps; they are not complete in the sense that they leave out the irrationals. A *continuous* set is a set with absolutely no gaps between elements. Such a set is "completely smooth." The set of all real numbers (i.e., the set of rationals together with the set of irrationals) is an example of such a set.

Digital computation is computation over a discrete set like the natural numbers, and, as I said above, it is the classical notion of computation. The mathematical theory underlying discrete computation is very robust. *Continuous computation* is computation over a continuous set. That is, continuous computation consists of simple, finitely specifiable, mechanical operations applied to elements of a continuous set. The notion of computing over a continuous set has not enjoyed as much publicity or mathematical scrutiny over the years as the traditional, digital notion of computation. However, the mathematical theory underlying continuous computation is reasonably well worked out. This was accomplished by extending the discrete notion of computation to continuous sets (e.g., see Blum, Shub, and Smale 1989).

Analog processing involves direct, quantitative relations between input and output: as the input varies continuously, so do the outputs. Analog processing, therefore, involves operations defined over continuous sets, but it is usually considered to be different from continuous computation (of course, it is different from digital computation). Continuous computation is an extension of the classical theory of digital computation to continuous sets. Analog processing does not involve the classical theory of computation, extended or otherwise. That is, it does not involve simple, mechanical operations applied to determinable tokens. That's why I call it "analog *processing*" rather than "analog *computing*": analog processing is not really computing, at least as this notion is classically understood. Researchers who study analog processes describe them as involving or obeying differential equations. That is, differential equations are required to fully analyze and explain a given analog process.

There are other distinctions between analog processing and computation. Some researchers regard time as crucial to the distinction. Computation is, in theory, independent of time. Analog processes crucially involve time. But time seems to be a red herring. No implemented computation, no *actual* computation is independent of time. Some analog processes are faster than some of their digital counterparts, but this doesn't seem important enough to forge a robust theoretical distinction between the two. Some researchers introduce "implementation-dependence" into the distinction. The very identity of a given analog process depends on how it is realized in some physical material; change the physical material and you can change which analog process it is. Again, this doesn't seem enlightening. As I mentioned above, a computation of multiplication can be implemented in myriad ways. But given an implementation, if you change it—say, by pouring Coca Cola on it—you change the identity of the computation. Still, there is a distinction between analog processing and computation. Continuity and complexity seem to be the hallmarks.

Perhaps some examples would help. A pendulum clock is an example of an analog processor. So is a slide rule. Another example is the rheostat in a dimmer switch: as the switch is continuously rotated, the lights it controls continuously change in brightness. A watch with minute, hour, and second hands is also an analog processor. Contrast these with a digital watch, a calculator, and an on-off light switch.

At the level of theory, the distinction between digital and continuous computation is clean and precise. The distinction between these two kinds of computation and analog processing is not as clean, but it is tolerable. (There isn't a robust mathematical theory of analog processing, unless you want to count physics.) In practice, however, the distinctions between these three are muddier. For example, from the point of view of measurement, both continuous computation and analog processing look discrete (see Fields, 1989). That is, any time we measure or probe any continuous process (or object) we produce a finite, discrete set of measurements. We cannot measure something to infinite precision due to such things as thermal noise and the Heisenberg Uncertainty Principle. The finite, discrete set of measurements, and the function that describes it, can, in principle, always be modeled on a computer. For example, if you measure, in some electrical device, continuously varying voltages at selected times, you produce a discrete set of time–voltage pairs that can be used to construct a digital computer model of the electrical device. We can make this digital model so detailed and precise that it will be impossible to produce measurements of the real electrical device that distinguish it from the model. None of this means that we want to describe all processes and all computations as discrete, but it does mean that we can do so, in principle.

This is as far as I will go in defining "computation" here, mainly because this notion is half of what all the shouting is about, and several chapters in this book discuss it in detail. It is fair to say that there is little agreement on what the definition means, what it encompasses, and what its significance is (see the special issue on computation of the journal *Minds and Machines*, Vol. 5, 1994 #4). If there were agreement, this book might not be necessary. From here on out, by "computation" I shall mean "digital computation," unless I explicitly say otherwise. I shall also restrict myself to discussing digital computers.

A natural definition of "computer" would seemingly be "a physical system that implements (instantiates, is described by) a computation." This definition of "computer" isn't the standard one, however; it's too broad. The term is usually reserved for physical systems that can, in principle, implement *any* computation. This requires a bit of fleshing out. To do so, I will use two important twentieth-century achievements. The first comes from a theorem and the second is a discovery. One of the important theorems in the mathematical theory of computation demonstrated that there are universal machines, i.e., machines that can simulate any abstract machine (see Turing 1936). "Machine" here means "abstract mathematical description of a computation." In fact, "machine" is often used as a synonym for "computation" or "algorithm" in the mathematical theory of computation. A universal machine is just a mathematical description of a universal computation. A universal machine is given as input the description of another machine—say, an adder—and some input for *that* machine say, 1 and 2. Then the universal machine will run the adder on 1 and 2, outputting 3. Any computation whatsoever can be given to a universal machine and the machine will run it (again, in an abstract, mathematical sense). The Turing machine, the one Turing used in his proof, is probably the most famous abstract universal machine. Its generality and power led the mathematician Alonzo Church to hypothesize that a Turing machine could compute any computable function whatsoever, i.e., that the Turing machine captured our intuitive notion of computation completely (Church 1936b). This famous hypothesis is called *Church's thesis* (or sometimes the *Church–Turing thesis*). This thesis is widely accepted because all other formalizations of intuitive notions of computation have been proved equivalent to Turing machines (I mentioned this point above when I discussed the reliance of the formal notion of computation on intuition.)

The discovery was that it is possible to build physical systems that for all intents and purposes are universal Turing machines. These are the computers we know and love. Computers are not actually physical instantiations of abstract universal machines because universal machines require infinite memory (in order to compute every possible computation). Since no physical system in our universe has or can have infinite memory, it is impossible to build a physical version of a universal machine. However, a whole bunch of memory works just as well as infinite memory for any practical purpose. What's important about a modern-day computer is that because of its architecture, it *would be* a universal computer provided that it had unlimited memory. Ordinary, garden-variety computers, like the Macintosh I'm now typing at, are examples of such physical systems. Given unlimited memory (and time), my Macintosh could compute any possible algorithm (assuming Church's thesis is true, which I will do). Of course, my Mac would take longer than the lifetime of the universe to execute most of these algorithms, and the vast majority of them aren't important to us, anyway. Contrast this with your four-function calculator. It can only compute addition, . subtraction, multiplication, and division (plus combinations of these), so it could never be a universal machine even if we could give it infinite memory.

Sometimes physical systems like your calculator are called "special-purpose computers" to contrast with would-be universal computers that are called "general-purpose computers." Special-purpose computers are typically efficient and quite fast at computing the functions they are designed for, and they are used in everything from radar ovens to the space shuttle. General-purpose computers are programmed the same way universal mathematical machines are: they are given a description of a computation—of another machine—and the input for that other machine. Such a description is what a program is. The computer then runs the described machine on its input. This may not seem to be what's going on when you run your word processor, but it is. When a computer is running another described machine, the latter is called a *virtual machine* with respect to the base computer. Any time a software package executes, a virtual machine comes into existence. This concept will be very important later and in other chapters in the book.

It is important to remember that computations typically exist at a level intermediate between extensionally defined functions and the hardware of a working computer. To understand a particular computation in the abstract, you need only understand the extensionally defined function and an abstract version of the algorithm. Hardware is irrelevant. Of course, if you ever want to run your algorithm, you will need to implement it, i.e., develop an algorithm that will run on an actual machine. Then you will need to understand hardware, or rely on someone else who understands hardware (the people who built your computer and developed the programming language you are using, for example). Understanding a physical, computational system, however, is more complicated. In this case, you must interpret the physical states of the system in a way that allows you to see the execution of the computation in the system's state changes. This is difficult when dealing with computers in the wild.

Well, what about computers in the wild? Not many naturally occurring physical systems are general-purpose computers (but they're now relatively easy to build). However, every physical system in the universe, from wheeling galaxies to bumping proteins, is a special-purpose computer in the sense that every physical system in the universe implements some computation or other (more than one, in fact). But note, not every computation is implemented by every physical system, a point I'll return to later. (This way of putting things is due to Chalmers, in press. He also proposes there an interesting notion of implementation, part of which I've borrowed.) Now we can generalize the point made in the preceding paragraph: understanding any natural physical system amounts to developing a computation that can be used to interpret its state changes. I hasten to add that most scientists don't see themselves as doing reverse engineering on computers in the wild (i.e., finding out which algorithm their system of interest executes and how it is executed). Still, that's what they are doing. Many, but certainly not all, cognitive scientists do explicitly see themselves as searching for algorithms. Those who think they are doing something else, including some of those doing among the most exciting work, confuse searching for algorithms with searching for evidence that the brain or mind functions like a modern-day computer. Since it is overwhelmingly implausible that the brain works like a modern-day computer, they therefore think they are also *not* discovering algorithms. This is incorrect. Algorithms are ubiquitous; modern-day computers are not: they are merely one type of (would-be) universal machine.

So, of the two notions—computation and computers—computation is the more fundamental, especially to cognitive science. The importance of computers lies in their use for experimental tests of ideas and hypotheses, and as demonstrations of our theories.

To return to and expand on a central point made earlier: everyone in computational cognitive science believes that all cognition is computation in the sense defined here, the classical, digital sense. All of our cognitive processes, from seeing, hearing, walking, and tasting to reading, writing, learning, reasoning, etc., are the computation of some function. And, going the other way, anything that computes these functions will think (see, hear, walk, taste, learn, write, reason, etc.). This view is called *computationalism.* Specifically, we all believe that explaining human (and any other animal's) cognitive capacities requires discovering which functions their brains compute and how they compute them (i.e., both which algorithms they use and how the algorithms are implemented in the neural hardware). And to build an intelligent, thinking computer, we need only to program it to compute these (or relevantly similar) functions. However, we don't necessarily have to implement on the machine the very same algorithms humans use (remember, there are many algorithms for a given function).

Many computationalists work primarily at an intermediate level of computation—intermediate between the brain (hardware) and extensionally defined functions (behavior). Of course, a robust theory of human and other animal cognition will include implementational details (i.e., neuroscience) as well as introspectively described extensional functions. (I don't disparage neuroscience here. I'm aware that neuroscientists and neural net researchers do not view their work as merely figuring out implementational details. Of course they're right: in this case, God is in the details.)

[Two caveats: First, the functions and algorithms psychologists develop as psychological explanations don't often look like computer programs (or even functions and algorithms, for that matter). Again, what is important is the function and its algorithm—the computation—not how it is written down. There are many ways in many languages (including English) to express an algorithm. Of course, the algorithms AI researchers use *do* look like computer programs, at least when they're actually implementing them. Second, the brain is probably a general-purpose computer. Humans did, after all, devise the universal machine; all we have to do to implement it is to simulate its behavior (though, of course, we only have finite memory). But note, our cognitive abilities do *not* depend on our brains being general-purpose computers, assuming they are. Rather, and to say it again, our cognitive abilities are due to the fact that our brains implement as algorithms functions responsible for cognition. We don't know in detail what these functions are, and we are not sure of their algorithmic instantiations. Cognitive scientists are trying to discover the relevant functions and their algorithms.]

I want to stress that computationalism is a hypothesis; it is not true by definition. (The point of this book is that one of the leading alleged refutations of computationalism is incorrect.) Of course, computationalism is a very basic hypothesis. Still, like any hypothesis, it is open to possible refutation, as is the claim that we can build a thinking computer. There are several functions that are known to be not computable by any kind of machine we know of, i.e., no *possible* Turing machine can produce all the required outputs for all the relevant inputs for these functions. Computationalism would be false if it could be shown that intelligence is or involves one of these functions. Computationalism would also be false if it could be shown both that the brain was an analog processor and that *this analog nature mattered crucially for cognition.* This is because computationalism is the hypothesis that cognition is computation, not analog processing. Finally, computationalism would have to be altered a fair amount (but not abandoned) if it could be shown both that the brain was a continuous device and that *this continuity mattered crucially for cognition.* This is because computationalism is the hypothesis that cognition is *digital* computation, not continuous computation.

Thinking of cognition as computation is of paramount importance. Computation is a *framework* on which to base our theories and experiments; it is the notion around which we organize our thoughts about cognitive phenomena. It accomplishes this by providing us with a language for describing, explaining, and predicting the flow of cognition. Such theoretical frameworks are essential for every science. Without the development of the notion of computation and the invention of the computer, it is quite likely that psychology would still be where it was forty years ago (or even seventy years ago), with no prospects for serious advancement. Indeed, psychologists themselves would have probably developed the notion of computation.

The foundational nature of computationalism is widely misunderstood. To compare a similarly basic hypothesis, consider the idea that numbers and mathematics can be used to describe the physical world. This idea evolved and grew from Neolithic times, was first robustly developed by the ancient Greeks, and was employed with tremendous skill by Isaac Newton (to name but one individual). It's now such a commonplace that we scarcely see it as a hypothetical framework, but it was. Darwin's theory of evolution is another unifying framework. The science of biology wouldn't exist without his theory; all of biology rests on it.

Some who think that computational cognitive science is inadequate to the job of explaining and replicating cognition try to use the ubiquity of computation as grist for their mill. They claim that if everything is a computer (specifically, a special-purpose, naturally occurring computer) then the notion is vacuous (e.g., Searle, 1990). But this is wrong. First, by itself, ubiquity can't make a concept vacuous. Saying that all physical systems are composed of atoms doesn't make the notion of atoms vacuous. But a better example is this: saying that all physical systems that we can gain any knowledge of consist of measurable properties (e.g., speed, height, thickness, density, watts, decibels) in no way means that measurement is vacuous. The same is true of computation. The notion is far from vacuous; it's just widely applicable. Computation would be vacuous if any given computation could describe every physical system, but this is not the case (cf. Chalmers, 1994). Note that measurement would be vacuous in exactly the same way: if everything could be described as being six feet long, the notion of length would be useless.

Now for the notion that precipitated all the trouble: *intentionality*. Let's begin at the beginning. Cognition is for coping with the world. Planning, recognizing, wanting, believing, hating, enjoying, fearing, learning, reasoning, deducing, and problem solving are all for coping with the world. But you can't cope with the world unless you can represent it (your local part of it, your environment). Successful cognitive coping requires representing. The brain is an organ for representation. Indeed, it might be unique in this capacity. The brain is thus much more than a complex system with complex internal states. The weather is a complex system with complex internal states, but the weather isn't thinking. Unlike the weather, the brain represents its world and, moreover, processes those representations. The ability of the brain to represent is called *intentionality*. Intentionality, therefore, is what is important about cognition; it is what separates the brain from the weather or any other merely complex physical system.

Typically, cognitive scientists attribute intentionality not to whole brains, but to states of brains—mental states, thoughts. So, typically we say that mental states have intentionality, i.e., they are about something in the world. For example, if you believe that Wyoming is north of Colorado, then you believe something *about* Wyoming and Colorado. If you believe that coffee is good, that you are now reading, and that the mean temperature of our planet's atmosphere is increasing, then you have beliefs *about* things in the world: coffee, planet earth, what you're currently doing, etc. Any mental state thus interpretable is said to have intentionality. So, to be absolutely clear: intentionality is that property of mental states by which they are about—refer to, denote—things in the world, including physical things like objects, states of affairs, properties, etc., as well as nonexistent things like unicorns or Hamlet.

Being about things or representing things in the world is having *meaning* or *semantics*. So another way to define intentionality is to say it is the semantics of mental states or thoughts.

The states of some systems are *not* about things in the world (or so it seems); they lack semantics. For example, the states of rocks do not seem to be about anything in the world—they don't represent or mean anything. States of your car engine also do not seem to represent anything in the world. Even some mental states lack intentionality: undirected anxieties or depressions, for example.

Of the things in the world with meaning, some seem to have it intrinsically, others seem to have it derivatively. Consider the words in a book or the words on this page. They clearly mean something; they are clearly about something in the world. But the words have their meanings because we humans supply them. "Snow is white" means what it does because of the conventional meanings we have supplied to the words making up that sentence. We use words to represent our thoughts or, to put it another way, to express the *meanings* of thoughts. So, the meanings of words and symbols depend on the meanings of our thoughts, our mental states. The meanings of mental states came first, therefore. Some philosophers use these facts to draw a distinction between the intentionality of thoughts and words. They say that thoughts have *original intentionality* (sometimes called *intrinsic intentionality)*, while external symbols have *derived intentionality* or *derived meaning*. Here's another way to draw this distinction: words in a book don't mean anything to the book itself; they mean something to us only as external observers of the book, but our thoughts do mean something to us, the very carriers of those representations; our mental representations represent what they do *for us*, not just for external observers of our behavior such as our friends or our neighborhood cognitive psychologist.

The problem of intentionality can now be put this way: given that derived intentionality depends on subjects, like humans, with original intentionality, where does original intentionality come from? Given that words have meanings because of the meanings of our thoughts, where do the meanings of thoughts come from? This problem is what the debate about intentionality, computers, and the mind is all about. Do thoughts, minds, have intentionality for some banal reason that applies to all computers as easily as it applies to all minds? Or do thoughts have intentionality for special reasons that preclude computers from having it? Perhaps the answer lies in the middle. Perhaps thoughts have intentionality for quasi-special reasons that preclude some types of computers from having it, but not others (e.g., robots). The answers to these questions are contained in this book.

The distinction between original intentionality and derived intentionality forces us to deal with the vexed question of *consciousness*—the most difficult problem in all of philosophy of mind. (I believe something much stronger: developing a theory of consciousness that explains what it is and how our brains are responsible for it is among the most challenging and disturbing problems in all of science.) I think that the problem of intentionality would not be so troubling and disputatious were it not so closely linked with consciousness.

By "consciousness" I shall mean the phenomenal experience we have of the world (e.g., the way roses smell, look, and feel) together with our ability to think about ourselves (called self-consciousness or self-awareness) and our ability to access the contents of some of our beliefs, hopes, desires, etc. (sometimes called cognitive consciousness). (See Block 1993, and Chalmers 1993, for more on this way of defining consciousness.)

Philosophers skeptical of computationalism typically distinguish between consciousness, semantics, and original intentionality (of course, some nonskeptical philosophers also draw these distinctions). The problem I have always had is this: I can't see any difference between original intentionality and consciousness; specifically, I do not see the distinction between original intentionality and cognitive consciousness. The whole problem comes down to the meaning of "original intentionality": what does it mean for a representation to mean something *to* or *for* the system that possesses it? Does it mean that the system can *use* the representation to do something? If so, then computers presumably have original intentionality. Or does it mean that the system is also *aware* of what the representation means? If so, then *perhaps* computers lack original intentionality. But on this latter interpretation original intentionality *is* or *is crucially involved in* consciousness, so of course it is a profound and deep problem, but one we already know about, and one we are pretty sure will have to be solved in a way completely different from our theories of semantics. If intentionality is defined as the semantic content of conscious mental states, then the problem of intentionality reduces to the problem of consciousness because what is special about those contents is that they are conscious, not that they are semantical.

Moreover, such conscious awareness seems unnecessary for making an intelligent machine: how could awareness of content have any bearing on how that content is used? The very existence of computers raises this question, for it is easy to suppose that computers are not conscious, but they do use representations in ways that depend on the content of those representations. Computers themselves create this "use-awareness" gap. Of course, computers are not today as intelligent as humans, but it is not clear that this is because we are conscious and they are not. Consciousness might be completely epiphenomenal: the wonderful richness of our lives due to our consciousness might be only a by-product of cognition, much like body heat is a by-product of cell metabolism.

My personal view is that the putative profundity of the problem of intentionality rests on drawing a distinction where none exists. There is no difference between original intentionality and cognitive consciousness. Cognitive consciousness, together with the rest of consciousness, really is a profound problem. Original intentionality *seems* profound because it is consciousness masquerading as semantics while refusing to be defined as either.

I do, however, think that there are three separate notions here, just not the ones traditionally drawn. The three I see are ordinary semantics (a symbol or representation meaning something to whomever), what I call *process semantics*, and consciousness. Briefly, in process semantics, representations are used by some dynamic process for some purpose, and the use to which the representation is put determines its meaning, in part. Other determiners of a representation's meaning come from the system's causal interactions with its environment. This view of representational content is, I believe, similar to Mark Bickhard's view (but not identical: Bickhard is not a computationalist, see his 1993 paper). For me, the advantage of this view is its "emergent, process perspective" on meaning. Meaning comes from which processes the representation is involved in. Also, this view seems more useful for developing theories of intelligent thinking, which is our ultimate endeavor, after all; discussions about meaning and intentionality are, or should be, means to this larger end.

I think conceptual clarity would be best served by redefining "original intentionality" as process semantics, and "derived intentionality" as ordinary semantics, semantics that just sits there—like the words in a book. I'm prepared to be convinced that computers are not conscious, but they have process semantics, and so by my suggested redefinition, original intentionality. But defining "original intentionality" as the process semantics of a system would prejudge matters in favor of computationalism. Instead, and for the rest of this introduction, I shall mean *at least* process semantics by "original intentionality," ("intentionality," for short), leaving the door open to the possibility that there might be more to intentionality than process semantics. I will also take great pains to avoid equivocating between intentionality and (cognitive) consciousness. Intentionality must be less than consciousness if it is to be a separate and genuine problem for cognitive science. We will see below that anticomputationalists are not always careful about keeping consciousness and intentionality separate. And some don't even want to. In fact, our major antagonist now doesn't (see Searle 1992; see also Harnad 1993). I suspect that at root, the fight over meaning and semantics for Searle and his cohorts is really the fight over whether or not there can be a computational theory of consciousness. I wouldn't even hazard a guess about that. Theories of consciousness, computational or otherwise, are exceedingly hard to come by (for one valiant attempt, see Dennett's book, *Consciousness Explained*, 1991). Cognitive science is *not* the science tasked with explaining consciousness, at least not as its priority job. We are supposed to explain cognition and its role in behavior. If we don't separate consciousness and meaning, then there is nothing to discuss except consciousness itself, and since it's too difficult for scientific scrutiny right now, the rest of us can go back to our labs—Searle has arrested us for entirely the wrong reason. I will return to this point, in Section 4, when I discuss robots.

I said at the outset I intended to provide controversy-free definitions that would allow us to discuss computational cognition. It perhaps comes as no surprise that when I came to defining the key term for this book—*intentionality*—I could not avoid controversy. My definition of intentionality as at least process semantics is nonstandard, but it's worse than useless to define intentionality as the equivocation between consciousness and semantics.

We can now restate the problem of intentionality in a better way: is process semantics all there is to original intentionality (in which case computers have at least a simple version of it), or is there some form of original intentionality richer than process semantics (and beyond computers) but less than (cognitive) consciousness?

We are done with definitions. Let's now turn to the error AI and cognitive science are accused of making.

3. THE PROBLEM OF INTENTIONALITY AND THE CHINESE ROOM

I said earlier that the brain might be unique in being the organ of intentionality. It seems clear that weather patterns or states of automobile engines lack intentionality. What about the states of devices like thermostats, radios, phones, TVs, or . . . computers? Do the states of these devices possess intentionality?

According to John Searle, the answer is a booming *No.* (For his most recent salvo, see Searle 1992.) According to Searle, only brains intrinsically represent— and those systems causally and structurally (and possibly even physically) isomorphic to brains. Every other system in the universe either fails to represent or only represents parasitically on brains. Except for brains and their isomorphic cousins, the states of every other system in the universe lack intentionality. Intentionality is quite rare.

But is intentionality that rare? The states of thermostats, e.g., seem to represent the air temperature of rooms in a causally efficacious way, even when no one is in the room. If all humans vanished tomorrow my thermostat would still represent the temperature in my study in a manner useful for controlling the temperature. In fact, maybe we were too quick earlier: perhaps the states of your automobile engine have intentionality. Maybe its states represent the event that causally preceded them. For example, maybe a piston's going down represents the firing of the spark plug for its cylinder.

No one really much cares about thermostats or car engines. The fight is over computation, computers, and the intentionality of computational states. If at least some computational states have intentionality naturally, then anything that is a computer will have intentional states. This will include ordinary computers, thermostats, and anything else that computes. Intentionality, real, honest-to-God intrinsic intentionality, could thus turn out to be common. It might even turn out to be ubiquitous, since, as we saw above, probably every physical system in the universe is a special-purpose computer, or at least analyzable as such a computer.

Searle is convinced that computational states cannot have intentionality. Thermostats, computers, etc. have at most derived intentionality: thermostats have meanings the same way words in books do—because we supply them. In 1980, he presented the AI and cognitive science community with an argument designed to show that no computer can possess intentional states, states that are intrinsically about the world regardless of our interpretations of them (Searle 1980). In other words, he attempted to show that though computers have semantics, they nevertheless lack intentionality. The question to keep in mind is this: does Searle's argument uncritically presuppose the insidious identification of original intentionality with cognitive consciousness, or does it show that there is more to original intentionality than process semantics?

Searle's argument is called the *Chinese Room* argument. It is probably one of the most famous philosophical arguments invented in the last twenty-five years. It is also one of the most vexing. I now turn to it. (I encourage reading the original: Searle 1980. His paper is also reprinted in several places: e.g., Haugeland 1981 and Hofstadter and Dennett 1981.)

Imagine that you are locked in a room. Chinese texts written on sheets of paper are slipped through a slot in the door. Your job is to take these sheets with Chinese on them, write Chinese characters in response to them, and shove your responses back out through the slot. Imagine also that you know no Chinese at all, either written or spoken; in fact, you cannot distinguish Chinese writing from Japanese writing. (If you do know Chinese, fill in your own language—e. g., Russian, ancient Greek, or Sanskrit.) Fortunately, you have with you a book written in English, which tells you what to write, given that you are seeing certain Chinese characters. Your book contains instructions that look like the following (since the particular language doesn't matter and to enable those who understand Chinese to get the argument, I'll follow custom and represent Chinese characters with combinations of the words "squiggle" and "squoggle"):

> If you see squiggle squiggle on your sheet, then write down squoggle squoggle.
>
> If you see squiggle squoggle, then turn to page 312 and check under squoggle squiggle; if you also have squiggle squiggle squiggle on your input sheet, then write down squiggle squoggle squiggle.

You follow the rules in your book, writing down what it tells you. You have no idea what you are doing except writing marks in response to other marks arriving via a slot in the door. This goes on for months, during which time you are otherwise well cared for.

Outside the room, native speakers of Chinese are engaged in a conversation on the history of China, and the room is participating. They think that whoever or whatever is in the room knows Chinese and Chinese history quite well: your responses, unbeknownst to you, are almost indistinguishable from those of a native speaker.

Now for the coup de grace. Recall that the point of Searle's argument is to show that computational states lack intentionality. If it could be shown that inside the room, you are doing exactly what a computer does when it executes a program, then Searle's result would no doubt follow. For inside the room, you *understand* no Chinese; you are merely doing pattern matching on, and writing down per the instructions, uninterpreted marks. The marks happen to be Chinese characters relevant and meaningful to a conversation about Chinese history, but you don't know that. You are merely imitating, without *understanding*, someone who does understand Chinese. If a computer is doing that, if this is an accurate description of computation, then computational states lack intentionality. (Note that while you are manipulating the rules mentioning Chinese characters your mental states do in fact have intentionality: they are about the book, the rules, the various marks you see, etc. You understand these perfectly. But your mental states are not about what the conversation is about.)

To complete the argument, Searle asserts that what you are doing in the room is *exactly* analogous to what a computer does when it computes: you in the room *are* a computer. Since your mental states are not about, and could not be about, the external world, neither could a computer's internal states. A computer's states, therefore, are not intrinsically about anything in the world; they lack intentionality. When computers "think," they aren't thinking about anything; hence, they aren't *really* thinking. Whatever thinking is, it isn't computation.

That's it. That's the argument that has caused well over a decade of heated debate about the cognitive capacities of machines (and the debate shows no sign of subsiding). The argument is seductive and deceptively simple. If you disagree with the conclusion, if you think that the Chinese Room argument does not show that computational states are meaningless, you must say where the argument goes astray, and it is damnably difficult to do that.

Actually, it is not difficult to say what's wrong with the argument, at least to oneself; rather it's hard to get one's colleagues to agree with one's particular diagnosis. Cognitive scientists who agree that Searle's argument is wrong, and agree that computers can think and will one day be as intelligent as we are, cannot seem to agree on what's wrong with Searle's argument. This is one of the most fascinating aspects of the Chinese Room argument. The disagreement between scientists who agree the argument is wrong is almost as vociferous as these same scientists' disagreement with Searle. The reason for this, I think, is that the argument taps into deeply held intuitions about the nature of human cognition and mechanisms—intuitions that place these two on opposite sides of a vast chasm. Since we are currently without a candidate mechanistic theory explaining all, or even most of, cognition, these intuitions remain personal and as much ruled by aesthetics as reason. Hence, how to deflate the argument and bridge the chasm is a matter about which there is no agreement, even where there is agreement that bridging the chasm is possible.

Let's delve into these matters more deeply.

4.   SYSTEMS, ROBOTS, AND OTHER REPLIES

First, let's put some pressure on the argument. In his 1980 paper, Searle couched his argument in terms of *understanding* and intentionality. That is why I italicized this word in my version of the Chinese Room argument. It's not clear what *understanding* is, but it is clear that it's related to consciousness. When you understand an English sentence—"The dog ran home"—you are conscious of what the words mean and what the sentence means. When you fail to understand a sentence in Chinese, you lack such consciousness (but you are conscious of the sounds and *not* understanding what has been said). So it does appear as if Searle is equivocating between consciousness and intentionality, implicitly defining intentionality as consciousness. It is then no wonder that the argument has the intuitive appeal that it does, as well as being so difficult to solve. After all, computers don't appear to be conscious, and we are completely in the dark about how to make them conscious.

To keep Searle's argument logically coherent, let's make two fundamental assumptions (which we've made already when I defined intentionality): that intentionality is a real property of cognitive states and that intentionality is not consciousness or logically tied to the notion of consciousness. With these two assumptions, let's turn to some of the replies to Searle's argument that have appeared over the years.

Perhaps the most obvious point of attack is the claim that you, in the room, looking up marks in your book, are analogous to a working computer. If this claim is false, then it wouldn't matter whether you understood the marks or not: what's true of you would be irrelevant to what's true of a computer. Now it is obvious to the most casual observer that you in the room are *not* similar to the hardware of a late twentieth-century computer. So the Chinese Room argument is defeated, right?

No. This line of attack won't work. Remember I pointed out that any physical system is a special-purpose computer of some sort. All something need do to be a computer is implement a computation. Something does this if it precisely and mechanically applies a certain set of operations to a set of tokens. This is exactly what you are doing in the room. So this tack won't work. From the abstract point of view of computation, you in the room resemble a computer—you are computing. Of course, you don't look like a modern digital machine, but that's irrelevant.

The second and better place to attack Searle's argument is the inference from the fact that you don't understand the conversation on Chinese history to the claim that there is no intentionality associated with the room. This inference is incorrect. The fact that, while in the room, your mental states are not about Chinese history (the conversation "the room" is involved in) does not imply that there are no computational states semantically tied to the conversation on Chinese history. Such computational states might not exist, but facts about the contents of your mental states don't imply this. The contents of your states are strictly irrelevant to this issue. This is simply a matter of logic: Searle's argument is invalid.

Granted the argument is invalid, perhaps the intuition behind it is nevertheless correct (one can sometimes get the right answer for the wrong reasons). Perhaps computational states do lack intentionality. Perhaps Searle has the right conclusion, but the wrong argument.

Now we come to what is to my mind the deepest aspect of Searle's argument. The conclusion is incorrect. There *are* computational states with intentionality—they're the room's. This is the famous *systems reply* to Searle's argument. You in the room are part of another system we can call "you-in-the-room," and it is this other system that has intentional, computational states—states semantically tied to the discourse on Chinese history. Put another way, the relevant system is the *virtual machine* made up of you and your rule book.

This reply is highly counterintuitive, but it is the correct reply provided that you grant Searle the two suppositions mentioned above. In fact, to my mind, almost the entire worth of Searle's argument—which I think is considerable—lies in its forcing us to see the systems reply and to wrestle with its meaning. Before Searle's argument, the claim that an intentional system was really a multiplicity of systems, each with its own intentional states and possibly different semantics, would have struck everyone as too outlandish (with the exception of Daniel Dennett, see 1987). But this deep truth has now been revealed to us by meditating on Searle's argument. Of course, the existence of multiplicities of systems with different semantics still strikes many as outlandish, but so does quantum mechanics. Some truths you never get used to; that doesn't affect their truth, though. Don't reject the systems reply out of hand. Read the papers that discuss it.

To makes matters weirder, note that the room can be eliminated—as Searle himself pointed out in his original paper. All you need to do is memorize the rules written in the book. (We're still imagining here, since actually memorizing the rules without accidentally learning Chinese is impossible in our ordinary world because you still have one set of perceptual and motor systems: you would soon make the requisite associations.) The way to imagine this is to imagine developing another entirely separate cognitive system. What this does is produce another person inaccessible to you inhabiting your same body. Again, a multiplicity of systems share a single physical body, each with its own semantics—its own intentionality.

I'll leave further discussion of the systems reply to other authors in the book (in the next section, I'll present a guide to the chapters). Other rebuttals attack one or both of our two assumptions: that intentionality is real and that intentionality is not consciousness. What if intentionality is not real because it is an incoherent concept, or what if it suffers from some other conceptual problem? Or what if intentionality is really consciousness in disguise? We've already seen briefly what damage implicitly identifying intentionality with consciousness can do. [In Searle's recent book *The Rediscovery of the Mind* (1992) he finally and explicitly relates the two: he thinks that consciousness is the foundation of all intentional thought—"Only a being that could have conscious intentional states could have intentional states at all, and every unconscious intentional state is at least potentially conscious" (p. 132). From this quote, it seems that Searle still claims to distinguish intentionality from consciousness. It is unclear from his writings how he does this.]

Perhaps the most favorite reply is the *robot reply.* This reply concedes to Searle that computers lack intentionality, but then insists that a robot would possess intentionality. According to the robot reply, computing the right functions is *not* sufficient for thinking. Rather, thinking requires perceptual and motor capacities, too. The trouble with computers is that they just sit there. But a robot that could, say, walk around a room avoiding obstacles would clearly have intentional states; otherwise, how could it avoid the obstacles? Perceptual and motor capacities are not just functions (not obviously, anyway). In order to perceive an apple, one has to do more than merely execute a function: one has to interact with the world; one has to process light reflected from the apple, e.g.. If a machine could do that, then it would have intentionality, and indeed an intentionality more robust than process semantics.

This reply preserves this much of the computationalist claim: that a machine can think. However, it gives up the central core of computationalism—namely, that thinking is computing certain functions and that anything that computes those functions thinks. According to the robot reply, computation plus interaction is thinking, but computation alone is not.

I've never cottoned to the robot reply. For starters, it just isn't true that computers just sit there. If they did only that we couldn't interact with them: we couldn't program them, and we couldn't get output from them. So one can't claim that computers can't think while maintaining that computation plus interaction is sufficient for cognition because computers *do* interact with their environments. Those favoring the robot reply must say that standard forms of computer interaction aren't the right kinds of interaction, *and they must say why not and what the right kinds are*. These latter two tasks have yet to be done satisfactorily. Stevan Harnad perhaps has made the most valiant attempt at saying why keyboards and printers don't provide computers with the right kinds of interactions with the world (Harnad 1989, 1993). [To my mind, Bickhard (1993) has the best arguments for why robots are necessary to achieve robust intelligence and representation for a system itself, i.e., a genuine artificial consciousness. But I regard his arguments as going well beyond the notion of intentionality—which, of course, we must do if we hope to develop a robust theory of mind and intelligence.]

Briefly, Harnad argues that transduction—the transformation by sensory organs, such as eyes and ears, of information about the world into a form an organism can use—is a noncomputational process and essential to cognition. Harnad believes that transduction is noncomputational because he believes that transduction is essentially analog (recall our discussion of analog, continuous, and digital computation). Harnad's key term is "analog processing." He avoids the term "analog computation" (as he should), restricting the term "computation" to digital computation (but this is too restrictive since, as we've seen, there is a perfectly fine notion of continuous computation, which is important). I don't wish to argue the importance of transduction to cognition; let's assume it is crucial. (I should note, however, that Harnad thinks transduction is crucial because only it solves the Chinese Room problem, but I think that problem is already solved by the systems reply. I think transduction is important to cognition for evolutionary and epistemological reasons, not for logical reasons.) What is not clear is that transduction is essentially analog.

Recall that a digital computer can do anything an analog processor can do except operate over the continuum complexly. More generally, it appears as if our two notions of computation, digital and continuous, are sufficient to describe, *as a computation,* any process we are confronted with no matter how complex. It seems implausible that there is an analog process that we couldn't capture arbitrarily well with digital or continuous computation. Think about a dimmer switch. It can be approximated arbitrarily well, computationally. Why can't we do this for our visual system? (By the way, neuroscientists frequently couch their theories of our visual system in computational terms.)

Harnad's position is that we cannot render our visual system as a computational system. He thinks that only an analog system can recover the right information (the infinitely precise information?) from an organism's environment. Apparently, then, he's saddled with the view that what's crucial about cognition is the information we cannot, as scientists, measure with our instruments, the information that we cannot gain access to (because it requires infinite precision), since it is only this information that distinguishes an analog process from a computational version of that process.

It appears that Harnad does embrace this strong thesis. Like Searle, he thinks that consciousness and semantics are intimately intertwined. He thinks that leaving out the unmeasurable information leaves out something crucial to consciousness. In fact, when feeling generous, he might be willing to agree that an appropriately programmed computer could be *behaviorally* identical to a human. He just thinks it wouldn't have a mind, i.e., it wouldn't be conscious, nor would it have intentionality. Harnad has also said that there is something special about cognition, and the ubiquity of computation renders computation useless for capturing this specialness (Harnad 1993). It is clear from his writings that he links these two. He thinks what's special about cognition and the mind is intentionality and consciousness. But we can grant Harnad the view that consciousness makes being human special, without granting him the further move that explaining this special phenomenon is what cognitive science is all about.

Cognitive science begins with the assumption that humans are *not* special, that cognition is a physical process, and that our great intelligence is continuous with much less intelligent behaviors found in simple animals throughout the animal kingdom. Cognitive science is the discipline seeking to understand how cognition intelligently mediates environmental stimuli and behavior. Cognitive science is the search for the right architecture. As I said before in Section 2, it is not out of the realm of possibility that consciousness (and its Siamese twin, intentionality) are irrelevant to this enterprise: consciousness might be purely epiphenomenal. Even if it's not, cognitive science is *not* the field that seeks to explain consciousness, at least not as its first job. Why? Because consciousness, again as I said in Section 2, is far too difficult a phenomenon to pin the hopes of a science on. We seek to explain the causes of intelligent behavior. Hopefully, we will one day make some progress on consciousness, but in the meantime we should concentrate on the cognitive causes of behavior. Computation might or might not eventually explain consciousness, but computation clearly is useful now for explaining cognition. And ultimately, cognition *is* for getting along in the world. Lingering doubts about whether something that in fact *gets* along in the world *really* has a mind or not seem to me to be misplaced, and something of a luxury.

So, Harnad's robot reply requires taking seriously information that we cannot get access to (the infinitely precise information that makes an analog process continuous) and using this information to explain what we have no business worrying about how to scientifically explain right now: consciousness. Instead, we should take seriously only the information we can measure, and we should use it to explain the semantic content of cognitive states.

There is more to say about the robot reply, but we need to press on. Later chapters deal with it further.

The systems and robot replies are the dominant and most hotly debated attacks on the Chinese Room argument, and except for denying the reality of intentionality or the distinction between intentionality and consciousness (which are also popular), most other replies are either variants of the two front-runners or fail on some point of computation. The "brain simulator" reply is an example of the latter. This reply says that if, in the room, you simulated the workings of the human brain instead of looking up Chinese characters in some book, your thoughts would indeed be about Chinese history. But it is fairly obvious that this is not true; you would just be simulating a brain, and your thoughts would be about that task. Again, however, it is of no consequence what *your* thoughts are about: it's what the virtual machine's thoughts (states) are about. The brain simulator reply forgets that what's important about cognition is the functions and algorithms of which it is composed, not how they're implemented.

This concludes my introduction to thinking machines and the problem of intentionality. I hope I have convinced you that computational cognitive science might well be innocent of the error Searle accuses us of making, and beyond that, that computational cognitive science might be, if not correct, at least in the ballpark. It is now time to get to the detailed defense—the other chapters in this book. I close this introduction with a synopsis of each.

5.   THE CHAPTERS

The chapters in the first section are by authors who are dubious about the very existence of intentionality as understood by most philosophers. Resnick's Chapter 2 finds an analogy between intentionality and phlogiston, the seventeenth-century principle of burning that was later mistakenly reified as a substance thought to be released from a burning object. Phlogiston theory is no longer with us, and for a very interesting reason, Resnick contends—a reason that applies to intentionality also. The standard knock on phlogiston theory is that it had the fatal flaw of many old, brave theories: it made empirical claims that turned out to be false. The substance, phlogiston, was supposed to have negative weight, a property logically required if phlogiston was to explain the relevant chemical facts. Resnick's chapter represents a good bit of historical sleuthing and shows us that the demise of phlogiston theory was long and complex, involving more than just empirically false claims. These historical details make phlogiston theory and intentionality analogous—to the detriment of intentionality.

Fields's Chapter 3 is in the systems reply camp and brings an experimental perspective to the problem of intentionality and computation. One objection to computationalism is that it cannot prevent arbitrary attributions of content to the various data structures and representations involved in a computational process. Apparently, then, we are free to interpret any computational process any way we want. Fields considers the process of constructing a computational interpretation from measurements of a system's behavior and shows that this objection is incorrect. The analysis of how contents are attributed to states based on experimental observations also shows that the requirement of a flow of control between states places strong constraints on the semantics. These constraints provide a distinction between arbitrarily attributed content and stipulated content. Intentionality, in Fields's view, is ubiquitous: any system that interacts with its environment is intentional. Intentionality cannot, therefore, be used as a criterion to draw principled distinctions between systems of different kinds.

Dennett believes that the notion of original intentionality is incoherent (Chapter 4). The distinction between the derived intentionality of books and our own sui generis intentionality emerging ex nihilo from our brains is unsustainable and, anyway, quite useless. He argues for this by first distinguishing between "real" and "as-if" intentionality, a distinction orthogonal to "original" versus "derived" intentionality. Then using a clever thought experiment of this own—a variant of the robot reply—he manages to turn Searle's result upside down: not even the person in the room has original intentionality. Mother Nature—evolution in all its glory—turns out to be the font of intentionality, and all intentionality is *derived*, including Mother Nature's. Assuredly we all, including Mother Nature, have *real* intentionality. But nothing has original intentionality. (One can read Dennett's chapter as claiming that Mother Nature alone possesses original intentionality, and the rest of us, plants, animals, books, and computers, possess derived intentionality only. Based on this reading, original intentionality would be a coherent concept, but no threat to computationalism.)

My own Chapter 5 goes in this group because, as I indicated in Section 2, I'm skeptical that the standard philosophical notion of intentionality is sufficiently independent both of consciousness and process semantics. I'm also impressed by the fact that if Searle's argument were correct, then original intentionality would be useless, because, by hypothesis, the room's behavior is indistinguishable from mine. The intelligence of the room, therefore, is completely independent of its intentionality. Intelligence is a phenomenon we can study scientifically.

The next group of chapters argues that, when one is careful about definitions, computers naturally have, or can have, intentionality of a useful sort. Most of the chapters supporting the systems reply are here.

Cole spends the first part of his Chapter 6 discussing and analyzing the non sequitur at the heart of Searle's argument. Then beginning at the CPU level (the central processing unit), he speculates on how computers could have semantics, understanding, sentience, and finally consciousness. Along the way, he clarifies all of these notions. Cole's position is that the alleged impossibility of computer cognition rests on misunderstandings of the definitions of these cognitive terms and concepts.

The Churchlands (Chapter 7) present a compelling and eye-opening analogy between Searle and an imagined, mid-nineteenth-century objector to Maxwell's claim that light is electromagnetic waves. Where Searle proposes his Chinese Room, Maxwell's opponent proposes "the luminous room." Exposing the conceptual error of the luminous room argument cleanly exhibits a similar error in the Chinese Room argument. The Churchlands' chapter is important for another, separate reason. The Churchlands are not friends of traditional AI. Their sympathies lie with artificial neural networks (ANNs). They believe that the only way to build an intelligent machine is to build a neural network. Neural networks, they point out, have a host of very interesting properties that standard AI algorithms lack. Some cognitive scientists with similar sympathies think that ANN-based machines, unlike digital computers, are immune to Searle's objection because such machines are continuous analog devices, like brains (of course, when modeled on a computer ANNs are not analog continuous devices; they are discrete and digital). These researchers believe that neural networks' continuity somehow enables hooking them up to the world in the way required for endowing them with semantics and hence intentionality. The Churchlands will have none of this. Their position is that cognition is an architectural achievement. ANNs, but not standard AI machines, come closer to the right architecture. However, both kinds of machines are plenty semantical and have the capability for complete intentionality.

Dyer's Chapter 8 contains one of the best versions of the systems reply I've read. He makes the point I briefly mentioned above that eliminating the room by having Searle memorize the rules for manipulating Chinese characters produces a split personality. One of them is Searle, a philosopher at the University of California at Berkeley; the other is, say, a Chinese historian who also happens to live in Berkeley. The split just happens to be very exact and complete. Both personalities have all the intentionality their hearts could desire. Dyer also rehearses several related intentionality-based arguments attacking computationalism as well as their rebuttals.

Perlis proposes in Chapter 9 an architecture that would enable an artificial reasoner to refer to objects in its external environment. Referring to such external objects is just another name for intentionality. When one successfully refers to my pet spider, Fang, one has an internal representation that stands for Fang, and one takes that representation to stand for Fang. This last condition—taking an internal representation to stand for something—is one of Perlis's key points: both the representation and the fact that it represents something must be in some sense internal to the reasoner. Put another way, Perlis's view is that in order to successfully refer (to have intentionality) a machine (or you, for that matter) must have a model of an *inner world* modeling an external world. Here he presents a way to build a system with such an internal structure.

Finally, Rapaport (Chapter 10) argues, contra Searle, that computers can understand natural language and thus be humanly intelligent (Rapaport believes that understanding a natural language is necessary and sufficient for human-level intelligence). He also takes on Fred Dretske, another philosopher who is convinced that computers can't think because they allegedly lack intentionality. Like Perlis, Rapaport stresses the *internal* relation between representations for semantics and cognition. But there is a twist. Searle and others of his ilk have long claimed that computers, but not humans, are purely *syntactic machines*: manipulating symbols without knowing what they mean; this is why machines lack intentionality. In fact, the purely syntactic nature of computation is what the Chinese Room argument is intended to show. Rapaport agrees that computers are syntactical but argues that syntax suffices for semantics, hence computers are not *purely* syntactical. The internal relationships between representations turn out to be sufficient for semantics. Rapaport's arguments are made all the more compelling because he and his colleagues have a system that understands some English. This system is called CASSIE and Rapaport discusses it in his chapter.

The last group of chapters is about intentionality in the larger world. Three topics are discussed: consciousness, psychological explanation, and psychology. As we've seen, consciousness is intimately related to intentionality, maybe too intimately. The two might be different names for the same thing. They would then be identical—the ultimate intimacy. Well, what about consciousness itself? Could consciousness be a computation? Can it be explained mechanistically? Many philosophers think not. Leonard Angel is not one of them. Angel, in Chapter 11, discusses five key arguments designed to show that whatever consciousness is, it can't be a computational phenomenon. He systematically takes each argument apart, exposing its flaws. Angel concentrates on three arguments: an argument presented recently by Searle is shown to rest on an ambiguity. A standard source of pessimism concerning AI aspirations is considered, and a response is given based on Angel's strategy for showing how "conventionalizing mutuality" is programmable. And an important argument first offered by Noam Chomsky, which has not received widespread attention, is reconstructed and a detailed critical analysis presented. The argument is found to rest on an incorrect premise. Angel concludes with a positive section, suggesting ways in which the computational view of cognition and the mind *enhances* our understanding of consciousness.

Charles Wallis (Chapter 12) is concerned with the explanatory role representation plays in theories in cognitive science. On Wallis's view, many cognitive scientists, most notably Jerry Fodor and Fred Dretske, have incorrect views about what phenomena representations explain and how they explain them. These confusions in turn fuel further confusion about the nature of intentionality. Wallis argues that representation is not required to explain behavior, as is traditionally supposed. He points out that representation explains cognitive capacities. He then argues that, at the foundational level, researchers have reversed the order of the phenomena that need to be explained. Typically, researchers explain representation in terms of what one can know (i.e., in terms of epistemology). Instead, Wallis argues, cognitive scientists should explain what one can know in terms of representation, i.e., in terms of what the organism can represent. Finally, he argues that, after everything is put in the right order, there is still an important role for epistemology in psychological theories and explanations.

Hayes, Ford, and Adams-Webber take on Joseph Rychlak (and, implicitly, Searle and Roger Penrose 1989) in Chapter 13. Rychlak claimed that an entire, and successful, theoretical framework in cognitive psychology is incompatible with the view that human brains are computers of some sort. They explain the theoretical framework, personal construct theory, and then show how it is, in fact, compatible with computationalism. Indeed, they argue that cognitive psychology and AI are methodologically joined at the hip and that this is good for both. In the course of their chapter, they also discuss in detail the notion of a *virtual machine* and its close cousin, the notion that though modern hardware is Boolean (two-valued: "true" and "false"), software need not be, and usually isn't. Finally, they spend time discussing the discomfort that computational models of mind and cognition cause and suggest remedies.

This concludes my opening statement. The defense of computationalism and computational cognitive science now begins in earnest. I hope that by the end of the book, you are persuaded that support for computationalism and cognitive science is strong enough to warrant releasing us on our own recognizance. Of course, we might still succeed in hanging ourselves. Only time and vigorous research will tell. But even if we do hang ourselves, it won't be because of some conceptual error we've made, as the anticomputationalist philosophers and psychologists would have you believe. If we do fail, it will be for methodological reasons—the deepest reasons of all.

6.   ACKNOWLEDGMENTS

I thank Alan Strudler for reading and commenting on earlier drafts of this chapter. I also thank Dave Chalmers, Dennis Pixton, Matt Brin, Tom Head, and Robin Hill for discussions on computation and cognition.

7.   REFERENCES

Barr, A., Cohen, P., and Feigenbaum, E. (eds.) (1989) *The Handbook of Artificial Intelligence Vols I–IV*. (Reading, MA: Addison-Wesley).

Bickhard, M. (1993) Representational content in humans and machines. *Journal of Experimental and Theoretical Artificial Intelligence,* 5, (4).

Block, N. (1993) Review of Daniel Dennett's *Consciousness Explained. Journal of Philosophy, XC,* (4): 181-193.

Blum, L., Shub, M., and Smale, S. (1989) On a theory of computation and complexity over the real numbers: NP-completeness, recursive functions, and universal machines. *Bulletin of the American Mathematical Society*, 21, (1): 1-46.

Brooks, R. (1986) A robust layered control system for a mobile robot. *IEEE Journal of Robotics and Automation*, 2: 14 – 23.

Brooks, R. (1991) Intelligence without representation. *Artificial Intelligence* 47: 139–159.

Chalmers, D. (1994) A computational foundation for cognition. *Minds and Machines.*, 5, (4).

Chalmers, D. (1993) *Toward a Theory of Consciousness.* Ph.D. dissertation, Indiana University, Bloomington. Also available from Center for Research on Concepts and Cognition, Indiana University.

Church, A. (1936a) A note on the entscheidungsproblem. *Journal of Symbolic Logic*, 1: 40-41, 101–102.

Church, A. (1936b) An unsolvable problem of elementary number theory. *American Journal of Mathematics*, 58: 345–363.

Dennett, D. (1991) *Consciousness Explained*. (Boston: Little, Brown).

Dennett, D. (1987) *The Intentional Stance*. (Cambridge, MA: Bradford/MlT Press).

Fields, C. (1989) Consequences of nonclassical measurement for the algorithmic description of continuous dynamical systems. *Journal of Experimental and Theoretical Artificial Intelligence*, 1: 171–189.

Fodor, J. (1968) *Psychological Explanation*. (New York: Random House).

Harnad, S. (1989) Minds, machines, and Searle. *Journal of Experimental and Theoretical Artificial Intelligence*, 1: 5–25.

Harnad, S. (1993) Grounding symbols in the analog world with neural nets. *Think*, 2: 12–20, 29–30.

Haugeland, J. (ed.) (1981) *Mind Design*. (Cambridge, MA: Bradford/MlT Press).

Hofstadter, D., and Dennett, D. (eds.) (1981) *The Mind's I*. (New York: Basic Books).

Ginsburg, M. (1993) *The Essentials of Artificial Intelligence*. (Los Altos, CA: Morgan Kaufman).

Newell, A. (1990) *Unified Theories of Cognition*. (Cambridge, MA: Harvard University Press).

Penrose, R. (1989) *The Emperor's New Mind*. (New York: Penguin Books).

Searle, J. (1980) Minds, brains, and programs. *Behavioral and Brain Sciences,* 3: 417–424.

Searle, J. (1990) Is the brain a digital computer? *Proceedings and Addresses of the American Philosophical Association,* 64: 21–37.

Searle, J. (1992) *The Rediscovery of the Mind.* (Cambridge, MA: MIT/Bradford Press).

Turing, A. (1936) On computable numbers with an application to the entscheidungs problem. *Proceedings of the London Mathematical Society,* series 2, (42): 230–265, (43): 544–546.

II

Intentionality
And Its Discontents

Intentionality Is Phlogiston

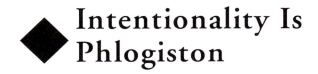

Peter Resnick

From a glance at the philosophical literature over the past ten years, one would think that intentionality[1] was one of the hottest new topics to hit philosophy since Quine or Wittgenstein. In fact, intentionality has been around for quite a long time in the philosophical literature. *Intentionality* is a technical philosophical term for the "aboutness" of mental states; that is, intentionality is what makes mental states *about* things. The theory of intentionality has had a rebirth of sorts in its application to recent issues in philosophy of mind. In fact, it is not only getting a lot of mileage in philosophy nowadays, but it can even be seen in the more philosophically oriented journals on cognitive science and artificial intelligence. As more and more of the foundational issues are fleshed out, the word *intentionality* is entering the vocabulary of cognitive scientists and intentionality is even becoming a part of

Thinking Computers and Virtual Persons
edited by Eric Dietrich
ISBN 0-12-215495-9

certain cognitive science research programs: scientists are now looking for the neurological microstructure responsible for intentionality.

There is an interesting parallel to intentionality in the eighteenth-century theory of phlogiston. Phlogiston was thought to be the principle of burning. Originally, *phlogiston* was used by a few chemists as a technical term to describe certain substances that were inflammable. Eventually, after phlogiston theory entered the scientific mainstream, scientists misconstrued phlogiston to be a substance that was released when things burned, and *phlogiston* was soon dismissed as a theoretical term.

My claim in this chapter is that intentionality will be found to be a useless scientific entity, just as phlogiston was in the eighteenth century, if the current direction of the research and literature continues. I will present an overview of the history of intentionality as well as a rather nonstandard view of the history of phlogiston and compare the theories and theorists in the respective fields in order to show that intentionality is probably fated to the same end reached by phlogiston. If scientific research continues to look for a *thing* called intentionality rather than intentionality being simply a property of certain mental phenomena, *intentionality* will almost certainly be rejected as a referring term.

1.   INTENTIONALITY

1.1   *Introduction—Definitions of Intentionality*

Intentionality is one of the most controversial terms in the recent history of philosophy of mind and philosophy of language. It has been used as everything from a description of a certain "state of mind" to a major part of speech-act theory. In its latest form, *intentionality* can even be found appearing in some of the cognitive psychological and linguistics literature, as well as in artificial intelligence research. Since the word *intentionality* first came into use, its definition has changed substantially. However, some important features still remain in common with its original meaning. In this first section, I have two major goals. The first is to develop some general definitions of *intentionality* and run through the history of the term to get an overview of the philosophical ideas involved. The second, which is part of my overall concern, is to establish what the ontological status of intentionality is. It is the ontology of intentionality that will allow us to compare it to phlogiston in the end.

Simply put, "Intentionality is aboutness" (*The Oxford Companion to the Mind* 1987, p. 383) By "aboutness," I mean that intentionality is the quality of certain mental states to be *about* things in the external world. In his book entitled *Intentionality*, John Searle gives an excellent account of this general definition.

> Intentionality is that property of mental states and events by which they are directed at or about or of objects and states of affairs in the world. If, for example, I have a belief, it must be a belief that such and such is the case; if I have a fear, it must be the fear of something or that something will occur; if I have a desire, it must be a desire to do something or that something should happen or be the case; if I have an intention, it must be an intention to do something. [Searle 1983, p. 1]

There are some who claim that many things, not just mental states, can have intentionality. Certainly books are *about* events and a discussion can be *about* a person. Dennett and Haugeland explain that there are three general categories whose members may be considered to have intentionality, including

> a great variety of *mental* states and events (ideas, beliefs, desires, thoughts, hopes, fears, perceptions, *dreams*, hallucinations . . .), also various *linguistic* items (sentences, questions, poems, headlines, instructions . . .), and perhaps other sorts of *representations* as well (pictures, charts, films, symphonic tone poems, computer programs . . . .). [*The Oxford Companion to the Mind* 1987, p. 384]

However, others like Searle claim that things other than mental states and events only have "derived" intentionality; what makes a headline about something or a picture be of something is that there is a person for whom these things do their intentional pointing. The concept of intentionality certainly has some tie to the idea of reference, i.e., that things (in the case of reference, words) in some way point to things in the external world. Many philosophers are quite content to say that reference, and for that matter intentionality, is something that mental states have and that other objects, words, or sentences have only by virtue of their status as triggers for mental states.

The idea that certain mental states are about the world is a very intuitive notion; as a part of folk psychology, intentionality in this philosophical sense is a simple and useful concept. When talking about desires or hopes, there must be some way to say what those desires are about. For instance, if a person were to say "I have a hope," the first question asked would most certainly be, "What are you hoping?" It would not do for the person to reply, "Nothing at all; I just have a hope." Mental states of this sort need to be about something. This kind of folk psychology, however, does not appear to be the origin of the term *intentionality*, at least in its most technical sense.

1.2   History of Intentionality

Before a discussion of recent problems in the study of intentionality can begin, I want to provide some historical background. *Intentionality* as a term had three distinct stages of development as I see it. The first stage was the use of the Latin *intentio* (intention) and *intendo* by Thomas Aquinas in the twelfth century. *Intentionality* then reappears with Franz Brentano and Edmund Husserl in the late nineteenth and early twentieth centuries for the second stage of development. Finally, I will examine the work of John Searle, who presents the current version of intentionality that will be my focus for the rest of this chapter.

The first use of intentionality seems to have appeared during the time of the Scholastics. It was derived from the Latin words *intendo* or *intentio* meaning "to point at" or to "tend towards." The terms were apparently first used in the philosophical technical sense by Saint Thomas Aquinas to describe the way people's souls were able to come in contact with objects in the world. Things having intentionality point to something other than themselves according to Aquinas. "Intention signifies a tending to another: that is the very ring of the term" (Aquinas 1970, la2æ. 12, 1). Borrowing from Aristotle and Avicenna, Aquinas believed the objects of intentionality to be "received into the soul" (*New Catholic Encyclopedia* 1967, p. 564). Through this object in the soul, which Aquinas refers to as an "intelligible *species*" (*New Catholic Encyclopedia* 1967, p. 564) a person is able to have thoughts about the object in the world.[2] This is not to say that the person has thoughts about the object in the soul, but uses that object to be intentional toward the real world object.

> Sense images are illuminated by the agent intellect and further, by its power, species are abstracted from them. They are illuminated because sense images, by the power of the agent intellect, are rendered apt to have intellectual intentions or species extracted from them, just as a man's sense part receives heightened power from being joined to his intellect part. [Aquinas 1968, la.85, 1 ad 4]

For Aquinas, intentionality was our ability to understand, in our intellect, the form or "species" of an external object. This notion of intentionality should be relatively uncontroversial and should not conflict with our commonsense beliefs about what our minds (or, as Aquinas would have it, our souls) normally do. Further concern with intentionality was not seen until the term was revived in the late nineteenth century by Franz Brentano and then further studied by his student, Edmund Husserl.

Franz Brentano was the first modern philosopher to use the term *intentionality*. For Brentano, an early phenomenologist and psychologist, intentionality was the defining property that differentiated the mental from all other things. Accordingly, intentionality became a more exact idea for Brentano than Aquinas had presented. Since Brentano was the first modern philosopher to work on this, his theories are at best underdeveloped and, unfortunately, somewhat confused. Brentano's earliest writings indicate that he believed intentionality to be the directedness of acts toward some sort of "object which is always there" (Føllesdal 1982a, p. 32). By this, he meant that when we act toward something or think about something, that thing is a constant object that, as Brentano put it, "intentionally inexists." Though the concept of "inexistence" (*Inexistenz*), is not well explained, the idea of constant *external* objects, even inexisting ones, did present some deep philosophical problems for Brentano. For Brentano to postulate truly external objects that our thoughts are about, he would have to have accounted for a connection between our minds and the objects in the world—some sort of metaphysical string connecting an intentional thought and what it is about. This problem of mental reference has been a bugbear in epistemology and philosophy of language throughout the history of the disciplines. Even if Brentano had been able to solve this problem, and according to many (Føllesdal 1982a; Gurwitsch 1982) he did not, there must also be an account of the fact that we have thoughts about things that do not exist. It is quite easy for me to have a thought about a purple elephant standing in my room, but clearly there is no corresponding external object that my thought is about. If Brentano had avoided the problems of external objects by claiming that the inexisting objects exist only in our minds, then he would have given up the idea of intentionality doing something in conjunction with the external world. Even so, it appears that with the idea of inexistence Brentano allowed for objects that exist only in the mind.

> [To Brentano,] objects of intentions, considered as such, are not the real forms of things, but only forms in the mind. Or, put in another way, every intention has an object, but considered simply as an object of an intention, such an object does not have to be anything extramental. [*New Catholic Encyclopedia* 1967,   p. 565]

These problems are the "problems of intentional objects" (Føllesdal 1982a, p. 33)

Unlike Brentano, Edmund Husserl avoided the problem of intentional objects by introducing the term *noema*. A noema is simply the object *as meant or intended* (Gurwitsch 1982, p. 63). Føllesdal explains:

> According to Husserl, there is associated with each act a noema, in virtue of which the act is directed toward its object, if it has any. When we think of a centaur, our act of thinking has a noema, but it has no object; there exists no object of which we think. Because of its noema, however, even such an act is directed. To be *directed* simply is to have a noema. [Føllesdal 1982b, p. 74]

Noema is not the object that our thought is about, but is the object *as it is intended* in our thought. Because of this, even if the object does not exist, there can still be a noema of the object as it would exist.

> Let us consider a different point of view between the perceptual noema and the thing perceived. The house may be torn down, but none of the pertinent noemata is affected thereby. Even after its destruction the house may still be remembered, and it may be remembered as presenting itself under one or the other of the aspects under which it had previously appeared in perceptual experience. To be sure, the noema is no longer a perceptual one; it is rather a noema of memory. [Gurwitsch 1982, p. 64]

Husserl attempted to solve the problem of intentional objects by creating the noema. Intentionality in this sense is basically a description of a type of mental experience, though it is unclear what sort of real-entity status Husserl gives to the noema. Early in his writings, Husserl doesn't make any claims about the ontological status of noema.

> It is important to reiterate, however, that in *L.I.* [*Logical Investigations*] Husserl has no ontological commitment to how the intentional content of an act is realized in the mind or brain, nor has he a view of what job the content performs other than that of individuating types of mental acts by describing the objects to which each type purportedly refers. [Dreyfus and Hall 1982, p. 4]

Later in his book *Ideas*, though, it may be that the noema was more of a complex entity than just a description of some function of the mind (Dreyfus and Hall 1982, p. 7). Commentators seem to disagree on this point, but this is beyond the scope of what I wish to discuss here. With this simple introduction to the history of intentionality in mind, we can now move on to look at the present status of intentionality theory.

Of all the philosophers in the history of intentionality I will discuss, John Searle presents the strongest view of intentionality. For Searle, things that have intentionality do not *point* in Aquinas's sense to objects in the world. More like Husserl and Brentano, Searle claims that intentional states have objects as their content in very much the same way that sentences have objects as their content. Directedness is the key to intentionality for Searle. This seems to be more along the lines of the lay use of the word *intention*, since when we intend something, we are directing our action toward a goal or object. Searle, however, is quick to point out that intentions and actions that are intentional are only two things that have intentionality.

> . . . intending and intentions are just one form of Intentionality among others, they have no special status. The obvious pun on "Intentionality" and "intention" suggests that intentions in the ordinary sense have some special role in the theory of Intentionality; but on my account intending to do

something is just one form of Intentionality along with belief, hope, fear, desire, and lots of others. [Searle 1983, p. 3]

Like statement-containing sentences, intentional states can either be satisfied or fail to be satisfied by states of affairs in the world. For instance, if I have a belief that it is raining (i.e., I believe it is raining), the "condition of satisfaction" for this belief is that it is in fact raining. In this example we also see what Searle refers to as the "psychological mode" of the intentional state: the action of believing that it is raining has a psychological mode of belief, as opposed to hope, desire, or wanting.

> . . . every Intentional state consists of an *Intentional content* in a *psychological mode*. Where that content is a whole proposition and where there is a direction of fit, the Intentional content determines the *conditions of satisfaction*. Conditions of satisfaction are those conditions which, as determined by the Intentional content, must obtain if the state is to be satisfied. [Searle 1983, p. 12-13]

Though Searle's theory gets rather elaborate, there is only one aspect that I need to discuss here since it brings Searle very close to the central theme of this chapter: he takes mental phenomena and intentionality to be products of the biological makeup of the brain.

> On my account, mental states are as real as any other biological phenomenon, as real as lactation, photosynthesis, mitosis, or digestion. Like these other phenomena, mental states are caused by biological phenomena and in turn cause other biological phenomena. [Searle, 1983, p. 264]

> . . . I am able to understand English and have other forms of intentionality as far as we know . . . because I am a certain sort of organism with a certain biological (i.e., chemical and physical) structure, and this structure under certain conditions is causally capable of producing perception, action, understanding, learning, and other intentional phenomena. And part of the point of the present argument is that only something that had those causal powers can have intentionality. [Searle 1980, p. 422][3]

This starts to go far beyond the conventional idea of intentionality as the property of having some sort of directedness toward the world. According to Searle, there is something special in humans (or perhaps he might say "higher animals")[4] that produces this *thing* called intentionality. Though Searle has never directly said anything on what the microstructure in the brain would be for intentionality, many of the scientists who take Searle's work seriously have made some attempts to find intentionality in some brain microstructure. These moves toward the scientific, biological object status of intentionality are my central concern.[5]

1.3   Intentionality in Science

The implications of Searle's assumptions for studies in cognitive science, artificial intelligence, and animal intelligence are enormous. Searle clearly wants to show that the only things that can have intentionality are those organisms that have some sort of "higher-level brains." As I stated earlier, the "aboutness" that newspaper headlines have for events and that thermometers have for the temperature is not intentionality for philosophers like Searle; at best it is a derived sort of intentionality. But to justify the claim that only "higher" organisms can have intentionality in virtue of their brains, science will have to show that intentionality is some kind of *thing* unique to the brains of these organisms. Furthermore, this brain phenomenon cannot be simple perceptual, sense-organ connectedness with the world; thermostats have that kind of intentionality, since they do possess a sense organ of a sort. Scientists, according to Searle, must start looking for a neural explanation for the first-order, nonderived intentionality that people (and some other living things) have that thermostats and newspaper headlines do not. This research plan has started to creep into recent scientific studies resulting in some interesting claims.

David Premack is a psychologist and biologist working on questions of language in nonhuman primates. He has done extensive work in testing these animals' abilities to arrange plastic tokens on a magnetic board to form meaningful sentencelike strings and has also made some interesting comparisons between ape and human intelligence (Premack 1976, 1986). Premack is also one of the modern scientists who has taken the notion of intentionality seriously in his scientific research.

> Communication, which we are only now beginning to study. . . , is of interest in part because it provides a setting in which to glimpse intentionality, and intentionality of interest in turn because it gives evidence of a concept of self. Indeed, communication and causal analysis can be brought together by the concept of self, both giving evidence of the concept but in different ways. [Premack 1976, p. 342]

More than any of the philosophers, and expectedly so for a nonphilosopher, Premack brings in the common use of intentions and intentional acts into his use of intentionality.

> Suppose Sarah [a chimpanzee] asked a trainer a question, and the trainer answered but then stood in front of the board, blocking Sarah's view of the answer. Any attempts Sarah made to recover the answer would be accepted as evidence of intentionality. . . . Comparable evidence could be provided by the converse case. If a trainer asked Sarah a question, and then utterly neglected her answer, Sarah could give evidence of intentionality by calling the trainers attention to the lapse, either by gently turning the trainers head toward the

board, or more impressively by an appropriate linguistic rebuke. Both cases would testify to Sarah's intentionality, showing that Sarah had "spoken"—in one case by asking and in the other by answering—with her listener in mind. [Premack 1976, p. 342]

This more common use of intentionality is not in conflict with the philosophers' definitions. Intentionality for Premack is the directedness and desire that he hopes to show exist in the chimpanzee. As Searle (1983) says, intentions are one type of intentionality. Just looking at intentionality in this way is not a problem as far as I am concerned. Interestingly, however, Premack also apparently aims to discover the biological microstructures involved in intentionality, and not the derived type that could be explained solely by perception. Given that Premack's interests are not philosophical but scientific, it is difficult to find a quote as perfectly philosophically crystallized as one would find, for instance, in Searle, but he does give many indications to this effect.[6]

> . . . although laymen may attribute states of mind (take the intentional stance) with respect to frogs, crocodiles, and the like, they are in considerable measure mistaken in doing so. Technical tests will show that at least some of these creatures are not intentional systems. (Thus, at least some creatures are entirely free of intentionality: they neither instantiate it or attribute it.) [Premack 1988, p. 523]

In laying out Premack's views, I am not trying to show that the scientific theories he is proposing are false. In fact, all that I am concerned with here is the fact that Premack has taken intentionality seriously as a scientific notion, and I believe that it can be established from context that he has also taken it as a material notion; it is something that could be found in the brain if we look hard enough and in the right places. Again, it is this kind of ontological status that will be most important to my conclusions.

Kenneth Sayre, though not a scientist like Premack, has given a view of cognitive science models that include looking into the biological and psychological bases of intentionality. And since Sayre is a philosopher, he makes no bones about this being an appropriate research direction. As he states in the abstract to his 1986 article:

> Visual representations are explained as patterns of cortical activity that are enabled to focus on objects in the changing visual environment by constantly adjusting to maintain levels of mutual information between pattern and object that are adequate for continuing perceptual control. In these terms, . . . the intentional functions of vision are those involved in the establishment and maintenance of such representations . . . The article concludes with proposals for extending this account of intentionality to the higher domains of conceptualization and reason, and with speculation about how semantic information-processing might be achieved in mechanical systems. [Sayre 1986, p. 121]

Sayre gives an elaborate account of how the mathematical theory of communication and the functions of certain parts of the brain interact to produce intentionality and semantic abilities in humans. The following excerpts from his conclusions show how involved a scientific empirical study Sayre is proposing.

> But what about intentionality and info(s) [semantic information]? The answer in general is that the relationship of identity in info(t) [mathematical information, in the technical sense] structure between O [the set of perceivable events at the object] and C [cortical events] *is* the intentionality of perception . . . it should be clear that not just any relationship of info(t) identity between input and output structures across a cascade of information channels constitutes a relationship of intentionality. It is not enough that the channel in question be involved in the perceptual guidance of the organism's behavior . . . What is required is a perceptual process that locks onto particular structures in the objective environment and tracks those structures through changing perceptual circumstances.
>
> . . . In terms used above, info(t) reaching the upper levels of the posterior branch of the visual cascade is processed in a variable coding format, the configurations of which are continuously being adjusted in the interests of efficiency. The relatively static formats in which the frog's brain receives reports from its visual sensors do not qualify for intentionality. [Sayre 1986, p. 135]

> . . . Although the issue is one for empirical determination, there is no reason by the present account why animals other than humans should not possess this feature [intentionality]. Although fishes and reptiles are probably excluded, higher primates and felines are not. [Sayre 1986, p. 136]

Again, I will make no claims about the actual scientific theory that Sayre is proposing,[7] but Sayre's theory assumes something very important about intentionality. For the theory to work, intentionality must be a special type of brain processing that only the "high-level" human cortex can handle, especially the "upper levels of the posterior branch of the visual cascade." According to Sayre, "low-level" brains like frogs and snakes possess could not perform these intentional perceptual connections to the outside world.

H. L. Roitblat, a specialist in animal cognition, is a scientist who makes some of the most straightforward claims concerning intentionality. As with Premack, he is not concerned with making any broad philosophical claims, but nonetheless, he does appear to be very interested in intentional phenomena in the brain.

> I would like to offer a fourth alternative strategy that holds the possibility of resolving both the strategic and the representational issue. . . . According to the hierarchical cognitive action theory, . . . the mind consists of hierarchically organized networks of highly interconnected units. Levels in the hierarchy correspond roughly to levels of abstraction. Nodes at the lowest level directly

control patterns of muscular and neuroendocrine activity. Nodes at somewhat higher levels represent abstractions of these actions. Nodes at the highest levels represent intentions, thoughts, expectancies, goals, and motivations. [Roitblat 1988, p. 525]

Note here that in these responses to Daniel Dennett's article on intentionality (1988), Roitblat appears not to be satisfied with a level of description, but is claiming that things like endocrine control and abstracted patterns of muscular activity[8] are the same types of *things* as intentions and thoughts. The nodes that he mentions are clearly (from the context) not theoretical nodes like in network systems theory, but are in fact neurons at different "levels" in the brain. That is, goals and intentions are neurological phenomena that are just at a higher level (i.e., using other neurons) than heartbeat and muscular control mechanisms. More importantly, Roitblat also seems to justify the claim that some "lower" species and nonbiological systems lack intentionality on the grounds that they do not have these necessary "high-level" brain parts. Again, these are implications of Roitblat's assumptions and not theories he himself would necessarily support. These examples seem to show quite clearly that the scientific community is using intentionality as a dividing line for intelligent and nonintelligent systems.

1.4   *What Is Becoming of Intentionality?*

The history of the term *intentionality* from Aquinas through Husserl should point to one clear fact: intentionality now means something very different from its original meaning. Intentionality in the older sense seems to be that unknown property that separated mental phenomena from physical ones, under the assumption that something like that kind of "unknown property" actually exists. Intentionality was a macrophenomenon explanation of mental and spiritual types of things. Aquinas and Brentano, and even Husserl to a certain extent, were not concerned with intentionality as some physical entity that existed somewhere in the brain. Aquinas was calling a certain function of the soul intentionality or *intentio*. Brentano was describing a certain feature of the mental, but it is not clear that he would have placed the mind necessarily in the brain. Even Husserl, who emphasized perception in his study of the noema (cf. Dreyfus and Hall 1982, pp. 97-123; Føllesdal 1982c, pp. 93-96), studied the objects of intentionality and did not make the notion very scientific. Certainly none of them were looking for corresponding microstructure to the macrophenomenon of intentionality.

Searle, on the other hand, views intentionality as a special kind of physical phenomenon. Intentionality is how the brain is able to make contact with things external to it. For Searle, intentionality is a way for semantic representations in the brain to take place, since it is through contact with the external that people are able to get the meanings of the objects they are having intentional thoughts about. The greatest implication of Searle's proposal for intentionality is that there should be some sort of objective phenomenon in the brain that corresponds to intentionality. For Searle (or at least for his followers), the fact that scientists who searched for a corresponding group of neurons for the pain experience found activations in the C-fibers[9] implies that there should be a real brain state corresponding to intentional mental states. The job now for Searle's theory is to find empirical scientific data to back up the existence of such an entity. And though Searle may not be going out to do the research that his theory implies should be done, there are researchers who have taken up the challenge.

And so we get to our unsuspecting scientists. Premack and Roitblat do a great deal of interesting scientific work on psychology, cognitive science, and animal learning. I will argue, however, that they have been lured into a mistaken research assumption by Searle's brand of intentionality. Premack and Roitblat are making claims and doing experiments under the assumption that certain things can be explained by the *brain* phenomenon of intentionality that, according to Searle among others, is unquestionably there in the neural structure. And since intentionality must be there, occasionally scientists like Roitblat and Premack (and Sayre, if he should be called a scientist) take the time to look for and explain it. I think I can now make some very interesting comparisons between the development of intentionality theory and the development of another interesting scientific theory, that of phlogiston.

2.   PHLOGISTON

The eighteenth-century chemical theory of phlogiston is often used by philosophers and historians as the paradigmatic example of a scientific theory that failed. Unfortunately, though the example of phlogiston is widely recognized, most philosophical and historical writing on the topic ignores important details of the rise and fall of phlogiston theory. The account of phlogiston theory that I am about to present is in large part due to J. H. White's book *The History of the Phlogiston Theory (1973)*. White's book is one of the few pieces of writing on the subject that goes through a complete historical account of most of the important figures and events during the heyday of phlogiston. Some people may find this account of phlogiston theory controversial. However, White's extensive review of the history, the consistent lack of such review in other works on the topic, and the fact that the original seventeenth-century literature on phlogiston, which I looked at, is quite consistent with White's account, all lead me to the conclusion that not only is White's version plausible, but is in fact the most plausible version of the history.

2.1   *History of Phlogiston*

As an extension of Aristotelian chemistry and alchemy, seventeenth- and eighteenth-century chemists proposed three elemental types[10] of which the four Aristotelian elements (earth, water, air, and fire) were made up: Mercury, Salt, and Sulphur. Mercury included the properties of volatility, liquidity, and the characteristic color and appearance for the metals; Salt had the characteristics of solidity and fixity; Sulphur was the "element" that displayed the principle of inflammability (White 1973, pp. l6-17). It was curiosity with what made sulphur inflammable that led to the inception of phlogiston theory.

Phlogiston is what is expelled from things when they burn. The term itself came from the Greek φλογιστόξ or φλογιστόν, meaning "burnt" or "inflammable" and may have been first used as early as 1606 by the chemist Hapelius. Phlogiston-based chemistry became popular in late seventeenth- and early eighteenth-century Europe. As far as the uncontroversial part of phlogiston theory goes, phlogiston is a principle or property associated with things that are combustible. According to the theory, when combustible materials, which include animal substances, vegetable substances, oils, and metals, are heated, they display two obvious phenomena: (1) burning (especially obvious in oils), producing spontaneous heat and/or light, and (2) breakdown into smaller particles, as in metals and wood. Therefore, whatever is in substances that burn must either break down into its constituent parts or leave the substance. The theory was intuitively easy to understand.

> It was a reasonable sort of explanation. Most of us today, with or without present knowledge built on past discoveries, would be quite ready to agree that, when a match is struck or a candle burns, some "fire-stuff" is released from each of them—and so likewise for other kinds of burning. [McKie 1951, p. 98]

Many of the early phlogistonists felt that phlogiston was something distinct from fire and flame, though obviously related to them. It was the problem of distinguishing phlogiston from fire (one of the four Aristotelian elements) that was in part responsible for the later demise of the theory.

Johann Joachim Becher is considered the father of phlogiston theory. Becher was a seventeenth-century chemist who published many chemical theories based on the old ideas of alchemy. In 1669, Becher wrote *Physica Subterranea* in which he proposes the views that led to the theory of phlogiston. In keeping with some

Aristotelian chemistry, Becher proposes that the world is not made up of earth, water, air, and fire, but instead is water and three types of earth.

> His first earthly principle is a "molten fluid and vitreous earth" (terra lapidia) which constitutes the basis of all things. The second is an "oily earth" (terra pinguis) present in all combustible substances of the animal and vegetable kingdom and in fossils or minerals in so far as they are capable of combustion. Thus this principle is really one of inflammability. The third and last principle is a "fluid earth" (terra-mercurialis). These three correspond to, he says, but are improperly termed Salt, Sulphur and Mercury respectively. Water he also regards as a type of "fluid earth," air as a "subtle earth," fire as a "rarefied earth," and ordinary earth as "dry earth." [White 1973, p. 48]

It is the *terra pinguis,* or oily earth, that is taken as the beginnings of phlogiston theory. Becher used the term φλογιστόν when referring to this oily (or combustible) earth principle.

> He also calls the combustible earth *sulphur adustible* and *sulphur* φλογιστὸν, the Greek work [*sic*][11] being used as the neuter of the verbal adjective in the sense of *ardens.* [Partington 1961, p. 646]

Notice that Becher only uses *phlogiston* as a description of the property of inflammability of the oily earth principle; at this time, *phlogiston* is no more than a descriptive term of a certain chemical principle. Contrary to some accounts of the history, though, it appears that Becher really had nothing more to do with the advent of phlogiston theory than the presentation of this oily earth principle. It was Becher's student, Georg Ernst Stahl, who actually used the term *phlogiston* more or less as we understand it today.

Georg Ernst Stahl was the originator of the phlogiston theory with which we are currently familiar. Stahl was a physiologist and chemist at Halle University in the late seventeenth and early eighteenth centuries. Also a student of Aristotelian chemistry as Becher was, Stahl felt that there must be some principle by which sulphur was inflammable, since fire was considered a particulate substance at the time.

> . . . in the *Specimen Becherianum* Stahl states that "flaming, burning and vehement fire" is very effective as an instrument for the fusion of a mixture, and enters as a part of the total constitution, i.e., the "materia et principium ignis" only and not the fire itself. "This I began to call Phlogiston," an inflammable principle capable of being influenced directly by heat and being also a useful solvent principle. (Sect. XVI)
>
> In Section XVII he says that the principle of fire does not properly undergo that motion which produces ordinary fire, unless by some means or other its corpuscles are joined with the Phlogistic principle which renders them capable of motion, as the particles of the fire principle are naturally immovable or tend to be so when closely packed. . . . This hypothetical

substance practically corresponded to and replaced the second earthly principle of Becher, the "terra pinguis." [White 1973, pp. 51-52]

However, it should not be assumed from this that Stahl believed that phlogiston was a substance. It is true that in his 1715 work *Opusculum Chymico-Physico-Medicum*, Stahl seems to use the word *phlogiston* as if it were a substance.

> For which reason indeed, in the preceding chapter, we've already noted that that *Phlogistos* substance [substantia illa *Phlogistos*], which is evident in the *fatness/oil* of a *fermenting* mixture, is no different in kind than every *Phlogistos* material, which has that property when it is most *spread out* and *evaporating*. [Stahl 1715, p. 136][12]

But throughout this work, Stahl consistently uses the term *phlogiston* in this odd construction, using the Greek adjective and usually setting it off by commas and the word *illa* or *hoc*. By contrast, he does not generally use this construction when referring to other substances like salt.

> Indeed all *salt* [omne *Sal*] is nothing else but a certain *fine earth* of such a proportion that it can be closely intermingled with particles of *water* and with them can be *moved* as if they were *one* and the *same*. [Stahl 1715, p. 129]

Even so, Stahl does seem to be pushing a somewhat substantial view of phlogiston. However, in his later 1731 work titled *Experimenta, Observationes, Animadversiones, CCC Numero, Chemicae et Physicae*, a book that is almost entirely devoted to work on burning and sulphur, Stahl always uses the word to mean something like "an inflammability property." More importantly, he almost exclusively uses the word *phlogiston* in its adjectival form and very infrequently uses it as a noun.

> *Upper Air*, of by far the most insubstantial material, and I mean consisting of *material*; but it is in no way *elastic* whether it is in a state of expansion or compression. To which approaches the pure *phlogistic* [phlogistica] substance, about which we have been speaking energetically up to this point: which in short when it has finally been either incorporated, as they say, or woven in to mixtures undertakes the formation in them of a catalyst for fire. [Stahl 1731, pp. 247-248, §198][13]

> While at least the highest rarefaction of the *phlogistic ingredient* [phlogisti principii] in the purest burning alcohol shines forth even from the standpoint that such an alcohol, for whatever reason it burns, exhibits not a trace of *brightness*. [Stahl 1731, p. 110, §77]

Notice here that my translators have translated the word *principii* as *ingredient*. I want to be somewhat conservative about how the word *ingredient* is to be taken. It has been argued by some that when Stahl uses the word *principium* in talking about phlogiston, he means some sort of substance; since *principium* means something like *first* or *origin*, it is said that it could also mean *element* in the sense of primary substance. I think this an incorrect interpretation of Stahl's meaning. First of all, he consistently uses the word *principium* when he is talking about the characteristic that makes something volatile—that is, the *property* of being phlogistic. Reading *principium* as *substance* does not fit with Stahl's overall use of the word. Second, the word *principium* was the Latin translation of the Greek ἀρχή as Aristotle uses it. As far as I can tell, Aristotle does not use the term *principium* to mean *substance*, and since Stahl was an Aristotelian chemist, it seems unlikely that he would have used the word in this nonstandard way, especially with no particular textual evidence to the contrary.

I think that the overall picture of Stahl's work indicates that Stahl did not consider phlogiston to be a substance, or at least in the end would not commit himself to that position. I think it is clear that at the very least, Stahl was waffling on the use of the term *phlogiston* in his later works, and more likely used *phlogistic* simply to describe these different chemical reactions. Stahl simply gave phlogiston the ontological status of a property or macroscopic phenomenon, though he did use terminology, from his earliest through his latest works, which implied that there was real scientific work to be done looking at the phlogistic substances.

He seems to have considered it similar to light, a phenomenon which could cause various effects and yet have no apparent substance. He states definitely that phlogiston is *not* composed of fire particles themselves, but is their "motus" or activating agent (White 1973, pp. 55-56).

It was later in the history of phlogiston that it was taken as a material contained in the burning substance.

2.2   *Phlogiston in Experimental Science*

Throughout his later works, Stahl experimented extensively on burning and inflammability, using the word *phlogiston* to refer to the properties of such reactions. It appears that at the same time (the early to mid-eighteenth century), as the word *phlogiston* entered the scientific literature more and more, especially due to Stahl, a camp of "phlogistonists" developed in the scientific community. These scientists, with Stahl among them, began to look intently at combustion and calcination reactions for mechanisms and explanations. Many of these phlogistonists, however, took Stahl's early use of the word quite seriously, and proceeded to look for phlogistic corpuscles, or the substance phlogiston, in these calcination and combustion reactions.

Problems of calcination and combustion in metals turned out to be the key issues in the controversy over phlogiston theory. Calcination is the process by which metals turn into a powdery substance by burning (combustion), heating, rusting, or tarnishing. It was well known by Stahl that the processes of calcination and combustion must be tied together in some way, and he believed that phlogiston was the unifying theory; heating metallic calces with a substance such as charcoal (a substance full of the phlogistic principle) regenerated the metal from which the calx was formed. Calcination does have one interesting feature: the calces of metals weigh *more* than the metals themselves. Given that combustion was supposed to be a release of phlogiston, the weight gain of calces needed to be explained, assuming that something else in the metals was expelled.

For Stahl, and some of his followers, the weight gain had to be independent of phlogiston. Stahl did not consider phlogiston to have weight at all. In fact, Becher, Stahl, and Robert Boyle all considered this weight gain to be caused by the addition of fire particles.

> . . . although Stahl made no reference to it, it is probable that he regarded the fire particles themselves as possessing weight, and that they, after the phlogiston had departed from them, increased the weight of the metal, following the explanation therefore of Boyle and Becher. [White 1973, p. 56]

Many of Stahl's followers gave no further explanation for the weight gain in calces. As far as they were concerned, it was a problem for future scientific study and they were offering no solutions. Indeed, the fact that phlogiston unified the theories of slow calcination and combustion seemed to be a great enough discovery to this one group of scientists. Some of Stahl's followers, however, tried to tie in phlogiston to the gain in weight of calces and made devastating changes to the theories Stahl had presented.

By 1730, Stahl had many followers in his phlogiston theory. The theory served to unify a rather confusing chemistry of the time into a simple explanation.

> When Stahl's ideas were first propounded there is no doubt that many of the chemists considered that chemical phenomena were becoming much more complex than they ought to be. Many of them were probably dimly realizing and groping after some unity underlying the varied phenomena. What more natural than that these workers should seize with alacrity on a theory, propounded by one who had proved himself trustworthy in many other respects, which was to explain so simply many diverse and complex observations and which, with a little imagination, could be made to embrace most of the chemical knowledge at the time. [White 1973, p. 57]

Then in 1730, Johann Juncker published a complete history of chemistry that included and supported the work of Stahl and Becher. A strong phlogistonist, Juncker mistakenly took Stahl's theory as stating that phlogiston was a substance. This was quite understandable since Stahl was quite evasive about phlogiston as a substance in his later works, and in his earlier works, Stahl seems to endorse phlogiston as a substance. But when Juncker discusses the question of the weight gain in calces, he makes the terrible mistake of claiming that phlogiston, since it is definitely material, must be different in that it has "negative weight."

> In the preface, he speaks in glowing terms of the efforts of Becher and Stahl to throw light on the dark tangle of chemical theory. Juncker, however, appears to misinterpret Stahl's idea of phlogiston, and regards it as being definitely material. Hence, dealing with the calx question he is driven to make that unfortunate assumption that phlogiston must possess the property of levity or the ability to render its compounds lighter. [White 1973, p. 70]

This assumption by Juncker was probably the major cause of phlogiston theory falling into disrepute. After Juncker, the problems for phlogiston theory continually worsened. Chemists at the time tried to develop phlogiston into a more cohesive theory, but ended up scrambling for parts of the theory to hold on to. Several chemists, including G. F. Venel and Guyton de Morveau, went along with Juncker believing that phlogiston was a substance that had negative weight. Many others believed that phlogiston was in fact a substance, but had no explanation whatsoever for the gain in weight of calces. Two scientists, Joseph Priestley and Karl Wilhelm Scheele, discovered a new gas that fire burned more brightly in (which we now know as oxygen) and explained this by stating that the gas had a great affinity for phlogiston while burning, perhaps being de-phlogisticated air. Priestley and Scheele both considered phlogiston a substance. P. J. Macquer, the French phlogistonist, proposed that this new gas must explain the gain in weight, but continued with the idea that phlogiston must be the cause of the combustion. Macquer also wavered between material phlogiston and phlogiston as a principle. All of this shuffling within phlogiston theory, as well as the ideas of gases being in some way involved in burning, led to the end of phlogiston theory. The experimentation of Antoine Lavoisier, which I will discuss next, was only a small addition to the pressures that brought about the eventual end to phlogiston theory.

2.3   The Demise of Phlogiston

The discovery of oxygen by Priestley and Scheele pushed experimentation in chemistry. The phlogistonists decided that this new gas must be de-phlogisticated air, since the burning substance had to release great quantities of phlogiston to burn so brightly and so was being absorbed easily by this gas. Priestley also discovered that this new air sustained life and if removed, animals would suffocate. He concluded that respiration must also be a phlogistic process. He also found that plants replaced the phlogiston into air that had lost it. As this was going on, Henry Cavendish did experiments on the new gas and a gas that he called "inflammable air." At first, Cavendish thought that the "inflammable air" was almost entirely phlogiston. When burned, though, it left behind a dew in its container, and Cavendish decided that "inflammable air" must be made up of phlogiston and water. Later, Cavendish decided that water was made up of "inflammable air," which turned out to be hydrogen, and oxygen, the new dephlogisticated gas, which absorbed a great deal of phlogiston from the hydrogen. Cavendish, in fact, wavered between these two positions (water as complex and hydrogen as phlogiston and water). All of these discoveries culminated with Lavoisier's experiments on oxygen and hydrogen.

In the late eighteenth century, starting about 1772, the French chemist Antoine Lavoisier realized that the weight gains that occurred in calcination and combustion were important phenomena that must have some common cause and that cause must be air.

> In a sealed note deposited with the Secretary of the French Academy on November 1, 1772, Lavoisier wrote:
>
> "About eight days ago, I discovered that sulphur in burning, far from losing weight, on the contrary, gains it; it is the same with phosphorous; this increase of weight arises from a prodigious quantity of air that is fixed during combustion and combines with the vapors.
>
> "This discovery, which I have established by experiments, that I regard as decisive, has led me to think that what is observed in the combustion of sulphur and phosphorous may well take place in the case of all substances that gain in weight by combustion and calcination; and I am persuaded that the increase in weight of metallic calxes is due to the same cause." [Conant 1950, pp. 16-17]

Through experiments in the years to follow, Lavoisier showed that the gas involved in calcination was Priestley and Scheele's new gas, which he coined *oxygen*. Without going into too much detail, Lavoisier used Cavendish's work to confirm that water was in fact made up of oxygen and hydrogen, as well as showing that all calcination included an addition of oxygen and a release of heat, which he termed *caloric*. In reality, caloric was just material phlogiston by another name, but it was not attributed all of the properties that Stahl's disciples gave to it. Francis Penrose, a late eighteenth-century antiphlogistonist is quoted:

> . . . although Stahl, Macquer, Dr. Black, etc., described phlogiston differently, yet the same matter was understood by the same name, which in the new chemistry is denominated *caloric*. It is still the matter of fire, of flame, of light and of heat which is liberated in combustion; they only differ from Stahl in this, that this principle is not disengaged from the body in combustion; but, from their experiments, they endeavor to prove that it is liberated from the vital air or oxygen, during the combustion, from the atmosphere. Yet it is still phlogiston, it is still the matter of heat; whether we call it phlogiston, caloric, or in plain English, *fire*. The difference between Stahl and Lavoisier appears to be that Stahl thought the matter of fire and light was no other than the

phlogiston which the body contained, and it was let loose in combustion. . . .
On the contrary, Mr. Lavoisier thinks that heat, light, and all other remarkable
phenomena of combustion, depend rather on a certain action of the air than
on the peculiar nature of the combustible bodies; . . . He ascribes to pure air
that decomposition which, according to Stahl, took place on the inflammable
substance. [White 1973, p. 144]

Contrary to the common belief of modern philosophers of science, a careful
study of the history reveals that Lavoisier did not destroy phlogiston with his
theories at all. In fact, all he did was set up phlogiston to be "cut off" by Occam's
razor when it was realized that his "caloric" was not a material substance, but
heat energy. Phlogiston theory slowly fell out of use, eventually being discarded
in the early nineteenth century.

Instead of a conceptual "principle" of burning or "property" of
inflammability, phlogiston was mistakenly considered a material contained in
inflammables. It was through nonempirical means that the microstructure
responsible for phlogistic phenomena had been posited by Stahl in his early
work. His disciples took the existence of these microstructures very seriously.
Had it not been for Juncker and his followers, *phlogiston* or *the phlogistic* may very
well have survived as principle terms, perhaps designating the commonality
between the two processes of combustion and calcination, both oxidation
processes in the current chemical account. Instead, science found *phlogiston* to be
a useless term for a material entity that did not exist. While phlogistonists were
looking for a substance that fit their name, chemists of the time had been
independently naming the microstructure substances that they had been
discovering and the phlogistonists were left holding an empty bag. It is here that
I will make the comparison to the current status of intentionality.

3.   Is Intentionality Phlogiston?

3.1   Introduction—Comparison to Be Made

The preceding two sections have been devoted to an overview history of the
intentionality and phlogiston theories. Each theory started out as a generalized
conceptual schema; *intentionality* and *phlogiston* were terms for certain
macroscopic phenomena. The respective central terms of each theory,
intentionality and *phlogiston*, were subsequently looked upon as material things,
i.e., microscopic substructure, that could be researched and experimented on
empirically. The shift from the macrophenomenon view of phlogiston to the
microstructure view caused *phlogiston* to be discarded as a useful scientific term.
What I want to claim is that *intentionality*, because it is making the same sort of

shift from macroproperty to substructure material, will also imminently be discarded if the current scientific trends continue. Saving intentionality will only be accomplished by removing many of the latest ontological claims. If scientists continue the current direction of psychological and biological research, the demise of intentionality is imminent.

3.2 The Cause of the Downfall of Phlogiston

Phlogiston theory began as a macroscopic description of the phenomenon of burning and calcination. *Phlogiston* started out as a loosely construed property term; that is, phlogiston was a useful concept to describe the common aspects of the combustion and calcination processes. The "principle" terminology that Becher and Hapelius used was a very loose descriptive nomenclature that apparently was not intended to make any ontological commitments to a substance. When Becher used the terms *inflammable principle* it is not clear that it in any way implied the existence of an entity. Hapelius refers to "τό φλογιστὸν," but talks about it as the "*essence* of that sulphur which is engrafted in all things" (italics mine) (White 1973, p. 51). When Stahl actually started to discuss phlogiston theory seriously, he invented a terminology for these principles of burning and calcination. It does not appear to have originally been any more than this kind of macroproperty theory.

Stahl, however, did do something that would become the eventual cause of the downfall of phlogiston. Stahl referred to phlogiston in terms of "phlogistic corpuscles" and of metals being composed of calx and phlogiston. The interpretation of the history that I am endorsing is that Stahl himself did not take phlogiston to be a substance: "Stahl conceived phlogiston as a principle; his disciples turned it into a material." (White 1973, p. 183). It is clear, however, that Stahl's positing of phlogistic corpuscles in metals implied to many scientists that phlogiston was certainly a substance and should be isolated and studied. It was this fact that led to the eventual end of phlogiston theory.

So long as phlogiston remained as a principle of burning, there was no problem with *what* in particular phlogiston was; it was defined in an epistemological framework and was simply the as yet unexplained property of burning things. In 1730, merely four years before Stahl's death, chemists like Scheele and Juncker began misinterpreting Stahl to mean something very different than what he had originally proposed. By the end of the eighteenth century, phlogiston was considered by several scientists of the time to be a substance.

> The substantial idea of phlogiston came later [after Stahl], and it is difficult to trace its origin to any one person. None of Stahl's immediate successors subscribed to it and yet, when we come to Scheele, we find him writing in his book published in 1777, "Since phlogiston is a substance (which always supposes some weight) . . . ", and by this time the idea is universal. [White 1973, p. 10]

As phlogiston made the transition from a macrophenomenon to a substance, scientists began to be forced to look for *its* properties and principles, and where it was to be found. With the wording of Stahl's writings, the obvious choice of where to look would be in the material that was undergoing calcination or combustion. Phlogiston was supposed to be released on combustion and therefore must have been in the burning material. Stahl had postulated that phlogiston was very subtle. This was taken to mean that it would be difficult or even impossible to make measurements on phlogiston or detect it at all. But the statement by Scheele (quoted above by White) shows that there was a notion at the time that all substances must possess some sort of weight and could therefore, in principle, be found.

The problem with the search for phlogiston was the origin of the search: phlogiston was not an independently discovered microstructure explanation for a macrophenomenon principle, but was instead a posited microstructure for the macrophenomenon due to a misinterpretation of the original statement of the principles of phlogiston. Although there always existed the possibility that a substance satisfying the definition of phlogiston could have been found, the *a priori,* unconditional probability for this seems very low: there were very few ways to be right about the substance that the phlogistonists were looking for; there were an immense number of ways to get it wrong. Making any kind of entity claim creates the possibility that the term will be discarded. The mere postulation of a microstructure for a macrophenomenon is clearly not the way other scientific discoveries are made.[14] A short review of some of these other scientific theories will clarify the point.

3.3   Uniqueness of Phlogiston— Comparison to Other Theories

The study of temperature in chemistry and physics seems to have a very similar history to phlogiston theory. Temperature began as a macroscopic principle of heat and coldness. Much study was devoted to temperature and how changes in temperature could be determined as well as its relationship to other phenomena such as pressure. Later in its history, it was discovered that temperature was actually the mean kinetic energy of the molecules of a substance. The question arises as to why temperature did not face the same kind of demise that phlogiston did. After all, temperature underwent the same sort of shift from a loosely defined macroproperty to a more tightly defined principle and then to a search for its microstructure characteristics. The clear difference between the two theories is how the microstructure of each was determined. Unlike phlogiston, scientists working in molecular theory discovered kinetic energy *independently* of any work on temperature. There was no assumption ever made in the theories of temperature phenomena that the energy in molecules was the actual microscopic phenomenon underlying temperature. It was only later that it was discovered that kinetic energy and temperature were actually the same thing. In phlogiston theory, the proposal for the microstructure was due to the assumption that there *must* be a single microscopic substance that is actually the same thing that the phlogistic principles had been explaining. When discussing the phenomena associated with temperature, scientists did not posit a substructure that must be found in the molecules; an independent discovery led to the connection between the substructure and the macroprinciple.

Another similar example is that of magnetism. Magnetism was the name for the attraction phenomenon that was experienced when people held lodestones near each other. There was a great deal of work on the strength of magnets, magnetizing substances, and magnetic fields. However, the discovery that magnetism was actually a function of the motion of electrons and the lining up of atoms in metals was established independently of the discussion of the macrophenomena. Scientists involved in electricity research discovered magnetic attractions between two pieces of charged material. Only then was a discovery of the connection between the studied microstructure of electric charges and the known macrophenomenon of magnetic attraction made. Again, in contrast, phlogiston was a posited microstructure for the loosely defined macrophenomenon of inflammability. The postulation of such a structure was not made due to independent discoveries made on inflammable materials.

An even more interesting example that compares to phlogiston theory is Mendel's theory of the gene. In this case, it appears as if Mendel posited some microscopic structure responsible for the phenomenon of inherited similarities between offspring and their parents, which was then later "discovered" by scientists doing cell biology research. Inheritance was clearly known as a macrophenomenon, and Mendel seems to have postulated the gene without making an independent discovery while working on microstructure. In fact, Mendel's work did involve one major difference from phlogiston theory, however. Mendel was interested in the transfer of inheritance information because he was breeding pea plants. Mendel *discovered* that transfer of microparticles, i.e., pollen, seemed directly responsible for the similarities and differences in the pea plants he was working with. Unlike phlogiston, Mendel had good reason to believe that a transferring microstructure was responsible for inheritance of different traits. Mendel made an independent discovery of microstructure due to his experimental methods in pea plant breeding.

It seems that most successful scientific theories develop in very much the same way that the theories of temperature and magnetism did. A macroscopic phenomenon is observed and named by a group of people or scientists. The evolution of the term is through the study of the macrophenomenon itself and its relationship to other phenomena. At the same time, scientists concerned with studying and labeling new scientific entities determine that some of these entities seem to be the underlying microstructure of independently established macrophenomena. In this way, independently observed phenomena are connected into larger cohesive scientific theories. The differences found between phlogiston and other scientific theories are not found in the comparison between phlogiston and intentionality.

3.4   The Similar History of Intentionality and Phlogiston

The ontological situation for early phlogiston seems very similar to the ontological status of intentionality at the time of the Scholastics and Aquinas. During that period, intentionality was a loose description of certain mental phenomena that had to do with people's experience with objects in the outside world. Although Aquinas uses words like "objects in the soul," it isn't apparent that these objects have the same sort of material status as scientific entities. In more modern terms, intentionality is the connectedness of our mind/soul with the object in the world; this is solely a statement of a property of the actions of minds and souls for the Scholastics.

Becher's early use of the word *phlogiston* and Stahl's later explication of phlogiston's importance runs somewhat parallel to Brentano and Husserl's theory of intentionality. Stahl, following Becher, considered phlogiston as a phlogistic principle and not as a material entity. Stahl elaborated on this in order to give some more exact criteria for what made up the principles of phlogiston, including his discussion of fatty bodies and other phlogistic substances. Stahl, however, did not apparently do any searching for a microstructure in materials that made these things phlogistic; he only proposed that things that burned and calcinated had phlogiston, the inflammable principle, in them. In a similar fashion, Brentano attempted to give a more exact explanation of and nomenclature for intentionality. He introduced the idea of the "intentional inexistence" of objects into his explanation of intentional phenomena. Though making claims as to the nature of the intentional phenomenon, Brentano never makes ontological claims about intentionality itself. Even Husserl, who introduced the notion of the noema, did not fall into the trap of making ontological claims; noema was the object as intended in the mind. The words that Brentano and Husserl use for things involved in intentionality, as well those used by Stahl in his theory of phlogiston, can easily be construed as implying the existence of some objects. However, none of them probably meant to imply that the principles with which they were concerned were actually *things*. Let me make a small aside about the ontology of the time.

After reading much of the material from the eighteenth and nineteenth centuries and their recent commentaries, I don't think it is clear what view of ontology was taken by philosophers and scientists of the time. Reading Stahl's writings on phlogiston especially, it was almost impossible to pin down with any certainty whether he was talking about an individual substance that he wanted to call *phlogiston* or simply a class of *phlogistic* (that is, inflammable) substances. In all of the texts on phlogiston that I have looked at, as well as writings of Aquinas, Husserl, and Brentano on intentionality, there is an extremely vague use of terms such as *principle* and *substance* or *species* in the case of intentionality. The use of these words seems to indicate that these philosophers and scientists gave much less weight to ontological claims than we do today. Also, of course, the notion of ontology was shifting as a philosophical idea during the eighteenth and nineteenth centuries. This makes commentaries like "There was, of course, . . . no chemical *proof* that the earth and water and air and fire were elements . . ." (McKie 1951, p. 97, my italics) seem somewhat unfair to the ideology of the time. Seventeenth- and early eighteenth-century scientists would probably have considered phlogiston a matter more of metaphysics than of chemistry and would not have even looked for such *proof*. The increasing concern with the implications of ontology in the nineteenth and twentieth centuries explains some of the reason for phlogiston's demise and the reasoning behind my conclusions on the status of intentionality.

3.5   Forcing Ontological Commitments—The Inevitable Demise

The best comparisons that I can make are those that can be made between Stahl and Searle, as well as between the scientific researchers who were their followers. Searle has proposed, in scientifically sketchy terms, that intentionality is a brain phenomenon and, even more directly, that intentionality itself is to be found somewhere in the brain. His continual move to make intentionality into a more scientific notion is very similar to Stahl's push to elaborate the notion of phlogiston. An even more interesting parallel is Searle's statement that intentionality must come directly from the "causal powers of the brain." The mystery behind what these causal powers might be seems very similar to Stahl's statement that phlogiston is very subtle and undetectable. Searle and Stahl leave each of these mysteries for future scientists to contend with, though neither makes an outright claim as to the ontological status of their respective theoretical entities. It is the scientists' research in the area of phlogiston that brought it to an end and the scientists in intentionality research that are of the greatest concern to its future.

Premack, Sayre, and especially Roitblat each have fallen into the same trap with intentionality that the late eighteenth-century phlogistonists fell into with phlogiston. To save phlogiston as a substance, the scientists began to add more and more constraints and extensions to the original phlogiston theory to make it fit with the observations, each time introducing more problems than were solved. The obvious mistake was to be looking for a material "thing" that was phlogiston. The three intentionality researchers, Premack, Sayre, and Roitblat, have misinterpreted at least Husserl and Brentano and, if we allow him the benefit of the doubt, even Searle. Sayre and Roitblat especially are closest to what had happened with the phlogistonists: they have pointed to things that appear to give evidence for some sort of brain structure for intentionality, but have increased the number of difficult questions in an attempt to answer the easy ones. Certainly they should have not even begun to look for the microscopic brain structures for intentionality.

4.   CONCLUSIONS

The term *phlogiston,* according to my account, was not discarded because it failed to refer, but because researchers in the field started looking for a microstructure associated with it far before they had any reason to believe that one existed in the form they were searching for. Though it seems clear that the term *phlogiston* does not refer to any object (cf. Putnam 1975a, b, 1984; Enç 1976), the view of history that proposes this as the *reason* that phlogiston was discarded leaves two very troubling questions. The first is what would have happened if phlogistonists had not proposed a microstructure but had continued to view phlogiston as that macroscopic property of inflammability. It seems quite plausible to think of *phlogiston* as a name for the bond energy released in calcinating and combusting substances. Lavoisier's *caloric*, though it clearly had problems in what it referred to, seems to have withstood time in the word *calories* or the term *high caloric food. Phlogiston* seems to have been rejected because it was mangled into an entity term too early in its lifetime. The second question that puts the strict reference interpretation into question is, What if Lavoisier had termed the new gas *substantial phlogiston* instead of *oxygen*—that is, if Lavoisier had decided that the phlogistonists were not looking for something that did not exist, but in fact had just thought mistakenly that phlogiston left substances when in fact it moved into them when they burned? Though there is probably room for some interesting study of the sociology of science of the time (i.e., maybe phlogiston *had* to be rejected because there were rival scientific factions), there is no question that the scenario is plausible. Both of these questions are designed to show that at least phlogiston was not *certainly* doomed because it did not refer. [15]

Now we return to the question of the final status of intentionality. Though the research is full of undeveloped and poorly defined terms, intentionality seems to be growing into what phlogiston did: a theory about a microstructure for a macrophenomenon that has developed before there is any good reason to believe the type of microstructure being sought even exists. Scientists are trying to push intentionality in the same way that the term *pain* is claimed to be equivalent to stimulated C-fiber neurons (and this is still a highly debated claim). Scientists like Roitblat and Premack have been told by philosophers like Searle that intentionality is in the brain and neurons somewhere. These scientists have taken these rather flippant microstructure claims very seriously. The odds of finding a microstructure to match the macrophenomenon with no independent research that gives any hint of a direction seem slim at best. This alone does not dismiss the possibility that intentionality is similarly reducible to neurophysiology, but it puts the prospects for success into some doubt. Given the amount of current neurological and cognitive science research currently being done, anything that has a chance of being a microstructure associated with the macrophenomenon of intentionality will most likely be named right out from under the feet of the intentionality researchers, much in the same way that *caloric* was named right out from under the phlogistonists. The timing seems perfect for this kind of move: in a parallel to the history of chemistry, where phlogiston was posited right at the time where chemistry was becoming a respectable empirical science with better defined research methodologies, intentionality is being introduced exactly at the time that cognitive psychology is coming into its own as a respectable science with defined empirical research methods. The time for the introduction of loosely defined substructure terms like *intentionality* has passed with the era of proposing the *id* and *ego*.

The final thing I want to look at, though, is the similarity between Stahl and Searle. Throughout, I have carefully stated that Searle is not the person who has actually made the mistake with intentionality. He has not proposed a microstructure for intentionality, just as Stahl did not propose a microstructure for phlogiston. However, Searle, like Stahl, has used rather loose (sometimes even not so loose) language that, if taken seriously by scientists, implies the existence of a certain kind of microstructure. Though White (1973) is quick to point out that Stahl never really believed in substantial phlogiston, Stahl suffered the fate of his disciples because his words prompted the search for phlogiston. In the same way, if intentionality goes the way of phlogiston because no *thing* can be found that satisfies what the researchers are looking for, and all substructures in psychology can be named without positing intentionality, Searle leaves himself open to the same kinds of attacks and disrepute that befell Stahl. Searle's encouragement of such research may be as bad for himself as it appears to be for psychology.

5.   POSTSCRIPT

I need to address two remaining issues with respect to intentionality. The first concerns its major difference from phlogiston: *intentionality* is a term used to describe a mental event or principle and not something chemical like phlogiston. Though the historical backdrop for intentionality and phlogiston has been very similar, intentionality has the added burden of being (at least for philosophers) an emotional issue of how people are separated from animals, computers, thermostats, and rocks. In fact, the power of the intentionality issue could be as great as the power of the geocentric theory of the universe. Because replacing that theory by the heliocentric theory also entailed giving up the primacy of humans, the geocentric model held on for years longer than it should have. It is conceivable that even if intentionality suffers the same fate as phlogiston, it will hang on a great deal longer that phlogiston ever did because it is a human issue rather than one of pure chemistry.

My other concern is what other choices there are for intentionality. Many philosophers, not the least of whom is Daniel Dennett, have proposed that intentionality should remain as a macrophenomenal term, describing the "aboutness" that was the original meaning of the term. Dennett proposes that intentionality be looked upon as a "stance" to be taken toward some things (like people, animals, and perhaps computers) and not to be taken toward others (like thermostats and rocks). If intentionality turns around like this, it seems more likely that down the road, a cognitive psychologist may find something and claim that it is the microstructure for intentionality (although it appears that Dennett may not accept even this). Clearly the term *intentionality* stands a better chance of surviving if it reverts back to a macrophenomenon instead of science continuing the search for it as a substructure. As a brain structure, intentionality certainly runs the high risk of ending up just like phlogiston.

6. NOTES

1. Throughout this chapter, I will use *intentionality* and *intentional* in the philosophical, technical sense of these terms. I will discuss the relationship that these words bear to the words *intention* and *intentional* in our common everyday language, but they should not be thought of as having the same meanings.

2. Aquinas (as well as Avicenna and Aristotle) sees these intelligible "species" as 'forms' that exist in the soul that, in turn, are of the 'forms' in the real world, in the Platonic sense of 'forms'. The use of the term *object* is my insertion for consistency sake.

3. Here, notice also that Searle claims that the mere ability to understand English is an intentional phenomenon. It must be kept in mind that Searle is basically a philosopher of language. He therefore asserts that understanding English requires an ability to connect propositions with their referents (or "conditions of satisfaction").

4. Throughout this discussion, I use scare quotes around "higher" and "lower" because these words make some distinctions that I do not wish to make even though the philosophers and scientists discussed here sometimes make them; these distinctions are not really supported by any theory.

5. My discussion of the history of intentionality would not be complete without at least mentioning Daniel Dennett. Dennett is a philosopher who has been going head to head with philosophers like Searle. He is quite clear on the ontological status of intentionality; intentionality is not a material entity, but an epistemological construct. It is a strategy by which we can describe certain things as having mental directedness. Intentionality is a way of talking about actions that we normally refer to as beliefs, desires, intentions, etc. He actually allows that intentionality exists, but only as an "objective phenomenon" that "can be discerned only from the point of view of one who adopts a certain *predictive strategy,* and its existence can be confirmed only by an assessment of the success of that strategy" (Dennett 1987, p. 15). Dennett is certainly not part of the problem that concerns this chapter (i.e., the current ontological status of intentionality), and therefore will not be included in any further detail, except for a postscript at the end.

6. Roitblat, whom I cite below, and in fact any number of scientists who write in *Behavioral and Brain Sciences*, tend to fall into this category. It is hard to pick a good philosophically strong quote out of any of these scientists' writings

simply because most scientists are not very concerned with making broad philosophical points (and rightly so). But one can interpret many of these scientists as stating that intentionality has a neurophysiological basis that separates biological or brained things from other types of things, and it is my considered opinion that many of these scientists do take this sort of intentionality quite seriously.

7.   For commentary on problems with the theory itself, see the 1986 *Behavioral and Brain Sciences* target article (Sayre 1986) as well as the Continuing Commentary articles in *B.B.S.*, (Sayre *et. al.*. 1987)

8.   By the latter, I think Roitblat means something like the set of neural firings for an entire arm movement, for example.

9.   I am making no claim as to whether this theory is true or false; it is just a well-known example that philosophers like to cite.

10.   I am purposely being vague by using the word *types* and below when I use the word *principles*. The kind of ontology that these early chemists used is very unclear. For instance, flame and fire are two different "things" in some of the writings (cf. White 1973, p. 64), and phlogiston is mentioned as a "principle" in many places in Stahl's later works. The lack of clarity in these terms seems telltale of a lack of exactness with the theoretical terms at this time. I will discuss this problem in detail when I get to Stahl's original writings and in my conclusions.

11.   I think this should be *word*.

12.   I am greatly indebted to Galit Sadan and J. Bradford Churchill of the Department of Classics at the University of Illinois at Urbana-Champaign for their wonderful work translating the sections of Stahl's writings in the *Opusculum* and the *Experimenta* from the Latin to English for me. I am especially grateful to Ms. Sadan for all of the time she spent with me working through the microcards and texts in the Rare Book Library and for her assistance analyzing the sense of many of Stahl's statements concerning phlogiston. (Italicized words in all of the Stahl quotes were italics in the original Latin.)

13.   For some reason, White cites passages in *Experimenta* by section number instead of page number, so I have included the section numbers for cross-reference purposes.

14. Mine is clearly a nonstandard view of how phlogiston theory was discarded. Most accounts of phlogiston include the statement that the term *phlogiston* just did not refer. Many philosophers (cf. Putnam 1975a, b, 1984; Enç 1976) give large theories of how theoretical terms do and do not refer to objects. For the most part, these theories come down to a "reasonableness standard" or a "principle of charity" where the terms are said to refer if their meanings can be reasonably preserved in the theory. My view is that phlogiston was discarded, not initially because it failed to refer (which it apparently, in the long run, did not), but that it was introduced as a microstructure term before there was any good reason to go looking for a corresponding microstructure to the inflammability principle. I argue extensively in the section on phlogiston for this nonstandard view of the history of phlogiston (see White 1973 for further information on this view). I will discuss reference only briefly in the conclusion.

15. These ideas coagulated with the help of some discussions on the topic with Dan Brabander at Brown University, Steve Straight, Eric Dietrich, Jerry Aronson, and Jim Blake, all at Binghamton University.

7. REFERENCES

Aquinas, St. T. (1968). *Human Intelligence*. Trans. Paul T. Durbin. In *Summa Theologiae*. Vol. 11. T. Gilby, (ed.) (Cambridge: Blackfriars).

Aquinas, St. T. (1970). *Psychology of Human Acts*. Trans. Thomas Gilby. *Summa Theologiae*. Vol. 17. T. Gilby, (ed.) (Cambridge: Blackfriars.)

Conant, J. B. (1950). *The Overthrow of the Phlogiston Theory: the Chemical Revolution of 1775-1789*, no. 2. (Cambridge, MA: Harvard University Press).

Dennett, D. C. (1987). *The Intentional Stance*. (Cambridge, MA: The MIT Press, A Bradford Book).

Dennett, D. C. (1988). Précis of *The Intentional Stance. Behavioral and Brain Sciences,* 11 (3) (September): 495-546.

Dreyfus, H. L., and Hall, H. (1982). *Husserl, Intentionality, and Cognitive Science*. (Cambridge, MA: MIT Press).

Enç, B. (1976). Reference of theoretical terms. *Noûs,* 10, (3) (September): 261-282.

Føllesdal, D. (1982a). Brentano and Husserl on intentional objects and perception. In H. L. Dreyfus and H. Hall, (eds.) *Husserl, Intentionality, and Cognitive Science*. (Cambridge, MA: MIT Press), 31-41.

Føllesdal, D. (1982b). Husserl's notion of *noema*. In H.L. Dreyfus and H. Hall, (eds.) *Husserl, Intentionality, and Cognitive Science* (Cambridge, MA: MIT Press), 73-80.

Føllesdal, D. (1982c). Husserl's theory of perception. H. L. Dreyfus and H. Hall, (eds.) *Husserl, Intentionality, and Cognitive Science*. (Cambridge, MA: MIT Press), 93-96.

Gurwitsch, A. (1982) Husserl's theory of the intentionality of consciousness. In H. L. Dreyfus and H. Hall, (eds.) *Husserl, Intentionality, and Cognitive Science*. (Cambridge, MA: MIT Press), 59-71.

McKie, D. (1951). The birth of modern chemistry. In *The History of Science: Origins and Results of the Scientific Revolution: A Symposium*. (London: Cohen & West), 97-107.

New Catholic Encyclopedia. (1967). Vol. 7, s.v. *Intentionality,* by H. B. Veatch. (New York: McGraw-Hill Book Company).

Oxford Companion to the Mind., The (1987). R. L. Gregory and O. L. Zangwill, (eds.) s.v. Intentionality, by D. C. Dennett and J. C. Haugeland. (Oxford: Oxford University Press).

Partington, J. R. (1961). *A History of Chemistry.* Vol. 2. (London: Macmillan & Co.)

Premack, D. (1976). *Intelligence in Ape and Man*. (Hillsdale, NJ: John Wiley & Sons, Halsted Press).

Premack, D. (1986). *Gavagai! or the Future History of the Animal Language Controversy.* The MIT Press Series in Learning, Development, and Conceptual Change. L. Glietman, S. Carey, E. Newport, and E. Spelke (eds.). (Cambridge, MA: MIT Press, A Bradford Book).

Premack, D. (1988). Intentionality: How to tell Mae West from a crocodile. (Open Peer Commentary response to Précis of *The Intentional Stance*, by D. C. Dennett.) *Behavioral and Brain Sciences,* 11 (3) (September): 522-525.

Putnam, H. (1975a). Explanation and reference. In *Mind, language and reality*, Vol. 2. (Cambridge: Cambridge University Press), 196-214.

Putnam, H. (1975b). Language and reality. In *Mind, language and reality*, Vol. 2. (Cambridge: Cambridge University Press), 272-290.

Putnam, H. (1984). What is realism? In J. Leplin (ed.) *Scientific Realism*, (Berkeley: University of California Press), 140-153.

Roitblat, H. L. (1988). How to build a mind. (Open Peer Commentary response to Précis of *The Intentional Stance*, by D. C. Dennett.) *Behavioral and Brain Sciences*, 11 (3) (September): 525-526.

Sayre, K. M. (1986). Intentionality and information processing: an alternative model for cognitive science. *Behavioral and Brain Sciences*, 9, (1) (March): 121-166.

Sayre, K. M. et al. (1987). Commentary on intentionality and information processing: an alternative model for cognitive science. *Behavioral and Brain Sciences*, 10 (4) (December): 755-765.

Searle, J. R. (1980). Minds, brains and programs. *Behavioral and Brain Sciences*, 3 (3) (September): 417-457.

Searle, J. R. (1983). *Intentionality*. (Cambridge: Cambridge University Press).

Stahl, G. E. (1715). *Opusculum Chymico-Physico-Medicum*. . . . (Halæ Magdeburgicæ (Halle): Orphanotrophei).

Stahl, G. E. (1731). *Experimenta, Observationes, Animadversiones, CCC Numero, Chymicae et Physicae* . . . (Berolini: Apud Ambrosuim Haude).

White, J. H. (1973). *The History of the Phlogiston Theory*. (New York: AMS Press). Originally presented as the author's thesis, University of London. Reprint (London: Edward Arnold & Co., 1932).

CHAPTER

3

◆ # Real Machines and Virtual Intentionality

An Experimentalist Takes on the Problem of Representational Contents

Chris Fields

The problem of intentionality—how states of systems can represent objects or features in an environment—is one of the defining foundational problems of cognitive science. Dietrich (1989, 1990) has shown that interpreting the behavior of a system as computation requires attributing semantics to its states; a system's behavior cannot be regarded as computation unless its states are regarded as representations of some problem domain. The principal explanatory strategy of both artificial intelligence and cognitive psychology thus requires that systems be viewed as intentional. Showing that computing systems must be viewed as intentional to understand their behavior as computation does not, however, directly address the question of whether such systems are intentional independently of any theoretical attributions, i.e., of

Thinking Computers and Virtual Persons
edited by Eric Dietrich
ISBN 0-12-215495-9

whether intentionality is a phenomenon or simply an artifact of the use of a particular explanatory strategy. If intentionality is not an artifact, the question of which features of the functional organizations of intentional systems make them intentional also arises. These questions motivate three common arguments against purely attributive accounts of intentionality: 1) the claim that organisms, not artifacts, are intrinsically intentional in virtue of their causal organization or embedding in the world (e.g., Searle 1980, Sayre 1986); (2) the claim that all and only systems with behavior that cannot be explained without explicit appeal to inferential processes defined over propositions are intentional (e.g., Fodor 1984, Pylyshyn 1984); and (3) the claim that intentionality is an irreducible feature of interactions between co-evolved organisms and natural environments (e.g., Gibson 1979, Michaels and Carello 1981).

Consideration of the process of experimentally determining the mechanisms by which a system interacts with its environment and what, if anything, its states represent as a result of such interactions is notably lacking from most discussions of intentionality. Even the Gibsonians frame most of their published arguments in this area in terms of a handful of idealized examples. Experimental analysis of natural and artificial systems is, however, both the source of serious claims about representational abilities and the greatest beneficiary of methodological and theoretical clarity on the issue. This chapter focuses on what is involved in characterizing interactions between a system and its environment experimentally, and how this process relates to computational interpretation. Experiments are controlled interactions with a system that are accompanied by observation and measurement of the values of one or more variables. Measurements of electrical activity in one or more neurons in a person's brain, or at one or more pins of a computer's processor, while interacting in some repeatable way with the person or computer, are examples of experiments. From an experimental perspective, attributions of representational content are stipulative but hardly arbitrary. The utility of such attributions depends on both explanatory goals and system complexity, but they are applicable to any system that is appropriately described as interacting with an environment. Intentionality, from this perspective, is both intrinsic and universal, and its ubiquity in descriptions of complex systems is no surprise.

1.   MECHANISTIC DESCRIPTIONS AND COMPUTATIONAL EXPLANATIONS

Faced with the task of describing what a system does and explaining how it does it, we choose a collection of state variables to measure, and then record what happens to the values of those state variables in the course of multiple rounds of placing the system (or a "copy" of the system from some ensemble of systems assumed to be identical in the relevant respects) in some state or other and letting it undergo state transitions until it reaches quasi-stability. This is a relatively simple process if the system can always be returned to a "resting" state $s[0]$ from which we can perturb it to some interesting initial state $s[1]$; it is more difficult if we can never get the system into the same state twice. Computers can be rebooted after each experiment; college sophomores and most other organisms tend to learn on each trial, so that re-use of the same subject renders the results ambiguous. Constructing ensembles is also more difficult with organisms, since their previous histories can never be known completely. The basic methodology of perturb and record the results is, however, universal in reverse engineering, fault diagnosis, neuroscience, behavioral biology, and cognitive psychology, as well as all other experimental (as opposed to purely observational) sciences [Ashby (1956) provides a good introduction to the general systems methodology.]

The starting state $s[0]$ in which a system is placed is typically regarded as having two components: the resting or default state of the subject considered in isolation from the experiment, and an input, which perturbs the default subject state into an initial system state $s[1]$. The subject is assumed to receive no other inputs during the course of the experiment, which in the case of experiments on organisms typically amounts to assuming that the subject's post-input behavior is not interrupted by additional relevant inputs. While the environment remains part of the system being analyzed, it is assumed to be inert once the primary input is received by the subject; it is the subject, not the entire system, that is generally regarded as behaving. The final state $s[n]$ in such an experiment may be defined simply as the state of the system after a certain amount of time has elapsed. The task of the experimenter is to select state variables that can be measured with minimal perturbing effect on the subject's behavior, but that reveal as much as possible about the states being traversed after the initial perturbation into $s[1]$. Measurement of the state variables may involve recording electrical activity at specific points in a hardware or neural circuit, observing characters printed on a screen, recording verbal protocols, or any other repeatable physical interaction with finite resolution in time and other relevant parameters. The goal of the exercise is to infer (1) a general, abstract description of the behavior of the system that can be compared with similar descriptions of the behaviors of other systems, and (2) a set of mechanisms that describe the system's individual state transitions in a way that allows them to be compared with state transitions in other systems.

The theory of effective procedures for computing functions provides a language for describing both behaviors (computing functions) and mechanisms (executing procedures). Showing that the actions of a set of state-transition mechanisms in some system S is isomorphic to the execution of a procedure on a set of inputs allows us to view S as computing a function, and hence to classify it as similar, in a relevant respect, to other systems that compute the function using that procedure. The computational language is both general and descriptively complete. Any measurable behavior of any system, whether discrete or continuous, classical or quantum mechanical, can be described as computation in a way that fully captures its dynamics as measured. The construction of a computational description of behavior is always possible because measurements are discrete events; hence any observed sequence of states can be characterized as resulting from a sequence of discrete state transitions (Fields 1989).[1] This method of classifying and analyzing the behavior of systems by functional interpretation has been advanced as the dominant form of scientific explanation in general and psychological explanation in particular (Cummins 1983), and computational cognitive science is firmly based on this strategy (Dietrich 1990). Computational interpretations are useful starting points for mechanistic explanations because they allow us both to organize instances of behavior into classes by computed function, and to develop predictive emulations of the behavior on general-purpose computers. Emulation, in turn, provides a formally rigorous method of testing mechanistic assumptions. The development of such testable links between observable regularities in behavior and actions of underlying mechanisms is the central task of explanatory theories.

Describing a behavior of a physical system S as the computation of a function F involves constructing an interpretation function that maps transitions between observed states of S to steps in a procedure P for calculating F, as shown in Figure 3.1 (Dietrich 1989, 1990). Given such an interpretation, the states of S can be described as representing the results of intermediate steps in the execution of P. The only physical requirements for constructing such interpretations are that the states be reproducibly observable using some measuring process, and that the transitions be locally definable over the states. These conditions allow us to tell that one of the transitions of interest is occurring, and to interpret them using well-defined functions. In order for the interpretation to be coherent, the interpretation function I must algebraically commute with both the state transition functions $\{h[i]\}$ and the steps in the procedure $\{g[i]\}$, i.e., for every i, it must be the case that $g[i](I(s[i])) = I(h[i](s[i])) = I(s[i+1])$.

A very natural sense of representation can be defined for functional interpretations of the kind shown in Figure 3.1: a state $s[i]$ of the system is said to *represent,* in the context of the functional interpretation I, the intermediate step $I(s[i])$ in the computation of F using procedure P. This is the sense in which a state of a calculator represents a sum: we interpret pressing the buttons on the calculator as entering numbers and the "+" function into its memory, and interpret the pattern of light and dark bands on the display as representing the number that "+" would produce as an answer. Given appropriate measurements of state variables, the internal states can be similarly interpreted as manipulating numbers [Dietrich (1989) works through this example in detail]. This interpretive sense of representation forms the basis of both the semantics of programming languages (e.g., Stoy 1977) and the notion of multiple levels of languages or virtual machines (e.g., Tanenbaum 1984). The state images $I(s[i])$ can, in particular, be regarded as states of a virtual machine V that computes F by procedure P, and the functions $g[i]$ can be regarded as state transitions in this virtual machine. Given the interpretation of the initial state and the commutivity of the interpretation function I, what each state $s[j]$ represents under the interpretation I is easy to write down as a composition of the actions of the previous $g[i]$ on the interpretation of the initial state $s[1]$:

$$I(s[j]) = g[j{-}1] g[j{-}2] \ldots g[1] I(s[1]).$$

Figure 3.1. An interpretation function I mapping the states $s[i]$ of a system S to virtual machine states $I(s[i])$. The transitions between the virtual machine states are steps in a procedure that calculates the function that I interprets S as executing. The system transition $h[0]$ is the input perturbation. Compare Dietrich (1989, Figure 1).

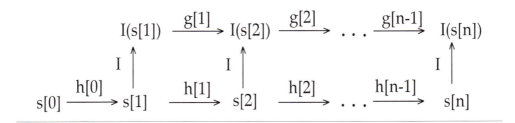

The computational interpretation I specifies the explanatory link between the observed behavior of S and the actions of the underlying mechanism at a level of abstraction that allows S to be compared with other similarly interpretable systems. Nothing else needs to be said about the representational contents of the individual states for the description to be complete, and saying what the contents of the individual states are does not add any information over and above that contained in the specification of I to the computational explanation of the system's behavior.

All of this is, however, very blithe from the point of view of an experimentalist. How, in particular, does this view of computational interpretation relate to the process of generating such an interpretation? How do we know that a proposed interpretation I is correct, i.e., how do we show that the internal dynamics of a system are actually organized in a way that can coherently be interpreted as executing the proposed procedure? Actually doing the experiments involves identifying particular kinds of states that are amenable to measurement with available technology, and correlating them with initial states that can be achieved by perturbations of the system. Often the instruments that are available do not have the bandwidth or the time resolution to capture long sequences of state transitions. Imagine, for example, trying to measure the voltages at all the pins on the processor in a typical workstation at 200 ns resolution (50 MHz) during a 1-second calculation: this would require keeping track of 50,000,000 voltage values for each of 48 or so pins! Nervous systems are even harder. Electrophysiology *in situ* always involves some disruption of tissue, and obtaining even action potential measurements, let alone the more informative post-synaptic potentials, for more than a handful of neurons simultaneously is a complex undertaking. Keeping track of the electrophysiological activity of all of the neurons in a vertebrate brain, or even a mollusc or insect brain, is currently out of the question. Noninvasive techniques such as positron-emission tomography or magnetic resonance imaging have millimeter resolutions, and only measure correlates of synaptic activity such as energy usage or magnetic field strengths. Such methods provide a useful view of average neuronal activity, but one that allows only a low-resolution, averaged representation of neuronal state. These difficulties render the identification of the states $s[i]$ of a nervous system that are amenable to computational interpretation a formidable challenge.[2]

In practice, we typically pick a few state variables that are amenable to measurement and that we think may be significant, and measure them for many inputs. If we are lucky, the selected variables will only change their values significantly for a small set of input perturbations: we then say that they are only sensitive to those initial states. Input perturbations that produce the same state transitions for the chosen variables form an equivalence class, the members of which cannot be distinguished by the measurements being made. The lower the resolution of the measurements, the larger the equivalence classes of indistinguishable states become. The goal of this method of measuring the response of a few variables for many perturbations is to sort states into execution traces, hence partitioning the state space of the system into paths, one for each equivalence class of inputs. Each path corresponds to a sequence $\{h[i]\}$ of equivalent (given our measurements) state transitions. Our task, for each path, is to find a procedure that is a plausible description of what the system is doing given prior interpretations of the relevant initial and final states, and a coherent interpretation of the observed $h[i]$ as an execution of that procedure.[3] As any reverse engineer, diagnostician, or experimental scientist will tell you, finding such interpretations and enough evidence to back them up is very hard work.

In the course of doing experiments of this kind, it is natural to characterize states by the initial perturbations to which they are sensitive. For example, we might notice that the voltage on a particular pin in our workstation shifted from 0V to 5V whenever the shift key was pressed together with any other key, and describe this situation by calling that pin the "shift-anything" pin. Or we might notice that the cells in a particular cortical minicolumn fired whenever left-moving edges were projected onto a subject's retina, and refer to that minicolumn as the "left -moving-edge" minicolumn. Such correlations give rise to a very natural informal semantics for these states, e.g., saying that activity in the left-moving-edge minicolumn represents left-moving edges. This informal notion of representation ties features of the environment that affect a component of a system to alterations in other, downstream parts of the system. Given that the activity of a minicolumn has downstream-activating or -inhibiting effects on other parts of the brain, for example, we often say that it represents left-moving edges to the downstream structures that it affects, or that it conveys the information that a left-moving edge is present in the environment to the downstream structure. This usage supports the view of intermediate states in a pathway as channels for the transmission of information from the environment to downstream processors and allows the calculation of information loss or gain during processing. It is important to note, however, that in such a case the minicolumn's activity does not represent edges or anything else to *us*—we just note the correlation between our manipulation of the environment and the subsequent changes in the minicolumn's activity. A recent paper in *Science* (Gallant et al. 1993) illustrates just this practice. It is this informal sense of representation as the holding or conveying of information about the external environment, not the formal, interpretive sense of representation discussed above, that arises most naturally when one considers the practical aspects of analyzing a system's behavior by experimentation. The intuitive attractiveness of the idea that states represent the changes in the environment with which they are correlated also motivates the criticism, by Gibsonians and by the likes of Searle and Sayre, that interpretive semantics is arbitrary, and hence inadequate as an account of intentionality.

2.   INTERPRETING INDIVIDUAL STATES

What is the relation between the abstract sense of representation obtained by constructing an interpretation function along the lines of Figure 3.1 and the informal, experimentalist's sense that captures the correlation between an observed state change in a system and a causally upstream, usually environmental event? A formal interpretation function is meant to describe the sequences of state transitions that follow particular inputs, while the informal, correlational sense of representation is generally applied to particular internal states. However, the informal notion of representation provides, in effect, a shorthand description of the relation of a state to the transition sequence to which it belongs—specifically, it allows us to view a state and its associated transitions as an information channel. In the case of the cortical minicolumn that responds selectively to left-moving edges that was considered above, the formal interpretation of the transition into a state of interest might be something like "inferring motion vectors for contrast edges," and the state itself might be interpreted as "contrast edge with vector v assigned"—not far at all from "left-moving edge." It would, in such a case, appear straightforward to simply identify the two senses of representation, and stipulate that the natural computational interpretation of a state is always the environmental cause of the system's being in that state.[4]

The easy identification of formal and informal senses of representation sketched above obscures some serious complications. These become clear when we consider the experimental analysis of not one, but a sequence of individual states, and attempt to match their informal, causal interpretations with those generated by the formal computational strategy. The visual system, which is relatively well understood, provides a good example [Maunsell and Newsome (1987) provide a good review of the biology; Churchland and Sejnowski (1992, Ch. 4) summarize the computational neuroscience]. Imagine measuring activity states of neurons along the primary visual pathway from the optic receptors through retinal ganglion cells, the lateral geniculate, and the various layers of the cortex as an edge is moved leftward across the visual field. Such measurements are, in fact, quite commonplace in experimental neuroscience. As outlined above, every one of the cells for which activities are measured in such an experiment can be described as representing a left-moving edge: a left-moving edge is the environmental cause and correlate of all of the measured activity. This is not a problem until one tries to assemble these interpretations into a computational description along the lines of Figure 3.1. When one does, one gets a sequence of transitions between states $s[i]$, all of which are interpreted as "left-moving edge." In the notation of Figure 3.1, $I(s[i]) = I(s[j])$ for every i and j; hence the functions $g[i]$ are all identity functions. The procedure executed by the system, which in Figure 3.1 transforms each interpretation into the next in the series, thus computes the identity function. This is not a very informative interpretation of the behavior of a visual system. It tells us nothing at all about what the system is *doing* to the signals that represent the left-moving edge.

In general, although it is very natural to interpret individual states as representing features in the environment that cause them—or with which they are informatively correlated (Sayre 1986)—this interpretation typically produces trivial sequences of transitions at the virtual machine level. Recall that in the canonical experiment, the input from the environment causes an initial, instantaneous perturbation of the system, after which the environment is assumed to remain inert while the state of the subject changes. The initial environmental event, which we can call $A(s[1])$ for the causal antecedent of $s[1]$, is the only external event with which the observed state changes in the system can be correlated by the experiment, since it is the only event to which the system is assumed to respond. If the states of the system are all interpreted as representing this initial environmental event, i.e., if the function I maps every state to the label $A(s[1])$, then the functions $g[i]$ will always be identity functions. A virtual machine specified by such $g[i]$ collapses into a single, static state; it does not *do* anything. This is paradoxical: one would expect that the intuitively sensible notion that states represent the environmental events that cause them would be consistent with the abstract, interpretive semantics developed to support the theory of virtual machines. The fact that these two notions do not seem to complement each other in a natural way calls the utility of the virtual machine concept as a tool for explaining the behaviors of systems like brains into question.

The depth of the incompatibility between the semantics sketched in Figure 3.1 and the intuitive notion that internal states represent their causal antecedents in the environment can be seen by asking what the behavior of a system would have to be like for an interpretive semantics not to collapse. In the notation of Figure 3.1, a system executes a nontrivial procedure if the composition of all of the functions $g[i]$ is not the identity function. This can be the case only if at least some of the interpretations $I(s[i])$ are distinct from each other. If these interpretations correspond to causal antecedents $A(s[i])$ in the environment, then at least some of these $A(s[i])$ have to be distinct. The system is assumed, however, only to respond, in a given experiment, to a single environmental event: $A(s[1])$. Any other environmental events are explicitly assumed either not to occur or to have no effect on the system. If the system gets into a state ordinarily correlated not with $A(s[1])$ but with some other event, a good initial hypothesis is that something must be wrong with the system. Consider the case of a visual system that is shown a left-moving edge. If in the course of measuring activities of cells, we found the system in a state typically caused by upward-moving edges, or typically caused only by static displays of dots or faces, we would consider that something was wrong. Sequences of states in which the set of typical environmental correlates $A(s[i])$ changes as i changes are *prima facie* evidence of a nondeterministic system that is jumping from one "normal" processing stream to another. If the behavior of a system interpreted along these lines cannot be explained with a reasonably simple stochastic model, one must begin to question the health of the system. Intermittent random state changes in a computer, for example, are evidence that it is broken.[5]

The problem with this interpretation scheme, and the source of the apparent paradox, is that the semantics sketched in Figure 3.1 ignores the experimental difficulties associated with defining a state, and hence characterizing the state space, of a system with complex anatomical or functional structure. Measuring the values of all of the available state variables of any interesting system is essentially impossible. In practice, only a relative handful of variables are measured after each input perturbation, and different variables may be measured at different times after a perturbation. In other words, practical experiments involve observations of transitions not between states, but between substates defined by subsets of the chosen state variables, which very often comprise different subsets of the state variables during different stages in an experimental procedure. Investigations of the visual system, for example, do not measure the state of the entire brain (much less the entire organism, as a Gibsonian might hope), but neither do they focus exclusively on a single component such as the retina. Activities in retinal cells are measured within a few milliseconds of stimulation, activities of cells in the geniculate some milliseconds later, and activities in different layers of the cortex still later. Measurement of different variables at different times following stimulation allows one to "follow" the course of activity through the system. Doing this successfully requires knowing something about the system's anatomy; measuring activity at the retina, and then the occipital lobe, and then the hypothalamus would presumably not be very effective for working out the function of the visual system.

In the course of a sequence of state transitions, each observed substate may represent, in the informal sense, the same causally antecedent environmental feature, and indeed each *complete* state may represent the same environmental feature or set of perceptually equivalent features, but different substates typically do the representational work at different stages in the processing. The experimenter's selection of the "right" substates for observation at different stages of processing can be represented mathematically by the action, on each state in the sequence, of a projection operator P. This situation is illustrated in Figure 3.2: while each state $s[i]$ is correlated with the same environmental feature $A(s[i])$, it is a different projected substate $P(s[i])$ with which the correlation with $A(s[i])$ is actually measured at step i. The system state transition functions $h[i]$ are, from the point of view of measurements of correlation with the input, transfers of activity between different substates. The $h[i]$ induce projected transitions $H[i]$ between the projected substates: $P(s[j]) = H[i](P(s[i]))$. These $H[i]$ are what experiments that track processing activity in response to an input effectively measure. Sending the representation of a feature of the environment to a different part of the system's state space—flow of control—is what does the work of computation.

The localization of processing in different parts of the state space requires that the notion of what a state or substate represents in the environment be extended to include not just the state's particular environmental antecedents, but also its location and role within the system. Understanding what a cell in the visual cortex is doing requires not just knowing that it is responding to a left-moving edge, but also that it is a cell in a particular cortical structure, and that it accepts input from particular upstream structures and sends output to particular downstream structures. This addition of functional context to representational content is made implicitly in localized measurements: neuroscientists, for example, take great pains to know what kind of cell (and in invertebrates, what *particular* cell) is being measured. Systems in which functional context cannot be inferred from physical position are, conversely, very difficult to reverse engineer; it can be extremely difficult, for example, to work out the functional context of a hidden unit in an artificial neural network or a bit register in a digital computer. Without the contextual information, however, descriptions of what the component's activity responds to, and hence of what it represents in the environment, are uninformative.

Figure 3.2. Interpretations of the states $s[i]$ of a system as representing the sets of environmental conditions $A(s[i])$ that cause them typically leads to a trivial set of transitions between the $A(s[i])$. Flow of control is between projected substates $P(s[i])$. The projected transitions $H[i]$ between these substates form a nontrivial sequence.

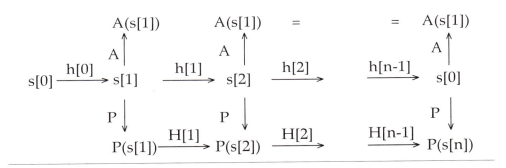

It is worth noting that the addition of anatomical or functional context to representational content is not a qualitative change in the semantics. The same effect can be achieved by reinterpreting the system to place the subject–environment division immediately upstream (in time) of the substate being measured. Each substate can then be regarded as representing its particular environmental input. By (radically) violating the usual assumption that the environment remains inert during the processing of the input, however, this formal reinterpretation destroys the usual, informal notion that it is the subject, not the combined subject–environment system, that is executing the computation. Not only does the identity of the subject change during each episode of processing when the system is interpreted in this way, it changes differently for each different input. Context-dependent representations of environmental events are required to avoid this sort of radical reinterpretation and maintain the usual, intuitive subject–environment distinction.

3.   REAL SYSTEMS AND VIRTUAL MACHINES

Comparing Figures 3.1 and 3.2, it is clear that the proper targets of interpretation in a system in which computation is localized are the projected substates. To maintain consistent nomenclature, let R be a representation function mapping projected states to virtual machine states, as shown in Figure 3.3. The system interpretation function is then a composition: $I = RP$. The inclusion of the substate projection P in I insures that the interpretation of each system state will include information about its context.

Figure 3.3. Construction of an interpretation function I as a composition of a substate projection P and a representation function R. Transitions in the virtual machine mirror transitions between the projected substates; i.e., they reflect flow of control.

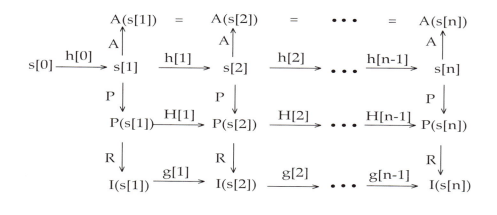

The projection P amounts to a functional modularization of S. The more natural the modules projected out by P, the easier it will be to find an R that maps these modules into functional modules of a virtual machine. The identification of well-defined, functionally self-contained modules requires good instruments, good experimental technique, and the recognition of architectural similarities in systems with similar overt behavior. One of the great insights of computational neuroscience is that anatomy can be used as a guide to functional localization: anatomically significant divisions of the brain correspond to functionally significant divisions of the state space of the system. Functions are continually being assigned to progressively smaller anatomical regions in the primate visual system, for example, effectively mapping a progressively more detailed virtual machine onto the anatomy (Maunsell and Newsome 1987); similar assignments have been made at the cellular level in several invertebrates. Functional analysis of general-purpose computers is hard precisely because the location of a component in such a machine gives so little information about its function. Reverse engineering a workstation with an oscilloscope to determine its operating system experimentally—the equivalent of an electrophysiological investigation of the function of a nervous system—is an engineer's nightmare.

Functional localization in the state space—sometimes accompanied by anatomical localization in physical space—forces modularization on virtual machines that describe physical systems. Modularization is an essential component of semantics. It is no surprise that procedures are described "at the high level" by flowcharts, entity-relationship diagrams, or other modular representations: such representations are the only way to capture the flow of control, and hence understand what the procedures are doing. Artificial neural network research provides a case in point: early back-propagation networks with completely distributed representations were viewed as black boxes that computed complicated functions in a single step (e.g., Hinton et al. 1986). More modular mathematical models, such as ART (Grossberg 1980), could be viewed as multistep virtual machines. As both virtual (e.g., Wilson and Bower 1991) and hardware (e.g., DeYong et al. 1992) artificial neural networks have become progressively more neuron-like, the functions encoded by the networks have become progressively more localized, and the systems progressively more understandable as virtual machines.

In summary, the interpretive and causal approaches to specifying the representational contents of the states of a system that interacts with an environment can be made coherent, and indeed complementary, by extending the usual notion of an interpretation function to include a projective component that specifies the functional context of each interpreted substate. In such a semantics, *what* is represented (the state of the environment that initiates processing) does not change during a computation, but *how* it is represented does change. Information processing, in this semantics, consists in changing the form of a representation with fixed contents. The physical transitions of which the transitions in the corresponding virtual machine are images are transitions between substates, not transitions between represented contents. It is these transitions, which manifest flow of control, that constitute processing. Such a semantics maintains both the formal notion of interpretation as a map from a system to a virtual machine, and the informal notion that internal states represent their causal antecedents to downstream processes. This semantics formalizes the notion of modularity that is critical both for defining control flow, and for devising practical experiments. Finally, this semantics is attributive but nonarbitrary: a collapse into triviality or nondeterminism can only be prevented by selecting the right substates to carry the represented contents at each stage of processing.

4.   WHAT KINDS OF SYSTEMS ARE INTENTIONAL?

The principal objection raised by critics of attributive approaches to semantics is that semantic attribution appears arbitrary in both scope and content. Consideration of the experimental basis for semantic attribution shows, however, that it is anything but arbitrary in content; a claim that cells of the primary visual cortex, for example, could just as well be interpreted as representing odors of fruits or computing tomorrow's weather could only be regarded as perverse. The idea that arbitrary contents can be attributed to a computing system probably derives from the observation that some architectures (e.g., the Turing or von Neumann machines) are universal and the widespread confusion of program execution with rule following (Cummins 1982). Universal architectures exist because a small number of basic operations are sufficient for any computation. The behavior of a machine realizing a universal architecture is, however, subject to the same basic constraint as the behavior of any other machine: the coding capacity of its input interface. A computer is not a mechanical ideal agent that can be told to do anything; it is a physical device with fixed structure and dynamics. Prior to receiving an input, "running a program" simply means being in a particular state: the state that, when perturbed by an allowed input, generates a sequence of state transitions that executes the relevant procedure. Loading a different program is putting the machine into a different resting state, in which a different set of input perturbations will lead to appropriate behavior. No machine, natural or artificial, follows arbitrary rules; what a system does after an input is received is entirely determined by its dynamics. Semantics could be arbitrary only if physics was arbitrary.

The complaint that attributive semantics is arbitrary in scope misses the true mark: attributive semantics is *universal* in scope. Any system that interacts with an environment—a source of input perturbations—can be described as computing. Whether it is useful to do so turns on whether what the system is doing in its environment is usefully regarded as behavior in the psychological sense. This question of explanatory context is not answered by carrying out a computational interpretation, and the procedure for performing such an interpretation does not depend on criteria of explanatory utility. When Fodor (1984) argues that computational analyses of the behavior of paramecia are pointless, he is arguing that the behavior of these organisms is not interesting, at least to him.

The principal agenda of arguments that attributive semantics is erroneously overgenerous in scope is the establishment of a dividing line between systems that are taken to be genuinely intentional and others that are not. Proponents of such arguments always include humans in the genuinely intentional category, but disagree about what else to so honor: Searle (1980) and Sayre (1986) include vertebrates but not computers, Harnad (1990) is willing to include some robots, and Fodor (1984) and Pylyshyn (1984) include "cognitively penetrable" software systems but not most animals. Neither attributive semantics nor computational explanation supports such distinctions. Organisms are embedded in their environments in exactly the same way that other physical systems are, and their states represent features of their environments in exactly the same way that states of other systems do. Conversely, computers have sensory systems (keyboards and mice) and effectors (screens and printers) just like organisms do, and their behavior is just as much "in the world" as any organism's.

Intentionality is a property of systems, not of their components. The subject–environment and peripheral–central distinctions are convenient, not principled. They can be misleading: Searle's (1980) confusion of a processing component with a system is a case in point. All physical processors, central or otherwise, have finite capabilities. No physical systems possess uniquely intentional "central processors" of the all-powerful sort envisioned by Fodor (1987); the idea of a computer with unrestricted access to information and arbitrary ability to assess relevance is incoherent (Dietrich and Fields 1992). All computing systems that execute multistep procedures are modular in the same sense and for the same reason: computing requires flow of control. Such modularity is required for computations to have semantics, and the semantics must explicitly recognize the modularity. The idea that the complex computations involved in high-level cognitive processing could be nonmodular in humans appears to derive from a lack of understanding of how higher cognitive functions are localized in the cortex, together with the same confusion of program execution with (arbitrary) rule following that underlies the idea that semantic attribution is arbitrary. Higher functions may or may not be anatomically localized in cortex or silicon, but neither computers nor people can solve arbitrary problems.

A final argument with considerable philosophical currency is that some systems are intentional independently of any attributions of semantics to their states. This is true of everything, but it is trivial. The question of whether the semantics of the states of a system is "real" in the absence of interpretive analysis is on a par with the question of whether planetary orbits are elliptical in the absence of mathematicians: neither the state transition mechanisms nor the large-scale behavior of the systems with respect to their environments is affected in any way by whether they are assigned interpretations by external observers. Intentionality in abstraction is a red herring: a rhetorical conundrum designed to divert attention from the hard work of characterizing mechanisms (Fields and Dietrich 1987).

5.   METHODOLOGY

It is not implausible to view the roughly three-decade history of cognitive science as a protracted struggle against naive reductionism on the one hand and vitalism on the other. The notions of representation and semantic interpretation have been disputed territory in this struggle. Thinking about the process of constructing a functional interpretation from the results of real experiments may clarify some of the methodological issues that arise in the early stages of dealing with systems for which almost no complete, system-wide functional descriptions have yet been worked out. A common pathology of sciences faced with such systems is counterfactual reductionism: the view that if a lower-level science achieved a complete description of a system's dynamics it would render all higher-level descriptions unnecessary and not worth pursuing. The counterfactual reductionist pathology is surprisingly common in cognitive science; for example, Hayes et al. (1992) worry that conventional cognitive science and artificial intelligence would be "relegated to history's dustbin" (p. 259) if biological descriptions of humans ever achieved dynamical completeness. This worry is very odd coming from computer scientists who presumably would not think of giving up high-level programming languages to work in assembler. From the perspective of standard psychological questions, a dynamically complete biological description would not only be a computational nightmare, it would be unthinkable experimentally. Whether such a description could be achieved in principle is of no relevance; it could not be employed to do anything useful.

Why is the counterfactual reductionist pathology so common among cognitive scientists? Disciplinary chauvinism alone does not seem adequate as an explanation. The prevalence of this attitude may be symptomatic of unease with the inability, thus far, of cognitive science to discover necessary and sufficient conditions for a system to count as cognitive. Much of the argument about intentionality, as reviewed above, is driven by attempts to discover a principled distinction between humans and humanlike systems and other (inferior) kinds. Reductionism may be particularly worrying to cognitive scientists because its possibility, even if unrealizable in practice, would strip humans of any principled distinction from the rest of the biological, and indeed the physical, world.

The account of intentionality and its sources outlined above will not comfort the victim of angst about the position of humans in the natural order. It should, however, encourage those who are optimistic about the opportunities for scientists with different interests and methods to collaborate in understanding how and why systems, including humans, behave as they do. What counts as interesting is identified pre-scientifically; science supplies the tools to do the work of explanation.

6.   NOTES

1.   This point is simple, but is often overlooked. Regardless of how we may standardly choose to formulate theories of a system's behavior, the data that the theories are meant to explain are always discrete. Hence what any individual system is actually observed to do can always be described as the undergoing of a sequence of discrete state transitions. Continuous descriptions of behavior that use real-valued functions—such as the descriptions of classical physics—are very convenient, but are not required by the data. The uncertainty principle in quantum mechanics gives this point universality: observations cannot, even in principle, have arbitrarily high resolution without perturbing the dynamics in a way that destroys both repeatability and predictability. The quantum mechanical description of the world may be continuous (e.g., using propagator theory), but the quantum mechanical description of what is observable is discrete (e.g., using a finite series of Feynman diagrams). Any sequence of discrete state transitions can be emulated by a Turing machine, and hence can be viewed as an instance of the execution of some procedure.

2.   One might object that cognitive science has been building computational models without the benefit of experimental descriptions of neural activity for several decades. The difference between phenomenological cognitive science and computational neuroscience is that with the latter one can make and test claims to the effect that particular data are represented by particular neurons and processed by particular synaptic circuitry. The methodological similarity between the activity of testing such claims and the activity of fault diagnosis or reverse engineering of computers or other electronic hardware is striking and pedagogically useful. I do not mean to imply that phenomenological cognitive science is not a valuable complement to computational neuroscience, as will be stressed explicitly below.

3.   The movement of a system's current state through the state space is commonly referred to in the AI literature as "search." This is one of the more unfortunate choices of words in cognitive science, due to its connotations of awareness and intention. As Korf (1992) points out in his definition for the *Encyclopedia of Artificial Intelligence, search* is simply behavior that can be described as execution of an algorithm that requires "systematic trial-and-error exploration of alternatives" (p. 1460); search is the procedure of choice only when insufficient information is available to design a more efficient algorithm. Saying that a system is executing an algorithm, whether a search or any other kind, is simply saying that the system's physical behavior can be

described in a particular way. No other connotations of the terms used are intended or warranted.

4.   It is a standard move to quibble with such blithe uses of the term *cause*, for example, by demanding to know how causes are to be individuated. In the current context, the experimenter is assumed to know what environmental variables are being manipulated and how. The point of the exercise is to describe what the system does once it has been placed in an initial state of interest by the environmental manipulation; as long as the manipulations are specified in a consistent way, it does not matter where in the environment "causes" are taken to reside.

5.   Note that this is not a point about what the system may be experiencing, and phenomena such as free association do not obviate it. The sequence of state transitions that a system undergoes following an input may be arbitrarily complicated; the only requirement of determinism is that the same input perturbation to the same resting state will, in the absence of other inputs, yield the same sequence of transitions. As noted earlier, achieving the same resting state and complete isolation from competing inputs may be impossible in practice for organisms; hence determinism is an idealized notion. A rough sense of repeatability is its usual replacement. The claim often made by Fodor (e.g., Fodor 1984) that higher cognition is not law-like is merely the claim that stimulus-response laws in which both stimulus and response are defined entirely externally—i.e., ignoring the resting state of the system—are inadequate. Thermostats are not law-like on this definition if one regards the trip setting as an internal variable.

7.   REFERENCES

Ashby, W. R. (1956) *An Introduction to Cybernetics* (London: Chapman and Hall).

Churchland, P. S., and Sejnowski, T. J. (1992) *The Computational Brain* (Cambridge, MA: MIT).

Cummins, R. (1982) The internal manual model of psychological explanation. *Cognition and Brain Theory*, 5: 257-268.

Cummins, R. (1983) *The Nature of Psychological Explanation* (Cambridge, MA: Bradford).

DeYong, M., Eskridge, T. C., and Fields, C. (1992) Temporal signal processing with high-speed hybrid analog-digital neural networks. *Analog Integrated Circuits and Signal Processing*, 2: 367-388.

Dietrich, E. (1989) Semantics and the computational paradigm in cognitive psychology. *Synthese*, 79: 119-141.

Dietrich, E. (1990) Computationalism. *Social Epistemology*, 4: 135-154.

Dietrich, E., and Fields, C. (1992) The wanton module and the Frame Problem: making Fodor's modularity thesis compatible with computationalism. In L. Burkholder (ed.) *Philosophy and the Computer*. (Boulder, CO:Westview), pp. 92-104.

Fields, C. (1989) Consequences of nonclassical measurement for the algorithmic description of continuous dynamical systems. *Journal of Experimental and Theoretical Artificial Intelligence*, 1: 171-178.

Fields, C., and Dietrich, E. (1987) Intentionality is a red herring. *Behavioral and Brain Sciences*, 10: 756-757.

Fodor, J. (1984) Why paramecia don't have mental representations. *Midwest Studies in Philosophy*, 10: 3-23.

Fodor, J. (1987) Modules, frames, fridgeons, sleeping dogs, and the music of the spheres. In Z. Pylyshyn (ed.) *The Robot's Dilemma* (Norwood, NJ: Ablex), pp. 139-149.

Gallant, J. L., Braun, J., and Van Essen, D. C. (1993) Selectivity for polar, hyperbolic, and Cartesian gratings in macaque visual cortex. *Science*, 259: 100-103.

Gibson, J. J. (1979) *The Ecological Approach to Visual Perception* (Boston: Houghton Mifflin).

Grossberg, S. (1980) How does the brain build a cognitive code? *Psychological Review*,,87: 1-51.

Harnad, S. (1990) The symbol grounding problem. *Physica*, D42: 335-346.

Hayes, P. J., Ford, K. M., and Adams-Webber, J. R. (1992) Human reasoning about artificial intelligence. *Journal of Experimental and Theoretical Artificial Intelligence*, 4: 247-263.

Hinton, G. E., McClelland, J. L., and Rumelhart, D. E. (1986) Distributed representations. In D. Rumelhart and J. McClelland (eds.) *Parallel Distributed Processing*. (Cambridge, MA: MIT) pp. 77–109.

Korf, R. E. (1992) Search. In S. Shapiro (ed.) *Encyclopedia of Artificial Intelligence*, 2nd ed. (New York: Wiley), pp. 1460-1467.

Michaels, C., and Carello, C. (1981) *Direct Perception* (Englewood Cliffs, NJ: Prentice-Hall).

Maunsell, J. H. R., and Newsome, W. T. (1987) Visual processing in monkey extrastriate cortex. *Annual Review of Neuroscience,* 10: 363-401.

Pylyshyn, Z. (1984) *Computation and Cognition* (Cambridge, MA: Bradford).

Sayre, K. (1986) Intentionality and information processing: an alternative view. *Behavioral and Brain Sciences,* 9: 121-166.

Searle, J. R. (1980) Minds, brains, and programs. *Behavioral and Brain Sciences,* 3: 417-457.

Stoy, J. (1977) Denotational Semantics (Cambridge, MA : MIT).

Tanenbaum, A. S., (1984) *Structured Computer Organization* (Englewood Cliffs, NJ: Prentice-Hall).

Wilson, M. A., and Bower, J. M. (1991) A computer simulation of oscillatory behavior in primary visual cortex. *Neural Computation,* 3: 498-509.

CHAPTER
4

◆ # The Myth of
Original Intentionality

Daniel C. Dennett

....

John Searle has proclaimed that 'strong' Artificial Intelligence is impossible because the brain has certain special causal powers, and 'no formal computer program *by itself*' would ever be sufficient to produce these causal powers. I will not take time to discuss the well-known 'Chinese Room' thought experiment with which Searle attempts to establish his case, since its host of fallacies have been pointed out many times by many people. (To my mind the definitive diagnosis of what is wrong with Searle's example is Hofstadter and Dennett (1981), pp. 348-82.) In fact, I don't know anyone except Searle who believes he has a good argument, but I know many people who think that, nevertheless, his conclusion is true. A frontal assault on the conclusion is what is required.

According to Searle, our brains 'are capable of causing mental phenomena with intentional or semantic content' (Searle 1982, p. 57). Sometimes Searle calls the effect wrought by these causal powers *original intentionality* (Searle 1980) and sometimes he calls it *intrinsic intentionality* (Searle 1982, p. 57). I too am impressed

Thinking Computers and Virtual Persons
edited by Eric Dietrich
ISBN 0-12-215495-9

by the causal powers of the human brain, but, as Searle notes, I do not believe in the effects he supposes to exist: 'Dennett . . . believes that nothing *literally* has any *intrinsic intentional* mental states . . .' (Searle 1982, p. 57). So my task is first to show how strange—how ultimately preposterous—Searle's imagined causal powers of the brain are, and secondly to expose the myth of original intentionality.

I will address my first task by contrasting Searle's claim about the causal powers of the brain with a similar and much more defensible claim. It is not unusual in philosophy for a confused and hopeless dogma to resemble an important truth; perhaps many of those who have been attracted by Searle's position:

> (S) Only an organic human brain—and certainly no electronic digital computer of the sort currently used in AI—could have the causal powers required to produce intentionality,

have mistaken it for the following position:

> (D) Only an organic human brain—and certainly no electronic digital computer of the sort currently used in AI—could have the causal powers required to produce the swift, intelligent sort of mental activity exhibited by normal human beings.

As the initials suggest, I shall endorse proposition *D* (somewhat tentatively), and then distinguish it sharply from Searle's proposition *S*. But first I must clear up a minor confusion in Searle's proposition. When Searle says that no 'formal' computer program by *itself* can produce these effects, there is a sense in which that is perfectly obvious: no computer program lying unimplemented on the shelf, a mere abstract sequence of symbols, can cause anything. By itself (in this sense) no computer program can even add 2 and 2 and get 4; in this sense, no computer program by itself can cause word processing to occur, let alone produce mental phenomena with intentional content. Searle's conviction that it is just obvious that no computer program could 'produce intentionality' might actually derive partly from confusing this obvious (and irrelevant) claim with something more substantive—and dubious: that no concretely implemented running computer program could 'produce intentionality'. But only the latter claim is a challenge to AI, and so for the sake of argument I will assume that Searle is utterly unconfused about this, and thinks that he has shown that no running, material embodiment of a 'formal' computer program could 'produce intentionality' purely in virtue of its being an embodiment of such a formal program. That is to say, the causal powers such a material embodiment would have in virtue of being an implementation of the program would never be capable of 'causing mental phenomena' (Searle 1982, p. 57). Perhaps more vividly: take a material object (any material object) that does *not* have the power of causing mental phenomena; you cannot turn it into an object that *does* have the power of producing mental phenomena simply by programming it—reorganizing the conditional dependencies of the transitions between its states.

How could I endorse proposition *D* without forswearing all my allegiances? Have I not defended strong AI as a methodology and ideology? Have I not insisted, moreover, that the commitment to AI is no more than a commitment to Church's Thesis and a resolve to strive for clarity in psychology (Dennett 1978)? Yes, but a commitment to strong AI does not conflict with proposition *D*, as we shall see.

Here then is my argument for proposition *D*. Edwin A. Abbott's amusing fantasy *Flatland: A Romance in Many Dimensions* (Abbott 1884) tells the story of intelligent beings living in a two-dimensional world. Some spoil-sport whose name I have fortunately forgotten once objected that the Flatland story could not be true (who ever thought otherwise?) because there could not be an intelligent being in only two dimensions. In order to be intelligent, this sceptic argued, one needs a richly interconnected brain (or nervous system or *some* kind of complex, highly interconnected control system) and in two dimensions you cannot wire together even so few as five things each to each other—at least one wire must cross another wire, which will require a third dimension.

This is plausible, but false. John von Neumann proved years ago that a universal Turing machine could be realized in two dimensions. And John Horton Conway has shown that one can construct a universal Turing machine in his amazing two-dimensional 'Life' world. Cross-overs are indeed desirable, but there are several ways of doing without them in a computer (or in a brain) (Dewdney 1984). One way is the way cross-overs are often eliminated in highway systems: by traffic-light intersections, where isolated parcels of information (or whatever) can take turns crossing each other's path. The price one pays, here as on the highway, is speed of transaction. But *in principle* (that is, if time were no object) an entity with a nervous system as interconnected as you please can be realized in two dimensions. But speed is of the essence for intelligence (in our world); if you can't figure out the relevant portions of the changing environment fast enough to fend for yourself, you are not intelligent, however complex you are. It is thus no accident that our brains make use of all three spatial dimensions.

Very well, nothing that wasn't three-dimensional could have the causal powers required to produce the swift, intelligent sort of mental activity exhibited by normal human beings. But digital computers are three-dimensional. True, but they are—almost all of them—fundamentally *linear* in a certain way; they are von Neumann machines, serial, not parallel in their architecture, and thus capable of doing just one thing at a time. It has become a commonplace these days that although a von Neumann machine, like the universal Turing machine it is descended from, can *in principle* compute anything any computer can compute, many interesting computations—especially in such important cognitive areas as pattern recognition and memory-searching—cannot be done in reasonable lengths of time by them. The only way of accomplishing these computations in interestingly macroscopic amounts of real time is to use massively parallel processing hardware. That indeed is why such hardware is now being designed and built. It is no news that the brain gives every evidence of having a massively parallel architecture—millions if not billions of channels wide, all capable of simultaneous activity. This too is no accident, presumably. So in order to achieve the causal powers required to produce the *swift*, intelligent sort of mental activity exhibited by normal human beings, one must have a massive parallel processor (such as a human brain) at one's disposal. (Note that I have not attempted an a priori proof of this; I am content to settle for scientific likelihood.)

Still, it may seem, there is no reason why one's massive parallel processor must be made of organic materials. In fact, transmission speeds in electronic systems are orders of magnitude greater than transmission speeds in nerve fibers, so an electronic parallel system should be faster (and more reliable) than any organic system. Perhaps, but then again perhaps not. Suppose—and this is not very likely, but hardly disproved—that the information-processing prowess of a single neuron (its relevant input-output function) depends on features or activities in subcellular organic molecules. If this were the case—that is, if information processed at the enzyme level (say) played a critical role in modulating the switching or information processing of individual neurons (each neuron a tiny computer itself)—then it might in fact *not* be possible to make a model or simulation of the neuron's behavior that could duplicate the neuron's feats *in real time.* This would be because if you try to model molecular behavior in real time, your computer model may indeed be tiny and swift, but not so tiny (and hence not so swift) as the molecule being modelled. Even with the speed advantage of electronics over electrochemical transmission in axonal branches, it might be that microchips were unable to keep pace with neuronal intracellular operations in the task of determining just how to modulate those ponderously slow output spikings. (A version of this idea is presented by Jacques Monod, who speaks of the '"cybernetic" (i.e. teleonomic) power at the disposal of a cell equipped with hundreds or thousands of these microscopic entities, all far more clever than the Maxwell–Szilard-Brillouin demon' (Monod 1971, p. 69).)

Of course on the other hand the complexity of molecular activity in neuron cell bodies may well have only local significance, in which case the point lapses. More decisively, as Rodolfo Llinas has claimed to me in conversation, there is no way for a neuron to harness the lightning speed and 'cybernetic power' of its molecules. Although the *individual* molecules can perform swift information processing, they cannot be made to propagate and amplify these effects swiftly. The spiking events they would have to modulate are orders of magnitude larger and more powerful than their 'output' state-changes, and diffusion and amplification of their 'signal' would squander all the time gained through miniaturization. So, in all likelihood, *this* line of argument for the inescapable biologicality of mental powers is forlorn. Still, it is mildly instructive. It is far from established that the nodes in one's massively parallel system *must* be neurons with the right stuff inside them, but, nevertheless, this might be the case. There are other ways in which it might prove to be the case that the inorganic reproduction of the *essential* information-processing functions of the human brain would have to run more slowly than their real-time inspirations. After all, we have discovered many complex processes—such as the weather—that cannot be accurately simulated in real time (in time for useful weather prediction, for instance) by even the fastest, largest supercomputers currently in existence. (It is not that the equations governing the transitions are not understood. Even using what we know now is impossible. The current sampling grid for North America breaks the atmosphere into volumes approximately 30 miles square and 10 000 feet deep. That yields in the neighborhood of 100 000 cells, each with less than a dozen intensities (temperature, barometric pressure, wind direction and velocity, relative humidity, . . .) characterizing each. How these intensities change as a function of the intensities in the neighboring cells is fairly well understood, but computing these changes in small enough temporal increments to keep some significance in the answers swamps today's supercomputers. One solution of course is to install 100 000 computers—one for each cell—and compute the prediction in parallel. But it is probably true that 30 miles is vastly too large a distance to average over, and that microclimatic disturbances (the sunlight bouncing off the windshield of a single parked car) propagate non-negligible effects. So then will we need a few billion computers in parallel . . . ?

Brainstorms may well prove just as hard to simulate, and hence predict. *If* they are, then since speed of operation really is critical to intelligence,

> (D) Only an organic human brain—and certainly no electronic digital computer of the sort currently used in AI—could have the causal powers required to produce the swift, intelligent sort of mental activity exhibited by normal human beings.

Hardly a knock-down argument, but the important point is that it would be foolish to bet against it, since it may very well turn out to be true.

But isn't this just the wager that AI has made? Not quite, although some AI enthusiasts have no doubt committed themselves to it. Like any effort at scientific modelling, AI modelling has been attempted in a spirit of opportunistic over-simplification. Things that are horribly complicated may be usefully and revealingly approximated by partitionings, averagings, idealizations, and other deliberate over-simplifications, in the hope that some molar behavior of the complex phenomenon will prove to be relatively independent of all the myriad microdetails, and hence will be reproduced in a model that glosses over those microdetails.

For instance, suppose an AI model of, say, action planning required at some point that a vision subsystem be consulted for information about the layout of the environment. Rather than attempt to model the entire visual system, whose operation is no doubt massively parallel and whose outputs are no doubt voluminously informative, the system designers insert a sort of cheap stand-in: a vision 'oracle' that can provide the supersystem with, say, any one of only 256 different 'reports' on the relevant layout of the environment. The designers are betting that they can design an action-planning system that will approximate the target competence (perhaps the competence of a 5-year-old or a dog, not a mature adult) while availing itself of only eight bits of visual information on environmental layout. Is this a good bet? Perhaps and perhaps not. There is plenty of evidence that human beings simplify their information-handling tasks and avail themselves of only a tiny fraction of the information obtainable by their senses; if this *particular* over-simplification turns out to be a bad bet, it will only mean that we should search for some other over-simplification. It is by no means obvious that any united combination of the sorts of simplified models and subsystems developed so far in AI can approximate the perspicuous behavior of a normal human being—in real time or even orders of magnitude slower—but that still does not impeach the research methodology of AI, any more than their incapacity to predict real-world weather accurately impeaches all meteorological over-simplifications as scientific models.

But have I now switched in effect to a defense of 'weak AI'—the mere modelling of psychological or mental phenomena by computer, as opposed to the creation of genuine (but artificial) mental phenomena by computer? Searle, it will be recalled, has no brief against what he calls weak AI: 'Perhaps this is a good place to express my enthusiasm for the prospects of weak AI, the use of the computer as a tool in the study of the mind' (Searle 1982, p. 57). What he is opposed to is the 'strong AI belief that the appropriately programmed computer literally has a mind, and its antibiological claim that the specific neurophysiology of the brain is irrelevant to the study of the mind' (p. 57).

There are several ways to interpret this characterization of strong AI, and in the interests of time I will force an interpretation by providing a more specific version of the strong AI claim.

> The only relevance of 'the specific neurophysiology of the brain' is in providing the right sort of hardware engineering for real-time intelligence. *If* it turns out that we can get enough speed out of parallel silicon-microchip architectures, then neurophysiology will be truly inessential, though certainly valuable for the hints it can provide about architecture.

Consider two different implementations of the same program—that is, consider two different physical systems, the transitions of each of which are accurately and appropriately describable in terms of a single 'formal' program, but one of which runs six orders of magnitude (about a million times) slower than the other. In one sense they both have the same capabilities—they both 'compute the same function'—but in virtue of its greater speed, one of them will have 'causal powers' the other lacks: namely, the causal *control* powers to guide a locomoting body through the real world. We may for this very reason claim that the fast one was 'literally a mind' while withholding that honorific from its slow twin. It is not that sheer speed ('intrinsic' speed?) above some critical level creates some mysterious emergent effect, but that relative speed is crucial in enabling the right sorts of environment–organism sequences of interaction to occur. The same effect could be produced by 'slowing down the outside world' sufficiently—if that made sense. An appropriately programmed computer—provided only that it is fast enough to interface with the sensory transducers and motor effecters of a 'body' (robot or organic)—literally has a mind, whatever its material instantiation, organic or inorganic.

This, I claim, is all that strong AI is committed to, and Searle has offered no reason to doubt it. We can see how it might still turn out to be true, as Searle and many others insist, that there is only one way to skin the mental cat after all, and that is with real, organic neural tissue. It might seem, then, that the issue separating Searle from strong AI and its defenders is a rather trifling difference of opinion about the precise role to be played by details of neurophysiology, but this is not so. A dramatic difference in implication between propositions S and D is revealed in a pair of concessions Searle has often made. First, he grants that 'just about any system has a level of description where you can describe it as a digital computer. You can describe it as instantiating a formal program. So in that sense, I suppose, all of our brains are digital computers' (Searle 1984, p. 153). Secondly, he has often conceded that one could, for all he knows, create a brain-like device out of silicon chips (or other AI-approved hardware) that perfectly mimics the real-time input-output behavior of a human brain. Such a device would presumably have the same description at the program or digital-computer level as the brain whose input-output behavior it mimicked. But only the organic brain would 'produce intentionality'. Actually, he often says that he does not know for sure that the silicon substitute would not produce intentionality—that is an empirical question. This is a puzzling claim; surely it is a strange kind of empirical question that is systematically bereft of all intersubjective empirical evidence. That is, you could throw a person's brain away, replace it with a suitably programmed computer (a 'merely formal system' that duplicated the brain at the digital-computer level, but embodied in some inorganic hardware), and that person's body would go on behaving *exactly* as it would have gone on behaving had it kept its brain—but without there being any mind or intentionality there at all. So Searle's position on the importance of neurophysiology is that although it is important, indeed all-important, its crucial contribution might be entirely undetectable from the outside. A human body without a real mind, without genuine intentionality, could fend for itself in the real world just as well as a human body with a real mind.

My position, on the other hand, as a supporter of proposition D, is that neurophysiology is (probably) so important that if ever I see any entity gadding about in the world with the real-time cleverness of, say, C3PO in *Star Wars*, I will be prepared to wager a considerable sum that it is controlled by an organic brain. Nothing else (I bet) can control such clever behavior in real time. That makes me a *sort* of 'behaviorist' in Searle's eyes. And it is this sort of behaviorism that lies at the heart of the disagreement between AI and Searle. This is why the causal powers Searle imagines are so mysterious: they have, by definition, no effect on behavior—unlike the causal powers AI takes so seriously: the powers required to guide a body through life, seeing, hearing, acting, talking, deciding, investigating, and so on. It is odd indeed to call such a thoroughly cognitivist and (for example) anti-Skinnerian doctrine behaviorist, but that is how Searle chooses to use the term.

L et us take stock. Searle criticizes AI for not taking neurophysiology (and biology generally) seriously, but then is prepared to concede that a non-biological control system might replace a brain in its niche with no loss of control powers. Many in AI would agree, for they are not committed to proposition *D*, nor need they be. It may indeed turn out that a non-organic input-output duplicate can be created. The point of disagreement is that Searle thinks that such a duplicate would not be (or 'cause' or 'produce') a mind. For it would not have 'original' or 'intrinsic' intentionality, being a mere instantiation of a 'formal' computer program.

We need now to see what original intentionality might be. Intentionality, for me and for Searle, is—in a word—*aboutness*. Some things are not about anything and some things are about something. A table isn't about anything, but Tom's belief that the table is wobbly is about the table; his desire to fix the table is also about the table (and not about the door, which may also need repair—but must be the subject of some different beliefs and desires). In general, mental phenomena are about things—things in the external world or things inside the mind or abstract things (the belief that π is irrational is about π). Perhaps some mental phenomena are not about anything. A nameless dread or a bout of depression might be mental phenomena that are not about anything at all. Some non-mental things are also about things: a pebble on the beach, or an apple, or a bicycle, is not about anything, but a sentence, a map, and even a computer program or a data structure in a computer can be about things. It is tempting to generalize and say that all things that exhibit intentionality are *representations* of one sort or another, but since we do not yet have an independent account of representation, this really means nothing more than that all things that exhibit intentionality are about ('represent'?) something.

According to Searle, however, only the mental phenomena exhibit *original* intentionality. The intentionality of an encyclopedia or a road sign or a photograph of the Eiffel Tower is only derived or secondary intentionality. This is certainly an intuitive and appealing first move towards a general theory of intentionality. Some of our artifacts exhibit intentionality of a sort, but only because we have decided to use these artifacts in certain ways, as our tools, our ploys, our devices. A sentence considered by itself as a string of ink marks or a sequence of acoustic vibrations has no intrinsic meaning or aboutness. It has a structure, or syntax, but in so far as it acquires meaning, or semantics, this is an endowment from us, its users. The sequence 'Snow is white' could mean anything or nothing; if we want to, we can decide to use the sequence 'foofoofoo' to mean it is time for lunch, or whatever we want; thereupon it will mean that.

This familiar idea is more plausible for some of our artifacts than for others. If words obtain their particular aboutness in an entirely arbitrary way, photographs generally seem to have quite natural and unconventional objects untouched by our intentions. But not always. There is a difference in intentionality between a photograph in an advertisement of a professional model smilingly pouring laundry detergent, and a photograph of the same woman in a wedding album or on a wanted poster—the latter pictures are about her, the individual, while the advertising picture is about the detergent, but not really about her. And while the symbols on maps can be entirely arbitrary (this symbol means *fire station* and that symbol means *public campsite*) many of the representational features of maps are not arbitrary at all. Moreover, not every structural feature of a representation is a syntactic feature; only those features variation in which can make a semantical difference count as syntactical features. If we find a book written in an alien language, we will not be able to tell whether the minor variations in ink color or character size are syntactic differences until we know the language's system of conventions, as determined by its speakers. Putting these points together, we can see that whereas some artifacts, such as books, are entirely inscrutable as representations unless we have a key describing the book's users' intentions, other artifacts, such as videotapes, impose strong natural limits on their possible semantical interpretation. (Whether the alien book is about chemical reactions or boxing matches may be impossible to determine in the absence of native users; a native user of the videotape may be needed just to confirm the obvious.)

In any event, these variations in conventionality do not seem at first to jeopardize Searle's distinction between original and derived intentionality. The reflection of a scene in a pond might be just as informative about the scene as a photograph of it would be, but the reflection in the pool has no derived intentionality, while the photograph does; it is *meant* to represent the scene; that is its *raison d'être*.

This idea has great appeal. We human beings, endowed with intrinsic and original intentionality, can transfer some faint shadow of this meaning to our creations, simply by willing it. One is reminded of the great panel in the Sistine Chapel ceiling by Michelangelo, in which God reaches out and touches Adam's hand, thereby endowing him with the divine spark of life and meaning. In similar fashion do we impose meaning on the squiggles of ink in our libraries, and on the maps and diagrams we fashion to serve our purposes. Where, though, do we get our 'original' and underived intentionality? From God, as

Michelangelo suggests? Or is it a mistake to ask such a question? After all, if our intentionality is truly original ('ursprünglich' as a German might say) then it is not derived from anything at all, but rather an ultimate font of meaning, an *Unmeant Meaner.* I take it that this is Searle's view. If it is not, then he certainly owes us an answer to the question of whence cometh our own intentionality.

But I, who think this doctrine of original intentionality is incoherent, am prepared to offer an account of the derivation of our own intentionality. In order to do this, I must first mark another plausible and familiar distinction between sorts or grades of intentionality: *real* intentionality and mere *façon de parler* intentionality. We have real (and original) intentionality, let us grant, and for the moment let us accept Searle's distinction and claim that no artifact of ours has real and original intentionality. But what of other creatures? Do dogs and cats and dolphins and chimps have real intentionality? Let us grant that they do; they have minds like ours, only simpler, and their beliefs and desires are as underivedly about things as ours. The dog's memory of where he buried his bone is as much about the bone as my thought is. What, though, about spiders or clams or amoebas? Do they have real intentionality? They process information. Is that enough? Apparently not, since computers—or at least robots—process information, and their intentionality is (*ex hypothesi*) only derived.

Spiders are not our artifacts. If a spider has an internal map of its web, that map was not created to serve *us*, even indirectly, so if it has intentionality, it will not be derived intentionality. But perhaps we should call it mere 'as if' or *façon de parler* intentionality. We can 'adopt a stance' and treat the spider's control mechanisms *as if* they represented portions of the world, and then go on to predict and explain features of the spider's activity in terms of this stance. (This is what I call the intentional stance.) Searle is contemptuous of the suggestion that it might account for *our* intentionality, but is less forthright about where and when such a stance might have its uses: 'Dennett . . . believes that nothing *literally* has any *intrinsic intentional* mental states, that when we say of someone that he has such mental states we are just adopting a certain "stance" toward him and his behavior, the "intentional stance"'. . . (Searle 1982, p. 57). But perhaps it is clear that spiders have real, intrinsic intentionality, as do the chimps and the dolphins. What, though, of plants? It must be obvious that when we talk about the modest information-processing talents of some plants (which turn to face the light, which 'seek' and 'find' suitable supports to cling to, etc.) we are merely using a convenient metaphor. And when it comes to micro-organisms, the same verdict seems obvious. Consider the following passages quoted from L. Stryer's *Biochemistry* (1981) by Alexander Rosenberg in his fascinating paper 'Intention and Action among the Macromolecules' (Rosenberg 1986):

> A much more demanding task for these enzymes is to discriminate between similar amino acids. . . . However, the observed error frequency in vivo is only I in 3000, indicating that there must be subsequent editing steps to enhance fidelity. In fact the synthetase corrects its own errors. . . . How does the

synthetase avoid hydrolyzing isoleucine-AMP, the desired intermediate? (Rosenberg's italics)

Here it seems obvious that this is mere *as if* intentionality, a theorist's fiction, useful no doubt, but not to be taken seriously and literally. Macromolecules do not literally avoid anything or desire anything or discriminate anything. We, the interpreters or theorists, *make sense* of these processes by endowing them with mentalistic interpretations, but the intentionality we attribute in these instances is neither real intrinsic intentionality, nor real derived intentionality, but mere *as if* intentionality.

So now we have, tentatively, two distinctions: the distinction between original and derived intentionality, and the distinction between real and *as if* intentionality. Searle apparently approves of both distinctions, but he is not alone. Both distinctions are widely popular and have a long history of exploitation in the literature, in spite of the boundary disputes and other quandaries that are occasioned by their use. (Where do we draw the line—and why—between real and mere as if? Is there an important distinction between the derived intentionality of a map intended for human use, and the derived intentionality of a map which is internal to, and for the use of, another artifact, such as a cruise missile? Might we 'reduce' derived intentionality to as if intentionality? Or vice versa? Etc.) Instead of pausing to adjudicate these quandaries, I will present a thought experiment designed to shake our faith in both distinctions simultaneously. It begins by supposing that both distinctions are to be honored.

Consider an encyclopedia. It has derived intentionality. It contains information about thousands of things in the world, but only in so far as it is a device designed and intended for our use. Suppose we 'automate' our encyclopedia, putting all its data into a computer, and turning its index into the basis for an elaborate question-answering system. No longer do we have to look up material in the volumes; we simply type in questions and receive answers. It might seem to naïve users as if they were communicating with another person, another entity endowed with original intentionality, but we would know better. A question-answering system is still just a tool, and whatever meaning or aboutness we reside in it is just a by-product of our practices in using the device to serve our own goals. It has no goals of its own, except for the artificial and derived goal of 'understanding' and 'answering' our questions correctly. (Note that here we introduce scare quotes around the mentalistic words, for this is not real but mere as if mentality or intentionality we now attribute to our artifact, which is thus firmly placed on the short end of both distinctions.)

But suppose we endow our computer with somewhat more autonomous, somewhat less slavish goals. For instance, a chess playing computer has the (artificial, derived) goal of *defeating* its human opponent, of *concealing* what it 'knows' from us, of *tricking* us perhaps. But still, surely, it is only our tool or toy, and although many of its internal states have a sort of aboutness or intentionality—for example, there are states that are about the current board positions, processes that investigate and hence are about various possible continuations, etc.—this is just derived intentionality, not intrinsic intentionality.

It seems in fact that this must be true of any artifact, any computer program, any robot we might design and build, no matter how strong the *illusion* we may create that it has become a *genuine* agent, an *autonomous* thinker with the same sort of original intentionality we enjoy. So let us take this assumption as given. No artifact of ours, no product of AI, could ever have original intentionality simply in virtue of the way it conducted itself in the world or in virtue of its 'formal' design. (We must remember that Searle supposes that if we happened to make our robot out of the *right stuff*, it might indeed have intrinsic intentionality, as a sort of bonus!) Although we may design a robot to have 'goals', 'purposes', 'strategies', 'ideas', and so forth, and although in the implementation of this simulacrum of mentality we will create formal states of the system that have derived intentionality, such an entity will lack genuine, original intentionality so long as it is not made of the right stuff.

Now comes the thought experiment. Suppose you decided, for whatever reasons, that you wanted to experience life in the twenty-fifth century, and suppose that the only known way of keeping your body alive that long required it to be placed in a hibernation device of sorts, where it would rest, slowed down and comatose, for as long as you liked. You could arrange to climb into the support capsule, be put to sleep, and then automatically awakened and released in 2401. This is a time-honored science-fiction theme, of course. Now designing the capsule itself is not your only engineering problem, for the capsule must be protected and supplied with the requisite energy (for refrigeration or whatever) for over 400 years. You will not be able to count on your children and grandchildren for this stewardship, of course, for they will be long dead before the year 2401, and you cannot presume that your more distant descendants, if any, may be relied upon to take a lively interest in your well-being.

So you must design a supersystem to protect your capsule, and to provide the energy it needs for 400 years. Here there are two basic strategies you might follow. On one, you should find the ideal location, as best you can foresee, for a fixed installation that will be well supplied with water, sunlight, and whatever else your capsule (and the supersystem itself) will need for the duration. The main drawback to such an installation or 'plant' is that it cannot be moved if harm comes its way—if, say, they decide to build a freeway right where it is located. The second alternative is much more sophisticated, but avoids this drawback: design a *mobile* facility to house your capsule and the requisite early-warning devices, so that it can move out of harm's way and seek out new energy sources as it needs them. In short, build a giant robot and install the capsule (with you inside) in it. These two basic strategies are obviously copied from nature: they correspond roughly to the division between plants and animals. Since the latter, more sophisticated strategy better fits my purposes, we shall suppose that you decide to build a robot to house your capsule. You try to design it (obviously) so that above all else it 'chooses' actions designed to further your best interests. 'Bad' moves and 'wrong' turns are those that will tend to incapacitate it for the role of protecting you until 2401—and that is its sole *raison d'être*. This is clearly a profoundly difficult engineering problem, calling for the highest level of expertise in designing a vision system to guide its locomotion, and other 'sensory' and locomotory systems. And since you will be comatose throughout and thus cannot stay awake to guide and plan its strategies, you will have to design it to generate its own plans in response to changing circumstances. It must 'know' how to seek out and recognize and then exploit energy sources, how to move to safer territory, how to anticipate and then avoid dangers. Your task will be made much more difficult, of course, by the fact that you cannot count on your robot being the only such robot around with such a mission. If your whim catches on, your robot may find itself competing with others (and with your human descendants) for limited supplies of energy, fresh water, lubricants, and the like. It would no doubt be wise to design it with enough sophistication in its control system to permit it to calculate the benefits and risks of cooperating with other robots, or forming alliances for mutual benefit.

The end of this design project would be a robot capable of exhibiting self-control (since you must cede fine-grained real-time control to your artifact once you put yourself to sleep). (For more on control and self-control, see Dennett 1984, ch. 3.) As such it will be capable of deriving its own subsidiary goals from its assessment of its current state and the importance of that state for its ultimate goal (which is preserving you). These secondary goals may take it far afield on century-long projects, and these projects may be ill advised, in spite of your best design efforts. Your robot may embark on actions antithetical to your purposes, even suicidal, having been convinced by another robot, perhaps, to subordinate its own life mission to some other.

But still, according to our assumptions, this robot has no original intentionality at all, but only the intentionality it derives from its artifactual role as your protector, and its simulacrum of mental states is just that—not real deciding and seeing and wondering and planning, but only *as if* deciding and seeing and wondering and planning. But if we cling to these assumptions the conclusion that seems forced upon us is that our own intentionality is exactly like that of the robot, for the science-fiction tale I have told is not new; it is just a variation on Richard Dawkins's vision of us (and all other biological species) as 'survival machines' designed to prolong the futures of our selfish genes (Dawkins 1976).

We now have an answer to the question of where we got our intentionality. We are artifacts, in effect, designed over the aeons as survival machines for genes that cannot act swiftly and informedly in their own interests. But our interests, as we conceive them, and the interests of our genes may well diverge—even though were it not for our genes' interests, we would not exist: their preservation is our original *raison d'être,* even if we can learn to ignore that goal and devise our own *summum bonum*, thanks to the intelligence our genes have installed in us.

So our intentionality is derived from the intentionality of our 'selfish' genes! *They* are the Unmeant Meaners, not us, and in so far as some theorist can interpret an event or structure in us as being about something or other (as, say, our inner-ear signals are about our orientation with regard to gravity and our acceleration), it is only because of the informative role that such signaling plays within the artifact, and the way it contributes to its self-preservation (Dennett 1982a). There is a stance available for the discernment of these relationships: the intentional stance, as I call it (Dennett 1978a, 1981a,b, 1982b, 1983). There is no need or room for a more absolute, 'intrinsic', and 'original' intentionality than this.

But this vision of things, while it provides a satisfying answer to the question of whence came our own intentionality, does seem to leave us with an embarrassment, for it derives our own intentionality from entities—genes— whose intentionality is surely a paradigm case of mere *as if* intentionality! How can the literal depend on the metaphorical? Moreover, there is surely this much disanalogy between my science-fiction tale and Dawkins's story: in my tale I supposed that there was conscious, deliberate, foresighted engineering involved in the creation of the robot, whereas even if we are, as Dawkins says, the product of a design process that has our genes as the primary beneficiaries, it is a design process that utterly lacks a conscious, deliberate, foresighted engineer. The chief beauty of the theory of natural selection is that it shows us how to eliminate this intelligent Artificer from our account of origins.

In fact, these two points go together: it is a bit outrageous to conceive of genes as *clever* designers; genes themselves could not be more stupid; *they* cannot reason or represent or figure out anything. They do not do the designing themselves; they are merely the beneficiaries of the design process. But then who or what does the designing? Mother Nature, of course, or more literally, the long, slow process of evolution by natural selection. And here is the somewhat startling consequence I wish to maintain: Mother Nature does exhibit genuine intentionality! That is, the process of natural selection has proved itself to be exquisitely sensitive to rationales, making myriads of discriminating 'choices', and 'recognizing' and 'appreciating' many subtle relationships.

For instance, it is not that the synthetase itself *desires* that isoleucine-AMP be the intermediate amino acid; it has no conception of isoleucine *qua* intermediate. But it is only *qua* intermediate that the isoleucine is 'desired'—as an unsubstitutable part in a design whose rationale is 'appreciated' by the process of natural selection itself.

Rosenberg (1986) endorses the view—developed by many, but especially argued for in Dennett (1969)—that a defining mark of intentionality is failure of substitution in the idioms that must be used to characterize the phenomena. He then notes that the biologists' attributions to macromolecules, selfish genes, and the like do not meet this condition; one can substitute ad lib without worry about a change in truth value, so long as the 'subject' (the believer or desirer) is a gene or a macromolecule or some such simple mechanism. Indeed the proof-reading enzyme does not recognize the error it corrects *qua* error, but—and this is my point—Mother Nature does. That is, it is only *qua* error that the items thus eliminated provoked the creation of the 'proof-reading' competence of the enzymes. The enzyme itself is just one of Nature's lowly soldiers, 'theirs not to reason why, theirs but to do or die', but *there is* a reason why they do what they do, a reason 'recognized' by natural selection itself.

Is there a reason, really, why these enzymes do what they do? Many biologists are reluctant to acknowledge such claims, but others—in particular, the adaptationists—are willing to defend such claims in terms of the functional roles that can be discerned under a frankly teleological analysis. If you want to assert such claims (and I side with those who do), you will find that they resist substitution in the classical manner of intentional contexts. Just as George IV wondered whether Scott was the author of Waverley without wondering whether Scott was Scott, so natural selection 'desired' that isoleucine be the intermediate without desiring that isoleucine be isoleucine. Certainly we can describe all processes of natural selection without appeal to such intentional language, but at enormous cost of cumbersomeness and unwanted detail. We would miss the pattern that was there, the pattern that permits prediction and supports counterfactuals. The 'why' questions we can ask about the engineering of our robot, which have answers that allude to the conscious, deliberate, explicit reasonings of the engineers (in most cases) have their parallels when the topic is organisms and their 'engineering'. If we work out the rationales of these bits of organic genius, we will be left having to attribute—but not in any mysterious way—an emergent appreciation or recognition of those rationales to natural selection itself; it does not consciously seek out these rationales, but when it stumbles on them, it recognizes their value.

The original reasons, and the original intelligent responses to them, were not ours, or our mammalian ancestors', but Nature's. Nature appreciated these reasons without representing them. And the design process itself is the source of our own intentionality. We, the reason representers, the self-representers, are a late and specialized product. What this representation of our reasons gives us is foresight: the real-time anticipatory power that Mother Nature wholly lacks. As a late and specialized product, a triumph of Mother Nature's high tech, our intentionality is highly derived, and in just the same way that the intentionality of our robots (and even our books and maps) is derived. A shopping list in the head has no more intrinsic intentionality than a shopping list on a piece of paper. What the items on the list mean (if anything) is fixed by the role they play in the larger scheme of purposes. We may call our own intentionality real, but we must recognize that it is derived from the intentionality of natural selection, which is just as real—but just less easily discerned because of the vast difference in time scale and size. And as for 'intrinsic' intentionality, there is no such thing.

I would not expect these considerations to persuade Searle. I expect that Searle would reply to them roughly as follows:

> Yes, we are the products of natural selection, but it happens that Nature's way of making us capable of fending for ourselves was giving us brains with certain marvelous causal powers of producing intentionality. There is no way of telling from outside (from the 'third-person point of view') whether or not an entity owes its talents for survival to genuine, intrinsic intentionality, or to some merely formal, merely syntactic system of internal engineering, but we conscious human beings know, from inside, that we have real, intrinsic intentionality.

I expect this is what he would say, since he has said this sort of thing often in the past. But if he still says this, we will be able to see more clearly now that his claims are unsupported by reasons, and are nothing more dignified than the glazed-eye dogmatisms of 'common sense'.

REFERENCES

Abbott, E. A. (1884) *Flatland: A Romance in Many Dimensions.*

Dawkins, R. (1976) *The Selfish Gene* (Oxford: Oxford University Press).

Dennett, D. C. (1978) *Brainstorms* (Cambridge, MA: MIT Press).

Dennett, D. C. (1981a) Three kinds of intentional psychology. In R. Healey (ed.) *Reduction? Time and Reality* (Cambridge: Cambridge University Press).

Dennett, D. C. (1981b), True believers: the intentional strategy and why it works. In A. F. Heath (ed.) *Scientific Explanation* (Oxford: Oxford University Press).

Dennett, D. C. (1982a) Comment on Rorty. *Synthese*, 53: 349- 356.

Dennett, D. C. (1982b) Beyond belief. In A. Woodfield (ed.) *Thought and Object* (Oxford: Oxford University Press).

Dennett, D. C. (1983) Intentional systems in cognitive ethology: the Panglossian Paradigm defended. *Behavioral and Brain Sciences*, 6: 343- 390.

Dennett, D. C. (1984) *Elbow Room: The Varieties of Free Will Worth Wanting* (Cambridge, MA: MIT Press).

Dewdney, A. K. (1984) *The Planiverse* (New York: Poseidon).

Hofstadter, D. R., and Dennett, D. C. (1981) *The Mind's I* (New York: Basic Books).

Monod, J. (1971) *Chance and Necessity* (New York: Knopf). First pub. (1970) as *Le Hasard et la necessite* (Paris: Editions du Seuil).

Rosenberg, A. (1986) Intention and action among the macromolecules. In N. Rescher (ed.) *Current Issues in Teleology* (Lanham, NY: University Presses of America).

Searle, J. (1980) Minds, brains and programs. *Behavioral and Brain Sciences,* 3: 417-458.

Searle, J. (1982) The myth of the computer: an exchange. *New York Review of Books,* 29(11) (24 June): 56- 57.

Searle, J. (1984) Panel Discussion: Has Artifical Intelligence Research Illuminated Human Thinking? In H. Pagels, (ed.) *Computer Culture: The Scientific, Intellectual, and Social Impact of the Computer* , Ann. N. Y. Acad. Sci. 426, 138–160.

Stryker, L. (1981) *Biochemistry* (San Francisco: Freeman).

CHAPTER
5

◆ # Computationalism

Eric Dietrich

··

1.   INTRODUCTION

Computationalism is the hypothesis that cognition is the computation of functions. If computationalism is correct, then scientific theories of cognition will explain it as the computation of functions. The job for the computationalist is to determine which functions cognition is, i.e. which specific functions explain specific cognitive phenomena.

A particular kind of computationalism—cognitivism—is the backbone of our current cognitive science (Haugeland 1978; Cummins 1983). And, though we should, and will, come to eschew cognitivism as cognitive science advances (or so I claim), we will still embrace computationalism. In fact, I am inclined to think that even when cognitive science is broadly construed, computationalism is still its foundational assumption. If we consider cognitive science to be the attempt to explain phenomena ranging from recognizing food or a conspecific to proving

Thinking Computers and Virtual Persons
edited by Eric Dietrich
ISBN 0-12-215495-9I

Fermat's Last Theorem, and concerned with systems ranging from paramecia to societies of humans, we find that computationalism is still at its foundation. And, though it is not foundational in disciplines such as developmental neurobiology, and molecular biology, ecology, economics, and neuropsychology and developmental psychology, computationalism is part of their methodological repertoire.

Computationalism is only foundational and methodological. By itself, it makes no claims about which functions are computed, except to say that they are all Turing computable (computationalists accept the Church–Turing thesis), nor does it make any specific claims as to how they got computed, except to say that the functions are systematic, productive, and interpretable in a certain way (see Section 2).[1] Computationalism, therefore, makes no specific predictions about any aspect of cognition beyond those implied by 'functionhood', nor does it explain any specific aspect of cognition. In fact, the computationalist thesis is compatible with a variety of more detailed theories of cognitive behavior which are themselves incompatible.[2]

Computationalism is an empirical thesis. It could be false—the only way to tell is to vigorously pursue a computationalist research strategy and see if we make any theoretical and empirical headway. But before this can happen, computationalism must be taken seriously. Taking computationalism seriously requires embracing, at least provisionally, all its consequences, and computationalism has some rather severe consequences. The purpose of this paper is to discuss two of these consequences. Specifically, I will argue that computationalism is incompatible with the notion that humans have any special semantical properties in virtue of which their thoughts are about things in their environment, and that the thesis is incompatible with the notion that humans make decisions. I am not, here, primarily concerned with whether computationalism is true or false, or explanatorily adequate or inadequate; that can only be determined by using it, and seeing if our cognitive science is better off with it than without it.

The two consequences just mentioned should be elaborated slightly. Computationalism claims that humans have no *special* semantic properties which attach them to their environment. Humans do indeed have such semantical properties but so do computers. More succinctly, if computationalism is correct, both humans and computers have *intentionality*. In fact, intentionality will turn out to be almost a commonplace. The second consequence is that humans have no special ability to make decisions, at least not when this term is given its ordinary meaning—as the capacity for willfully selecting among alternatives. Decisions are not made by any special exercise of the will.

As I formulate them, these two consequences have an interesting asymmetry. It is widely believed that humans possess intentionality but that computers do not (Searle 1980; Fodor 1981; Dretske 1985; Sayre 1986). It is also widely assumed that both computers and humans make decisions. If computationalism is correct, this is almost exactly backwards: both humans and computers possess intentionality, but neither make decisions. Intentionality is, therefore, not rare, and exercising one's will is so rare as to be non-existent.

2. THE NATURE OF COMPUTATIONALISM

In this section I shall describe computationalism in some detail and distinguish it from two other theses about cognition.

2.1. *Properties of Computational Explanations*

Computationalists claim that explanatorily adequate theories of cognition will use computational explanations. Such an explanation has the following properties. First, it is an explanation of an ability or capacity of a system to exhibit certain behavior. Thus, a computational explanation differs from a causal law which describes the causal state changes of a system (for more details, see Haugeland (1978) and Cummins (1983)). Because the observed behavior is regular, the underlying capacity can be described as the capacity to compute a mathematical function from inputs to outputs. For many systems, we forego describing the relation between inputs and outputs as a mathematical function, opting instead for descriptions such as 'the system plays chess' or 'understands English'. Nevertheless, to be amenable to computational explanation, a system's behavior must be describable as the computation of Turing-computable, mathematical functions. Conversely, attributing a function to a particular system is seeing that system as doing something regular.

The requirement that the observed behavior be regular and due to a certain ability may seem too weak because *any* system which changes states (i.e. everything) can be described as computing a function—the function that describes its behavior. Yet we clearly do not want computational explanations to apply to everything; computationalism cannot replace physics. For example, we could see an object and a volume of water as a system which computes Archimedes's principle when the object is placed in the water. Or we could see a bicycle pump, a flat tire, and a pumping cyclist as a system which computes the ideal-gas law. But this seems wrong. We can explain why the object displaces the amount of water that it does by using Archimedes's principle, but we do not see the object–water system as actually computing a function. There are proposed solutions to this problem, but it is not clear any of them work. This problem need not concern us, though. There are clear, unproblematical cases where we explain a system's behavior by saying it computes a function. We will stick to such cases.[3]

The first property of computational explanations guarantees that capacities for exhibiting certain behavior are understood (by the explainers) as capacities for computing certain functions, and that exhibiting the behavior is seen as computing the function. The function so attributed to the system is 'system-sized'; it describes the behavior of the whole system.

The second property of computational explanations begins where the first leaves off. A computational explanation must be systematic, i.e. it must exhibit the system in question as, indeed, a system. To do this, the explanation must posit interdependent functions which interact to produce the output from the input. In other words, the explanation must analyze the system-sized function into subfunctions and show how the different subfunctions interact to produce the output (the behavior) in question (cf. Haugeland 1978). Moreover, the subfunctions must constitute a rather fixed set of functions out of which the larger functions are built. Procedures and standard computer programs are systematic in just this sense. In fact, one way of phrasing the second property is to say that, in order for an explanation to be computational, it must allow theorists to see the system's state changes as the execution of a procedure. (Computer programs, i.e., procedures implemented in some computer language, are also systematic, but they are not explanations in the sense used here; they are not theoretical explanations of behavior. It is easy to see this. Many different programs can implement the same procedure. If programs were theoretical explanations, then we would have an embarrassment of theories for each capacity we wished to theorize about, and we would have no reason for selecting one of these 'theories' over the other (see Dietrich 1990). Of course, all procedures must be couched in some language or other. But some languages are more scientifically useful than others. Computationalism needs a scientifically useful language, not a software engineering language. Logics of various sorts and statistical mechanics are the currently preferred languages of computationalism.

This is a good place to introduce the notion of *control flow*. The specific ordering arrangement of functions which are computed is called the control flow of the system's computation. In Section 4, this notion will be quite important. For now, I just want to note that the flow of control is fixed by the functions which the system can compute and by the initial state of the system, i.e. its initial input. In other words, once a procedure is specified (by a programmer or by evolution) then flow of control is determined (except for random events) by the initial state of the system.

The first and the second property together mean that the ability of the system to produce or exhibit some particular kind of behavior on a regular basis is the ability to execute certain procedures, and whenever the system exhibits the behavior in question it is executing the relevant procedure.

Third, a computational explanation is interpretive. This property of computational explanations is logically entailed by the first. The capacity for a certain behavior is manifested as a characteristic part of the actual behavior. In order to see (or describe) a part of behavior as the computation of a certain function, F, we, as theorists, must see the system generate, over time, output equal to F(input). However, in order to see this, we must be able to interpret the initial state of the system as being the requisite input for F, and the final state of the system as being the requisite output, F (input). So, computational explanations are inherently interpretive.

The three properties of computational explanations may be summed up as follows. Explaining a system's behavior as computing some function requires interpreting the initial and final states of the system as inputs and outputs for the proposed function, and then analyzing the proposed function into a sequence of subfunctions each of which carries with it its own interpretation of its initial and final states. Finally, whenever the system exhibits the behavior in question, it is computing the relevant sequence of subfunctions, i.e. it is executing a procedure. (All of the preceding is relatively well-known thanks to the work of Haugeland (1978) and Cummins (1983); see also Fodor (1965).)

The three properties just discussed do not fully capture the notion of a computational explanation. One other property is required. I call this property *productivity*: the functions whose computation is attributed to the system in question must be productive, a property which can be understood by contrasting it with non-productive procedures.

Consider two devices which take numbers as input and output their product. The question is: are both devices multipliers? Suppose the first device uses the well-known iterative-sum procedure: given 4 x 7, it totals up four sevens. Suppose the second device stores a two-dimensional, n x n matrix as in Figure 5.1. When the second device is given 4 x 7 it merely finds the product which is already present in the matrix.

Only the first device can potentially handle any posed multiplication problem because only it executes a multiplication procedure, hence only the first device is a multiplier. The second device is not a multiplier because it does not execute a multiplication procedure. In order for the second device to be useful, the products must be built in, and in order to do this they must already be known or computed. Hence, to build the second device, one requires the first device (or some other device that uses a productive multiplication procedure).

Figure 5.1. The n x n two-dimensional matrix for the second device.

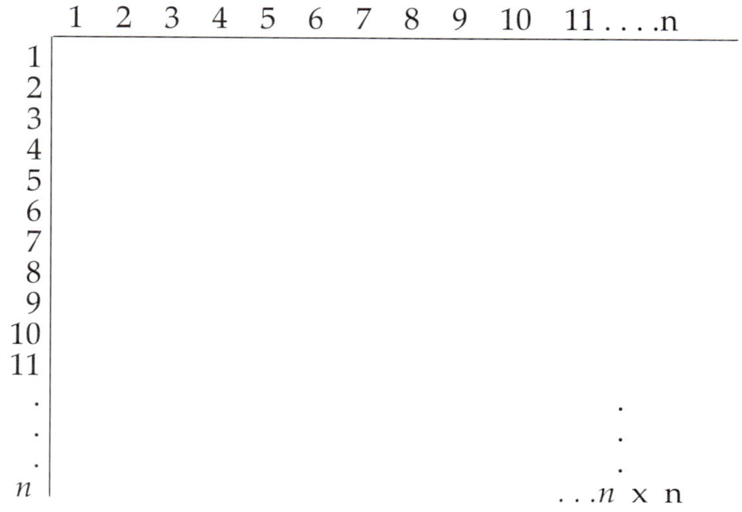

```
        1  2  3  4  5  6  7  8  9  10  11 . . . .n
      1
      2
      3
      4
      5
      6
      7
      8
      9
     10
     11
      .                                    .
      .                                    .
      .                                    .
      n                                . . .n x n
```

Of course, the second device is a computer, albeit a simple one, because it does compute functions: it computes matrix-look-up functions and it does this by executing matrix-look-up procedures. Hence, we can produce computational explanations of the second device because the procedure attributed to it is productive: it continues to work as the size of the matrix, is increased. But it is not a multiplier, and computational explanations attributing computing the multiplication function to it are wrong.

Some are tempted to say here the second device computes the multiplication function, but not by executing the iterative-sum procedure. Here is the argument. Both devices have a finite capacity for multiplying numbers. The first device only has a finite (random-access) memory. Consequently, it can multiply only a finite set of numbers. The second device only has a finitely large matrix. Suppose that the behavior of the two devices is indistinguishable. That is, suppose that the second device's matrix is large enough to accommodate any multiplication problem which the first device can handle. On this supposition, we can attribute the computation of the multiplication function to both devices, but only the first device is executing the iterative-sum procedure.

The temptation to argue this way must be resisted because we have little reason to attribute the computation of the multiplication function to the second device unless we have some idea of *how* it is computing it, and this requires determining how the multiplication function is analyzed into subfunctions. We must see the second device as executing some multiplication procedure, i.e., some procedure which productively multiplies numbers. Of course, we might *use* the device to compute the function just as we might use a calculator as a doorstop, but this does not mean calculators are doorstops. In general, we have little reason to attribute the computation of a function F to a system unless we can see the computation of F as systematic and productive (the second and fourth properties), i.e. unless we see the system as something which can compute F. An infinite number of functions can be attributed to a system if we are simply shown a finite sequence of its input–output behavior. Though this is also true when we systematically analyze the computation of F into component functions, we are nevertheless justified in settling on F as the function the system computes (instead of, say, G) once an understandable procedure begins to emerge which satisfactorily shows us that F explains the system's behavior.

The last claim commits me to the view that computational explanations are relative to what theorists understand and find satisfactory. But all scientific explanations, in fact, *all* explanations, are relativized this way. This relativization means that, in certain circumstances, we might view both devices as computing the multiplication function. If the devices' behavior really is indistinguishable (i.e. if they multiply exactly the same set of numbers in exactly the same amount of time, giving off exactly the same amount of heat, and we cannot open them up to run further tests) then we would find it irresistable to attribute the multiplication function to both, and it seems reasonable to do so. If this suits our other explanatory goals, then such an attribution is all the more reasonable. But such a case would be extraordinary, and we should not reject the productivity property because of it.

We now, finally, have all the properties of computational explanations. The four properties work together to form an explanatory strategy which is scientifically respectable and robust. And now, we can be a little more rigorous.

The goal of the computationalist is to attribute to a physical system, S, the computation of a certain function, F. To do this, it must be determined (or assumed) that S computes F, and it must be determined how S computes F. Attributing the computation of F to S is successful when it is possible to explain S's computation of F in terms of a sequence of functions $<g_1, \ldots, g_n> (n > 1)$ such that: (1) $F = g_n \circ g_{n-1} \circ \ldots \circ g_1$; (2) the sequence $<g_1, \ldots, g_n>$ is productive; (3) S passes through a sequence of states each of which corresponds via an interpretation function I to either the domain or range of one of the g_i's, and each state between the first and final states is the range of some g_i and the domain of some g_{i+1} and (4) we antecedently understand the g_i's. Succinctly, a computational explanation has the form described in Figure 5.2. When $F = g_n \circ g_{n-1} \circ \ldots \circ g_1$'s and the g_i's are non-trivial, it is natural to say that the sequence of functions $<g_1, \ldots, g_n>$ *analyzes* the computation of F by S and explains the capacity of S to compute F (cf. Haugeland 1978 and Cummins 1983: 28–44).[4]

Figure 5.2. Interpreting the state transitions of S as computing the sequence of functions $<g_1, \ldots g_n>$.

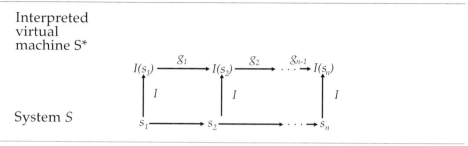

Interpreted
virtual
machine S*

System S

2.2. *Computationalism versus Other '-isms'*

Computationalism is distinct from both 'computerism' and cognitivism. 'Computerism' is the thesis that explanations of cognition will look like procedures for our current (late 20th century) computers. Computerism is thus tied to a specific computer hardware architecture, in particular a serial architecture. Note that the computerist is interested in more than the functions which get computed; she is interested in how they are computed. It is not clear that anyone actually believes computerism, but frequently, when computationalism, artificial intelligence, and computational psychology are attacked, it is 'computerist' notions that are attacked instead (see, for example, Carello, *et al.* (1984) and Reeke and Edelman (1988)).

Almost all computers today are Von Neumann machines, meaning that they compute functions serially, executing one program instruction at a time. To claim that some machine is a Von Neumann machine is to make a claim about its *architecture*, and hence about the kinds of procedures which can be written *directly* for that architecture (i.e. what kinds of procedures can be written in the *assembly language* of that architecture).

Specifically, assembly language procedures must be constructed using combinations of these three kinds of control: looping, branching, and sequencing (this is true of almost all programming languages, also.)[5] These three kinds of control, in turn, limit the kinds of assembly language instructions which may be used: the instructions must be simple, deterministic, and discrete. So, the computerist believes that the procedures relevant to explaining cognition use sequences of simple, deterministic instructions. Hence, for the computerist, the g_i in Figure 5.2 would be instructions like those we find in assembly language computer programs which exist today: simple, deterministic instructions such as REP MOVS DEST, SRCE (move what's in SRCE to location DEST) and STOS DISPLAY (store what is in a specific register at DISPLAY) which are instructions for the Intel 8088 microprocessor (Intel 1983).

Computerism is false on empirical grounds: the brain is not a Von Neumann machine, not even approximately. In fact, when seen as attacks on computerism, the works by Dreyfus, Carello, etc., are compelling. The mathematical functions which the computationalist believes explain cognition can only be tortuously described by simple, deterministic instructions, at best. Put simply, computerism adopts the wrong kind of description language for the phenomena it is supposed to describe because it assumes an impoverished explanatory ontology.

Computationalism as depicted in Figure 5.2 is neutral on the Von Neumann–non-Von Neumann issue. Computationalism is not tied to any specific architecture, nor is it committed to the view that procedures which are composed of simple, deterministic instructions explain cognition. Computationalism is compatible with massively parallel architectures such as those studied by the connectionists (see Bechtel 1988 and Smolensky 1988), and those studied by neural modelers such as Grossberg 1987) [see Dietrich and Fields (1988)].

Cognitivism is the thesis that the functions which explain cognition are rational functions defined over propositions (or sentences). Rational functions relate propositions in an epistemologically appropriate way. Thus, for cognitivists, the objects which are computationally manipulated are propositions (or sentences), and it is propositions which are the inputs and outputs of such systems (this is why some cognitivists do not consider early perception part of cognition). Cognition is the production of output propositions which are rationally related to input propositions. For the cognitivist, inference is the paradigmatic cognitive function. For example, Cummins (1983) says: '. . . cognitive capacities are inferentially characterized capacities . . . : the transition law specifying a cognitive capacity is a rule of inference' (p. 53). Cognitivism is far away the most prevalent, general hypothesis about cognition. [Cognitivism and its prospects have been discussed in detail by Haugeland (1978, 1981); see also, Cummins (1983) and Cummins and Schwarz (1988).]

Computationalism is not cognitivism. Computationalists are not committed to the claim that cognition is inferentially processing propositional or sentential structures. Nor are they committed to the claim that rationality or epistemological adequacy is the fundamental relationship between inputs and outputs of cognitive systems. Rationality plays a major role in cognitivism, but it plays only a minor role in computationalism, and even then, it is a special type of rationality (see Section 4).

Cognitivism will be false if it turns out that the most important cognitive functions are not inferences. Yet in such a case, computationalism could still be true. This would happen if thinking turned out to be, for example, manipulating algebra, vectors, or automata of various types. In such cases, the functions explaining cognition would be algebraic morphisms, operations on vectors, or operations on automata, respectively. This is not mere hand waving, either. It is plausible that at least one kind of creative thought—the 'a-ha' experience—is not an inference at all, and in fact could not happen in a system only capable of inferences (Dietrich and Fields 1986; Fields and Dietrich 1987b). In general, theories of cognition couched in *mathematical* languages will be compatible with computationalism, but not compatible with cognitivism. Mathematics is not the science of inferences; 1 + 1 = 2 is not a rational inference.

Most philosophers balk at this, utterly. For example, Cummins says

> What makes a [cognitive] capacity [cognitive] is surely that its exercises are epistemologically assessable, and this commits one to the view that such exercises are amenable to sentential interpretation. . . . Talk of cognition in the absence of actual or sentential interpretation of inputs and outputs is mere hand waving. (Cummins 1983: 198–199)

The limits of a philosopher's imagination are frequently where he or she uses the word 'surely'. The view that thinking is basically inferencing is a vestige of logical positivism—one of philosophy's dark ages. Computationalism offers ontological and methodological riches unimagined by the cognitivist, which we will squander as long as we believe thinking is inferencing.

Computerism and cognitivism differ from computationalism along two different dimensions. Computationalism, again, is the claim that cognition is the computation of certain Turing-computable functions which are to be determined by cognitive *science*. Cognitivism is a further claim about *which* functions are computed. It is the claim that the functions are inferences of one sort or another, that the objects which the functions process are sentence-like propositions, and that rationality is a fundamental property of cognition. Computerism, however, is a claim about *how* the functions are computed, i.e. it is a claim about what the architecture of the brain (or maybe the mind) is. All three claims are empirical and are based on various combinations of evidence, theoretical assumptions, 'what-else-could-it-be' arguments, wishful thinking, and lack of imagination, and all three could be false (i.e. the three do not exhaust the space of cognitive theories). Only computationalism manages to keep its claims modest by tying them to the evidence, and to avoid premature commitments to theories and research strategies. It does this by strictly adhering to the notion of computation found in computer science, and letting evidence determine both which functions are computed and how they are computed. In spite of its modesty, however, computationalism has (at least) two strong consequences which are explained in the following two sections.

3.   INTENTIONALITY

Intentionality is sometimes defined as the property of mental states to be about things (Haugeland 1978, 1981: 32; Sayre 1986). The things need not exist (for example, one can have thoughts about the Grail), nor do the things need to be logically possible (one can have thoughts about round squares, for example—one can think they do not exist). When understood in this way, intentionally is a semantic notion: intentionality is the psychological property of having semantic content.

At other times, intentionality is defined as the property of a system to understand its own representations (Searle 1980; Fodor 1981; Dreyfus 1982; Follesdal 1982; Cummins 1983; Dretske 1985; Haugeland (1981) also discusses this definition of intentionality under the term 'original intentionality'). This notion of intentionality is, or is very close to, the notion of a system consciously understanding the world around it.

However it is defined, intentionality is regarded as a crucial aspect of cognition (but see Stich (1983)), and, therefore, it must be explained if we are to understand cognition thoroughly. Since computationalism purports to be a theoretical framework for cognitive theories, the question naturally arises as to how computationalism should deal with intentionality. This question is a matter of some importance, since computationalism is widely regarded as being *incapable* of supporting any explanations of intentionality. Arguments purporting to demonstrate computationalism's deficiency in this matter have been offered for a variety of intentional psychological phenomena. Examples include understanding a language (Searle 1980), perceiving an environment (Sayre 1986), and, finally, thinking itself (Searle 1980; Dretske 1985). In short, computationalism is considered to be incapable of producing explanations of the phenomena we intuitively regard as genuinely mental, and is, therefore, rejected.

3.1.   *Intentionality as a Semantic Property*

In this section I consider how computationalism copes with intentionality defined as a semantic property of mental states. If computationalism is true, mental states have semantic content. In fact, providing a computational explanation of a system's behavior *requires* attributing semantic contents to the system's states. Recall that computational explanations require interpreting the inputs, outputs, and states of a system as elements in the domains and ranges of a series of functions. In fact, computationalism provides us with a *strategy* for semantic interpretation. I call this strategy the *computational strategy,* and the way in which it works is described briefly below (for more details, see Dietrich, 1989).

Recall Figure 5.2, when S passes from state s_i to s_j, function g_i is computed and its output is then input for succeeding function g_j. We (as theorists) understand the state transition of S from s_i to s_j by seeing the transition as the execution of g_i. Doing this is just interpreting the states of S because it is treating the states of S as symbols which are transformed. When we do this, we see S not merely as a physical system, but as an interpreted virtual machine, i.e. as a system S^* that computes F by passing through a sequence of virtual states which are the inputs and outputs of the g_i terms (for the notion of a virtual machine, see Tanenbaum (1984)). The correspondence between the S states and the g_i is made precise by the interpretation function, I, which maps states of S on to the g_j. Once we can view S as an interpreted virtual machine, we can switch between this view and the physical state transition view (cf. Stabler 1983)[6].

There are five pertinent consequences of using the computational strategy in order to attribute semantics to systems. The two most important consequences concern psychology, computer science, and philosophy of mind. First, if psychology is to embrace the computational paradigm, it must (*contra* Stich (1983)) ascribe contents to mental states and processes because ascribing contents is necessary for understanding which function is being computed by the psychological processes in question, and understanding this is necessary for understanding the behavioral and psychological capacities of the system. Secondly, we cannot view computers as merely formal symbol manipulators and understand their behavior. That is, we cannot view computers as merely syntax machines performing their computations on the basis of the syntactic properties of the symbols they manipulate. In order to understand their behavior we must interpret their states (this is well-known to computer scientists, see Wulf *et al.* (1981: chap. 5) and Stoy (1977)). This is quite contrary to the received dogma. The view that computers *are* formal symbol manipulators and that we can understand them as such is the prevalent view. This view has allowed philosophers to divorce semantics from computational explanations. Semantic content, then, becomes something one adds to computational explanations to get psychological explanations (Searle 1980). Other philosophers have claimed that we can get by without semantics at all (Stich 1983). If computationalism is correct, both these views are wrong (for more on these two consequences, see Dietrich 1989).

A third consequence is that there are no arbitrary or extra-theoretical restrictions placed on the contents that can be attributed to a system. The only general requirement is that the attributed contents explain observed behavior and hypothesized cognitive capacities. This renders otiose some well-known relations that are supposed to be important to semantic contents. For example, the causal connections of referring terms have no role in the computational strategy. Hence, we can simply avoid issues such as what the causally correct referent of a referring term is. Which function a system is computing is the only matter of importance because it is this that determines the contents of its states.

Causation, in general, is relegated to a supporting role from the computationalist's view. This is a welcome result because causation cannot do the work some philosophers think it can. Some philosophers seem to think that computers are not causally connected to the world, or at least not causally connected in the 'right way'. (This is one of the things Sayre taxed us with missing in our commentary on his paper. See Sayre (1986, 1987) and Fields and Dietrich (1987a).) The 'right way' is frequently expressed in terms of information theory, but this just will not work. The information computers get from the world when described by information theory is as real as the information our perceptual systems obtain. Computers are as 'causally embedded' in the world as humans are. So, as far as information theory is concerned, humans are not causally special. Computationalists can accommodate this result easily: the role of causation is to describe the physical-state changes and properties of the system S (see Figure 5.2).

A fourth consequence is that attributing a particular content to a particular mental state (or state of a system) is *not* paramount, as it is in other strategies for semantic attribution. The computational strategist wants to understand systems. Semantic contents are thus viewed in the context of entire systems. On the computational strategy, no mental state, indeed no symbol whatsoever, is (usefully) interpreted in isolation. Rather, whole systems of states must be ascribed contents so that a cogent explanation results.

A fifth consequence is that the attributing semantics via the explanatory strategy is not a folk art or a matter for casual speculation. One must be intimate with the systems under study in order to attribute contents that are scientifically useful. This is just another way of saying that understanding and attribution are achieved concomitantly.

Finally, note that when intentionality is defined as a semantic notion it is nearly ubiquitous. If a computational explanation explains a system's behavior, then that system's states have semantic content. All kinds of systems, from humans to the lowly and oft-maligned thermostat, will have contentful, computational states.

3.2.   Intentionality as a System's Understanding of Its Own Representations

I will now consider how computationalism copes with the definition of intentionality as the capacity of a system to understand its own representations. (In this section I use the word 'intentionality' to mean only the notion of a system understanding its own symbols.) This is the most well-known notion of intentionality, and it is the notion discussed by Cummins (1983) and used by Searle (1980) and Dretske (1985) in their arguments that machines cannot think.

In his famous and important paper on intentionality, Searle says:

> . . . the programmed computer does not do "information processing". Rather, what it does is manipulate formal symbols. (Searle 1980: 303)

For the computationalist, the phrase 'formal symbol' is an oxymoron. However, for Searle and others of his ilk, a formal symbol is something which is a contentful symbol to us, but a contentless object to a computer or other syntax machine. In his equally stimulating paper, Dretske (1985) states

> To understand what a system is doing when it manipulates symbols, it is necessary to know, not just what these symbols mean, what interpretation they have been, or can be, *assigned*, but what they mean to the system performing the operations. (Dretske's emphasis; Dretske 1985: 27)

Similarly, Cummins says when a system has intentionality

> the representations in question are representations for (or to) the system that has them, and not merely for (or to) a user or theorist . . . . (Cummins 1983: 76)

Intentionality is thus the unification of meaning and manipulation: the symbols being manipulated mean something to the system doing the manipulations.

What is intentionality for? What good is it? Nearly everyone writing about intentionality assumes that intentionality is crucial for cognition. Humans and other genuine cognitive agents do not have formal symbols. A human's mental symbols have meaning not only to theorists such as psychologists, but to it, itself, and it is because of this, apparently, that humans can think. But no one has actually shown that intentionality is crucial for cognition. Searle certainly has not. At best, he has shown that the Chinese Room lacks intentionality. But his argument depends on the behavior of the room being indistinguishable from the behavior of a genuine Chinese speaker. Searle has succeeded in showing that intentionality is useless.[7]

Before proceeding, I want to point out that intentionality is supposed to be different from consciousness or conscious understanding (see Searle (1980) and Dretske (1985: esp. p. 30)). This is important for what follows because intentionality is problematic exactly to the extent it is thought to be different from consciousness. If intentionality were just another word for consciousness, most of us could at least agree that it exists, though we still would not know what it is, nor what it is for. I also want to mention again that computers are supposed to lack intentionality, i.e. their symbols do not mean anything to them.

We can question the very cogency of the notion of a system understanding its own symbols or representations. First, it is a notion that is supposed to apply to me as a thinking creature. But I can assure you that I do not understand my own symbols. I understand the symbols I am currently writing now, but these are not mine; they are on this page and are public symbols. I can introspect, but intentionality is supposed to be more general and ubiquitous than introspection, and, anyway, computers can introspect. So, it is not clear that intentionality is a notion that applies to me while not applying to computers.

Secondly, it seems as if no system could have intentionality on pain of generating an infinite regress. If understanding involves symbols, then if a system understands its own symbols it is using symbols. Does it understand these 'second-order' symbols? If not, then the system—the whole system—lacks intentionality because it does not understand its own symbols, some of them, anyway. If it does understand its 'second-order' symbols, then it must understand its 'third-order' symbols, or, again, it lacks intentionality. It follows that a system must understand an infinite hierarchy of symbols. However, it is not obvious that any sort of physical system can do this.

An obvious objection to my argument is that a system need not understand all its symbols; it need only understand a few of them at a time—the ones on which its attention is currently focused, for example. This objection is rather plausible, but it has two problems for believers in intentionality. First, computers can generate hierarchies of symbols as well as processes (Dietrich 1985). So, once again, intentionality applies equally to humans and computers. The believers in intentionality would counter by insisting that intentionality is more than the capacity to generate hierarchies of symbols. It involves the notion of special, internal understanding, and computers lack such an understanding. However, now it seems as if the notion of consciousness, not a separate notion of intentionality is doing the real work in this objection. In fact, it seems to me as if this latter claim relies on the notion of *self*. Believers in intentionality seem to be saying that a system must have a concept of itself as an enduring whole in order to have intentionality. This also seems plausible to me, but it clearly depends on notions which philosophers such as Searle and Dretske regard as completely independent of intentionality.

Let us get our bearings. It seems as if intentionality either does not apply to humans, or applies equally to computers and humans, or is a hodgepodge of notions such as consciousness and the self masquerading as a single concept. I think that intentionality is really a masquerading hodgepodge, and the hodgepodge comprises the concepts we should really be interested in. Here is my argument. We can dismiss any notion that intentionality does not apply to humans. This leaves the second and third options. There is a robust notion of 'understanding your own symbols' which applies to humans and computers (I will show this shortly). However, believers in intentionality will reject this as not being what they mean by intentionality. Hence, consciousness, etc., must be the real notions. I will now show that there are processes within operating computers to which internal symbols have meaning. If I am right, then computers are not merely formal symbol manipulators, and computationalism can easily accommodate part of the notion of a system understanding some of its internal symbols.

It seems to me that the ordinary notions of a variable (variable binding and variable substitution) suffice to establish the claim that computers are not merely formal symbol manipulators. In an obvious sense of the term, to manipulate symbols in a purely formal manner is to manipulate them without regard to what they refer to, mean, or denote, nor must the manipulations depend on the fact that a symbol has a meaning or denotation. For example, manipulating a symbol solely by virtue of whether it is a token of some numeral, letter, or part of speech is one way to treat a symbol purely formally.

Consider the notion of a variable in this instance of the Lisp function '+': $(+ \ x \ 1)$. Loosely speaking, this function adds 1 to whatever x is bound to. However, for this argument, it is important that we be more precise about what the entities under discussion are. A computer running a Lisp interpreter (the Lisp execution program) defines a virtual machine called the Lisp virtual machine (LVM). The LVM operates solely in terms of Lisp expressions, the syntax for which can be specified by a grammar; no numbers or other "external" objects are involved. (I will mention Lisp expressions by placing single quotes around them. The primary reason for couching the argument in terms of an LVM is that it will be easier to understand. Nothing turns on this. The same argument could be made at the bit level, though at this level the argument would be all but lost in the detail.)

The LVM takes as input expressions such as '$(+ \ x \ 1)$', evaluates them, and returns expressions as outputs. We interpret the inputs, outputs, and intermediate expressions as, for example, computing (an instance of) the function plus, and producing the number 7 as its value. We also attribute the semantic content 1 or "representing the number 1" to Lisp expressions such as '1'. These interpretations are enhanced by making the syntactic form of the Lisp expressions look like expression in languages we already know.

Evaluating the expression '$(+ \ x \ 1)$' requires the LVM to determine the value of the variable 'x', which is some other Lisp expression, say '6'. If the LVM could not do this, the expression would be syntactically ill-formed: '+' is not defined for expressions we interpret as non-variable letters. But note that the LVM itself, in treating 'x' as a variable, regardless of our interpretations (which are, in fact, quite different), is treating 'x' as denoting the expression '6'. It follows from this that the LVM treats 'x' as having a meaning. Hence, the operation of the LVM depends on 'x' having a meaning for the LVM, and not just for us. Of course, the meaning 'x' has for the LVM (*viz.* '6') is not the meaning 'x' has for us (we typically interpret 'x' as representing the number 6, not the Lisp expression '6'), and the LVM is not conscious of the meaning 'x' has. Nevertheless, the LVM's manipulations depend on the fact that 'x' has a meaning, and, indeed, on the meaning that it has. This is enough to make false the claim that computers are formal symbol manipulators, at least on the straightforward interpretation of this claim I have assumed.

To sum up, I have shown, that: (1) computers are not merely formal symbol manipulators because they 'look up' the values of variables, and anything capable of doing this is also not merely a formal symbol manipulator; (2) since computers are not formal symbol manipulators and since computational explanations explain the behavior of computers as *genuine* symbol manipulators, computational explanations can explain the behavior of systems which are more than mere formal symbol manipulators; and therefore, (3) computational explanations can explain much more of human behavior than is commonly believed. If looking up the values of variables captured the notion of intentionality satisfactorily, then we could see why intentionality would be important for cognition. A cognitive system cannot have a function for every situation which might arise in its environment, so a few functions must have wide applicability. This is accomplished by having variables and variable binding and look-up procedures.

I want to close this section by returning to consciousness and related notions. As I said, I suspect that the notion of intentionality studied by Searle, Dretske, and others is a hodgepodge of other notions and intuitions, some of which we want to maintain. Consciousness is certainly one of these notions. Humans, but not computers, are conscious; we are aware of some of the states and contents of our own minds. Personally, I like Nagel's notion of consciousness (1974): there is something it is like to be a human, but being a computer *seems* as if it would be like being an intelligent rock. Consciousness, whatever it is, certainly needs explaining. Of course, computational explanations would be entirely appropriate (see Dietrich 1985). Another notion is intelligence. Humans are simply smarter than computers. In fact, computers occupy a new class in the intelligence hierarchy; they are a new class of idiot savants. Expert systems demonstrate this clearly. They are less intelligent than snails on virtually every dimension we care about, yet are smarter than most humans on a few special dimensions (for more on this, see Harnad 1989). Finally, in a fascinating paper, Haugeland (1979) argued that computers will not succeed in understanding natural language until they can be given (or otherwise develop) a sense of the world they inhabit, the creatures they interact with, and, most importantly, a sense of themselves as enduring wholes. Those that think computers are merely formal symbol manipulators (and, hence, that computationalism is too weak) may in fact be noticing that computers are not conscious, not very intelligent, and are not selves.

If intentionality is only a semantic property, it is virtually ubiquitous. If intentionality is variable binding and look-up, then it is quite common. If intentionality is consciousness, etc., then it is quite rare. The literature on intentionality defines it as one of the first two notions, but reading between the lines, consciousness and related notions are the real phenomena of interest.

4.   MAKING DECISIONS

Computationalism is incompatible with our ordinary, day-to-day view that humans make decisions. Hence, for a computationalist, decision-making is not a cognitive capacity. In fact, if humans really do make decisions in the way we ordinarily think decisions are made, then computationalism is false.

On the ordinary view, humans and other intelligent systems frequently decide to take a certain course of action or to form a certain intention. Of course, not all of our actions or goals are arrived at by deciding, but some are. A few months ago, I decided to write this paper; I decided to work on it today. But as I type this paragraph I am not deciding to breathe or to maintain tonus; these are done automatically.

The computationalist wants to, and should want to, maintain the distinction between the two kinds of action just mentioned. However, whereas both our folk psychology and our current cognitive psychology couch the distinction in terms of deciding and not deciding, the computationalist couches it in terms of the kinds of procedures executed. This makes all the difference in the world. I will describe this class of procedures shortly; for now, let us consider ordinary deciding.

Deciding is, I think, most naturally seen as the exercise of the will. Typically, the system has three or four options before it, and it willfully chooses the one which has the highest score provided by a process of evaluating the options along some dimension (or dimensions). Generally speaking, the dimensions measure the desirability of the outcomes produced or their ability to satisfy some previously set goal or established intention. For example, I can continue to write or I can go to watch football on television. I ponder over these options. I would rather go to watch football; it is relaxing and fun. Writing this paper is not relaxing. However, writing this paper is fulfilling in a way that watching football is not. I continue to ponder. Aesthetics, relaxation, and enjoyment turn out to be secondary. I have a duty to write this paper: a duty to myself (for my career and philosophical integrity), to specific others (those I have made promises to regarding this paper), and unspecified others (the philosophical and cognitive science communities at large). I sum everything up and 'see' that my duties outweigh my desires for fun and relaxation, so I choose to work on my paper. My will enters here in the last step. Once I see which option has the highest score, I am not thereby destined or forced to work on my paper. I must willfully choose to work on my paper. That this is true can perhaps be seen more readily if we suppose that I am one of those who generally ranks duties below enjoyment no matter what my duty. In this case, the fact that I must willfully choose to work on my paper is more apparent.

As I just mentioned, will can be exercised with varying intensity. Suppose I see that my duties are not all that strong. Suppose I already have plenty of research grants and publications, my promises were 'weak' promises or promises with unspecified dates, and the philosophical and psychological communities at large already accept the scientific bankruptcy of the notion of deciding. In such a case, my desire for fun might get the highest score, so I choose to watch football. Even in this case, I exercise my will. For example, I might be a workaholic and have to make an effort to relax. But even if I am one of those who is disposed to relax and have fun when I have no other pressing duties, I must still exercise my will in order to watch football on television, though in this case, I need not exercise my will very much. If I do not exercise my will, I will just sit here in front of my monitor maintaining tonus and breathing, typing nothing and doing nothing. What is the will? No one knows (though not from want of trying). Perhaps one day psychologists will discover what it is. Perhaps one day artificial intelligence researchers will be able to program will into a computer. Perhaps we will never know (cf. Fodor (1983)). But humans clearly have wills, and they exercise them frequently in the course of their daily lives.

This, I submit, is the ordinary view of human decision-making—and, it is the view which gets extended to cover all other intelligent systems from ants, to cockroaches, to dolphins, to chimpanzees, and to computers.

Computationalists have a different view of deciding. Their view is that decisions are the computation of branching functions. Branching functions map expressions constructed using computable, boolean functions (which are called *conditions*) onto some other computable function. Thus if F is a set of computable functions, we have:

$$B: \{\text{conditions}\} \text{---} > F.$$

The action of B is then

$$B \, (\text{condition}) = \begin{cases} f_1, \text{ if condition is true} \\ f_2, \text{ if condition is false} \end{cases}$$

where both f_1 and f_2 are elements of F. In computer science, branching functions are typically rendered as IF statements (which are procedures)[8]

IF (condition) THEN f_1,
ELSE f_2[8].

At this point, we need to recall the notion of *control flow*. As mentioned in Section 2, the specific sequence of functions which get computed is called the control flow of the system's computation. In *sequential control flow*, no branching functions are executed: computing the function f_i is always a sufficient condition for computing the function f_{i+1}. (Here, we must assume that the system is working properly and that it is not a stochastic system, i.e. that its state changes are not probabilistic relative to our explanatory goals.) Described at the state level, we can say that being in state s_1 is always sufficient for entering state s_2 (again, assuming the system is working correctly and is not stochastic). However, branching functions can change the flow of control in a system's procedure execution. Computing a branching function B does not always result in next computing a specific function. Depending on the values of the relevant variables, computing B could result in computing f_1 next or f_2 next. However, as also noted in Section 2, once a procedure is specified, flow of control is determined by the initial state of the system, and this is true even if the procedure contains branching statements. In fact, given a branching function B, its condition C, and C's input i, $B(C(i))$ uniquely determines an output function f which is then simply executed automatically. Computationalism is incompatible with the notion that cognitive agents such as humans decide precisely because there is nothing for the will to do. The automatic nature of control flow and the notion of branching functions capture everything there is to the notion of deciding.

I now return to my decision to work on this paper instead of watching football on television. To the computationalist, I computed some branching function which determined that my duties outweighed my desire for fun and relaxation. That is I executed this procedure;

> IF (duties outweigh desire for fun),
> THEN work on paper,
> ELSE watch football.

Given that my duties do outweigh my desire for fun, I simply compute next the work-on-paper function or, more precisely, the first function in the sequence of functions which constitutes my work-on-paper function and which explains my working on my paper as I do. Notice that there is no need for will. Once the branching function computes the Boolean expression which makes up the condition <duties outweigh desire for fun> I compute the next function automatically, just as the computer does.

But what about the case where my duties rank lower than my desire for fun, yet I choose to work on my paper instead? Will seems required to explain this. In the computationalist view, however, if the procedure mentioned above adequately explains my behavior and I work on my paper instead of watching football, then I have not, in fact, ranked my duties lower than my desire for fun. However, does this mean that computationalism cannot take seriously the distinction underlying the above question? Some decisions do seem harder to make than others. Computationalism either ought to account for this or to show that the supposed phenomenon is an illusion. I believe that computationalists will be able to explain this phenomenon. Of course, the best way to argue this point would be to produce such an explanation here. But something less will do, too—I need only show that computationalism *can* explain this phenomenon which I can do by producing a plausible explanation.

Some function computations are *goal-driven*. A goal-driven computation is just like an ordinary computation (as in Figure 5.2) except for the way in which the sequence of functions came into existence. For goal-driven computations, the system itself builds the sequence (actually some subsystem builds the sequence, but we can be relatively sloppy about this point). The constraint on building a sequence is that the sequence should, when executed, result in achieving the goal. (Goal-driven computations are well-known in artificial intelligence (see Rich (1983: 57 ff.) for an introduction. Goal-directed computation is also known as top-down processing, expectation-driven processing, and backward reasoning, etc.)

In general, in a goal-driven computation, whether or not the goal should be achieved is not open to debate. The goal results in a sequence of functions, control is passed to the first function in the sequence, and the goal is achieved (assuming the sequence is in fact capable of producing the goal). However, sometimes a system has 'dueling goals', i.e. different goals which compete against each other for current resources. Suppose there are two kinds of dueling goals: candidate goals and interfering goals. In both kinds of goals, goals compete against each other. The difference is in how genteel the competition is. Candidate goals are goals which, as it were, agree to abide the decision of a branching function—rather like polite political candidates, or factions in a legal dispute. Interfering goals, however, are not 'willing' to abide by the decision of a branching function. They, as it were, influence the voting. Such goals are like heads of rival criminal organizations of corrupt political adversaries. Specifically, interfering goals create looping branching functions.

Returning again to my decision to work on this paper. Suppose that I have dueling goals: to work on this paper or to watch football on television. In the case where I fairly easily decide to work on this paper, my two goals are candidate goals. My *goal adjudication system* takes the two goals as input and constructs the following branching procedure (which is quite similar to the one described above):

> IF (duties outweigh desire for fun),
> THEN Activate: work-on-paper,
> ELSE Activate: watch-football.

This branching procedure is executed, and the winning function, 'Activate: work on paper', say, activates my goal to work on my paper. This, in turn, spawns the appropriate sequence of functions, and I do indeed work on my paper.

However, suppose that my goals are interfering goals. Their interference causes my goal adjudication system to create a looping branching procedure:

IF (duties outweigh desire for fun),
THEN decrease the importance of my duties and re-execute this
        procedure,
ELSE increase the importance of my duties and re-execute this
        procedure.

The watching-football goal is responsible for the THEN clause, and the work-on-paper goal is responsible for the ELSE clause. The difficulty of the decision depends on the intensity of the increase/decrease war implicit in the branching procedure. In the worst case, every decrease could be met by an increase of exactly the same amount, and an infinite loop could result. Then my *emergency looping branching procedure repair system* would have to be called (the calling condition would be something like 'branching function has looped more than 10^6 times'), and it would be responsible for taking control away from the looping branching procedure, and trying to restore order. In the very worst cases, my emergency looping branching procedure repair system might simply have to 'flip a coin' and pass control to the winner while actively preventing control from being usurped by the loser. When viewed from my conscious level, I could very plausibly describe all this as 'agonizing over my decision whether to work on my paper or to watch football', and as 'exercising my will to work on my paper'.

We can now, perhaps, finally abandon the notion of willful decision-making. With the demise of willful decision-making goes any robust notion of a person scanning an array of options and choosing one. Humans do not choose, they merely compute. The procedures we execute are extraordinarily complex and quite plastic, but like any computational mechanism, we decide to do some things and not others entirely on the basis of our initial state and the branching procedures we execute.[9]

5.   CONCLUSION

In this paper, I have defined computationalism, shown that computationalism makes any *distinct* notion of intentionality widely applicable, and I have shown that computationalism is incompatible with our ordinary notion of willful decision-making. From the computationalist perspective, humans are very different from what we thought. Thus, computationalism is incompatible with folk psychology. Given the batting average of folk theories, this is a point in computationalism's favor.

6.   NOTES

1.   A brief discussion of algorithms, procedures, functions, and the Church-Turing thesis is required. Computer scientists distinguish between *effective procedures* and *algorithms* (e.g. see Brainerd and Landweber 1974). An effective procedure ('procedure' for short) is a finite, unambiguous description of a finite set of effective operations. An operation is effective if there is a strictly mechanical method for executing it. (This is as precise as the definition can be made, which is why the Church–Turing thesis cannot be proved.) All computer programs are (effective) procedures.

Depending on what input they are given, procedures will halt in a 'yes' or 'no' state in a finite amount of time or go into an infinite loop. If a procedure always halts no matter what input it is given, then it is called an *algorithm*. In other words, an algorithm never enters an infinite loop; instead, it always produces a definitive answer to an input question, though it need not produce the right answer. Only some computer programs are algorithms. In this paper, 'procedure' will be used most of the time because we have no empirical evidence that any cognitive procedure always halts.

The Church–Turing thesis says that Turing machines can compute any function for which an effective procedure exists. The converse of this statement is known to be true. Computationalists are committed only to the claim that cognition is the execution of procedures. This is the weakest claim compatible with computationalism. It is this claim and the Church–Turing thesis that commits them to the further claim that all cognitive functions are Turing computable. Computationalists need not, and should not, commit to the stronger claim that cognition is the execution of algorithms because we have no evidence that every procedure which humans execute always produces a definite answer.

Computer scientists frequently distinguish between computing a function and executing a procedure because every procedure realizes exactly one function, but each function can be realized in several different procedures. For example, the function $2*x$ which doubles any number can be realized as a procedure which adds x to itself, or as a procedure which multiplies x by 2. Another example, is the function *sort A* which sorts an array of items from the lowest to the highest (e.g. if the items are character strings, *sort A* sorts them into alphabetical order). *Sort A* could be realized using the bubble sort procedure or the selection sort procedure. However, this distinction is not too important in computationalism because computationalists must analyze the functions they attribute to systems into subfunctions (see Section 2). Doing this forces them to view functions as built from certain subfunctions in certain ways, hence they are forced to view functions as procedures. Therefore, I shall use the words 'function' and 'procedure' more or less interchangeably.

2. For example, there are competing theories of how humans make analogies. One kind of theory claims that analogies are made by accessing pairs of representations (or data structures) in memory which denote relations such as causal relations (see, e.g., Schank 1982). Another kind of theory claims that the accessing strategy is rather wanton, accessing almost any representation it can regardless of what it denotes [see, e.g., Dietrich and Fields (1986), Gentner and Landers (1985) and Gick and Holyoak (1983)]. On the former theory, when required to do so, humans should by and large produce only a few plausible analogies from which a 'best' analogy is selected. On the latter theory, when required to do so, humans should produce a large number of candidate analogies many of which will be spurious. These theories make incompatible predictions, yet both are compatible with the computationalist thesis. Indeed, both kinds of theory are couched in computationalist language.

3. This is not a cop out. All sciences are beset by the problem of how to carve the world in order to get systems for which good explanations are forthcoming. The current problem is merely computationalism's version of this. Presumably, computationalism can handle it as well as physics, for example.

4. Completing steps 1–4 (i.e. determining that S computes F and that $F = g_n \circ g_{n-1} \circ \dots \circ g_1$, where we understand the g_i terms) is generally quite difficult and typically requires creativity and insight. A theory of how steps 1–4 are accomplished would, therefore, require a theory of how humans come to see systems as executing F instead of E, and why F, say, provides a more satisfying explanation of the behavior of S than E does. To date, very little is known about this phenomenon.

5. Looping is executing a sequence of instructions over and over again. Branching is jumping from the current position in the program to some other place in the program; this is typically accomplished by using a test statement, e.g. 'IF x > 5 GOTO STMT 100'. Sequencing is executing the next in a sequence of instructions unconditionally.

6. In computer science, I is typically the composition of two functions ($I = I_2 \circ I_1$). I_1 maps states of S onto instructions in some programming language. This

function is left largely implicit, and is realized by engineers who design computers, beginning with those who design computer chips and ending with those who design operating systems and applications software. I_2 is provided by, e.g. a denotational semantics (or some other kind of semantical function) which provides semantic valuation functions mapping syntactic contructs in the programming language onto the abstract values they denote (see Stoy 1977). I_2 is also often left implicit.

7. Dretske (1981, 1985) has argued that intentionality is crucial to learning. If he is right, then he has shown why intentionality is crucial to cognition. But computers can learn, and they are supposed to lack intentionality.

8. An important manifestation of branching functions involves the nesting of conditions. Such nestings have this form (I shall use the procedure notation since it is more familiar):

> IF <condition 1> THEN f_1
> ELSEIF <condition 2> THEN f_2
> .
> .
> .
> ELSEIF <condition n-I > THEN f_{n-1}
> ELSE f_n

In such nestings, the first condition to be evaluated to be true determines which of the functions f_1 to f_n becomes executed. There are always a finite (and typically small) number of conditions to test for, and one of the conditions must be chosen: the ELSE clause (the final clause) is executed in case no other clause is; the ELSE clause is thus the trap clause.

9. Some philosophers have suggested that I have only succeeded in producing another argument for determinism The attitude seems to be that my argument can be met by trotting out some argument for freewill. But this completely misses the point. The object of the game is to explain human cognition scientifically, not to save some cherished notion of human agency. If the notion of will can be made scientifically respectable and we discover that our theories of cognition are inadequate without this revised notion, then will the concept of will take its proper place among other scientifically respectable entities such as mass, energy, the proton, the quark, DNA, etc. In fact, such a scenario is compatible with adopting computationalism as the foundation of cognitive science. But I suspect that any notion of will with a

scientific foundation will not be considered the real thing. So, if we can explain human cognition without the will, then we ought to do so.

7.   REFERENCES

Bechtel W. (1988) Connectionism and the philosophy of mind: an overview. *The Southern Journal of Philosophy* , XXVI (Suppl.) 2: 17 -41.

Brainerd, W., and Landweber, L. (1974) *Theory of Computation* (New York: Wiley)

Carello, C., Turvey, M., Kugler, P., and Shaw, R. (1984) Inadequacies of the computer metaphor. In M. Gazzaniga (ed.) *Handbook of Cognitive Neuroscience* (New York: Plenum Press): 231-248.

Cummins, R. (1983) *The Nature of Psychological Explanation.* (Cambridge, MA: MlT/Bradford).

Cummins, R., and Schwarz, G. (1988) Radical Connectionism. In T. Horgan and J. Tieson (eds.) *The Southern Journal of Philosophy,* XXVI (Suppl.): 43-61.

Dietrich, E. (1985) *Computer Thought: Propositional Attitudes and Metaknowledge.* Ph.D. Dissertation. University of Arizona, Tucson, AZ.

Dietrich, E. (1990) Programs in the search for intelligent machines: the mistaken foundation of AI. In D. Partridge and Y. Wilks (eds.) *The Foundations of Artificial Intelligence* (Cambridge: Cambridge University Press): 223-233.

Dietrich, E. (1989) Semantics and the computational paradigm in cognitive psychology. *Synthese,* 79 (1): 119-141.

Dietrich, E., and Fields, C. (1986) Creative problem solving using the wanton inference strategy. In *Proceedings of the First Annual Rocky Mountain Conference on Artificial Intelligence* (Boulder, CO: University of Colorado/Breit): 31-41.

Dietrich, E., and Fields, C. (1988) Some assumptions underlying Smolensky's treatment of connectionism. *Behavioral and Brain Sciences,* 11: 29–31.

Dretske, F. (1985) *Knowledge and Flow of Information* (Cambridge, MA: MlT/Bradford).

Dretske, F. (1985) Machines and the mental. *Proceedings and Addresses of the American Philosophical Association,* 59(1): 23-33.

Dreyfus, H. (ed.) (1982) *Husserl, Intentionality, and Cognitive Science* (Cambridge, MA: MlT/Bradford).

Fields, C., and Dietrich, E. (1987a) Intentionality is a red herring. *Behavioral and Brain Sciences*, l0: 756-757.

Fields, C., and Dietrich, E. (1987b) Multi-domain problem solving: a test case for computational theories of intelligence. In *Proceedings of the Second Annual Rocky Mountain Conference on Artificial Intelligence* (Boulder, CO: University of Colorado/Colorado Institute for AI): 205-223.

Fodor, J. (1965) Explanation in psychology. In M. Black (ed.) *Philosophy in America* (Ithaca, NY: Cornell University Press).

Fodor, J. (1981) *Representations* (Cambridge, MA: MIT/Bradford).

Fodor, J. (1983) *The Modularity of Mind: an Essay on Faculty Psychology* (Cambridge, MA: MIT/Bradford).

Follesdal, D. (1982) Husserl's notion of noema. In H. Dreyfus (ed.) *Husserl, Intentionality, and Cognitive Science* (Cambridge, MA: MIT/Bradford): 73-80.

Gentner, D., and Landers, R. (1985) Analogical reminding: a good match is hard to find. *Proceedings of The International Conference on Systems, Man, and Cybernetics* (Tucson, AZ).

Gick, M., and Holyoak, K. (1983) Schema induction and analogical transfer. *Cognitive Psychology,* 12: 306-355.

Grossberg, S. (1987) Competitive learning: from interactive activation to adaptive resonance. *Cognitive Science,* 11: 23-63.

Harnad, S. (1989) Minds, machines, and searle. *Journal of Experimental and Theoretical Artificial intelligence,* 1: 5-25.

Haugeland, J. (1981) Semantic engines: an introduction of mind design. In J. Haugeland (ed.) *Mind Design* (Montgomery, VT: Bradford): 1-34.

Haugeland, J. (1978) The nature and plausibility of cognitivism. *Behavioral and Brain Sciences,* 1: 215-226.

Haugeland, J. (1979) Understanding natural language. *Journal of Philosophy*, 76: 619-632.

INTEL (1983) *Introduction to iAPX 88* (Reston, VA: Reston).

Nagel, T. (1974) What is it like to be a bat? *The Philosophical Review,* 4 LXXXIII: 435-450.

Reeke, G., and Edelman, C. (1988) Real brains and artificial intelligence. *Daedalus*, 117 (1): 143-173.

Rich, E. (1983) *Artificial Intelligence* (New York: McGraw-Hill).

Sayre, K. (1986) Intentionality and information processing: an alternative view. *Behavioral and Brain Sciences*, 9: 121-166.

Sayre, K. (1987) Various senses of 'intentional systems. *Behavioral and Brain Sciences*, 10: 760-765.

Schank, R. (1982) *Dynamic Memory* (New York: Cambridge University Press).

Searle, J. (1980) Minds, brains, and programs. *Behavioral and Brain Sciences*, 3: 417-457.

Smolensky, P. (1988) On the proper treatment of connectionism. *Behavioral and Brain Sciences,* 11: 1-23.

Stabler, E. (1983) How are grammars represented? *Behavioral and Brain Sciences*, 3: 391-402.

Stich, S. (1983) *From Folk Psychology to Cognitive Science: The Case Against Belief* (Cambridge, MA: MIT/Bradford).

Stoy, J. (1977) *Denotational Semantics: The Scott-Strachey Approach to Programming Languages* (Cambridge, MA: MIT).

Tenenbaum, A. (1984) *Structure Computer Organization* (Englewood Cliffs, NJ: Prentice-Hall).

Wulf, W., Shaw, M., Hilfinger, P., and Flon, L. (1981) *Fundamental Structures of Computer Science* (Reading, MA: Addison-Wesley).

III

 The Natural Intentionality of Machines

137

CHAPTER
6

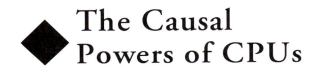

The Causal Powers of CPUs

David Cole

Much of the philosophical dispute over the potential mental abilities of machines has focused on a few arguments and critiques of those arguments. Most prominent among the arguments against the possibility of digital computers ever actually having mental states (intentionality, understanding, etc.) has been John Searle's Chinese Room argument. Searle argued that he could do just what a digital computer does in running a program that allegedly produces understanding of a subset of a natural language, and yet he wouldn't understand that language—so the computer doing the same thing wouldn't understand either. How is it then, that Searle CAN understand a natural language? Of course no one can supply a detailed explanation of how humans accomplish these feats, but Searle suggests that the causal powers of the brain are responsible, and that these differ in important ways from the powers of CPUs in digital computers.

Thinking Computers and Virtual Persons
edited by Eric Dietrich
ISBN 0-12-215495-9

Over the past decade Searle's argument has been the target of a series of criticisms, my own included. Here I briefly recap what I take to be the most serious objection to Searle's Chinese Room argument, and then focus on more positive, and speculative, suggestions as to how a computer might realize understanding, belief, consciousness, "original intentionality," and even sentience, having feelings or sensations. These issues crucially involve theories of meaning, consciousness, intentionality, and sentience, and so speculation is informed by partial analyses of these. In the course of this I consider Searle's claims about the relation of syntax to understanding and meaning, and I argue that the late Shakey the Robot achieved a certain degree of consciousness.

1.   HU'S IN THERE!? WHAT THE CHINESE ROOM ARGUMENT DOESN'T SHOW

I am sometimes surprised to discover disagreement about the structure of Searle's argument. The Chinese Room argument is about as clear as arguments get in philosophy. As Searle puts it in a 1990 paper, the argument that refutes strong AI can be summarized in a single sentence: "A system, me for example, could implement a program for understanding Chinese, for example, without understanding any Chinese at all" (p. 585). The Chinese Room argument is just that, with some details filled in about how the implementation works, how things appear to outsiders, the evidence that the system (Searle) wouldn't really understand Chinese, despite appearances, and so forth.

Searle begins his original statement of the full argument a decade earlier with the remark:

> One way to test any theory of the mind is to ask oneself what it would be like if my mind actually worked on the principles that the theory says all minds work on. Let us apply this test . . . with the following Gedanken experiment.

This introductory remark, and the one-sentence summary of the argument quoted above, highlights the way in which I think the Chinese Room argument is fundamentally confused. *Searle's* mind is the one grappling in the room with bits of paper, following English instructions for responding to Chinese symbols. The mind, if any, that results from such manipulation is *not* Searle's. The understanding of Chinese, if any, that results from Searle's activities in the Chinese Room would not be *Searle's* understanding. The mind, if any, that understands Chinese will have memories, traits and dispositions, beliefs and desires, aptitudes and quirks, as provided by the program. The mind that understands Chinese, if any, will not have Searle's memories, personality traits and dispositions, beliefs and desires, quirks and aptitudes—including linguistic abilities. The mind, if any, that answers the Chinese questions will not understand *English*, unlike Searle. It will not be the mind that wrote Speech Acts, and it will probably not be a mind acquainted with contemporary analytic philosophy. Thus the one thing that Searle does not give us in the Chinese Room argument is an account of "what it would be like" for *his* mind to work along the lines of a computational theory.

In short, it seemed to me that there is a question of the identity of persons lurking in the Chinese Room argument, and that Searle's argument simply assumes that if there were a mind that understood Chinese in the room it would have to be his (he is *alone,* isn't he?), and since he wouldn't understand Chinese simply by following English instructions for manipulating Chinese symbols, there was no understanding created. But all that he is actually entitled to is the conclusion that *he* would not understand Chinese, not that there was no understanding created.

In considering this, there is another position that the Chinese Room argument does refute: the view that a suitably programmed computer could understand— really understand—a language. That claim *is* refuted by the Chinese Room argument. But that claim is not the correct claim for someone interested in defending AI to make, and again it reflects a mistake about personal identity. I understand English—but my body doesn't, nor does my head. I am not the same thing as my body. If my death is typical, my body will continue to exist when I do not. That could only be the case if I am not identical with my body. And psychiatric evidence suggests that it is possible for my body to be the home of two distinct persons who have quite different psychological properties. Thus no computer will understand Chinese in just the same way that no body will. Minds are abstract in the sense that their identity conditions are not the same as those of any physical object. But this statement should not be viewed as invocation, to be accompanied by theremin music, of mysterious entities. It is not a rejection of physicalism.

All things are ultimately physical. But "ultimately" is constrained by the preceding considerations, which preclude simple type-type reductions of minds to the physical systems that realize them.

This personal identity critique is distinct, perhaps subtly, from the "system reply" to Searle's argument. The system reply maintains that the entity that understands in the Chinese Room is not Searle but is the *system* consisting of Searle and the "program" (English instructions), along with the intermediate bookkeeping on bits of paper that Searle modifies in the course of following the instructions for the syntactic manipulation of Chinese input. Searle is correct in holding that he could in principle internalize all the rules of the "program" and do the bookkeeping in his head—and that *he* still would not understand Chinese. But, as I have indicated above, it does not follow from this that *no one* understands Chinese. No argument has been given to show that no mind is created by this activity. But it does follow that it is not Searle who is doing the understanding of Chinese. Hence it seems to me that it also follows that in the case of a computer running a language understanding program, it is not the computer that is doing the understanding, or the system consisting of the computer and whatever software it is running. It is a person who understands, and the person is not to be identified with the physical subsystem that realizes it. The system might realize *two* or more distinct persons—and since they would be distinct, it can't be the case that both are identical with the physical substratum, and so there will be at least one mind that is not to be identified with its substratum or "body."

I suggest, then, that in the Chinese Room, the operator may well realize a mind that is distinct from that of the operator of the room. Thus no failure on the part of the operator to have a given psychological trait can be taken as evidence that no such trait exists as a result of the operator's activity. The mental states that result from the operator's activity would not exist, ceteris paribus, but for that activity. They are caused to exist by that activity. But they are not the mental states *of* the operator of the room. They belong to another mind, a virtual mind produced by the activity in the room. And in the case of the original Chinese Room, that virtual mind may well understand Chinese. Nothing in Searle's argument shows that it doesn't.

The realization of one mind by another is presumably rare. But it is a possibility that is perhaps easier to imagine where the virtual mind conspicuously has a familiar sort of body, unlike the mind answering questions in Chinese. In an earlier paper, "Thought and Thought Experiments," I noted that if one of the neurons in Searle's brain were conscious, and actually followed instructions for when to squirt neurotransmitter, it would not have the same psychological properties as Searle has. But even if all of Searle's neurons were conscious rule followers, none of them would be Searle. Yet Searle would not have a mind but for their activity. This relationship of virtual mind to its realization may be a special case of supervenience (see Pollock 1989). But that question cannot adequately be explored here.

Note that even if Searle's neurons were all conscious agents, under the stipulated condition that they successfully follow rules for squirting neurotransmitter, the gross behavior of each neuron would be unchanged. If the ability of the brain to realize intentional states, beliefs, and consciousness is the result of the behavior of neurons, as seems very likely, then these relevant and interesting "causal powers" of the brain would not be affected by the supposition that the neurons behaved as they did as a result of conscious rule following. Like any physical system, the gross properties depend upon the microproperties only down to some level. Below that, the substitution of functional equivalents makes no difference to the performance of the system. If a CPU could be substituted for a neuron, it should make no difference to the mind realized by the system of which that neuron was a part. If CPUs can have the causal powers of neurons, they can have the causal powers of brains. This is a hypothesis that the relevant causal powers are found at this level of organization or above, and, in particular, not at the subatomic or quantum level.

2.   SYNTAX, SEMANTICS, AND CAUSAL POWERS

In formal logic, one deals with formal calculi. These are ideal, not physical, objects. They are stipulated as having certain syntactic properties, so then one may go on to stipulate some semantic properties as well. Finally, if one is ambitious, one proves that some relationships hold between the two, such as that the syntactic relations mirror some semantic relations, for example, entailment. Or one can stipulate that the system has no semantic properties at all. And, of course, an abstract formal system is devoid of intrinsic causal properties—it does nothing on its own; its only effects are the result of a human using the calculus for some purpose or reacting to it, being inspired, confused, etc., by it.

With real-world systems, the situation is very different. If an actual causal system is causally sensitive to states of affairs in some part of the world, then one is not simply free to stipulate what semantic properties it has, or whether it has semantic properties at all. Semantic properties are not just in the eye of the beholder. Searle appears to hold that intentionality is the result of the causal properties of the brain. What he denies is that intentionality or beliefs can result from a purely syntactic system, such as a computer. But what is a syntactic system, and is a computer such a beast?

The answer to the latter may seem to be obviously affirmative—for we can and often do describe the computer in purely syntactic terms. But any causal system is describable in "purely syntactic" terms. My toaster instantiates a rule that "rewrites" white squares as brown squares. And any realized syntactic system will be rife with causal powers, as it transforms one state into another.

There is a superficial attractiveness to the following inference: computers are syntactic engines, they operate by solely syntactic manipulation; a look at formal systems shows us that syntax is independent from semantics, in that syntactic systems have no semantic properties unless they are attributed to them by an outside observer; therefore computers do not have intentionality—their states do not have meaning apart from that attributed to them by others.

But in what sense are computers syntactic systems? What does the microprocessor in my Buick have to do with syntax? Most CPUs are microprocessors used in machines for control purposes. Like all CPUs, they are causal systems. It is heuristically useful to think of CPUs as performing syntactic manipulations. But even if syntax is a highly abstract physical feature, abstract shape, say, it is still misleading to think of CPUs as syntactic manipulators. CPUs do not follow any syntactic rules. They cannot literally manipulate 1s and 0s. They cannot manipulate anything in virtue of its syntactic structure because they don't understand syntax, at the level of machine language, any more than they understand semantics. But they are causal systems that have causal properties that mirror—are isomorphic with—syntactic transformations.

And they may well have semantic properties and intentional states as well. It is not a question of trying to get semantics from syntax, it is a question of getting both from causal properties. Since the CPU is not a syntactic engine, it is a moot point whether one can get from syntax to semantics. And it is clearly the case that some causal systems understand meaning—we do. The question remains as to what properties are necessary for understanding. The point to observe is that no one has shown that CPUs lack those properties. Syntax, and its association with inert abstract systems, is a red herring.

A computer is first and foremost a *causal* system. It is millions of transistors arranged to *do* certain things. Most CPUs are not discernibly concerned with syntax at all—they are controlling air-fuel mixtures in automobile engines, they are animating figures on television screens under the control of video game programs. In what sense are these, or any, computer syntactic systems? If I label the switch on the wall next to my office door with "logical 1" above the toggle handle and "logical 0" below the toggle handle, does it become a syntactic manipulator that turns on a light—my office light—when it receives a logical 1 as input? Does a computer manipulate symbols in response solely to their syntactic features?

Reflection on these questions suggests that Searle's claim that the Chinese Room shows what it would be like for his mind to work along the lines of the strong AI theory is doubly misleading. Not only is it the case that there is reason to believe that any mind that would result from such an implementation of the theory would *not* be Searle's, there is the further problem that the theory does not suppose that the computer manipulates syntactic symbols in the way that Searle does. A computer does not understand that any of its states have any syntactic properties. A computer program does not consist of instructions for syntactic manipulation that are followed by the computer—unlike the books of English instructions that Searle imagines in the Chinese Room. It is only the interpreting human that can take the state of the computer as being a binary numeral, or as having any syntactic properties at all. Syntactic properties, such as being a noun, or a Boolean connective, or a sentence, are not properties that CPUs respond to. Recognition of these properties, which are abstract, requires interpretation. CPUs are electrical devices. Their inputs and outputs and internal states are electrical. Now the only sense in which they are syntactic engines is that those states *mirror* syntactic relations. And *we* can describe the operations at a certain level of abstraction from the electrical details as syntactic.

Thus it seems that Searle should not even think of computers as manipulators of syntax—on just the same grounds that he denies that a computer has intentional properties. The computer does not know that "hamburger" means hamburger. But the computer doesn't *know* that "hamburger" is a noun, or even a word, and it doesn't *know* that any internal state is a binary numeral. So it seems odd to me at least that Searle seems to have regarded computers as involved in syntactic operations and then argues that you can't get semantics from syntax. But if we were to follow this line, the computer is revealed for what it is—a brute causal system.

The whole issue of syntax here seems to me to be a red herring. The syntactic properties of computer states are neither here nor there for the semantic, intentional properties. An internal state of the computer represents the barometric pressure at Denver. It does that not in virtue of its syntactic properties, and not in virtue of anyone's interpretation of the state, rather the state has the representational property it has because of the causal connection between the state and the barometric pressure. The state tracks the barometric pressure. Thus the meaning of the state does *not* derive from its syntactic properties, any more than does the meaning of the idiot light on my dash.

Causal theories have a "feature" worth noting: things indicate what causes them. Thus erroneous indication becomes impossible. The meaning of the sign just expands to include whatever causes it—and something causes everything. Thus "cow" tokenings generally are caused by cows, but on one or more occasions are caused by bulls (that is, a language user sees bulls and fails to distinguish them from cows) and so "cow" now comes to mean "cow or bull."

Or does it? The meaning is specific to the occasion. What a token means depends upon what causes it, and that is, ex hypothesis, a bull on this occasion. So it doesn't mean cow or bull, rather, it sometimes means cow and sometimes means bull. What this does, of course, is introduce serious epistemological problems—it becomes difficult, if not impossible, to tell (exactly) what it means when such a language user tokens "cow." She is like an idiot light with a loose wire swinging around behind the dash. Now it means the oil is low, now that the battery is discharging, now merely that the ignition is on.

Of course, the proper pedantic response to someone who tokens "cow" in the presence of bulls is to correct her. If we can see what is causing the tokening, we can know what she means, and we can tell her that she is misusing the word. (Up to this point, I think that I do not diverge greatly from the line taken by Fodor 1990 in *A Theory of Content.*) What does misuse mean here? Well, all that appears to be required is some consistency across the community in the use of words. All we need point out, in our pedantry, is that most people use "cow" to mean the females of that species only, not the males. The Humpty Dumpty reply, that words shall mean whatever he wants them to mean, is revealed as unsatisfactory here, by the fact that the preceding remark is clearly in part a reproach—you run a serious risk of misleading people if you do not conform to general patterns of usage. Of course, risk aversion varies with the circumstance. If it is *very* important that we keep the sexes of farm animals straight, we may require conformity with a more precise usage than that generally prevailing among our language community. Thus even if most English speakers call all cattle "cows," we may require that a distinction be observed between cow, bull, and steer.

So it seems we ordinarily respond to the problem of disjoint causes of tokenings by invoking *norms*. The norms are needed to make communication appropriately informative. The norms are frequently invoked, as noted above, in correcting the usage of language users. Now Wittgenstein seems to have thought there were no rules but that there were regularities in the behavior of language users and that users judged what was acceptable linguistic behavior. Wittgenstein seems to have had a peculiar lack of interest in what produced judgments of acceptable linguistic behavior, but he seems to have been convinced it wasn't mental rules. I don't find Wittgenstein's reasoning here very convincing, but will be content to note that when we do make judgments of linguistic propriety, it is not unreasonable to say that we are expressing rules of proper usage. In any case, the expression at least has causal efficacy, that is, it modifies the linguistic behavior of others. And we typically hold ourselves to the same high standards to which we hold others.

The preceding is meant as a defense of causal theories of meaning against problems raised by Fodor (1990) in *A Theory of Content*. In any case, it seems clear that an AI natural language processor could have its behavior modified by correction delivered as natural language input. Whether corrected or not, the output of a language-using system, human or artificial, will have an idiolect that may mean something in that its output indicates how things are. The *semantic* properties of the output of such a causal system are to be discovered, not stipulated. To see this more clearly, let us look at the nature of meaning.

3.   MEANING

Paul Grice, Searle's longtime colleague at Berkeley, distinguished two kinds of meaning, natural and nonnatural. The former is typified by "those spots mean measles" or "those clouds mean rain." The latter is the result of speaker intentions.

Grice (1957) argues that meaning something involves an intention to create an effect on the auditor via the recognition of the intention, a delightful reciprocal pas à deux of intention. Presumably, understanding what someone means is the inverse of this process; it involves the recognition of the speaker's intention that the auditor recognize the speaker's intention to have the would-be understander recognize the speaker's intention. Since computers do not recognize intentions, it seems fair to say that computers never understand *that* anyone means anything by what they say, and ipso facto fail to understand *what* anyone means.

Thus we have a new argument that computers fail to understand language, and one that is quite independent of the Chinese Room considerations. The

Chinese Room, a hotbed of syntactic manipulation, was, so the argument goes, quite devoid of any awareness of semantics, of what the words stand for in the world. But Grice's analysis is meant to show that nonnatural meaning, the sort of meaning characteristic of language as opposed to spotty skin, is dependent not just on semantic but essentially pragmatic considerations, and mentalistic ones at that. Thus Grice's account was a sharp and self-conscious rejection of behaviorism and, Grice seems to indicate, of *causal* accounts of meaning in general.

There are two obvious possible responses to Gricean considerations that friends of CPUs might make. One is to deny the analysis; the other is to argue that computers can meet the conditions on understanding that the analysis sets out. Both of these responses seem to me to be reasonable, and I will pursue each in turn.

Grice's account is very interesting, and has been endorsed in its essentials by many, including some philosophers of mind like Michael Devitt and Kim Sterelny (1987) who espouse a robust naturalism in their approach to language. But embracing Grice's account has its costs. The danger of inflating the conditions on understanding, of course, is not just that we will show some weaker account to be inadequate, but we may well end up denying that we can be understood. The intention recognition that Grice sees as essential to linguistic communication—meaning and understanding that meaning—is sophisticated. Presumably, it is beyond the wherewithal of a 2-to-3-year-old child. Yet we do say of toddlers that they understand what someone said. Do they know what one meant by saying such and such? Does, e.g., a 2-year-old know what I mean by saying "Drink your milk"? Before reading Grice, one would think so. But if the wee tad must recognize my intention to have it recognize my intention, it might well dehydrate and wither for want of the cognitive ability to get my drift. And presumably my dog Andrew will never know what I mean by anything I say. I must admit that the facts of Andrew's performance do not constitute a stunning refutation of the intentional account of meaning, but it is nevertheless natural to say that the dog does, sometimes, under optimal conditions, seem to know what I mean when I say "Let's go outside," or "Get your bowl." The upshot, it seems to me, is that the defender of the intentional account is left with a bit of a dilemma; either intention recognition is not always necessary for understanding, or, on the other hand, intention recognition is not very cognitively demanding. If dogs do it, then despite the apparent obstacle that at first blush the intentional account presents, there is hope that CPUs might do it as well.

Before we explore that general line of response to the intentional objection, let us briefly consider the prospects for a less inflated account of the requirements on understanding. It appears that the division between human and natural signifying is not as clear as the Gricean analysis suggests—it seems we do attribute meaning to humans that is not different in kind from natural. For example, one can say "When Tom says 'there's no accounting for taste,' it means he does not care for whatever you are showing him." This may or may not be what Tom *intends* to communicate by this expression—his intentions are irrelevant to what it means when he says this. This contrasts with cases where we say that Tom means x by y, where Tom's intentions do make a difference. Also note that where speakers are sincere and enjoy epistemic success—they are right about the way things are—there is no difference between the answer to the question of what the speaker means by saying X and what the speaker's saying X means. For example, what Tom means by saying that the cat is on the mat and what Tom's saying the cat is on the mat means is, in both cases, that the cat is on the mat.

The fact is, most of the time people mean what they say. It is in the cases of metaphor and, especially, irony, that one must be sensitive to speakers' intentions in order to understand what is going on. And metaphor and irony are cases where the dog and the young child are conspicuously unsuccessful. Thus the difference between what a speaker means by utterance U and what his uttering U means is created by the possibility of a gap between what something usually or optimally means(n) and its failure, because of deceit or epistemic failure, to mean(n) that in this case. To fill the gap, representation properties, meanings, propositions, are postulated.

The upshot is that there appears no problem in creating machines whose output means(n). It should be noted that this meaning is not in any way dependent upon a human interpreter. What the spots on the face mean is something for would-be diagnosticians to discover. Same with the output of a computer.

In many ordinary cases, when one says "it is raining" or "snow is white," what one means by that is that it is raining or, in the second case, that snow is white. It MAY be that one intends that one's auditors understand that snow is white through recognition of one's intention that this is what you want them to understand, or some such. But why suppose all this? In ordinary cases, my intentions are irrelevant, as is your recognition of them. I merely wish to let you know something. I do this by acting as a reliable indicator of the way things are—not what I believe, but the way things are. I can, of course, let you know what I believe, and I can do that by telling you "I believe such and such." But most of the time, I am telling you about the great world outside of my head. Thus I mean what I say. What I say is a reliable indicator of the way things are, in just the way a good thermometer reliably indicates temperature, a good oil-pressure idiot light indicates adequate oil pressure. And so we appear to be back to natural meaning and causal accounts as adequate to mundane, informative communication, contrary to what Grice says, but in accord with Dretshe (1988).

Now it might be argued that we are not: for each of the indicators I have described is an artifact, and as such represents the intentions of its creators. But that appears to me to be a genetic fallacy. It is true that the oil pressure light would not exist and would not represent what it does in the absence of the intentions of its designers—normally. But nothing follows about what makes it represent what it does. The designers cause it to have certain causal, functional properties. But it is the latter, not the former that determine its representational properties. The connections to the engine are what make the light mean what it means. The designers determine what it is supposed to mean, which, when things go right, determines what it means by getting the connections right. But the gap between genesis and actual representational properties, between what something means and what it is supposed to mean, become apparent when things don't go right, that is, as the designers intended. Suppose, for example, that there is a mix-up on the part of an inexperienced assembler and the oil pressure light is in fact connected to a cooling system sensor that completes the circuit when the engine is too hot. Then when the light labeled "oil pressure" comes on, it will not mean that the oil pressure is inadequate. It will mean that the engine is too hot. Of course, that is not what it is supposed to mean. But the very fact that there can be a difference between what it is supposed to mean, that is, what the designers intended, and what it does mean shows that intentions are not the proximate determinate of meaning in this sense of meaning, causal role is, just as it is in the natural meaning of spotty skin and cloudy skies.

I conclude that there is reason to think that the intentional account complications that are highly relevant in some very interesting cases, such as metaphor, allusion, irony, sarcasm, and so forth, are not necessarily general conditions on understanding what someone means. For people normally mean what they say, and what they say functions as a generally reliable indicator of the way things are. People often function in communication as very complicated indicators. One can understand what they say without considering that they are intending to be indicators, just as I can use other products of human artifice as an indicator and understand what it indicates without reflecting on the intentions of its designers. Good news for toddlers and dogs.

Suppose now we explore the other horn of the dilemma and consider how a machine might actually meet the standards of the intentional account of meaning and understanding. It can surely be objected that although it is possible to produce machines that are syntactic engines and that nevertheless have states that mean this or that, the machines themselves mean nothing by what they "say." They remain mindless relayers of information, glorified idiot lights. They have no communicative intentions. And so they don't even rise to the competence of a dog, who may mean this or that by his barking, or his trotting over with his empty food dish, all the while monitoring the behavior of the intended recipient of his message for signs of recognition.

This objection to computer meaning seems to me to be surely valid. However, it appears to have a straightforward technological fix. In order for something to mean something by what it says, the thing must have a model of its auditor, and must choose its message in light of anticipated effects on the auditor. It does not seem necessary that there be feedback or assessment of the actual success; one can mean something by something, as in a suicide note, where there is no expectation of monitoring the effects of the message.

What seems to be required is that any system that is to understand what someone means must have a complete model of the communicative transaction, including the speaker and itself. In order to recognize speakers' intentions, it must, let us suppose, be able to represent them. This requires a representation of the speaker and what she is trying to accomplish. Since in this special case the other's intentions are to produce in the auditor a recognition of the speaker's intention, in order to represent the speaker's intention, the auditor must also be able to represent its own mental states and, in particular, its own representation of the intention of the speaker. While all this seems very fancy, as Mr. Rogers might say, it seems to me to pose no particular problem for a machine beyond the familiar problem of representation itself. That is, if a machine can represent objects with properties, it should pose no additional insurmountable hurdle that some of those objects are persons and that some of the properties they have are goals or intentions. Indeed, the systems described by Roger Schank that were Searle's particular target in the original Chinese Room piece purportedly represented the purposes with which people normally entered restaurants, yet that particular feature was not singled out as any more problematic than representing hamburgers themselves. And, as many have observed, there seems to be no particular problem with self-representation. Thus it seems to me there is no cause for alarm even if a most baroque form of the intentional account is correct in setting out the conditions of understanding, and, as indicated above, there is some reason to doubt that it can be a general account of understanding.

4.   CONSCIOUSNESS

Having raised the possibility of a system that represents itself, let us turn to explicit consideration of consciousness. There is an important distinction that seems to be very often neglected between consciousness and self-consciousness. While self-consciousness is a special case of consciousness, something can be conscious that is not and cannot be self-conscious. The things that can be conscious are those to which the conscious/unconscious distinction applies. Thus many animals, including reptiles, can be conscious but apparently cannot, for want of concepts of themselves, be self-conscious.

One encouraging sign that there is progress in philosophy is that different generations identify different deficiencies as the great scandal. So at least there is movement in what we identity as the area in which there is no movement. For Kant, it was the failure to prove the existence of the external world. For Wittgenstein and Gilbert Ryle, it was bewitchment by language and thinking of the mind as hidden. For Searle, as bemoaned in his 1990 paper, it is failure to pay due attention to consciousness. Yet there has been a host of recent works on consciousness, and, as I will argue below, they may be too little too late to be of much help in producing Artificial Consciousness.

Consciousness may appear to be the most elusive of mental phenomena. But I don't think that is the case. A brief excursion into ordinary language considerations will ease us, perhaps, into a less inflated view. "Conscious" is typically used with an object—one is conscious *of* this or conscious *of* that. To say that something is conscious *simpliciter* seems to indicate that it is *disposed* to be conscious of this or that, but if the point is merely to say that the thing is conscious rather than unconscious, there does not seem to be a requirement that it occurrently be conscious *of* anything. Second, note that the class of close synonyms of "conscious of" in ordinary contexts includes "aware of" and "notices." Consciousness is elusive at least in part because it does not denote any overt behavior. But mindful that fairly lowly organisms can be conscious simpliciter and notice and fail to notice things in their environment, we may be more disposed to see consciousness as a surmountable programming challenge.

And it is one that may have already been met. Consider Shakey, the robot that once roamed Stanford Research Institute (SRI). Shakey had a single television camera for vision, set atop an armless boxlike torso containing batteries, motors, and some control and radio electronics. He could move about on wheels, and he had curb feeler-like "whiskers" that sensed contact with objects. The computers that controlled him were not onboard, but were linked to the robot body by radio (shades of Dennett's 1978a "Where am I?"). Shakey produced internal predicate calculus statements that reflected his discoveries about his world. The predicate calculus model of the state of the world, including his own position, was updated using the camera and the whiskers as sensory apparatus. The information in the predicate calculus model was then used to carry out requests delivered at a teletype terminal in one of the rooms. Of course, there wasn't a whole lot the armless Shakey could do, but he could go to a room that one requested him to go to, and he could push things. The rooms were full of large obstacles, and doorways, so navigation was a considerable challenge.

Now it seems to be very natural to say that Shakey was sometimes unaware of certain objects in his environment. The vision system was rough and took single still life snapshots that were analyzed and converted to propositional form. Things could be missed, including obstacles in his path. He would then plow into them when he began to move. Of course, the whiskers allowed him to stop, take another picture, and reassess the situation. He might then take note of an object or distinguish what had formerly been treated as a single object. Shakey could make mistakes. He could fail to notice. He could be unaware of something and bump into it and then take account of it by correcting his predicate calculus model of the world so that the presence of the object was now represented.

In that sense, then, it seems to me that Shakey was conscious of some features of his environment. And thus I conclude not only that machines *can* be conscious, but some already have been. Two things should be noted: first, it is not *much* of a consciousness that we are dealing with here. I do not wish to suggest that being Shakey would be like being anything, that it would have a subjective quality. But I don't think it is like anything to be a frog, either—Descartes is more or less right about frogs. More on that later. Second, in particular there is no reason to suppose that any machine has ever had a human-type consciousness, that is, has ever been aware of things in the way a human can be, with rich associations, keen appreciation of the sort of thing something is, memories of past similars, and so forth. In particular, Shakey, so far as I know, has no strong claim to having been *self*-conscious. Although he did represent his location, and had a nominal token for himself ("robot") that was used in his predicate calc world representation, he did not represent his own representing, and thus lacked that peculiar reflexivity that marks self-consciousness. Presumably some lower animals that navigate the maze of twisty little passages that is the terrestrial world do so by means of maps in which their location is represented, but there is no need for them to have (nor reason to suppose that they do have) a representation of their own representing. Such animals are (often) conscious, but they are not self-conscious—Shakey rides with these critters.

Note that at this point, the discussion of consciousness and the discussion of intentional accounts of meaning come together. In order to have Gricean intentions, a system must have intentions about intentions, and thus representations of its own and others' representing—consciousness of its own and others' mental states.

But above I argued both that such reflexive representation presented no novel challenge beyond the general problem of representation, and also that such representation did not actually seem to be required for understanding in central, straightforward (no irony, etc.) cases of language use. Here I argue that consciousness does not require self-consciousness, and so is easier to produce than it would be if in order to be conscious one must also have higher-order consciousness (again, good news for dogs and tykes). But the present considerations suggest that achieving self-consciousness will turn out not to present problems that go much beyond the general problem of creating systems that have perception and belief.

5.   SENSE AND SENTIENCE

It is perhaps a bit disconcerting to think of it this way, but most computers inhabiting office desktops have but a single sense organ, one that detects fingerstrokes. Some computers used in control and other applications (such as imaging) have much richer sensory apparatus. But despite this sensory richness they still don't have sensations, they are not sentient. Could they be? Is this a deficiency that could be corrected by ingenious programming?

So far I have argued that no theoretical obstacle stands in the way of a program that achieves real understanding of what people mean, and that consciousness is so little of an obstacle that it may already have been achieved. Sentience, the having of sensations, is rather more difficult, it seems to me. But that commits me to the view that something can be conscious yet not sentient. And I think that is correct. However, some further explanation is in order.

Sentience is a particular response to things and so might be a familiar aspect of consciousness, but it does not appear to be necessary. If consciousness is awareness, a taking account of something, then there is no need to posit some kind of subjective character. As Descartes observed, much of animal behavior (conscious behavior, I might note) can be accounted for as reflex or other "automatic" response. There appears no need for some intervening subjective state. Now I certainly don't think humans and higher animals are devoid of sentience, and I suggest that in their case at least some conscious responses to things DO require us to posit more than a reflex. What is so often characteristic of lower animals is that a certain property of something in the environment will *trigger* a stereotypical response. The organism does not seem to have *any* awareness of other features of the environment, and it seems to be incapable of taking any stance toward the triggering stimulus other than displaying the behavior it evokes. In particular, it cannot put any distance between itself and the stimulus, it cannot reflect upon the stimulus, it cannot analyze the stimulus in a search for hypotheses to explain puzzling features of the situation, it cannot search for the right words to describe the stimulus, it cannot regard the stimulus with aesthetic detachment or pleasure. It *just* responds.

Computers cannot, at the state of the art, do most of these interesting things either. But they are no worse off than most organisms, including those that are clearly conscious. The conscious frog is a bundle of reflexes triggered by stimuli. If we wonder, as we stare into those bulbous eyes, what it is *like* to be a frog, what the consciousness of a frog would be if experienced from the "inside," as it were, I think the reality would be profoundly disappointing. To be a system that is simply a reflex system is like being a thermostat—or a computer, such as the one on my desk, that just responds unthinkingly and certainly without sensations to my digital stimulation of its sole sense "organ." Descartes was essentially right in his denial of sentience to lower animals.

Paradoxically, it appears that the possession of sense organs is both necessary and unnecessary for having sensations. On the one hand, sense organs seem to be the required source of the information and content of sensations. On the other hand, it seems that a live brain in a vat could have sensations, even if it had no body (or, more dramatically but more remote from contemporary materialism, even an immaterial Cartesian Res Cogitans could have sensations in the absence of any physical sense organs). Although meaning may not be in the head, sensations are. The apparent paradox dissolves when we observe that there are two senses of *necessary* at work here. The first is a practical necessity—typically, sense organs are needed to produce sensations. But the latter considerations make the point that in principle, and in fairly rare actual circumstances, the organs are not necessary: phantom limbs, hallucinations, and (hopefully) remote possible worlds where ALL limbs are phantom limbs. Both are correct and the two lines of thought are compatible. Thus, the value of the robot reply, it seems to me, is that if we really intend to produce sensations in computers, we had better hang on some interestingly capable sensors, similar to our own. But once we have learned the trick, we can throw away the latter and induce computer hallucinations and experience of virtual reality to our heart's content. The point is a practical one. We are (extremely) unlikely to ever properly understand what is involved in analyzing sensory data in the absence of using actual sensors in real-world situations. So robots are a practical necessity.

It may seem that I am endorsing the robot reply to the Chinese Room argument. But two points. The first is the reminder that the thing that understands is more abstract than the robot as well. If robots have minds, then the robots themselves, those piles of nuts, bolts, and silicon, will not be the things that are understanding. The understander is a virtual entity not identical with the system realizing it. Once again, I think Searle is quite correct in denying that tacking some sensors onto the room would give *him,* the occupant of the room, any understanding. But of course, his is not the mind that would realize by this arrangement.

Second, I resist the suggestion that *direct* connection to sensors is necessary to produce understanding. There needs to be causal connection with the world for there to be representation and consciousness of that world. But there seems to me to be no in principle reason why this connection cannot be mediated by human data suppliers. The Baker Street irregulars were Holmes's eyes and ears on occasion, and Helen Keller depended on the sensory abilities of others throughout her life. Yet Holmes and Keller were aware of and could think about things they had never seen directly. Consider also that should the idiot light on the dash of my Buick fail, and should it turn out that it is cheaper to hire an undergraduate to crouch under the hood, monitor the position of the oil pressure sensor, and then manually complete the circuit when and only when the sensor indicates low pressure, then there is no net effect upon what is meant when the oil pressure light is on. Direct connection to the world is not a necessary condition on awareness or sentience.

Sentience arises in—indeed, it is a form of—the analysis of data from the senses (or other source of similarly structured data, as in hallucination and phantom limb). But not all analyses of sensory data are sentience. My suggestion is that the analysis becomes sentience only when it involves hypothesis testing. And it only becomes similar to familiar, human, sentience when the range of possible hypotheses is wide. Thus, sentience presupposes considerable cognitive wherewithal (rather than being the substratum upon which cognition is built, as the empiricists supposed). Hypothesis testing is key here because it involves an appearance/reality distinction—I am appeared to in such and such a way, perhaps that means that H is true. In light of this, we see links between sentience and the capacity for self-consciousness (a link that Kant also asserted in the First Critique, but his reasoning is opaque to me). I won't explore the implications for the rights of animals here. I am content to note that nothing in the proposed understanding of sentience precludes *robot* sentience. Indeed, it is presented as a programming problem, and a phenomenon that will be emergent as artificial perceptual systems involving hypothesis testing evolve.

6.   CONCLUSION

I have covered a great deal of ground but have trod lightly. I intend to develop fuller discussion of these issues in the future (see Cole 1994). But now a recap of our itinerary is in order. First, I argued that the Chinese Room argument, taken as a refutation of Good Old-Fashioned Artificial Intelligence, is invalid—Searle's failure to understand Chinese in the room is simply irrelevant to whether or not running the program has succeeded in producing understanding of Chinese. Second, I argued that CPUs are causal systems, and only at a certain level of description are they syntactic systems. Hence the question of how to get from syntax to semantics simply should not arise. The question is how to get from causal connections to the world to semantics and meaning, and that question I explored in the next section. Meaning ain't in the CPU. This is what makes meaning easier for CPUs to come by. While I think that Grice's analysis of meaning is very interesting, it is too black and white in its bifurcation of meaning between the natural and the nonnatural. A result was the conclusion that a machine, like a toddler, might understand what someone says without mastering Gricean reflexive intentions. But, I have argued, even *that* mastery appears to be achievable. Next, the distinction between consciousness and self-consciousness was emphasized, and deflationary accounts of both were offered. Finally, I suggested that sentience cannot exist in simple systems, but emerges only in systems complex enough to take various stances with regard to the data offered up by their sense devices. All suggests that the future of AI is bright indeed.

7.   REFERENCES

Cole, D. (1984) Thought and thought experiments. *Philosophical Studies,* 45: 431-444.

Cole, D. (1991) Artificial intelligence and personal identity. *Synthese,* September.

Dennett, D. (1978a) Where am I? In *Brainstorms* (Cambridge, MA: Bradford Books): 310-323.

Dennett, D. (1978b) Why you can't make a robot that feels pain. In *Brainstorms* (Cambridge, MA: Bradford Books): 190-229.

Dennett, D. (1991) *Consciousness Explained* (Boston: Little, Brown and Co.).

Devitt, M. and Sterelny K. (1987) *Language and Reality* (Cambridge, MA: MIT Press).

Dretske, F. (1985) Mentality and machines. *Proceedings and Addresses of the American Philosophical Association* 59:1.

Dretske, F. (1988) *Explaining Behavior* (Cambridge, MA: MIT Press).

Fodor, J. (1987) *Psychosemantics* (Cambridge, MA: MIT Press).

Fodor, J. (1990) *A Theory of Content and Other Essays* (Cambridge, MA: MIT Press).

Grice, H. P. (1957) Meaning. *Philosophical Review,* 66 (3): 377-388.

Pollock, J. (1989) *How to Build a Person* (Cambridge, MA: MIT Press).

Rapaport, W. (1988) Syntactic semantics: foundations of computational natural-language understanding. In James Fetzer (ed.) *Aspects of Artificial Intelligence* (Kluwer Academic Publishers), pp. 81-131.

Searle, J. *Speech Acts* (Cambridge: Cambridge University Press).

Searle, J. (1981) Minds, brains and programs. *Behavioral and Brain Sciences,*

Searle, J. (1983) *Intentionality* (Cambridge: Cambridge University Press).

Searle, J. (1990) Consciousness, explanatory inversion, and cognitive science. *The Behavioral and Brain Sciences*, 13: 585-596.

Wittgenstein, L. (1953) *Philosophical Investigations* (New York: Macmillan).

CHAPTER

7

 ## Could a Machine Think?

Classical AI Is Unlikely to Yield Conscious Machines; Systems That Mimic the Brain Might

Paul Churchland and Patricia Churchland

A rtificial-intelligence research is undergoing a revolution. To explain how and why, and to put John R. Searle's argument in perspective, we first need a flashback.

By the early 1950's the old, vague question, Could a machine think? had been replaced by the more approachable question, Could a machine that manipulated physical symbols according to structure-sensitive rules think? This question was an improvement because formal logic and computational theory had seen major developments in the preceding half-century. Theorists had come to appreciate the enormous power of abstract systems of symbols that undergo rule-governed transformations. If those systems could just be automated, then their abstract computational power, it seemed, would be displayed in a real physical system.

Thinking Computers and Virtual Persons
edited by Eric Dietrich
ISBN 0-12-215495-9

This insight spawned a well-defined research program with deep theoretical underpinnings.

Could a machine think? There were many reasons for saying yes. One of the earliest and deepest reasons lay in two important results in computational theory. The first was Church's thesis, which states that every effectively computable function is recursively computable. Effectively computable means that there is a "rote" procedure for determining, in finite time, the output of the function for a given input. Recursively computable means more specifically that there is a finite set of operations that can be applied to a given input, and then applied again and again to the successive results of such applications, to yield the function's output in finite time. The notion of a rote procedure is nonformal and intuitive; thus, Church's thesis does not admit of a formal proof. But it does go to the heart of what it is to compute, and many lines of evidence converge in supporting it.

The second important result was Alan M. Turing's demonstration that any recursively computable function can be computed in finite time by a maximally simple sort of symbol-manipulating machine that has come to be called a universal Turing machine. This machine is guided by a set of recursively applicable rules that are sensitive to the identity, order and arrangement of the elementary symbols it encounters as input.

These two results entail something remarkable, namely that a standard digital computer, given only the right program, a large enough memory and sufficient time, can compute *any* rule-governed input-output function. That is, it can display any systematic pattern of responses to the environment whatsoever.

More specifically, these results imply that a suitably programmed symbol-manipulating machine (hereafter, SM machine) should be able to pass the Turing test for conscious intelligence. The Turing test is a purely behavioral test for conscious intelligence, but it is a very demanding test even so. (Whether it is a fair test will be addressed below, where we shall also encounter a second and quite different "test" for conscious intelligence.) In the original version of the Turing test, the inputs to the SM machine are conversational questions and remarks typed into a console by you or me, and the outputs are typewritten responses from the SM machine. The machine passes this test for conscious intelligence if its responses cannot be discriminated from the typewritten responses of a real, intelligent person. Of course, at present no one knows the function that would produce the output behavior of a conscious person. But the Church and Turing results assure us that, whatever that (presumably effective) function might be, a suitable SM machine could compute it.

This is a significant conclusion, especially since Turing's portrayal of a purely teletyped interaction is an unnecessary restriction. The same conclusion follows even if the SM machine interacts with the world in more complex ways: by direct vision, real speech and so forth. After all, a more complex recursive function is still Turing-computable. The only remaining problem is to identify the undoubtedly complex function that governs the human pattern of response to the environment and then write the program (the set of recursively applicable rules) by which the SM machine will compute it. These goals form the fundamental research program of classical AI.

Initial results were positive. SM machines with clever programs performed a variety of ostensibly cognitive activities. They responded to complex instructions, solved complex arithmetic, algebraic and tactical problems, played checkers and chess, proved theorems and engaged in simple dialogue. Performance continued to improve with the appearance of larger memories and faster machines and with the use of longer and more cunning programs. Classical, or "program-writing," AI was a vigorous and successful research effort from almost every perspective. The occasional denial that an SM machine might eventually think appeared uninformed and ill motivated. The case for a positive answer to our title question was overwhelming.

There were a few puzzles, of course. For one thing, SM machines were admittedly not very brainlike. Even here, however, the classical approach had a convincing answer. First, the physical material of any SM machine has nothing essential to do with what function it computes. That is fixed by its program. Second, the engineering details of any machine's functional architecture are also irrelevant, since different architectures running quite different programs can still be computing the same input-output function.

Accordingly, AI sought to find the input-output *function* characteristic of intelligence and the most efficient of the many possible programs for computing it. The idiosyncratic way in which the brain computes the function just doesn't matter, it was said. This completes the rationale for classical AI and for a positive answer to our title question.

Could a machine think? There were also some arguments for saying no. Through the 1960's interesting negative arguments were relatively rare. The objection was occasionally made that thinking was a nonphysical process in an immaterial soul. But such dualistic resistance was neither evolutionarily nor explanatorily plausible. It had a negligible impact on AI research.

A quite different line of objection was more successful in gaining the AI community's attention. In 1972 Hubert L. Dreyfus published a book that was highly critical of the parade-case simulations of cognitive activity. He argued for their inadequacy as simulations of genuine cognition, and he pointed to a pattern of failure in these attempts. What they were missing, he suggested, was the vast store of inarticulate background knowledge every person possesses and the common-sense capacity for drawing on relevant aspects of that knowledge as changing circumstance demands. Dreyfus did not deny the possibility that an artificial physical system of some kind might think, but he was highly critical of the idea that this could be achieved solely by symbol manipulation at the hands of recursively applicable rules.

Dreyfus's complaints were broadly perceived within the AI community, and within the discipline of philosophy as well, as shortsighted and unsympathetic, as harping on the inevitable simplifications of a research effort still in its youth. These deficits might be real, but surely they were temporary. Bigger machines and better programs should repair them in due course. Time, it was felt, was on AI's side. Here again the impact on research was negligible.

But time was on Dreyfus's side as well: the rate of cognitive return on increasing speed and memory began to slacken in the late 1970's and early 1980's. The simulation of object recognition in the visual system, for example, proved computationally intensive to an unexpected degree. Realistic results required longer and longer periods of computer time, periods far in excess of what a real visual system requires. This relative slowness of the simulations was darkly curious; signal propagation in a computer is roughly a million times faster than in the brain, and the clock frequency of a computer's central processor is greater than any frequency found in the brain by a similarly dramatic margin. And yet, on realistic problems, the tortoise easily outran the hare.

Furthermore, realistic performance required that the computer program have access to an extremely large knowledge base. Constructing the relevant knowledge base was problem enough, and it was compounded by the problem of how to access just the contextually relevant parts of that knowledge base in real time. As the knowledge base got bigger and better, the access problem got worse. Exhaustive search took too much time, and heuristics for relevance did poorly. Worries of the sort Dreyfus had raised finally began to take hold here and there even among AI researchers.

At about this time (1980) John Searle authored a new and quite different criticism aimed at the most basic assumption of the classical research program: the idea that the appropriate manipulation of structured symbols by the recursive application of structure-sensitive rules could constitute conscious intelligence.

Searle's argument is based on a thought experiment that displays two crucial features. First, he describes a SM machine that realizes, we are to suppose, an input-output function adequate to sustain a successful Turing test conversation conducted entirely in Chinese. Second, the internal structure of the machine is such that, however it behaves, an observer remains certain that neither the machine nor any part of it understands Chinese. All it contains is a monolingual English speaker following a written set of instructions for manipulating the Chinese symbols that arrive and leave through a mail slot. In short, the system is supposed to pass the Turing test, while the system itself lacks any genuine understanding of Chinese or real Chinese semantic content.

The general lesson drawn is that any system that merely manipulates physical symbols in accordance with structure-sensitive rules will be at best a hollow mock-up of real conscious intelligence, because it is impossible to generate "real semantics" merely by cranking away on "empty syntax." Here, we should point out, Searle is imposing a nonbehavioral test for consciousness: the elements of conscious intelligence must possess real semantic content.

One is tempted to complain that Searle's thought experiment is unfair because his Rube Goldberg system will compute with absurd slowness. Searle insists, however, that speed is strictly irrelevant here. A slow thinker should still be a real thinker. Everything essential to the duplication of thought, as per classical AI, is said to be present in the Chinese room.

Searle's paper provoked a lively reaction from AI researchers, psychologists and philosophers alike. On the whole, however, he was met with an even more hostile reception than Dreyfus had experienced. In a later piece ("Is the Brain's Mind a Computer Program?" *Scientific American* Jan. 1990, 20-25), Searle forthrightly listed a number of these critical responses. We think many of them are reasonable, especially those that "bite the bullet" by insisting that, although it is appallingly slow, the overall system of the room-plus-contents does understand Chinese.

We think those are good responses, but not because we think that the room understands Chinese. We agree with Searle that it does not. Rather they are good responses because they reflect a refusal to accept the crucial third axiom of Searle's argument (see Figure 7.1, page 163): "*Syntax by itself is neither constitutive of nor sufficient for semantics.*" Perhaps this axiom is true, but Searle cannot rightly pretend to know that it is. Moreover, to assume its truth is tantamount to begging the question against the research program of classical AI, for that program is predicated on the very interesting assumption that if one can just set in motion an appropriately structured internal dance of syntactic elements, appropriately connected to inputs and outputs, it can produce the same cognitive states and achievements found in human beings.

The question-begging character of Searle's axiom 3 becomes clear when it is compared directly with his conclusion 1: "*Programs are neither constitutive of nor sufficient for minds.*" Plainly, his third axiom is already carrying 90 percent of the weight of this almost identical conclusion. That is why Searle's thought experiment is devoted to shoring up axiom 3 specifically. That is the point of the Chinese room.

Although the story of the Chinese room makes axiom 3 tempting to the unwary, we do not think it succeeds in establishing axiom 3, and we offer a parallel argument below in illustration of its failure. A single transparently fallacious instance of a disputed argument form often provides far more insight than a book full of logic chopping.

Searle's style of skepticism has ample precedent in the history of science. The 18th-century Irish bishop George Berkeley found it unintelligible that compression waves in the air, by themselves, could constitute or be sufficient for objective sound. The English poet-artist William Blake and the German poet-naturalist Johann W. von Goethe found it inconceivable that small particles by themselves could constitute or be sufficient for the objective phenomenon of light. Even in this century, there have been people who found it beyond imagining that inanimate matter by itself, and however organized, could ever constitute or be sufficient for life. Plainly, what people can or cannot imagine often has nothing to do with what is or is not the case, even where the people involved are highly intelligent.

To see how this lesson applies to Searle's case, consider a deliberately manufactured parallel to his argument and its supporting thought experiment.

> Axiom 1. *Electricity and magnetism are forces.*
>
> Axiom 2. *The essential property of light is luminance.*
>
> Axiom 3. *Forces by themselves are neither constitutive of nor sufficient for luminance.*
>
> Conclusion 1. *Electricity and magnetism are neither constitutive of nor sufficient for light.*

Imagine this argument raised shortly after James Clerk Maxwell's 1864 suggestion that light and electromagnetic waves are identical, but before the world's full appreciation of the systematic *parallels* between the properties of light and the properties of electromagnetic waves. This argument could have served as a compelling objection to Maxwell's imaginative hypothesis, especially if it were accompanied by the following commentary in support of axiom 3.

"Consider a dark room containing a man holding a bar magnet or charged object. If the man pumps the magnet up and down, then, according to Maxwell's theory of artificial luminance (AL), it will initiate a spreading circle of electromagnetic waves and will thus be luminous. But as all of us who have toyed with magnets or charged balls well know, their forces (or any other forces for that matter), even when set in motion, produce no luminance at all. It is inconceivable that you might constitute real luminance just by moving forces around!"

Figure 7.1. Oscillating electromagnetic forces constitute light even though a magnet pumped by a person appears to produce no light whatsoever. Similarly, rule-based symbol manipulation might constitute intelligence even though the rule-based system inside John R. Searle's "Chinese room" appears to lack real understanding.

THE CHINESE ROOM

Axiom 1. Computer programs are formal (syntactic).

Axiom 2. Human minds have mental contents (semantics).

Axiom 3. Syntax by itself is neither constitutive of nor sufficient for semantics.

Conclusion 1. Programs are neither constitutive of nor sufficient for minds.

THE LUMINOUS ROOM

Axiom 1. Electricity and magnetism are forces.

Axiom 2. The essential property of light is luminance.

Axiom 3. Forces by themselves are neither constitutive of nor sufficient for luminance.

Conclusion 1. Electricity and magnetism are neither constitutive of nor sufficient for light.

How should Maxwell respond to this challenge? He might begin by insisting that the "luminous room" experiment is a misleading display of the phenomenon of luminance because the frequency of oscillation of the magnet is absurdly low, too low by a factor of 10^{15}. This might well elicit the impatient response that frequency has nothing to do with it, that the room with the bobbing magnet already contains everything essential to light, according to Maxwell's own theory.

In response Maxwell might bite the bullet and claim, quite correctly, that the room really is bathed in luminance, albeit a grade or quality too feeble to appreciate. (Given the low frequency with which the man can oscillate the magnet, the wavelength of the electromagnetic waves produced is far too long and their intensity is much too weak for human retinas to respond to them.) But in the climate of understanding here contemplated— the 1860's—this tactic is likely to elicit laughter and hoots of derision. "Luminous room, my foot, Mr. Maxwell. It's pitch-black in there!"

Alas, poor Maxwell has no easy route out of this predicament. All he can do is insist on the following three points. First, axiom 3 of the above argument is false. Indeed, it begs the question despite its intuitive plausibility. Second, the luminous room experiment demonstrates nothing of interest one way or the other about the nature of light. And third, what is needed to settle the problem of light and the possibility of artificial luminance is an ongoing research program to determine whether, under the appropriate conditions, the behavior of electromagnetic waves does indeed mirror perfectly the behavior of light.

This is also the response that classical AI should give to Searle's argument. Even though Searle's Chinese room may appear to be "semantically dark," he is in no position to insist, on the strength of this appearance, that rule-governed symbol manipulation can never constitute semantic phenomena, especially when people have only an uninformed common-sense understanding of the semantic and cognitive phenomena that need to be explained. Rather than exploit one's understanding of these things, Searle's argument freely exploits one's ignorance of them.

With these criticisms of Searle's argument in place, we return to the question of whether the research program of classical AI has a realistic chance of solving the problem of conscious intelligence and of producing a machine that thinks. We believe that the prospects are poor, but we rest this opinion on reasons very different from Searle's. Our reasons derive from the specific performance failures of the classical research program in AI and from a variety of lessons learned from the biological brain and a new class of computational models inspired by its structure. We have already indicated some of the failures of classical AI regarding tasks that the brain performs swiftly and efficiently. The emerging consensus on these failures is that the functional architecture of classical SM machines is simply the wrong architecture for the very demanding jobs required.

Figure 7.2. Nervous systems span many scales of organization, from neurotransmitter molecules (*bottom*) to the entire brain and spinal cord. Intermediate levels include single neurons and circuits made up of a few neurons, such as those that produce orientation selectivity to a visual stimulus (*middle*), and systems made up of circuits such as those that subserve language (*top right*). Only research can decide how closely an artificial system must mimic the biological one to be capable of intelligence.

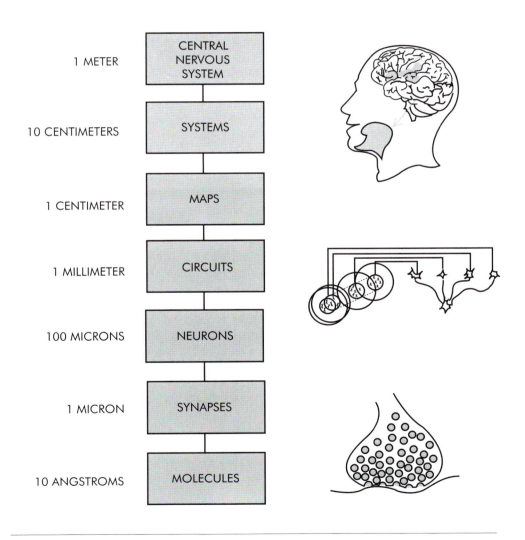

W hat we need to know is this: How does the *brain* achieve cognition? Reverse engineering is a common practice in industry. When a new piece of technology comes on the market, competitors find out how it works by taking it apart and divining its structural rationale. In the case of the brain, this strategy presents an unusually stiff challenge, for the brain is the most complicated and sophisticated thing on the planet. Even so, the neurosciences have revealed much about the brain on a wide variety of structural levels. Three anatomic points will provide a basic contrast with the architecture of conventional electronic computers.

First, nervous systems are parallel machines, in the sense that signals are processed in millions of different pathways simultaneously (see Figure 7.2, page 165). The retina, for example, presents its complex input to the brain not in chunks of eight, 16 or 32 elements, as in a desktop computer, but rather in the form of almost a million distinct signal elements arriving simultaneously at the target of the optic nerve (the lateral geniculate nucleus), there to be processed collectively, simultaneously and in one fell swoop. Second, the brain's basic processing unit, the neuron, is comparatively simple. Furthermore, its response to incoming signals is analog, not digital, inasmuch as its output spiking frequency varies continuously with its input signals. Third, in the brain, axons projecting from one neuronal population to another are often matched by axons returning from their target population. These descending or recurrent projections allow the brain to modulate the character of its sensory processing. More important still, their existence makes the brain a genuine dynamical system whose continuing behavior is both highly complex and to some degree independent of its peripheral stimuli.

Highly simplified model networks have been useful in suggesting how real neural networks might work and in revealing the computational properties of parallel architectures. For example, consider a three-layer model consisting of neuronlike units fully connected by axonlike connections to the units at the next layer, (see Figure 7.3, page 167). An input stimulus produces some activation level in a given input unit, which conveys a signal of proportional strength along its "axon" to its many "synaptic" connections to the hidden units. The global effect is that a pattern of activations across the set of input units produces a distinct pattern of activations across the set of hidden units.

The same story applies to the output units. As before, an activation pattern across the hidden units produces a distinct activation pattern across the output units. All told, this network is a device for transforming any one of a great many possible input vectors (activation patterns) into a uniquely corresponding output vector. It is a device for computing a specific function. Exactly which function it computes is fixed by the global configuration of its synaptic weights.

There are various procedures for adjusting the weights so as to yield a network that computes almost any function—that is, any vector-to-vector transformation—that one might desire. In fact, one can even impose on it a

Figure 7.3. Neural Networks model a central feature of the brain's microstructure. In this three-layer net, input neurons (*bottom left*) process a pattern of activations (*bottom right*) and pass it along weighted connections to a hidden layer. Elements in the hidden layer sum their many inputs to produce a new layer of activations. This is passed to the output layer, which performs a further transformation. Overall the network transforms any input pattern into a corresponding output pattern as dictated by the arrangement and strength of the many connections between neurons.

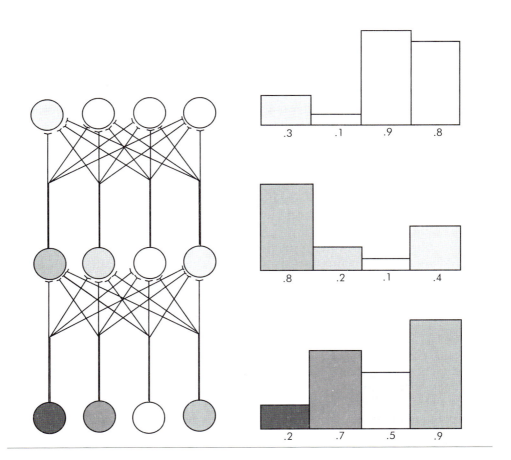

function one is unable to specify, so long as one can supply a set of examples of the desired input-output pairs. This process, called "training up the network," proceeds by successive adjustment of the network's weights until it performs the input-output transformations desired.

Although this model network vastly oversimplifies the structure of the brain, it does illustrate several important ideas. First, a parallel architecture provides a dramatic speed advantage over a conventional computer, for the many synapses at each level perform many small computations simultaneously instead of in laborious sequence. This advantage gets larger as the number of neurons increases at each layer. Strikingly, the speed of processing is entirely independent of both the number of units involved in each layer and the complexity of the function they are computing. Each layer could have four units or a hundred million; its configuration of synaptic weights could be computing simple one-digit sums or second-order differential equations. It would make no difference. The computation time would be exactly the same.

Second, massive parallelism means that the system is fault-tolerant and functionally persistent; the loss of a few connections, even quite a few, has a negligible effect on the character of the overall transformation performed by the surviving network.

Third, a parallel system stores large amounts of information in a distributed fashion, any part of which can be accessed in milliseconds. That information is stored in the specific configuration of synaptic connection strengths, as shaped by past learning. Relevant information is "released" as the input vector passes through—and is transformed by—that configuration of connections.

Parallel processing is not ideal for all types of computation. On tasks that require only a small input vector, but many millions of swiftly iterated recursive computations, the brain performs very badly, whereas classical SM machines excel. This class of computations is very large and important, so classical machines will always be useful, indeed, vital. There is, however, an equally large class of computations for which the brain's architecture is the superior technology. These are the computations that typically confront living creatures: recognizing a predator's outline in a noisy environment; recalling instantly how to avoid its gaze, flee its approach or fend off its attack; distinguishing food from nonfood and mates from nonmates; navigating through a complex and ever-changing physical/social environment, and so on.

Finally, it is important to note that the parallel system described is not manipulating symbols according to structure-sensitive rules. Rather, symbol manipulation appears to be just one of many cognitive skills that a network may or may not learn to display. Rule-governed symbol manipulation is not its basic mode of operation. Searle's argument is directed against rule-governed SM machines; vector transformers of the kind we describe are therefore not threatened by his Chinese room argument even if it were sound, which we have found independent reason to doubt.

Searle is aware of parallel processors but thinks they too will be devoid of real semantic content. To illustrate their inevitable failure, he outlines a second thought experiment, the Chinese gym, which has a gymnasium full of people organized into a parallel network. From there his argument proceeds as in the Chinese room.

We find this second story far less responsive or compelling than his first. For one, it is irrelevant that no unit in his system understands Chinese, since the same is true of nervous systems: no neuron in my brain understands English, although my whole brain does. For another, Searle neglects to mention that his simulation (using one person per neuron, plus a fleet-footed child for each synaptic connection) will require at least 10^{14} people, since the human brain has 10^{11} neurons, each of which averages over 10^3 connections. His system will require the entire human populations of over 10,000 earths. One gymnasium will not begin to hold a fair simulation.

On the other hand, if such a system were to be assembled on a suitably cosmic scale, with all its pathways faithfully modeled on the human case, we might then have a large, slow, oddly made but still functional brain on our hands. In that case the default assumption is surely that, given proper inputs, it *would* think, not that it couldn't. There is no guarantee that its activity would constitute real thought, because the vector-processing theory sketched above may not be the correct theory of how brains work. But neither is there any a priori guarantee that it could not be thinking. Searle is once more mistaking the limits on his (or the reader's) current imagination for the limits on objective reality.

The brain is a kind of computer, although most of its properties remain to be discovered. Characterizing the brain as a kind of computer is neither trivial nor frivolous. The brain does compute functions, functions of great complexity, but not in the classical AI fashion. When brains are said to be computers, it should not be implied that they are serial, digital computers, that they are programmed, that they exhibit the distinction between hardware and software or that they must be symbol manipulators or rule followers. Brains are computers in a radically different style.

How the brain manages meaning is still unknown, but it is clear that the problem reaches beyond language use and beyond humans. A small mound of fresh dirt signifies to a person, and also to coyotes, that a gopher is around; an echo with a certain spectral character signifies to a bat the presence of a moth. To develop a theory of meaning, more must be known about how neurons code and transform sensory signals, about the neural basis of memory, learning and emotion and about the interaction of these capacities and the motor system. A neurally grounded theory of meaning may require revision of the very intuitions that now seem so secure and that are so freely exploited in Searle's arguments. Such revisions are common in the history of science.

Could science construct an artificial intelligence by exploiting what is known about the nervous system? We see no principled reason why not. Searle appears to agree, although he qualifies his claim by saying that "any other system capable of causing minds would have to have causal powers (at least) equivalent to those of brains." We close by addressing this claim. We presume that Searle is not claiming that a successful artificial mind must have *all* the causal powers of the brain, such as the power to smell bad when rotting, to harbor slow viruses such as kuru, to stain yellow with horseradish peroxidase and so forth. Requiring perfect parity would be like requiring that an artificial flying device lay eggs.

Presumably he means only to require of an artificial mind all of the causal powers relevant, as he says, to conscious intelligence. But which exactly are they? We are back to quarreling about what is and is not relevant. This is an entirely reasonable place for a disagreement, but it is an empirical matter, to be tried and tested. Because so little is known about what goes into the process of cognition and semantics, it is premature to be very confident about what features are essential. Searle hints at various points that every level, including the biochemical, must be represented in any machine that is a candidate for artificial intelligence. This claim is almost surely too strong. An artificial brain might use something other than biochemicals to achieve the same ends.

This possibility is illustrated by Carver A. Mead's research at the California Institute of Technology. Mead and his colleagues have used analog VLSI techniques to build an artificial retina and an artificial cochlea. (In animals the retina and cochlea are not mere transducers: both systems embody a complex processing network.) These are not mere simulations in a minicomputer of the kind that Searle derides; they are real information-processing units responding in real time to real light, in the case of the artificial retina, and to real sound, in the case of the artificial cochlea. Their circuitry is based on the known anatomy and physiology of the cat retina and the barn owl cochlea, and their output is dramatically similar to the known output of the organs at issue.

These chips do not use any neurochemicals, so neurochemicals are clearly not necessary to achieve the evident results. Of course, the artificial retina cannot be said to see anything, because its output does not have an artificial thalamus or cortex to go to. Whether Mead's program could be sustained to build an entire artificial brain remains to be seen, but there is no evidence now that the absence of biochemicals renders it quixotic.

W e, and Searle, reject the Turing test as a sufficient condition for conscious intelligence. At one level our reasons for doing so are similar: we agree that it is also very important how the input-output function is achieved; it is important that the right sorts of things be going on inside the artificial machine. At another level, our reasons are quite different. Searle bases his position on commonsense intuitions about the presence or absence of semantic content. We base ours on the specific behavioral failures of the classical SM machines and on the specific virtues of machines with a more brainlike architecture. These contrasts show that certain computational strategies have vast and decisive advantages over others where typical cognitive tasks are concerned, advantages that are empirically inescapable. Clearly, the brain is making systematic use of these computational advantages. But it need not be the only physical system capable of doing so. Artificial intelligence, in a nonbiological but massively parallel machine, remains a compelling and discernible prospect.

FURTHER READING

Churchland, P. M. (1989) *A Neurocomputational Perspective: The Nature of Mind and the Structure of Science* (Cambridge, MA: MIT Press).

Churchland, P. S. (1986) *Neurophilosophy: Toward a Unified Understanding of the Mind/Brain* (Cambridge, MA: MIT Press).

Dennett, D. C. (1987) Fast thinking. In Dennett (ed.) *The Intentional Stance* (Cambridge, MA: MIT Press).

Dreyfus, H. L. (1972) *What Computers Can't Do: A Critique of Artificial Reason* (New York: Harper & Row).

Turing, A. M. (1950) Computing machinery and intelligence. *Mind*, 59: 433-460.

◆ Intentionality and Computationalism

Minds, Machines, Searle, and Harnad

Michael G. Dyer

....

1. INTRODUCTION

One major, long-term goal of Artificial Intelligence (AI) researchers is to pass 'Turing's Test' (Turing 1964), in which a group of testers (T) engage both a computer (C) and a person (P) in an extended conversation over a dual teletype-style communication medium. The conditions for the test are:

Thinking Computers and Virtual Persons
edited by Eric Dietrich
ISBN 0-12-215495-9

(1) One teletype links C to T and the other links P to T.

(2) Both C and P will attempt to convince T that each is the person.

(3) Each member of T knows that one teletype link is to a computer and the other to a person, and that both C and P are trying to convince T that each is a person.

(4) There is no limitation (other than time) placed on the nature of the conversations allowed.

(5) C passes the test if members of T are about evenly divided on which teletype is linked to C and which to P.

Notice that condition (3) is essential, since without it, members of T may uncritically accept output from each candidate as being that of a person, or they may fail to explicitly test the limits of each candidate's cognitive capabilities.

A major, working assumption of AI is that Mind is realizable as an executing computer program. This assumption has been called both the 'Strong AI' position (Searle 1980a) and the 'physical symbol system hypothesis (PSSH)' (Newell 1980).

Not all cognitive scientists accept Turing's Test as a definitive task for proof of the existence of Mind, or the PSSH as a reasonable hypothesis. Over the last decade, Searle (1980a, 1982a, 1985a, 1989) has produced a number of arguments attacking the PSSH. These arguments purport to show that computer programs, while they may act as if they are intelligent, actually lack *intentionality* (i.e. they do not know 'what they are talking about') and thus constitute simply an elaborate deception at the input/output level. Recently, Harnad (1989) has accepted a subset of Searle's arguments as having 'shaken the foundations of Artificial Intelligence' (p. 5). In response, Harnad has argued both that Turing's Test must be modified and that *noncomputational devices* (i.e. sensory and motor transducers) are a prerequisite for intentionality, through their role in achieving what Harnad considers a more fundamental task, that of *symbol grounding* (i.e. establishing a correspondence between internal representations and the real world).

This paper critically examines both Searle's and Harnad's arguments and concludes that the foundations of 'Strong AI' remain unchanged by their arguments, that the Turing Test is still adequate as a test of intentionality, and that *computationalism* (i.e., the position that Mind, Life and even Matter are entirely describable in terms of computations) continues to appear adequate to the task of realizing intentionality in both brains and machines.

2. SEARLE'S ARGUMENTS AND REBUTTALS

The arguments summarized below have been put forth by Searle (1980a, b; 1982a, b, c;1985a, b; 1989). Here I have summarized these arguments in my own words. For organizational and reference purposes, I have assigned each argument both a descriptive title and a label.

2.1. The 'Doing versus Knowing' Argument (SA-1)

Humans have 'intentionality'. Computers do not. What is intentionality? It is whatever humans have that make them 'know what they are doing'. Since computers do what they do without knowing what they are doing, computers lack intentionality. For example, computers multiply 7 x 9 to get 63 without knowing *that* they are multiplying numbers. Humans, on the other hand, know *that* they are multiplying numbers; know what numbers are; know what 63 signifies, etc. In contrast, computers manipulate numbers but do not know *about* numbers.

2.1.1. Rebuttal to SA-l (the 'sufficient domain knowledge' reply)

True, a normal computer does not know what it is doing with respect to numerical manipulations. However, it is possible, using current 'expert systems' technology, to build an AI system, let us call it COUNT, composed of a large number of schemas or frames (Minsky 1985), connected into semantic networks via relations, constraints and rules. Each schema would contain knowledge about the domain, i.e. about numbers; about numeric operations (such as counting, pairing, comparison, addition, etc.) and about number-related concepts, such as the difference between a numeral and its cardinality. In addition, COUNT would contain: (a) an episodic memory of events; for instance, of the last time that it counted up to a hundred, (b) facts concerning numbers, e.g. that 4 is even, and (c) of enablement conditions for numeric operations, e.g. that to count, one must place the objects counted in one-to-one correspondence with the numerals in ascending order, and so on. Schema instances would be organized in an associative memory, for content-addressable recall. COUNT would also have an English lexicon, mapping English words about the numerical domain to number-related concepts (i.e. to the network of schemas). COUNT would also have natural language understanding and generation subsystems, so that it could answer questions in English about number related concepts, numerical operations and its past experiences with numbers.

Now, suppose we ask COUNT to multiply 7 x 9. First COUNT must recall schemas concerning the concepts MULTIPLY, and NUMBER, along with schemas for the specific concepts of 7 and 9. Once COUNT realized that the question was concerning an operation upon two particular numbers, it could decide how to answer the query. In this case, COUNT would simply recall the answer from its associative memory, based on the concepts of MULTIPLY, 7 and 9 as indices to memory. After retrieving the answer, COUNT might recall one or more related memories, perhaps of the last time it multiplied two numbers together or the time it last had a conversation concerning those numbers, or that operation, etc. COUNT would also be able to answer other questions about its 'number world', such as:

> What is an example of a small number?
>
> Are there any special properties of the number 7?
>
> What do you think of the number 63?
>
> How can you tell even numbers from odd numbers?
>
> etc.

Prototypes of such programs, like the one hypothesized here, have been constructed for other domains, such as the domain of script and plan-based story comprehension and question answering (Dyer 1983, Lehnert 1978, Schank and Abelson 1977, Wilensky 1983) and editorial comprehension (Alvarado 1990).

As the sophistication of COUNT's concepts and cognitive processes in the numerical domain approaches that of humans, people would be less and less inclined to conclude that COUNT 'does not know what it's doing'.

Clearly, when COUNT is executing, in some sense it cannot help but do what it has been set up to do. COUNT has access only to its schemas. The internal programs that are executing are inaccessible to COUNT while at the same time essential for COUNT's performance. But, of course, the same is true for humans. Humans are just as automatic, in the sense that they cannot stop or control the firing patterns of their own neurons. Humans also have limited access to their own concepts about numbers. Although we can retrieve and manipulate concepts concerning numbers, we do not know how these concepts are represented or manipulated in the brain. But these unknown processes are every bit as automatic as an executing program, just many orders of magnitude more complex. Just as we would not be interested in talking to a hand calculator about the world of numbers (but we might enjoy talking to COUNT, depending on how sophisticated its concepts are); likewise, we would not be interested in talking to some isolated cluster of someone's neurons, since this cluster also 'does not know what it is doing'.

Thus, COUNT need not understand its base-level schemas, nor its own schema construction or other schema-processing mechanisms. For COUNT to perform in an 'intentional' manner, it only need have the ability to automatically *construct* useful schemas (e.g. during learning) and to automatically *apply* (access, generate deductions from, adapt, etc.) relevant schemas at appropriate times. In cases where COUNT's schemas refer to other schemas, COUNT will 'know about what it knows.' The same situation appears to be true of humans. Humans are not aware of how they represent, construct, modify or access their own forms of knowledge. Humans exhibit 'knowing that they know' only to the limited extent that they happen to have acquired knowledge about their knowledge of a given domain. Likewise, expert systems exhibit 'knowing that they know' to the extent that they have schemas concerning other schemas in memory. If 'knowing that one knows X' is anything more than schemas referring to other schemas (along with lots of automatic, inaccessible processing mechanisms), then it is up to those in the Searle camp to specify of what this extra magical 'stuff' of 'intentionality' consists.

2.2.   The 'Chinese Room' Argument (SA-2)

This argument relies on a thought experiment in which a person P sits inside a room and reads one or more books containing program instructions. These instructions can ask P to flip to other pages of instructions, look up symbols or numbers in various tables, and perform various kinds of numerical and/or logical operations. In addition, there can be blank pages for storing and referring to the results of prior calculations. P receives Chinese characters as input from people who insert pieces of paper into a slot in the room. P then reads and carries out the program instructions and these instructions tell P how to interpret the Chinese characters and respond with other Chinese characters. As a result, one can carry on a conversation in written Chinese with this room. However, if we ask P, in English, whether or not P knows Chinese, P will reply: 'I know no Chinese, I am just mindlessly following the instructions specified in these books'.

P clearly does not understand Chinese. The instructions clearly do not understand Chinese (they just reside in a static book), so where is the comprehension? According to Searle it just *appears* that there is comprehension. P is just acting as an interpreter of a set of instructions. Modern, program-store computers also consist of both a program and an interpreter which executes the instructions of the program. Thus, a computer built to read and answer questions in Chinese is no more understanding Chinese than P. Thus, to the extent that computers are composed of a (mindless) interpreter and a static set of instructions, they must also be only appearing to understand, but are not 'really' understanding.

2.2.1.   Rebuttal to SA-2 (the 'systems' reply)

Although P does not understand, the entire room, *as a system* consisting of both Searle and the instructions, does understand. We cannot expect Searle, who is acting as only one component in a two-component system, to understand Chinese, since the understanding is a consequence of the interaction of multiple components. For example, a radio is composed of various circuits, whose overall organization produces 'radio-ness'. We could fancifully imagine asking each part: 'Are you a radio?' and each would reply 'No. I'm just a capacitor (or transistor, or resistor, etc.)'. Yet the radio arises as a result of the organization of these parts. Likewise, we can imagine asking each neuron in a person's brain if it knows what it's like to think a thought. Individual neurons would not even be able to understand the question, while very large numbers of interacting neurons can realize numerous cognitive tasks.

Let us use a variant of Searle's Chinese room argument to 'convince' ourselves that a computer cannot really add two numbers, but is only appearing to do so. To show this, we take the addition circuitry of our hand calculator and *replace each component with a human.* Depending on the size of the numbers we want to add, we may need thousands of humans. Assume we place all of these humans in a giant football field. Each human will be told how to act, based on the actions of those humans near him. We will use a binary representation scheme to encode numbers. When a human has his hand raised, that is a '1', when lowered, a '0'. By setting the hands on a row of humans, we can encode a binary number. If we need a bus of wires between, say, the registers and the arithmetic/logic circuitry, we can set up such a bus by telling certain humans, e.g. 'When the person in front of you raises his hand, then so many seconds later, you raise your hand also, and then drop it'. In this way we could simulate the propagation of bit patterns down a bus of wires, to other circuits (layouts of humans) in the football field. We could actually then calculate the sum of two binary numbers, as long as each human faithfully acts as each piece of wire or other circuit component needed for our adder.

After successfully adding two binary numbers, we could now ask each human if he knows what he is doing. He will say 'No. I don't know what this football field of humans is accomplishing. I am just here raising and lowering my arm according to the rules I was given'. Does his response mean that addition did *not* occur? Of course not! The processes of addition have occurred, and in a manner isomorphic to that occurring in the hand calculator. Likewise, if we knew how neurons interact in that portion of our brains that realizes human-style numerical addition, then we could theoretically construct another 'human network', composed of perhaps billions of humans (requiring a gigantic football field), where each human would play the part of one or more neurons (synapses, neurotransmitters, etc.). In this case, also, each individual human would not know what he/she is doing, but the overall operation of addition would be occurring nonetheless.

In computer science, it is not at all unusual to build a smart system out of dumb components. We should just not be confused when many overly smart components are used to build a smart system.

2.3.   The 'Total Interpreter' Argument (SA-3)

Argument SA-3 is an attempt by Searle to refute the 'systems' reply: In this thought experiment, Searle imagines that P has memorized the instructions specified in the Chinese room books. Upon receiving bits of paper with Chinese symbols, P is able to mentally flip through the pages of these books, performing the calculations specified, and thus carry on a conversation in Chinese. In fact, P has memorized these instructions so well that P no longer even has a sense of consciously carrying out the Chinese room instructions, but does them subconsciously and automatically. Again, P writes down Chinese characters without having any sense of what P is doing and thus has no subjective sense of understanding Chinese.

Notice, in this thought experiment, P is no longer just acting as one component in a two-component system. P is performing *all tasks* of the system and acting as an interpreter of the entire [interpreter + instructions] Chinese room system, still without experiencing understanding of Chinese.

2.3.1.   Rebuttal to SA-3 (the 'split levels' reply)

In SA-3, P's brain (with its memory and processing abilities) is being used to create a system capable of interpreting Chinese. To make this system's capabilities more clearly distinct from those of P, let us assume that the Chinese room instructions create, not only Chinese comprehension but an alternative personality who holds completely different political beliefs, general world knowledge, attitudes, etc. from those of P. Thus, if P believes in democracy, then let us assume the alternative personality, CP, believes in communism. If P is ignorant about life in China, then let us assume, when P writes down Chinese characters in response to Chinese input characters, the system CP demonstrates great knowledge of Chinese culture.

When we talk in English to P, we have one sort of conversation, but when we feed written Chinese to P, we have completely different conversations (with CP). P, not understanding Chinese, of course does not know what these conversations are about. Likewise, CP may not understand English. That is, if we try to talk to CP by writing down English on scraps of paper, we get responses only from P, who can read the English.

Now, according to Searle, the fact that P does not understand Chinese (or the content of these Chinese conversations), while at the same time doing *all* computations involved in bringing CP into existence within P's brain, is an argument against there actually being a system CP that 'really' understands, i.e. that has 'intentionality'. Is this a reasonable conclusion?

Let us ask CP (in Chinese) what it is like to be CP. Suppose that the instructions P is carrying out are so sophisticated that CP is able to pass the Turing Test; that is, CP can give long discourses on what it is like to be human, to be Chinese and to be a communist. Why should we deny that CP exists, simply because, when we talk to P, P claims no knowledge of such an entity?

Imagine, for a moment, that we find out that *all of our own* neurons are controlled by a tiny creature, TC, who is highly intelligent. This creature actually samples the inputs to each of our neurons, and at *very* high speed, decides what outputs our neurons should send to other neurons. That is, our neurons are not under the control of electro-biochemical laws, but under the control of TC. Furthermore, TC claims not to understand what it is doing. TC is actually following a big book of instructions, which explains what kinds of outputs to produce for each of our neurons, based on each neuron's inputs. Assume scientists have recently discovered this fact about *our own* brains and we have just read about it in *Science*. Now, do these facts:—i.e. (1) that our mental existence is maintained by TC, (2) that TC is highly intelligent and can hold a conversation with us, and (3) that TC does not know what it is doing—lead us to conclude that *we* do not have intentionality; that *we* do not understand English but are only acting as if we do? Does the existence of an intelligent subsystem, that is doing all of the necessary computations to bring *us* about, obviate our acceptance of *ourselves* as having intentionality?

The existence of multiple and interdependent systems (referred to in computer science as *virtual* systems), simultaneously active within a single underlying system, is a standard notion in both the cognitive and computational sciences, e.g. (Minsky 1986). Virtual systems are usually created via time sharing (interleaving of calculations) or memory sharing (swapping memories in and out between main memory and the disk).

Consider a hypothetical AI natural language comprehension system, called NLP-L, whose domain of knowledge is the AI programming language Lisp. That is, NLP-L has knowledge about concepts involving Lisp. Assume that NLP-L itself is *built out* of Lisp programs that are being executed by a Lisp interpreter. Now, let us ask NLP-L something in English about Lisp:

Q: What is CAR?
NLP-L: It's a function that returns the first element in a list.

However, if we try to talk directly to the underlying Lisp interpreter (which is only designed to execute Lisp expressions), then we get garbage:

> Q: What is CAR?
> Lisp: "What"—unbound variable.

The kind of capability we see depends on what *level* or portion of a system we are communicating with. The Lisp interpreter executes Lisp but does not know *that* it is executing Lisp, so lacks intentional states with respect to Lisp. NPL-L, however, *does* have some intentional states (at least about Lisp). Yet NLP-L cannot exhibit its intelligent behavior without being brought into existence by the underlying execution of the Lisp interpreter.

It is easy to be confused by the existence of two separate systems, being maintained by P's single brain, B. But that is because we naively imagine that B has time to execute the computations that give rise to CP and still execute the computations that give rise to P. We imagine P being able to carry on a conversation with us, in English, of the sort where P every now and then performs CP-creating computations and then stops and says:

> I sure don't know what is going on when I see Chinese symbols on scraps of paper, but my brain does something and then suddenly I write down Chinese symbols. I remember when I used to more consciously carry out calculations specified in those Chinese Box books and that sure was boring work!

But let us look at this scenario from a different perspective. Imagine that when P is resident on B, it is because P-creating computations are going on within B (i.e. the brain). But who is to say that it is 'P's brain' and not actually 'CP's brain'? When Chinese characters are presented to B, this brain now executes CP-creating computations. During this period (no matter how short), where is P? While CP-creating computations are being carried out by this brain, perhaps we are being told by CP (in Chinese) that it is P who lacks intentionality! That is, *whose brain is it?*

Let us imagine that we are performing every computation being performed by every neuron of this brain, B. We are now simulating B in its entirety. Sometimes the computations bring about P and sometimes CP. If we imagine we are just controlling the firing of neurons, how will we know what is going on, even though we are performing *every* operation in the system? Thus, our own introspection, of what it is like to completely support *all* operations that give rise to intentional behavior, gives us no insight into which system is active, or whether or not the resulting systems are intentional.

We are led thus to a paradoxical situation: if I simulate you and experience *being you*, then, by definition of what it means *to be you*, I am no longer *me* and therefore cannot answer questions about what it's like *to be me*, since *I am you*. However, if I am *still me* and am simulating *you*, then I am *not really succeeding* at simulating you, since it is *really me* who is responding to questions about *what it is like to be you*. I cannot be me (and only me) at the same time that I am executing computations that bring about you. So there are three possibilities:

(1) Temporally split personalities—P and CP are being time sliced on B.

(2) Spatially split personalities—P and CP reside within different regions of B.

(3) Merged personalities—a new form of consciousness is resident.

In cases 1 and 2, the intentionality you get depends on which portion (or level) of the total system you talk to. That is, there are two distinct, intentional entities resident on the same brain. In case 3, however, we have neither P nor CP, since a merger of both is a form of consciousness (with its corresponding intelligence, knowledge and 'intentionality') that is distinct from either individual consciousness.

So, if B is carrying out CP-creating computations so automatically that we can talk to it (via the Chinese input channel), we cannot deny this intentionality just because later B is carrying out P-creating computations (just as automatically) that create a personality which denies the experience of understanding Chinese. What is confusing is that, in Searle's thought experiment, these alternative personalities switch back and forth rather rapidly, depending on the input channel (written Chinese versus spoken English) and we are naively led by Searle to believe that somehow the P personality is primary. But the brain B that is executing P-creating computations is no more (or less) primary than the same brain B executing CP-creating computations. Furthermore, when imagining carrying out (even *all* of) the complex computations needed to create intentional behavior, why should we be allowed to conclude that no intentionality exists, just because we cannot understand the nature of the intentionality we are bringing into existence? While 'P's brain' B is doing all and *only* those CP-creating computations, then, for that time period, P does not exist. Only CP exists.

If Searle is simulating the Chinese personality *that* automatically, then, during that time period, Searle's intentionality is missing and only that of the Chinese personality exists, so of course Searle will have no insight into what it is like to understand (or be) Chinese.

My own brain right now is taken up (100% of the time, I think) with Dyer-forming computations. I would hate to have Searle deny me *my* experience of being conscious and 'intentional' just because Searle can imagine doing the computations my brain is doing right now and then claim that *he* would still not feel like *me*. If I act as if I am conscious and can argue cogently that I am conscious, then you should accept me as being conscious, no matter what Searle thinks his introspective experience of simulating me would be like.

2.4.   The 'Mere Simulation' Argument
(SA-4)

Consider computer simulations of a car hitting a wall, or the destruction of a building caused by a tornado. Clearly, these simulations are not the same as the real things! Likewise, the simulation of intentionality is not really manifesting intelligence. Since a computer cannot create the actual phenomenon of car accidents or tornadoes, it cannot create the actual phenomenon of intentionality.

2.4.1.   Rebuttal to SA-4
(the 'information processing' reply)

The actions performed by automobiles and tornadoes involve highly specific substances (e.g., air, concrete), so a simulation of a tornado on a computer, where only information *about* the destruction caused by the tornado is modelled, would not be equivalent to the actual tornado (with its whirling air and flying debris, etc.).

However, *if* thought processes consist in the manipulations of *patterns* of substances, then we only need to build a system capable of creating these identical patterns through its physical organization, without requiring exactly the same set of substances. *If* thought is information processing, then the 'simulation' of thought on a computer *would be the same as* thought on a brain, since the same *patterns* would be created (even if they were electromagnetic patterns in the computer and electrochemical patterns in the brain). Remember, the computer, when executing, is producing *patterns of physical things* (which could be photons, electrons or some other stuff). Right now, what differentiates an AI model running on a computer, from a human mind running on a brain, is the nature, complexity and sheer volume of brain patterns. But there is no reason to believe that this difference constitutes any *fundamental* sort of barrier.

Where does intelligence reside? It cannot reside solely in the patterns. It must also reside in the *causal architecture* that gives rise to physical embodiments of those patterns. Why is this the case? Consider a person who videotapes all of the patterns produced by some computer executing some AI system. When he plays these patterns back on a TV monitor, no one would accept that the display sequence of all of these patterns constitutes artificial intelligence, and yet the video camera, in some sense, is 'producing' the same patterns that the AI system was producing! The reason we do not accept the TV stream of patterns as artificially intelligent is the same reason we do not equate a video of a person with the actual person. Namely, the video display is lacking in the underlying physical architecture that gave rise to those patterns in the first place. Only this physical architecture can generate an open-ended set of novel patterns. So the paradigm of AI demands that the *patterns be embodied* in the physical world and produced by causal/physical relationships within some physical system.

A computer is just such a physical device, capable of creating novel patterns based on the causal architecture set up in its physical memory. Two computers that are the exact same model, built by the same manufacturer, are *not* identical when they hold different programs. The reason is that those programs are stored in each computer by making different *physical* changes to the memory circuits of each machine, so each machine ends up with a different *physical* structure, leading it to perform physically in distinct ways. This is why Newel (1980) refers to AI systems as '*physical* symbol systems'. As long as these patterns have some embodiment and recreate the same causal architecture, the substance used to make up these patterns need not be restricted to a particular kind of substance. Ironically, Searle himself (1980a) has argued for the necessity of such a 'causal architecture' while simultaneously rejecting a computer as capable of realizing 'intentionality'.

Consider buildings. The bricks that make up, say, a Gothic church may be made of cement, clay, plastic, ceramics, graphite, or some other substance. As long as each brick can satisfy weight bearing constraints, and as long as each type of brick can be combined to construct the same range of buildings, then what makes a building be in the style of what is called 'a Gothic church' is determined by the way in which the bricks are organized, not in the substance of which each brick is made.

If intentionality (i.e. consciousness, intelligence—Mind in general) arises from the way in which patterns of 'real stuff' interact, then the simulation of intentionality *is the same as* embodying intentionality, because the *'simulation' of information processing on a computer is information processing.* This is the case because a computer is a physical device that manipulates patterns of 'real stuff' to realize information processing.

The working assumption of AI is that Mind is the result of information processing. Given this assumption, simulations of intelligence are not 'mere simulations'—they are the real thing. Since tornadoes, however, are not assumed (here) to consist of information processing, a simulation of a tornado would not be a tornado. At this point, it appears that there is an accumulating body of evidence, indicating that complex, intentional behavior can be realized through information processing. It is up to those who reject the 'mind-is-information-processing' hypothesis to amass any kind of evidence that Mind requires something more.

3.   HARNAD'S ARGUMENTS AND REBUTTALS

Harnad (1989, 1990) accepts SA-3 and thus believes that computers cannot realize 'intentionality'. Given this state of affairs, Harnad then poses questions concerning what is essential to the notion of 'intentionality' and what must be added to computers in order to obtain this 'intentionality'.

3.1.   The 'Chinese Dictionary' Argument (HA-1)

Consider a person trying to learn what Chinese symbols (words) mean by looking at a Chinese dictionary, where each Chinese symbol refers only to lists of other Chinese symbols in the same dictionary. A person will never know what a Chinese symbol means, simply by knowing how it relates to other Chinese symbols, because none of these symbols refer to anything *outside* of the dictionary. Understanding the true meaning of a symbol requires *symbol grounding* —i.e. setting up a physical correspondence between the symbols in the dictionary and actual objects and actions in the real world.

3.1.1.   Rebuttal to HA-1 (the 'internal representations' reply)

In current natural language processing (NLP) systems, words are *not* related directly to each other, but map instead to *internal representations,* which have a correspondence to one another in ways that are analogous to how the real objects (they stand for) relate to one another in the real world. This correspondence does not have to be perfect —only good enough to allow the organism with these representations to perform in the real world, by manipulating these internal representations. If the representations (and computations over them) are in some sense analogous to real objects and actions in the real world, then the organism will have a better chance of surviving. For example, if a real chair has four legs, then the internal representation will include constituents that represent legs. If chairs are made of wood, and pieces of wood can become splinters in someone's skin, then there will be representations for kinds of materials, for pieces of larger objects, for pointed shapes, for penetration by pointed objects that come into contact with them, for coverings (such as skin) of the surface of objects, and so on. For these internal representations to support the kind of visualizations that humans are capable of (e.g. recalling components of an object by examining one's visual memory of an object), they will need to encode spatial dimensions, spatial trajectories, and spatial interactions.

When I recall a chair, I manipulate internal representations of chairs, which contain visual, kinesthetic, and other sensory memories, along with episodic events and generalized facts or abstractions concerning chairs (e.g. when a given chair broke; that people sit on them, etc.). I use these representations to perform tasks related to indicating my understanding of chairs. If the Chinese word for 'chair' maps to such internal representations, and if the system manipulates these representations in ways identical to how my brain manipulates its representations, then there would be no difference between what a system knows and understands about chairs than what I know and understand about chairs.

So while it may be true that relating Chinese symbols to one another will not allow a system to know what a chair (in Chinese) really is, there is no reason to believe that 'chair' must be grounded in the real world. 'Chair' *need only be grounded in internal representations* that allow the system to behave *as if* it has a memory of having seen a real chair. Such a system could then describe in detail (say, in English) what the Chinese word for 'chair' signifies.

3.2.   The 'Transducer' Argument (HA-2)

If one accepts SA-3 as correct, then a way to deal with this argument is to find an additional, necessary component for 'intentionality' and show that Searle is incapable of simulating it. This additional component consists of the sensory and motor transducers that allow a robot to interact with the real world. Now, although Searle can imagine simulating the interpreter and the Chinese room instructions, he *cannot* simulate the sensory and motor transducers, since what these transducers are doing involves energy transformations that are not computational in nature. That is, an arm moving through space is not normally considered a computation, nor is the operation of a photosensitive cell which is transforming light into electrical impulses. If transducers are essential to 'intentionality', then Searle can no longer argue that he is simulating the *entire* system, thus defeating SA-3. Conveniently, these transducers are exactly the components needed to ground the robot in the real world.

A major consequence of this argument is that the Turing Test (TT) is no longer an adequate test of intentionality, since it does not require that a robot perform sensory and motor tasks in the real world. Searle is thus correct (so Harnad's argument goes) in stating that a machine which passes the TT is simply behaving as if it is intentional, but is really lacking intentionality. What is needed instead is the 'Total Turing Test' (TTT), in which the computer must control a robot and the tasks demanded of it include both interactive dialog *and* performance of scene recognition and coordinated physical actions.

3.2.1.   Rebuttal to HA-2
(the 'simulated environment' reply)

First of all, if one accepts the 'split levels' reply to SA-3, then one need not postulate an additional component, such as transducers. Leaving this response aside, however, we can still ask just how crucial transducers are to modeling intentionality and how adequate the TT is.

Transducers are not critical if the robot's *environment* and sensory/motor behaviors are simulated in addition to the robot's brain. Suppose the robot is standing in a room and looking at a chair. The simulation now includes information (to whatever level of detail one requires) concerning the spatial and other physical properties of the chair, along with a simulation of the patterns of information that the robot's real (visual and kinesthetic) transducers would have sent as input to the rest of the robot's brain, if the robot had real transducers and were standing in a real room. As the robot's brain performs computations to move its body, the simulation will calculate how the robot's position in space has changed and then simulate the changing visual and kinesthetic patterns that the robot's brain will receive as input (identical to those patterns that the real transducers would have sent to the robot, had it really moved about in a real room). In this manner, the robot's brain can be grounded in an environment, but without requiring a real environment or the (supposedly) noncomputational features of real transducers. The simulated environment may or may not have a physics identical to the physics of the real world. But no matter what physics are simulated, the simulated robot will be grounded (and performing a TTT) in that environment, and *without transducers.*

How crucial is the TTT to testing 'intentionality'? A more careful examination of the standard TT reveals that it is adequate to the task of testing symbol grounding. Remember, the testers can ask *any* questions via the teletypes, including those intended to test symbol grounding. For example:

> 'Imagine you are holding an apple in your hand. How does it feel if you rub it against your cheek?'

> 'Recall when you last splashed water in the tub. You cup your hand more and hit the water faster. How does the sound change? What happens to the water?'

> 'I assume you are wearing clothing. Right now, pull your shirt up and hold it with your chin. Describe how much of your stomach is uncovered'.

> 'Try to touch the left side of your face with your right hand, by first placing your right hand behind your neck and then bringing your hand around, while moving your face toward your hand. How much of your face can you touch by doing this?'

These questions require a computer to have internal representations that allow it either (a) to control an actual robot body to perform these sensory/motor tasks, (b) to simulate them in a simulated world, or (c) to imagine them via mental simulation in a robot's memory. Such tasks are a more adequate test of 'intentionality' than merely observing a robot perform coordinated activities in the real world. A dog or cat can perform exquisite feats of sensory/motor behavior and yet they do not have 'intentionality' (i.e. they do not know that they know). By having the robot respond in natural language, it must not only mentally relate representations of visual/kinesthetic memories and experiences, but also understand language descriptions *about* such experiences. Thus, although the TTT is a useful, final proof of robot coordination and mobility, the TT is perfectly adequate to the task of testing symbol grounding.

3.3. The 'Noncomputational Brain' Argument (HA-3)

If one concludes that symbol grounding via transducers is a crucial element of 'intentional' systems, then it becomes a crucial observation that the entire brain consists simply of layers and layers of transducers. That is, each neuron is a transducer that is essentially noncomputational in nature. The brain consists of billions of such analog and analog-to-digital devices that each performs energy transformations, which are fundamentally noncomputational in nature. If we look for computations in any layer of the brain, we will not find any, only projections to other transducers. Thus, it may not be that just the input (sensory) and output (motor) layers are noncomputational transducers; the entire brain is noncomputational.

3.3.1. Rebuttal to HA-3 (the 'noncomputational computer' reply)

A computer *also* consists of a great many transducers. Each circuit element is a transducer, that transforms energy in an analog and analog-to-digital manner. By using HA-3, one can argue that the *computer itself is noncomputational*, since the input (keyboard) is a transducer and it simply projects to other transducers (e.g. transistors), and so on, until projecting to the output, display device (also a transducer). But this observation is simply that the computer is a physical entity, and that, like the brain, obeys the laws of physics. It is an amazing fact that AI systems can exhibit Mind-like behavior without violating any physical laws. That is, the I/O level acts intelligently while the transducers, that make up the machine, inexorably behave according to physical laws. For this point of view, there is no magic (no dualism; no 'ghost' in the machine), other than the (often counterintuitive) emergent properties of the entire system, through the interactions of its many components.

The reason we speak of a computer as 'computing' is that it is manipulating patterns of physical stuff (energy/matter) in ways such that one pattern, through causal relationships, brings about other physical patterns in systematic ways. But the brain can be described as consisting of noncomputational transducers that are doing exactly the same kinds of things. Thus, the brain is as computational (or noncomputational) as is the computer, depending on how one wants to look at it.

4. MIND, LIFE, MATTER, AND COMPUTATIONALISM

Throughout this paper we have assumed that a *computation* is the creation and manipulation of physical patterns in a physical device with a causal architecture, such that the novel patterns produced are determined by the physical patterns already resident in the device. The working assumption of 'Strong AI' is that (a) Mind emerges from the brain's computations and (b) that Mind emerges in computers to the extent that they perform similar computations.

The recent disputes, between connectionism and traditional AI (Pinker and Mehler 1988; Dyer 1988, 1991; Graubard 1988; Smolensky 1988), are not disputes over the fundamental computational power of these approaches, since any neural network (whether chemically based, optically based, etc.) can be simulated by a modern computer (and therefore by a Turing Machine). Rather, they are disputes over which approaches offer the most appropriate languages and metaphors for describing cognition.

The position of *computationalism* is that the notion of computation is powerful enough to describe, not only Mind, but Life and Matter also. Below are two final arguments against computationalism, with rebuttals.

4.1. The 'Intentionality Presumes Life' Argument (SA-5)

Digestion consists of complicated biochemicals interacting in a 'wet' and 'goopey' environment, totally unlike the insides of a computer. This 'goopeyness' is a major reason why a computer cannot realize digestion. Likewise, the brain consists of neurotransmitters and complex biochemical materials. It is normally assumed that Mind is only *loosely coupled* to the living processes ongoing in the neural cells, dendritic aborizations, blood and other chemical life-support processes to the cellular structures of the brain. The assumption is that the life processes, while they keep the cells alive, are not involved in the computations that bring about Mind. What if, however, the 'life-state' of each cell is *intimately* involved in the embodiment of Mind in the brain? What if Mind is more like digestion than like computation? In such a case, Mind would be impossible to embody in a computer.

4.1.1.   Rebuttal to SA-5
(the 'artificial life correspondence' reply)

This 'cognition is digestion' argument hinges on the biochemistry that is essential in digestion, and that is assumed to be essential in the cognitive aspects of brain function. If the biochemistry of life is somehow essential to cognition, then SA-5 can be rephrased as: 'A prerequisite for a system to have intentionality is that it must first be alive'. Two major issues are raised by this kind of argument: 'What is Life?' and 'Is an intelligent-acting robot alive?'

At first glance, there appear to be two levels at which Life arises in natural systems: (a) the population level—involving recombination, cloning, mutation, natural selection, etc., and (b) the metabolic level—involving cellular activities, including digestion, growth, healing, embryonic development, etc. A computer-controlled metallic robot R then would be 'alive', from a population point of view, only to the extent that there existed a population of related robots, capable of reproduction, mutation, and so on. Likewise, R would be 'alive', from a metabolic perspective, only to the extent that there were cellular processes going on.

But defining 'life' turns out to be as difficult as defining 'intentionality'. The last member of the Dodo species would still be considered 'alive', even though a population of Dodos no longer exists. Even a metallic, computer-controlled robot can be viewed as having some kind of a metabolism, since it consumes energy and expends heat in order to sense its environment and move.

Historically, vitalists in biology argued that a special 'life force' distinguished living creatures from dead ones. Today, biologists view life as a systems phenomenon, arising from the complex interaction of millions of chemical and molecular elements. Theoretically, therefore, life could arise in other than carbon-based materials. Recently, a new field, called 'Artificial Life (AL)' has been gaining momentum, in which *artificial* physics–including chemical, cellular, genetic and evolutionary environments–are being modelled with computers (Langton 1988). The following question then arises: 'Could AL systems ever 'really' be alive?' This question is analogous to 'Could AI systems ever 'really' be intelligent or intentional?'

Suppose the firing of a neuron *is* tightly coupled to a neuron's metabolism. Suppose that this metabolism is the result of how chains of molecules twist and fold in upon one another, mediated by numerous enzymes. Now let us imagine that we replace each molecule with a binary representation of all aspects of its three-dimensional topology and chemistry. These binary representations will be enormously large, in comparison to the size of the actual molecular chain, but they will still be finite in size. That is, there will be a *systematic correspondence* between real molecular chains and these binary representations. Suppose we now also build a program that simulates all of the laws of molecular-chemical interaction. This program may be computationally extremely expensive, but again, there will be a systematic correspondence: between manipulations of binary representations by the program and the real twists and turns of interacting chains of real molecules. Such a simulation would allow one to discover how molecules interact without having to use actual molecules. *If* one defines Life as a systems phenomenon, then AL systems are 'really' alive, in that they involve the same level of causal relatedness among correspondingly complex representations, even though the materials of which these representations consist are completely different in substance. As Langton (1988) states:

> Life is a property of form, not matter, a result of the organization of matter rather than something that inheres in the matter itself. Neither nucleotides nor amino acids nor any other carbon-chain molecule is alive—yet put them together in the right way, and the dynamic behavior that emerges out of their interactions is what we call life (p. 41).

At this point, terminology and assumptions become all important. *If* we define the term 'alive' to mean *only* what systems of actual molecules do, then AL systems are clearly not 'alive' in this sense, since we have already precluded the ability to apply the term in this way. If, however, we define 'alive' to mean physical patterns of interaction that are systematic in certain ways (e.g. can be placed in causal correspondence and exhibit the same levels of complexity), then the term 'alive' *will* apply to such AL systems.

It is interesting to note that the arguments that are beginning to emerge within the AL community, concerning whether or not such systems will ever 'really' realize Life, are following a parallel line of development in relation to arguments concerning whether or not AI systems will ever 'really' realize intelligence, consciousness, or 'intentionality'. As one might expect, some of the initial arguments against AL systems ever realizing 'true' Life rely heavily on Searle's and Harnad's arguments (e.g. see Pattee 1988).

4.2.   The 'Unsimulatable World' Argument (HA-4)

What if each neuron's behavior is intimately affected by what is happening down to the quark level, i.e. to the bottom-most level of the physics of reality? There must be some point at which computationalists give up. Assume for example that a computer can simulate physics down to the quantum level. A simulation of gold in the computer will still not have the value of real gold. Since the real brain exists in the real world, and since the real world is unsimulatable, therefore the real brain cannot be replaced by a computer simulation.

4.2.1.   The 'nonclassical measurement' reply

Recently, Fields (1989) has argued that, if one gives up computationalism, then one must abandon nonclassical (i.e. quantum) physics. Continuous measurement to an infinite level of precision is not allowed in nonclassical physics, due to the effect that measurement has on the phenomena being observed. Once continuous functions of infinite precision are no longer allowed, then any arbitrary level of finite precision can be simulated by a Turing Machine. Thus, reality itself can be simulated. Now, it is true that one will still value real gold much more highly than simulated gold (even if one can simulate accurately the melting, gravitational pull, decay and other (sub)atomic properties of the simulated gold), but that is because social convention determines that only the real gold is an acceptable object for currency. If one imagines that simulated gold were chosen as a form of currency, then perhaps those with access to the most complex hardware would be the richest individuals in this hypothetical society. That is, social convention can only determine the social status of an object, not its other properties; otherwise, we could determine whether or not machines 'really' think by taking a vote.

While it may be difficult to imagine reality itself being simulated by a Turing Machine, with its state transitions and paper tape, it is not quite as difficult to imagine reality being simulated by some massively parallel computer (MPC). For example, suppose future physicists complete the development of a 'grand unified theory' of reality, where reality is composed of minuscule, space/time units and where different forms of matter/energy consist of different configurations of state values in minuscule space/time units and their interactions with neighboring space/time units. Then such a reality (even with chaos effects, non-locality properties, etc.) could be simulated on an MPC in an isomorphic relation to reality, as long as a systematic correspondence were maintained between MPC processors and one or more space/time units and their physical laws of interaction. It might take an MPC with, say, 10^{16} very fast processors an entire year of computation to simulate (for just a few time units) a tiny segment of this 'artificial reality', but the simulation would maintain complete fidelity, in the sense that the results of any 'artificial reality' experiments would conform completely with their corresponding direct, physical experiments. This hypothetical MPC is ultimately simulatable on a Turing Machine because each element/process of the MPC itself can be placed in correspondence with a state (or set of states) of the Turing Machine's tape symbols and state transitions.

This approach is reasonable only if reality is not continuous (i.e. infinite) at every point of space/time. As Fields argues, the non-classical (i.e.

noncontinuous) paradigm within physics has become more and more accepted within this century and recent results within physics indicate that this paradigm will remain robust for the foreseeable future. For a more detailed discussion of the 'non-classical measurement' reply, see Fields (1989).

5.   CONCLUSIONS

The working hypothesis of AI, connectionism, and cognitive science in general is that Mind (i.e. intelligence, intentionality, consciousness, perception of pain, etc.) arises from the way in which simple processing elements, each of which lacks Mind, can be *organized* in such a way as to exhibit Mind.

The extent to which cognitive scientists can build a convincing system with intentional behavior is ultimately an *empirical and political issue,* rather than philosophical one. That is, once systems exhibit intentional behavior, either they will convince humans to accept them as being intentional, or they will have to fight humans for their civil rights.

Postulating a special 'intentionality' in people—that *in principle* cannot exist in computing machinery—is similar to reactions in the past by others unhappy with theories that reduce mankind's sense of self importance. For example: (a) The Copernican revolution replaced man from being at the center of the universe; (b) the Darwinian revolution removed man from holding a special biological position in the animal kingdom; (c) genetic theory and molecular biochemistry eliminated the notion of 'vitalism' as a special substance separating living systems from dead matter. The notion of 'intentionality' as residing in the substances of the brain is now serving the same purpose as that served by 'vitalism' for 19th century scientists alarmed by reduction of life to the 'mere' organization of matter.

Before we abandon computationalism and the systems assumption for what appears to be a form of 'cognitive vitalism', we need truly convincing arguments (i.e. that nonbiological machines lack intentionality). Until then, if a computational entity acts like it knows what it is talking about, then we should treat it as such. This kind of a pragmatic approach will keep us from mistreating all alien forms of intelligence, whether they are the result of evolution (or of artificial intelligence and neural network research) on our own planet or within other distant solar systems.

6. REFERENCES

Alvarado, S. J. (1989) Understanding editorial text: a computer model of argument comprehension. Ph.D. Dissertation. Computer Science Department, UCLA.

Dyer, M. G. (1983) *In-Depth Understanding* (Cambridge, MA: MIT Press).

Dyer, M. G. (1988) The promise and problems of connectionism. *Behavioral and Brain Sciences,* 11(1): 32-33.

Dyer, M. G. (1991) Symbolic neuroengineering for natural language processing: a multilevel research approach. In J. A. Barnden and J. B. Pollack (eds.) *High-Level Connectionist Models* (Norwood, NJ: Ablex), 32-86.

Fields, C. (1989) Consequences of nonclassical measurement for the algorithmic description of continuous dynamical systems. *Journal of Experimental and Theoretical Artificial Intelligence,* 1: 171-178.

Graubard, S. R. (ed.) (1988) *The Artificial Intelligence Debate* (Cambridge, MA: MIT Press).

Harnad, S. (1989) Minds, machines and Searle. *Journal of Experimental and Theoretical Artificial Intelligence,* 1: 5-25.

Harnad, S. (1990) The symbol grounding problem. *Physica D,* 42: 335-346.

Langton, C. (ed.) (1988) *Artificial Life* (Reading, MA: Addison-Wesley).

Lehnert, W. (1978) *The Process of Question Answering* (Hillsdale, NJ: Lawrence Erlbaum).

Minsky, M. (1985) A framework for representing knowledge. In R. J. Brachman and H. J. Levesque (eds.) *Readings in Knowledge Representation* (Los Altos, CA: Morgan Kaufmann).

Minsky, M. (1986) *The Society of Mind* (New York: Simon and Schuster).

Newell, A. (1980) Physical symbol systems. *Cognitive Science,* 4(2): 135-183.

Pattee, H. H. (1988) Simulations, realizations and theories of life. In C. Langton (ed.) *Artificial Life* (Reading, MA: Addison-Wesley), 63–77.

Pinker, S., and Mehler, J. (1988) *Connections and Symbols* (Cambridge, MA: MIT Press).

Schank, R. C., and Abelson R. P. (1977) *Scripts, Plans, Goals, and Understanding* (Hillsdale, NJ: Lawrence Erlbaum).

Searle, J. R. (1980a) Minds, brains and programs. *Behavioral and Brain Sciences,* 3(3): 417-424.

Searle, J. R. (1980b) Intrinsic intentionality. *Behavioral and Brain Sciences,* 3(3): 450-457.

Searle, J. R. (1982a) The Chinese room revisited. *Behavioral and Brain Sciences,* 5(2): 345-348.

Searle, J. R. (1982b) The myth of the computer. *New York Review of Books,* 29(7): 3–7.

Searle, J. R. (1982c) The myth of the computer: an exchange. *New York Review of Books,* 29(11): 56-57.

Searle, J. R. (1985a) Patterns, symbols and understanding. *Behavioral and Brain Sciences,* 8: 742-743.

Searle, J. R. (1985b) *Minds, Brains and Science* (Cambridge, MA: Harvard University Press).

Searle, J. R. (1989) Does cognitive science rest on a mistake? Presentation to the Cognitive Science Research Program, UCLA, 17 November.

Smolensky, P. (1988) On the proper treatment of connectionism. *Behavioral and Brain Sciences,* 11(1): 1-23.

Turing, A. M. (1964) Computing machinery and intelligence. In A. R. Anderson (ed.) *Minds and Machines* (Engelwood Cliffs, NJ: Prentice-Hall).

Wilensky, R. (1983) *Planning and Understanding* (Reading, MA: Addison-Wesley).

Putting One's Foot in One's Head—Part II: How?

Donald Perlis

1. INTRODUCTION

This is the second of a two-part work on intentional states. My thesis is that an *internal* notion of reference is far more salient for philosophy of mind and language, as well as for artificial intelligence, than is the usual external one, and that the former provides a key to the latter. This involves in a central way the embedding of the thinking agent in a causal physical environment, and thus has much in common with functionalist views. However, it also involves a self-referential feature that can be brought to bear on the subjective (narrow or individualist) character of thought, as well as on the problem of error, and which provides the aforementioned key between internal and external reference.

I*n Part I: Why* of the broader work (Perlis 1991b), I argued the need for (and suggested an account of) internal reference, as part of any successful theory of external reference. Here I take up issues left aside in *Part I*. In particular, I focus on *how* a meaning agent can accomplish tasks of external reference (largely via internal reference). My proposal is a combination of several others well-discussed in the literature—covariant, historical, imagist, and description-theoretic—plus

Thinking Computers and Virtual Persons
edited by Eric Dietrich
ISBN 0-12-215495-9

some new features (involving self-reference and some modest insights from neurophysiology).

In the "prequel" (*Part I* of the broader work), much was said about *why* it is important to have an inner world model, including a model of the external referential relation itself, in any entity that purports to have intentional states. However, little was said there as to *how* this might be accomplished, i.e., how it contributes to an account of *external* reference. In this current work (*Part II* of the longer work) I will address this matter and propose a specific architecture toward that end. This architecture should be viewed as an addition onto the familiar functionalist architecture and not a departure from its basic conceptual framework.[1]

I will attempt to provide an account of external reference along the following lines: an external object R is related to the meaner (reasoning agent) P in much the same way that the notional object Rp is related to P's self-notion Pp.[2] Thus we introduce a self-notion in part for this purpose. The basic (easiest) case is that in which R is part of P's body (e.g., R is P's foot). Then the "in much the same way that" allusion two sentences above can be given physiological force via the actual pathways between foot and brain (e.g., leading to the tectum). Once we have a semblance of body meaning along these lines, we can try to extend it further outward by a kind of "body geometry." (In this we are not far from the spirit of Johnson 1987.)

First, I remind the reader of some of the main points from *Part I*, concerning *iref* (internal reference) and how it is intended to fit into a larger framework of *eref* (external reference). Figure 9.1 shows a sketch of the theory of internal reference given in *Part I*. There the symbol S is some internal token, which (we wish to explicate) somehow has content R external to the reasoning agent P. This occurs in two parts: *iref* maps S to another internal entity Rp, which is the reasoner's version of R (i.e., in the reasoner's worldview or scene), and R is the actual external object that Rp corresponds to (via a relation called *eref*). I won't go into why the internal architecture is proposed; this is dealt with in detail in *Part I*.

The point is that, in order for the reasoner P to refer (as opposed to merely intone, say) when she says "S," she must have something in mind that she means (in *Part I* this is called the Generalized Kripke Condition). The latter thing-in-mind is Rp. Yet for this to have any external content, there must actually be some external thing, R, that S and P and Rp somehow are suitably related to.[3] The remainder of this chapter is devoted to an account of this latter relationship (*eref*). My account will treat *eref* as dependent upon *iref* in a crucial way. The upshot will be an account that can be given the following formal dress:

$$content_p(S) = eref_P(iref_p(S)) = erefP(Rp) = R$$

That is, the content of the symbol S as used by P, is the external correlate R of that which P takes S to mean (Rp). Just how a canonical external correlate may (sometimes) be singled out is the major brunt of the argument to follow.

Figure 9.1. Elementary model of *iref* and *eref*.

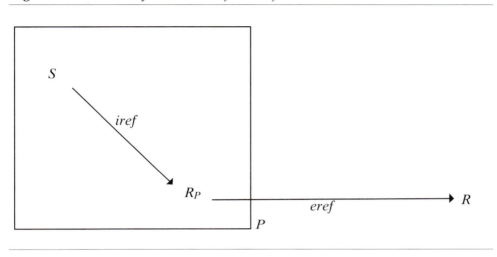

A question that naturally arises is what good is the extra layer of tokens; why not just as well go right from *S* to *R*? There are several reasons for this, discussed at length in *Part I*. But for our present purposes, it is especially important to recall one of them: error recognition and correction. If a reasoner is to be able, at times, to come to believe that a prior belief or view (*V*) of his may have been in error, then he needs a way to represent that belief or view as an object (a former belief) and state of affairs *A* it supposedly described, and also the newly believed information to the effect that there is a discrepancy between *A* and *V*: *V* is (contrary to prior belief) not reality. In terms of our notation, for instance, if *S* is the word *dog* then the belief that *Rp* is a dog may later come under suspicion and be replaced by a belief that *R p* is really a fox but appeared to be a dog at first. This is treated in Section 5.

2. SOME RELATED IDEAS

2.1. *Dealing with Putnam's Internal Realism*

Putnam (1981, 1987) argues that objective accounts of meaning must fail, and he proposes instead an "internal realism" that seems to correspond to the "subjective inner view" that each individual has, as we might say, of "the world," although Putnam is denying that there is any one correct match between these inner views and the outer world. As a consequence, says Putnam, our words can never be (in any robust sense) genuinely about external things. We can refer only to internal things, things in our views.

If Putnam is right, we can't be a brain at all, not even in a body! Our internal meanings do not pertain to things outside, such as our bodies out there. Our notion of body is "in here" in the sensorium, the mental space our minds inhabit. So to us, according to Putnam, *body* cannot mean something out there beyond our thoughts; all our thoughts mean things in our world of thoughts. This is much more than the mere thesis that there is a *puzzle* about how internal things like thoughts get tied to external things like tables and chairs. The latter is a recognized hard problem, sometimes called Brentano's problem, and is usually taken as something to try to solve. But Putnam is presenting an argument that purports to show there *can be* no solution to Brentano's problem: it is folly to think our thoughts get mapped outside in any coherent, objective way, he says. This is a very radical thesis. It seems to require giving up the standard scientific view of an objective external reality about which we think.

What does our *iref*/*eref* distinction have to say about it? We will need to elaborate our account of *eref* before a clear statement can be made, but in rough form it is as follows. Putnam's argument involves some considerations that apply to *iref*, and others to *eref*. His argument uses the following criterion that is supposed to apply to any possible theory of meaning: the meaning of a sentence depends crucially on the meanings of its parts (words). That is, we cannot in general alter the words (or their meanings) without altering the meaning of the whole sentence (in at least some way). This criterion is sometimes called "compositionality." Putnam argues that in fact nearly *arbitrary* changes in any purported external word meaning can be allowed and yet preserve sentence meaning, thus violating compositionality.

Now, *iref* does obey compositionality, and it does indeed provide a way to link symbol to symboled. If we make a sentence using symbols, the (*iref*) meaning of the whole will reflect the (*iref*) meanings of the individual symbols. However, the (*iref*) meaning here is determined by the user (this is what *iref* amounts to), and so any change in word (*iref*) meaning will in general change the overall internal user meaning of sentences having those words. This is so since *iref* maintains the reference relation in an internal structure, not in some unreachable external world. If the meaning of *foot* is changed, it is changed because the user has so changed it, i.e., she has decided to now take *foot* to refer to, say, her hand (as construed by her in her inner view of her limbs).

Where Putnam's claims have force is in the case of *eref*. If we readjust the agent's world so that in fact *erefp*(*foot p*) is no longer the agent's foot, and similarly for *hand* p, say, it is possible *à la* Putnam to get a sentence such as "my hand is on my foot" to have the same *eref*-erential meaning as before the readjustment. But the readjustment is a matter of engineering the way the agent fits into the world (e.g., rewiring the agent's nervous tissue between brain and limbs) and does not in itself affect what the words mean to the agent (i.e., does not affect *iref*). This may be in part Putnam's point: (the compositional part of) reference is internal. But he ignores the possibility of a robust external component that allows for an objective external referent after all, but that is not (and has no need to be) compositional. *Eref* accounts for what links between (internal) mind and (external) world make the former's behavior fit well into (survival in) the latter.

What an external account is, then, is evidential. We do not pin down an external (*eref*) account for certain. We make educated guesses and rely on evidence to provide us with more or less confidence in our theories about externals. I will provide below an external account that is in rough accord with common sense (I claim), but certainly is not to be regarded as an *ultimate* determination of external reference. Indeed, there may well be no such ultimate determination, for our concepts may in large measure be usefully related to the external world only at a special human-sized scale. But this is no mark against such an account of meaning. We can indeed mean tables by *table* even though a sufficiently detailed account of matter may convince us that instead of "real" tables there are gyrating conglomerations of atoms held together loosely by potential force fields, that merely look table-ish to us. Certainly the modern notion of tables has undergone considerable change from older views of tables as solid homogeneous masses. Yet people back then surely did refer, as much as we do now, by the word *table*, in the sense that their behavior calls for an explanation pretty much the same as ours. The discovery of atoms did not surely, suddenly, and totally alter the basic nature of language and mind.

We form theories as to an external world. These theories are internal. We revise then as we get more data. This is true both in everyday life and in the technical realm of science. The revision process is a complex one, in which we "reflect" our own processes into a more subtle representation of our thinking.

The extent to which an external reality may or may not actually correspond to our thoughts is not one we have means to ascertain except tentatively by a kind of educated guesswork. However, we do have by our own lights a variety of tools to decide if our theories are adequate in terms of what we know and expect of them and our data. Moreover, these tools include measurements, and measurements implicitly involve interaction with the environment. It is this interaction that is the basis for the theory of external reference (*eref*) that I will develop below.

Relative to a viewpoint, we can determine *eref* and hence content. This is Putnam's point, in a way. But we alter our viewpoint as we get new data—the viewpoint is in part honed by us to be useful, succinct, to fit the data into packages we can deal with. We can even often get away with the pretense that there is a single stable scientific viewpoint within which we carry on our theoretical discussion of mind and language.

2.2.   *Fodor's Long Way Around;*
         Thought Ascription

Fodor (1987, 1990) has been working long and hard on Brentano's problem, insisting on a rigorous mentalism: he takes beliefs and other cognitive states seriously, thinks they are real indeed, and also that they nevertheless are quite naturalistic events, ultimately explainable in nonmentalist (and objective) terms. However, his efforts also tend to have large doses of distality in them. Instead of looking squarely at behavior, he looks elsewhere to get a side view through counterfactual glasses, based in part on the distal (causal-historical) theory of Kripke (1980). By "distal" I mean an account that focuses mainly on external reference, with relative neglect of internal reference. By contrast, a proximal approach looks more closely at internal workings of the mind, and in particular at the internal referents of symbols.

There is a clear appeal to distal approaches. We know little about the mind *per se*; and many different mental operations would seem to be able to be "about" the same external object—so different, in fact, that it seems clear no one account of the mental could possibly capture cleanly all kinds of thoughts about ducks, say. To understand this, we need to break down duck-thoughts into two types.

One type of duck-thought is *ascribed* duck-thought: we say of someone else that she is thinking about a duck; this even though she may not know the word duck or even have a concept at all similar to our duck concept. She may be thinking of a particular bird flying overhead that happens to be a duck (unknown to her). We still can fairly say that she is thinking about a duck, but nothing in her brain (or mind) has anything to do with a duck-concept (we shall suppose). So far, so good. In this ascriptive sense, it will be impossible to give an internal (individualist) account of which thoughts are duck-thoughts. However, this is not what we really want to do anyway. Ascribed duck-thoughts are things for our benefit and are not very revealing about the person to whom duck-thoughts are ascribed. This is the same point I make in *Part I*: if we want to understand P's behavior, it is P's view we need to analyze, not ours.

The other kind of duck-thought is one that is a duck-thought to P herself. This is determined by her (*iref*) use of the word *duck*. Here there seems every reason to believe that all thoughts that are duck-thoughts to P have something in common in her brain. After all, they are all identified by her as "duck-thoughts."[4]

2.3. *Qua Problem*

The *qua* problem is as follows: does *foot* mean my whole foot or just part of it? (This also is the famous problem of indeterminism, Quine 1953.) But as far as *iref* is concerned, there seems to be an easy answer. *Foot* means whatever is actually tagged (*foot*$_P$) by the tag "foot" in my mental space (i.e., tagged by the *iref* relation). This sheds some light on *iref*: the tagging should be viewed not merely as a matter of tying a string to R_P with a card at the other end having the tag S written on it.[5] Rather, the entire taggee R_P should "light up" when the S tag (or button?) is pulled (pushed?). That which is lighted is then the whole internal referent of the tag.[6] We can then extend this to external reference (*eref*) by the means to be presented below.

Now, this is an easy case, for we have been dealing only with singular terms (names). What about *feet* as a kind term? Does it apply only to feet or to any bodily appendages? Again, we can tell by seeing how it is used internally with respect to parts of the inner homunculus. And again, the meaner (P) has control over this. She can decide to use *feet* to refer to appendages if she wants. Then not only *foot*$_P$ but also *hand*$_P$ will light up in her mental space whenever the "feet" tag is invoked.

2.4. *McCarthy Machines*

McCarthy has offered an example to illustrate the precarious nature of intentionality.[7] I will present the example and then turn it around to argue against the Dennett–McCarthy intentional stance.

McCarthy's example (altered, but in the spirit of the original) is as follows. Suppose that a machine is constructed so that whenever one or more persons are nearby it does a quick scan of their DNA pattern (with futuristic technology), and if that pattern matches a fixed one that had been randomly selected and kept in its database years ago, then it loudly intones "Get him!" and releases a robot that grabs whoever is present. Suppose further that the stored DNA pattern is exactly mine and no one else's. Is it the case then that the machine's intoning "Get him!" *means* me? Is the term *mean* here a significant theoretical concept or a bit of fluff that we can dispense with? I think in this example it is fluff. All that is significant, all that there is to the matter, is that if I do not remove myself quickly from the neighborhood, I will be captured. The machine is a DNA pattern recognizer with a subsidiary grabber: that tells the whole story. Whether we call that meaning or not is immaterial. It tells us nothing new to say that the machine's use of *him* is symbolic of me. The intonation of "Get him" results from a certain DNA pattern triggering a highly predictable sequence of actions, that is all. McCarthy and Dennett, I think, would agree with this. We can say that the machine means me, if we wish; it is convenient to talk that way but reveals nothing about the machine in itself. On the other hand, if my identical twin comes by, the machine will treat him the same as me, so it seems misleading to say the machine really means me, specifically, by *him*.

However, there are cases in which it is not immaterial at all, but central to the events, and in fact is necessary to understand what is happening. These are cases of the genuine use of symbols as symbols, i.e., for the purpose of standing in for something else. Now, how do purposes get in here? And what good are stand-ins? Macbeth's dagger is a good example.[8] The dagger percept is not a dagger, and he knows this. What he wonders is whether there is a real dagger that is giving him the dagger percept. That is, he knows the percept is not the real thing, whereas McCarthy's machine has no such information or ability to process it (unless it is constructed so as to have these, in which case it then is using symbols as symbols).

Yet Macbeth is in certain ways similar to the McCarthy machine. He too does a comparison of input (DNA pattern or dagger pattern) to stored data (DNA pattern or dagger pattern). The difference is in whether any relating is done to a "presumed external entity," i.e., whether the machine has a world model in which its own processing is represented as part of that model and potentially external things as other parts of that model, with the capability of representing error. Only then is it representing a stand-in relation i.e., a meaning relation, a difference between its percept (the input DNA pattern) and what it takes to be the external cause (me, say).

Now, to fulfill McCarthy's original scenario, none of this sophistication of double representation (of separating the thought or symbol from the thing thought about or symbolized) is needed. And for the same reason, that machine cannot question whether it got the wrong person: it has no mechanism to distinguish people (or DNA or daggers) from its data patterns that we would regard as being about people (or DNA or daggers). If the pattern matches, then that is that; there is no notion, for it, of there being an error in the scanner that read the DNA pattern, i.e., that the real DNA being scanned has a different pattern from that which is being read as input.[9] It has nothing with respect to which there can be an error: no inner model providing what for it would be a correct outcome that can fail to occur.

On the other hand, a more sophisticated version of the machine, as hinted at two paragraphs earlier, might indeed be able to detect what it would regard as errors; for instance, if the robot cannot grab anyone despite the pattern match, it has the internal representational material to formulate the notion that there is no external cause of the pattern, that it is an illusion, or that the external cause is nevertheless not the person with the indicated DNA pattern, because of a processing error.

It is instructive to consider three kinds of McCarthy machines. The first, $McMac_1$, merely has a DNA pattern matcher and a robot hand that grabs in a wide sweep, catching whoever is close by. To escape is easy: simply stand beyond the range of the hand-sweep. The second, $McMac_2$, also has the pattern matcher and, in addition, a mobile robot that chases in the direction of any detected human-sized objects. To escape $McMac_2$ we need to get out of its sight. But if it catches us we will not be released, even if we are not the person whose DNA triggered the operation. $McMac_3$, however, has a robot that is cleverer still. It reanalyzes the DNA of everything it grabs, and it may decide it got the wrong guy. $McMac_3$, I suggest, will have a far richer behavioral repertoire, enough so that we will want to use different terminology in describing it. Indeed, I just did: $McMac_3$ is capable of getting the wrong guy. Note that I do not mean "wrong" in the sense of the intent of $McMac_3$'s *designer*, but wrong by $McMac_3$'s own lights.[10] To be able to decide that it got the wrong guy, $McMac_3$ must have a notion of the distinction between its (former) thought that this is the right guy and its (present) changed view that this after all is someone other than the person sought. Thus this is *iref*. And such a machine is structurally different from, and more sophisticated than, the more rigid $McMac_1$ and $McMac_2$.

Why cannot $McMac_1$ simply have a further piece of its program that rechecks the DNA of each captured individual and lets him go if it is not the same as the stored one? Surely this can be the case, without all the fancy machinery I am requiring for $McMac_3$. But what such a souped-up $McMac_1$ (or $McMac_2$) could not do is to begin to suspect, after several false captures, that the DNA reader on its robot needs to have its lens cleaned or replaced. That is, it has no means to represent that its reasoning or information is at fault—different from external reality—and hence no means to initiate recalibration (more on this below).

3.   BODY REFERENCE

In this section I present the bare bones of my theory of *eref*, in a restricted case: namely, the "external" referent of a token is part of the reasoner's own body. The reason for this is as follows: it is tempting to say that the relationship between Rp

and an external R is to be found by considering first the relationship between R and P and looking for the same sort of relationship between Rp and Pp. This is especially suggestive in light of our insistence in *Part I* that the reasoner, P, must have an inner model of herself (Pp), as well of her surroundings, if she is to have beliefs about these. For a picture, see Figure 9.2. Thus to get from Rp to R, we find how to get from Rp to Pp, and then use the same process in reverse starting from P to get to R.

Figure 9.2. One's inner model.

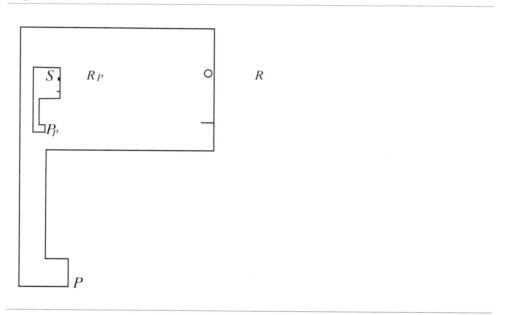

In the form of an algebraic ratio, we have Pp is to Rp as P is to R. The trouble is that there is no obvious metric by which the "Pp to Rp" relation is given. Our task is then to find such a metric. This appears to be easier when R is itself a part of P's body. Then later we can see how this might be extended beyond the body to distant objects. But even when R is a body part, how can we explicate an inner relation that is like an outer (bodily) one? Pictures surely will not do. While a definitive answer will be a true feat of neuroengineering, I think that at least a plausible outline can be developed. And, in a way, pictures are the key. For whatever our minds do, they can conjure up in the mind's eye inner representations that we use to get around with.

3.1.   The Inner Metric

We will take one simple example. Suppose the word *foot* plays the role of our symbol S above. Then R will be P's actual foot, and we seek an account of the relation between these two, via P's inner foot notion, what we might write as *foot* $_P$. Again a picture is instructive; see Figure 9.3. *foot* p is a sort of "footunculus," to be discussed more below. We thus focus on a situation that is hard-wired into our bodies, namely, self-perception. Consider what it is to refer to one's foot. One has the name *foot* (or whatever or however one chooses to call or token it) and also the internal foot, that is, the thing we take (in our mental space) to be the foot. Now, the former, the symbol (say, *foot*) is under our control. We can instead employ *pied* or *shmoot* or anything we like. But our bodies/brains provide us with a hard-wired footunculus that is created as a result of wiring between the brain and (you guessed it) the actual foot extremity itself.[11]

Figure 9.3. The foot in one's head.

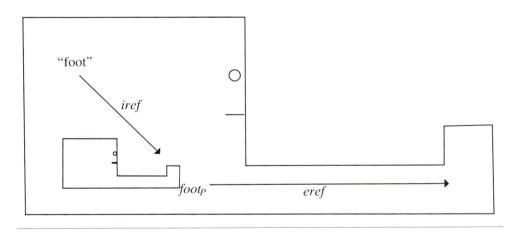

Note that *foot* p is not the word *foot*, nor is it the equivalent mentalese of *foot*. *foot* p is the visio-proprioceptive "reliable sign" of P's foot in P's head. This latter tie is not *iref*, it is *eref*. Note also that not merely feet but much of one's body is so mapped via the nervous system to an inner homunculus (actually several homunculi, which we ignore here). These inner bracketed body parts can then be named by us (attended to as "this part" and "that part") and thus thought about. Whenever we "think about our foot" we are invoking or activating a relation between our footunculus and some name or other ostensive tag that—among other things—declares our attention to it. It is the ostensive tag that is the symbol; we can use whatever we like as a tag, as long as we make sure that we in fact so use it, i.e., we tie it appropriately to whatever we want it to tag. This amounts to a procedure that we create and invoke: it takes us from the tag to the taggee, and our job is then to remember the procedure (i.e., remember which tag goes with which taggee).[12]

The internal metric that provides the congruence between the S-to-Rp relation and the Rp-to-R relation is simply that given by the neural wiring: whatever internal structures allow us to make assessments of, say, the length of our foot, determine the metric. The "length" of our footunculus is (mapped to) the length of our foot. If there is a discrepancy, this will cause us problems, which either we learn to correct, or will leave us in some confusion and without a sharp semantics for, say, *length*. It is easiest to suppose an actual inner body map, much like our actual bodies, although this is physiologically misleading. Some other story, but presumably not wholly unrelated, remains to be uncovered by physiologists.

Any device or brain that can carry out the above operations must have a genuine space or field of tokens we (the reasoner) can employ for tags and be able to tell them apart and keep track of how we have decided to hook them to inner referents, as well as notions of temporal distance between such decisions, and so on. All this must be actual physical structure that we can recall and shape to our needs. Thus the mental engines of thought are fundamentally embedded in a physical context and rely on accurate access to the context to inform of present versus past and of this tag versus that. There is then a primitive space-time semantics built into the inner ostending machinery. It distinguishes times, places, tags, and taggees. And this, I hope, is enough to regain the world as we know it. It must be—modulo alterations of letter but not of spirit—if my position is to stand.

3.2.   A Difficulty

Now we address the situation of the amputee. On a naive reading, my account so far would seem to say that if I lose my foot, then I lose meaning for the expression *my foot,* for I am no longer appropriately wired to it. I may still have my footunculus *foot p,* but this is mere *iref*. Yet our intuition is that I can still refer to my missing foot. Partly this is a problem of extra-bodily *eref*, that we will get to in the next section. But since I will build those treatments based on bodily *eref,* how can my theory hold up in the case of an amputee?

Here we are to suppose that one's foot-reference is not the only semantic tie one has to one's body. Suppose we also have ties to hands, fingers, arms, eyes, etc. Then if we lose a foot, we can still interpret our bodies via these many other intact regimes, and from there try to get on to full extra-bodily eref. On the other hand, a creature with only a footuncular inner self would indeed, on my theory, lose its semantic attachments when it loses its foot. By the same token, if we lose all our homunculi-to-body wirings (super-paraplegic), then we do lose our semantics as well. Without eyes, ears, limbs, skin, etc., I cannot relate my inner body notion to a body (for there is no body to speak of, and I am just a brain in a vat, indeed an unfriendly vat in which I do not get the right sort of inputs when I perform certain output commands).

3.3.   Some Neuroscience

It is instructive to ask whether the internal layer of representation I am espousing has any basis in biology. Certainly we do not, in any literal sense, have little people in our heads. However, it is no joke that a sort of homuncular view of the mind/brain is central to much of modern neuroscience. There are in fact a number of distinct homuncular maps between the body overall and portions of the brain, whereby certain brain structures correspond (in the neural wiring) to highly detailed parts of the rest of the body. Thus there is a "motor cortex" that involves a collection of neurons that are linked (via motor neurons) to bodily muscles; a "sensory cortex" is similarly linked to sense organs. These cortices are furthermore laid out spatially in the brain in rough correspondence to the shape of the corresponding distal body parts. In addition, there is another homunculus, in the midbrain (the tectum, to be precise) where various sensory modalities, including proprioceptive information, are combined into a map of the current body position and motion within the immediate surrounds (see Kolb and Whishaw 1990). Thus the notion of an inner self is not so farfetched. However, this is a far cry from isolating precise structures that play the roles I am outlining in this chapter.

4.   BEYOND THE BODY

Now, we get to *eref* at last. How do we go beyond direct wiring (body parts) to other pieces of the world? How do we get out to our dog Sandy? Here I propose that we use geometry. Our mental space has a foot(-unculus) in it. Let us use that to mentally step off several feet in our mental space until we get *to Sandy p*. The result is the number of feet (so to speak) that we take *Sandyp* to be in front of us.

Of course, all this is in our mental space, not out there in the real external space between us and Sandy. But there is an obvious extension to the external space: the actual number of actual foot lengths between us and the actual Sandy. We can even get at this by physically laying out rulers (or shoes or our own foot again and again) until we bump into the dog (actually and also seen/felt in our mental space). We might then find that our guess was right or off the mark (see Figure 9.4).

Figure 9.4. Getting outside oneself.

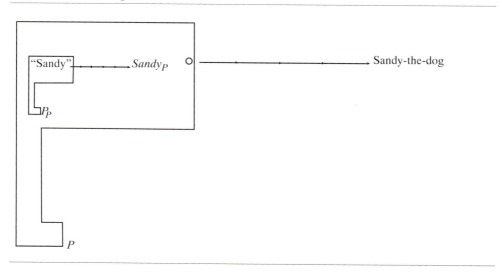

Here "*Sandy*" is the word/sound/token of the dog's name inside P's mind. *Sandy*p is the dog Sandy as far as P is concerned; it is P's mental representation of Sandy (visual and/or whatever other forms it may involve). Note that "*Sandy*"—but not *Sandy*p—is represented by P as being in P's mind/head (i.e., in her self-homunculus). This reflects a further property of internal reference: P takes herself to be a meaner, an entity where symbols are maintained, typically distant from their referents. P does not (usually) regard *Sandy*p as being in herself—after all, this is (to her) a dog! But P's uses of the dog's name are (for her) events initiated in her head. On occasion, to be sure, P might consider *Sandy*p, to be in her own head, e.g., if someone calls this to her attention ("it's really just a visual image") or if something makes P suspect that she is deceived about what is really out there.

We can measure, in our mind's eye, how many of our foot lengths would appear to be required to step off the distance between us (i.e., our inner self image) and Sandy (i.e., our inner *Sandy p*). This may or may not correspond to the actual number of actual foot lengths to the actual Sandy. In Figure 9.4, we have indicated an inner measure of five foot lengths between the inner self *Pp* and the inner *Sandyp*; and four real foot lengths between *P* and Sandy the dog. It appears to *P* that the dog is five feet away, but she is deceived, and if she steps out foot lengths she will bump into Sandy after only four steps. *P*'s belief that "Sandy is five feet in front of me" is false. If this happens a lot to *P*, she probably will learn to recalibrate the way she "steps off"" foot lengths in her mind's eye. This can be thought of as a change in (part of) her notion of foot length. She "recalibrates" her *iref* so that it is a better fit with reality.[13] Thus we use an inner metric (footuncular lengths, say) that has a canonical map to a real physical measure (our real foot lengths). The latter can be checked by carrying out a physical measurement (stepping off so many foot lengths to Sandy), and thus we can determine whether our estimate was accurate. The meaning, then, of "that thing five of my foot lengths in front of me" is whatever may happen to be five of my actual foot lengths in front of me. This depends on our knowing that *my foot* means my foot, but this is determined by links in my head (*iref*) between that phrase and my footunculus. For the footunculus *is* connected to my actual foot; and the *iref* is, we may suppose, largely formed from contacts with my sociolinguistic community: I learn to link the sound "foot" to my footunculus.

We build our inner world and carry on referring behavior with respect to it. Often this behavior fits well with the outer world around us, in the sense that we get the expected outcomes. When we do not, we invoke calibration behavior to reset our worldview; that is, we create a larger world in which our old world is a datum to which "didn't fit" is applied. Thus I can distinguish things as imaginings or as real within my world. I want to sit down, so I reach for the chair behind me, in my world. My real arm also moves behind the real me, and if the latter does not meet a real chair, I will (typically) not get the expected hand-meets-chair result in my world, so I recalibrate my world by taking the chair behind me away. That is, I stop believing there is a chair close behind me, but I continue to keep the chair-close-behind-me idea, now marked as false (poor fit).

However, this does not really offer any insight into *how* the inner measuring is done. I have no detailed theory to offer, but perhaps some further comment is useful. To think one is thinking is to attend to one's attending, that is, to have an object in mental space that plays the role of—stands for—one's attending mechanism. There is then a natural covariance between the mental-space attender (one's inner self-concept) and the actual attending mechanism. This is the beginning of a map between inner and outer worlds. Next we need an inner metric and a way to calibrate it with external inputs. (Actually, for mere comparison to another's mind, we might not need calibration; this is unclear to me.) But the inner metric is given in the inner world; it comes with a measuring device, with ground zero being the model attender. I suggest that time of scan may provide a basis for the metric. To scan from the (inner) attender out through mental space to (inner) object q takes time t, and then t is a sort of distance d that q is from the attender. Now this is fraught with problems, for I can think about (attend to) stars that are light-years away (even in my conception of them) in as little time as I can think about my home one mile away. So I am tempted to propose a basic contiguous-scan device that moves out through mental space without taking shortcuts. But this is in some sense irrelevant since it is all adjustable according to recalibration as hinted at above and further described below.

Now how do we link up inner and outer units? Perhaps we use standard units, such as one's own body size. My mental foot has an inner-measured size, and the outer foot has a real length; I move my foot according to my mental measures and recalibrate if things go wrong. What makes something my mental foot? Simply that it moves when and only when my real foot moves.[14]

If I am totally disconnected from bodily parts that I can move and sense, then it may be that I cannot refer to objects in the outer world. I will have no basis for measuring, so ability to judge that this is close or far, that this is up or down, large or small, in front or behind, no way to calibrate. But I suspect that even more damage than this is required to totally break the map.

How is calibration done? Once an expectation exists as to what a given portion of the inner world will do, its failure to do so occasions an effort to revise some portion of one's beliefs (i.e., of one's inner world) so as to fit (and explain) what was observed. There is no one right way, of course. Things like Occam's Razor will probably be important. And now we can see that we are in effect simply being everyday scientists, revising our theories when data so dictate. If I do not get a hand-on-chair observation, I revise my belief that the chair is within arm's length of me. I move it from arm's length to a farther distance. And so doing is a calibration.

How does this help with intentionality? How does it let us specify when I mean the same chair as you? If we both have thoughts involving portions of our worlds, respectively, that are an arm's length behind *me*, then we are thinking of whatever occupies the same piece of space, assuming our arm's-length notions are calibrated. We may, for instance, both have been present when my arm was measured for a shirt and both heard that it is 32 inches long. We may also each have an inch notion, calibrated again and again by us as children through the use of rulers in art class.

It would be highly instructive to set up a simple, one-dimensional world and work out the details for a simple organism that can think and calibrate. Once such simple cases are understood, we can turn to apparently much more difficult issues such as mapping from internal notions to external objects currently out of sight or even of objects whose whereabouts are unknown. While I think there are promising candidates for how to proceed here, I do not yet have a well-developed theory.

Figure 9.5. Error recovery.

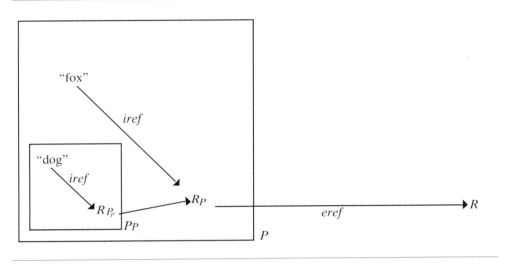

5.   ERROR AND RECOVERY

We return briefly to the issue of error, since it is a key one in the literature on intentionality and, in particular, a central theme of our *Part I*. We consider the example of seeing something, thinking it is a dog, and then deciding it really is a fox but appeared at first to be a dog. In terms of our pictorial models, a complex picture is formed, as indicated in Figure 9.5. The idea is that P first thought "there is a dog" but then (the state as pictured) "I thought that was a dog, but it's a fox." The inner homunculus here displays what was formerly believed, i.e., it displays things formerly simply believed outright but now seen as things in the mind (that turned out) not in line with what is presently taken to be reality.[15]

Thus there is a fundamental belief layer, in which the current view is taken at face value and only later can be called into question by means of passage to a new (perhaps more introspective) view (which then in turn is taken at face value). Whatever the current view is, it is believed and indeed taken as being reality.[16] That is, instead of there being a "true" box that marks those sentences in one's head that are judged true, there is rather a "doubt" box that marks those that have come to be doubted. The default is to believe. It takes a reflective act to show a belief to be, after all, merely something in one's head. Only at this point is the belief separated—in the reasoner's mind—from that which it is about. Up to that point there is no distinction made.[17]

Default reasoning is a hot topic in artificial intelligence. And it is largely about drawing defeasible conclusions: ones that might be in error, and that additional information might cause us to retract. Thus the present proposal can also be construed as a suggestion toward a mechanism for default reasoning.[18]

Fodor (1990) compares Macbeth reaching for a presumed dagger and a frog snapping at a moving dot (a fly or a BB). Macbeth, he says, can come to see his error, but the frog cannot be said in any serious sense to be able to err: it is built so that it snaps at moving dots, and presumably has no inner distinction to make about something failing to be a fly (or even being found not to be a moving dot after all once snapped at). According to Fodor, the frog merely has moving-dot-appearance detectors, whereas Macbeth has real dagger detectors.

Despite Fodor, we also merely have dagger-appearance detectors; that's all we ever detect: appearances. But we have other processes that can assess whether a given appearance detector's firing is veridical with respect to other criteria (e.g., Does it cut? Can it be grasped? Do others see it?) that are also appearance detection. We also have mechanisms for trying to sort out things when confusion (nonveridicality) sets in. This is how "though (Macbeth) and I both make mistakes, we are both in a position to recover," as Fodor says (1990, p. 107). Recovery is a key notion, although Fodor does not dwell on it. He is less interested in looking inward at our behaviors than outward toward the distal stimuli. But recovery is an inner comparison between what is and what isn't, in the agent's world; that is, between what the agent takes to be really out there and what she takes to be in her mind. To do this she needs to have both of these represented in her mind, i.e., she needs a robust world-model that includes a self-model. The self-model is where the not-really-out-there things go: they are one's thoughts, feelings, etc. And if we are to attribute our mistakes to them, then we need them to be active parts of us.

Let us consider error for kind terms. Let us use Fodor's example of *horse*—not just my horse Henry, but the general notion of a horse. In the view I am advancing here, I have a complex description that constitutes my meaning for the term *horse*. Part of it is explicit (nonvicarious): animal, typically four-legged, looks more or less like *this*. And part of it is vicarious: the biological kind specified by technical features of genetics, evolution, and other things experts know but I do not.

Now I see an object in front of me in dim light. I cannot verify[19] all parts of my *horse* description, not even all the explicit parts. But I verify enough of them to decide it is a horse. I am guessing, but not wildly.

Now there are several ways error might have occurred here:

1. Error of public/expert use: I may discover others do not use *horse* the way I do. (This is the case of Sue's Purdue discussed in *Part I*.)

2. Error of term picking: I may have slipped up in manipulating my tags
    and taggees and picked the wrong tag, having gotten "horse" instead of
    "donkey." I would then claim to have meant the right thing (donkey) but
    grabbed the wrong word (*horse*). I had the right Rp.

3. Error of identification: The lights may brighten and I may now see that
    there are stripes on the animal: it is a zebra. I decide that what I *thought*
    was a horse is in fact a zebra. I did not merely pick the wrong word, I
    had the wrong Rp.

At least one issue is left unclear in this example, however. For the tag used for a
taggee is itself, at least sometimes, part of (or even all of) what we know as the
description of the taggee. In that case, we cannot get the tag wrong but the taggee
right (case 2 above). Putnam's elms (Putnam 1975) come to mind. If all we know
about elms is that they are something or other tagged by the term *elms*, then we
cannot get the tag wrong without also getting the taggee wrong. This seems to
require some modification of my earlier claim that we have no control over Rp: in
a case like this we do have some control. In fact, a case like this is largely one of
pure formalism (if we really know *nothing at all* about elms, not even that they
are physical objects). The entire meaning is then in terms of a tag applied to
something created only for the purpose of attaching that tag to it! So we create
both tag and taggee here.

This also points up that I have been quite vague as to what, in general,
constitutes a taggee or object in mental space.[20] I cannot offer any better analysis
at this time, however.

I am similarly vague about where descriptions fit into the S-to-Rp picture of
iref. I am not sure there is a definite answer here: perhaps descriptions can play
three roles: as S (name), as Rp (named), and as part of what cements S to Rp. One
problem with giving a straightforward explanation of this is that the entire
mechanism is dynamic, as is brought out more forcefully in my discussion of
error and especially of reflection in the final section.

6.   FUNCTIONAL ROLE SEMANTICS VERSUS *IREF*

The above view of meaning suggests some alterations in functionalist treatments
of reference. For instance, it suggests that we can have reference or content of
thoughts *without* external embedding other than the space-time features
specified. We need a temporally manipulable space of tags and taggees, but any
computer has this. Inputs and outputs external to the system are not essential; *iref*
may still be present. Notice the word *may*. There is no claim here—indeed a

denial—that every computer (programmed and running) has *iref*. But the presence of *iref* depends not at all on events outside the system. It depends only on the right sort of setup *inside* the system.

This opens up the possibility that two meaners could be thinking the same thing (about a game of chess, say) with no contact whatsoever with the outer world. The chess-game versus war-game scenario[21] of Rey (1980) does not apply here, since it is not multiple external maps that determine reference (chess versus war) but internal tagging structure, and it may happen that these are the very same in the two meaners. What would make the activities chess games rather than war games would be details about the tag network, such as the feature that there is a *general* rule being applied as to how a knight always moves, for instance, rather than a one-time rule that says this knight moves in this way only in this particular game. Of course, truly distinguishing between war and chess in a thoroughly convincing way involves a myriad of very human details that we cannot begin to analyze in the present state of theory.[22]

Do the players in the "game" think of it as war or chess? Only they can tell! It's their world. But can there be an intrinsic meaning? Can there even be a sense in which an outsider (outside their vat, so to speak, to relate this to the new Putnam) can make sense of the notion that inside that vat the beings are thinking of war (or chess)? There's a strong intuition that even if it should turn out that all my thoughts and memories are dreams (or ruminations) and there is no outer world at all, still I have chess and war ideas and so could someone else, and my chess and her chess would both be chess, i.e., the same in crucial respects; one would not be chess and the other war. Indeed, the geometric reference idea seems to let us both match unicorn concepts, for that matter. We do not need an external world to appeal to here.

Another modification *iref* suggests is simply itself: another dimension should be adjoined to the nature of mental states. It is not enough to covary with an external entity and be the object of inferential manipulations. For this can be done by a one-tiered system, which has no internal meaning (of its own) and hence no error (of its own). *iref* buys us error (and with it the chance of undoing error) and also buys us ourselves, i.e., the tag mechanism allows the possibility of constructing a division of the mental space into two parts: the tags and the taggees; when error pushes us to revise the tagging network, we compare the old ("errorful") status and take it to be false, not true of the world, not real. But if not real, then what is it? It is that part of the world that represents (sometimes incorrectly) other parts: it is a meaner (us!). In seeing how our ideas differ from reality we see a thing (ourselves) as approximating but different from (part of but not the whole) world.

As a consequence, two *functionally* equivalent engines may have distinct mental states: indeed one may be one-tiered and have no mental state at all (on the view I am advocating here) and the other may be *two-tiered* (with *iref*) and have rich mental states.

Finally, the internal semantics urged here (*iref*) is no mere stance (*à la* Dennett). It is a real design feature of the system in question.

7.   REFLECTION AND GEOMETRIC SEMANTICS: A SUMMARY

We have summarized our proposal in a formula:

$$content\,p(S) = eref\,p(irefp\,(S)) = erefp\,(R\,p) = R$$

Roughly, we can get outside to the real world by taking our internal measured universe and mapping it outside through our (real) feet!

A simpler case than that of Sandy the dog is basic geometry, e.g., a rectangle. What makes a bit of my brain process amount to my thinking of a rectangle? Surely I could do this even if I had never seen or heard of a rectangle. Yet how could my brain chemistry then have anything to do with things quite different from it? For there are no rectangles in my brain, or at least none of roughly human size, which—let us suppose—is how I imagine my rectangle to be. Here is my answer: we use geometry to measure our brain-chemical process, in terms of other such standard processes, e.g., the my-foot-idea that is also a brain process.

One might ask how the latter brain-chemical process can be justifiably called a foot-idea? Doesn't that just beg the question? No, for there is an important difference: my real foot is wired to the my-foot-idea in such a way that they covary extremely well. And now, from the foot measuring stick, we can (I suggest) reconstruct the universe as we see it: indeed, that is what it is for us to have a view of the world!

To get content out there, we first need to get it in here. My immediate meaning for *John* is the John in my world, which is something in my head. That John in my head is related to the real John out there, but how? By the real John's being situated in the real world pretty much the way my world's John is situated in my world. How do we even begin to compare the real world and my world to see if there are similar situatednesses? By the canonical pinning point: me. My world's right foot maps canonically to my real right foot, as we saw before. My body is highly mapped this way, to homunculi in my brain, a very sophisticated and robust system of covariances. My "John" thoughts, however, do not covary nearly as well with the real John's presence, and this is where distal attempts founder. By going right out there to distal objects, the robust proximal maps are ignored and with them the basis for a robust geometry that can in fact capture the distal objects.

We must avoid a verbal difficulty; when I speak of the John in my world, I mean as an outsider would describe my world. To me, of course, that simply is John, except when I grow philosophical and try to catch my thoughts as objects. Then I do make a distinction between the real John and the my-world John, but I do so only by going deeper inside, not by going out to the real John. What I do is "reflect": I create another layer in my world that has a model of me in it and the (as I would then style it) my-world John sitting in the my-world head while the real John (as I would style it) sits outside that head. This is probably the sort of thing that drove Kant (and now Putnam) to their dismal conclusion that we can never know or even think about things-in-themselves. But this is not so bad: the whole of science shows how we can make robust progress despite the possibility of total confusion. We get evidence that our inner worlds match pretty well with the real world; not proof, but impressive evidence.

We need to say more about something mentioned here and there in the foregoing discussion, namely, what constitutes *thinking* (about something). Merely to tag Rp with S is not to *think* about Rp, at least not in the sense of thinking aimed at getting a better understanding of Rp. On our view, getting a better understanding amounts to recognizing potential errors or gaps in Rp (as the thinker's view of some hypothesized external R) and trying to bring Rp more in line with the real R. But how can this be? It seems to fly in the face of all we have said here: the thinker P is constrained to do all her mental activity only with the materials at hand, namely, things in her mind or mental space. There is no R there.

This is where reflection comes in. Recall that error (in one form) amounts to finding a discrepancy in one's own (delayed verification of one's) descriptions. What is the thinker to do on discovering such? The answer that I propose is as follows: she creates a new item in her mental space that is (to her, now) the real thing out there—this was what Rp *was* to her formerly but now she decides that the old Rp was a mistaken identification of reality, merely how reality (which she now views her *new* inner item as being) *appeared* to her through her confused conceptual/perceptual mechanisms (her glasses were dirty, the light was bad, whatever). See Figure 9.5 for an example, where Rp_p is the former Rp.

She has thus "reflected" the entire tagging apparatus into an object for scrutiny. She has not really gotten "out there" to the real R in itself (as Kant warned cannot be done). But she may have gotten closer to it (a better approximation to it).[23] Perhaps, then, in a sense, we never do refer to real external things. Perhaps we can yield on this point to the "renegade Putnam" (as Devitt and Sterelny 1987 style Putnam's recent thinking). But also perhaps we do not need such reference, if *iref* can through reflection and space-time-situated error lead us to better and better world models. Indeed, our obvious success in dealing with (surviving in) the world speaks strongly for exactly this.

Thinking, then, I suggest, amounts to considering alternatives, e.g., weighing them as to their more plausible "reality" (as seen in our mental space).

Performing this involves frequent reflections (in-turnings) of taggee into seen-as-taggee, i.e., a further flexing of our control of symbolism.

This notion of meaner control of meaning often appears in the literature, but in the form of asides or casual remarks (e.g., Fodor 1979, p. 191). Here I have argued that this is one of the primary features of mind and meaning and provides us with the luxury of making mistakes and thereby improving our world pictures. One curious feature of the view urged here is that there is no reference without self-reference. The meaner herself is an essential part of her own mental space, for she takes the measure of reality (in her own inner terms) by means of her own situatedness not only as a physical object but as a thinker to whom things can appear different from what they are.[24]

In sum, we have progressed through three different pictures of meaning, from a one-tiered model (which is the basic distal view) to the two-tiered, to the internal body-in-the-world model where we can recapture external (distal) reference via internal geometry and where active representation is possible as well as reflection/thought. I suggest that this line of investigation may lead to a characterization of what thinking is. Much of what I have proposed may seem obvious to a neuroscientist; certainly the tectal maps are well known. But the reflection capability is, as far as I know, new, and apparently nothing has as yet been discovered in the brain that may play such a role.

8.   VIRTUAL REALITY MACHINES

Recently there have been studies involving so-called virtual reality machines. (See, e.g., Stix 1991.) These machines present a user with sensory input very much like that in a normal sensory setting in which an external object is "sensed" via the usual signals (optical and otherwise). In the case of these machines, however, there is no external object (at least of the usual sort). Instead the machine simulates the sensory inputs that would normally be produced by the external object; thus visual and other inputs are manufactured in the machine and presented to the user. The effect can be quite startling. Early versions of such machines include the widely used aircraft simulators pilots use to gain experience in takeoffs and landings. The newer machines are more sophisticated and have applications far beyond piloting aircraft.

What is of interest for us is that such machines provide a setting in which, in a sense, *eref* fails but *iref* succeeds. External objects appear to be present, but they are not. We might phrase this by saying that the objects are there in the subject's view. Yet this is always the case. A rainbow is, in some significant sense, not there at all in the world. There is in fact no particular physical entity situated just where there appears to be a rainbow. The appearance results from our limited visual field and the angles of refraction of light on water droplets. There is of course something there, but the something is not very much like what we "see." What is actually there are water droplets and refracted light going in rather subtle directions resulting in an ordered array of wavelengths being perceived at any small region where a viewer stands. It is, in an important sense, an illusion. And yet we can point to it, discuss it, analyze it.

A virtual reality experience is a similar illusion. Two users can agree (or disagree) on details of the perceived world. Their words are, then, surely about something, but the something is complicated. We can even say the same about a dream, even though this is not a shared access to perceptual data; a dream has features that can be discussed. Finally, even in the most ordinary of settings, e.g., seeing an actual table right in front of oneself, there is here, too, a view that is best understood in terms of the viewer. After all, we now know that a (wooden) table is not a totally solid homogeneous mass; rather it is mostly water in countless cells that in turn are jostling atoms, and so on. Our everyday sense of it is perfectly adequate (even, perhaps, excellent) for everyday purposes, but then so is our sense of a rainbow and our sense of the virtual reality experiences. Only when we need to look deeper do we find it useful to relinquish these views for others. And we most likely have not yet discovered a "final" level that is the "one true" reality. Yet we surely should not conclude, then, that we have not yet ever experienced reference in our thinking and talking!

What is, I think, essential for there to be reference, is a reliable recourse to data. As long as we can reliably point to color data (i.e., take another look at the colors), we can speak meaningfully of a rainbow and know what we mean. Experiential rainbowhood is there, whether or not we wish to argue that a spatially delimited mass is there that will stand up to all investigation.

Now, this is not enough. For we do want to be able to distinguish between experiences we regard as real and those that are illusory. However, we never get a final answer on this. We go by the evidence. As long as the evidence appears consistent with some interpretation, we may feel comfortable with it and go on using it. But when the evidence (in the form of more data) reaches a certain discomfort level, we start to change our view.[25]

9.   ACKNOWLEDGMENTS

I would like to thank Georges Rey and Michael Miller for helpful comments, although this in no way should be taken to suggest they agree with me on any of this.

This research was supported in part by the U. S. Army Research Office (DAAL03-88-K0087) and the National Science Foundation (IRI-8907122).

10. NOTES

1. Although functionalists must decide for themselves whether they regard my additions as a basic departure or not!

2. Pp is P's inner "homunculus"; this will be clarified later.

3. Of course, it can occur that there is no such external R, yet internal reference can still occur. Thus, I may think about a unicorn (i.e., I think "unicornly").

4. Fodor suggests an "asymmetric dependence" account of what it is for an event internal to P (a thought) to have external content, in the case of kind terms (e.g., ducks). This account is a highly distal one, making no mention of structures internal to P. Crucial to his account is the notion of error—indeed, asymmetric dependence is precisely an attempt to account for the possibility of error. The account is complex, and I will not attempt to describe it here; however, I suspect that it may come closer to a characterization of belief-content *ascription* than of belief-content itself.

5. Then the *qua* problem would resurrect itself: what is the extent or boundary of the thing at Rp's end of the string? All of Rp, or part of it, or more than it?

6. We should avoid too narrow a reading of "lighted up"; this is not a visual image in any naive sense. For instance, we may envision or think of Rp as a solid object entirely lit up on both its surface and its interior. What matters is what we take to be referred to; we apparently have a great skill at imagining various things, and that is what lets us think so subtly.

7. Personal communication. In particular, McCarthy's example purports to show, *à la* Dennlett (1987) (but see also McCarthy 1979), that whether an agent's behavior exhibits intentionality is a stance we, the observers, take and is not a matter of fact about the agent herself.

8. We shall return to this when we discuss more of Fodor's ideas below.

9. For instance, if the reading device is inaccurate, errors will be introduced, yet the machine will have no way to represent this possibility.

10. It may seem odd that being able to be wrong is a sign of intelligence, but I really mean having a sufficiently rich inner view to allow distinguishing appropriate from inappropriate results.

11.   In fact, there are several such footunculi in various parts of the brain. For instance, the tectum (part of the midbrain) involves so-called tectal maps, which facilitate computing spatiotemporal trajectories based on inputs from visual, auditory, and proprioceptive systems. We need the footunculus and its motion in our mental space to reliably covary with real foot motion.

12.   This footuncular map may obtain even when we are not looking at our foot, but merely thinking about it, for the map is not solely tied to the visual system. For the present I ignore difficult cases such as that of an amputee who has no foot or of someone who has a foot but whose neural wiring does not provide an inner footunculus; I return to this later.

13.   Thus the case of a missing limb: at first we may refuse to believe the limb is not there because we may still "feel" it there. But eventually experience starts to erode that view, as we recalibrate our inner metric: the proprioceptive foot length no longer is a good measure for us, so we rely more on other measures.

14.   That is, in the normal course of things. If I am an amputee, I may have foot-motion sensations, but there will be a telltale lack of regularity, in that I will not have control over the foot. I cannot make my inner foot move at will anymore because the motor nerves do not reach muscles. In this case I will have evidence that my inner foot does not correspond to a fully functioning external foot.

15.   We need minds, then, to have a place where wrong ideas can be kept. Of course, right ideas go there, too; but if all our ideas were right (i.e., if by our lights we could not regard any as wrong), we would not need to distinguish our reality view from anything else, and a one-tiered mechanism would suffice.

16.   Pictorial representations are not always useful here, and I do not mean to suggest that the entire issue of belief and belief correction is a mere matter of pictures.

17.   This has interesting points of agreement with research in cognitive psychology (e.g. Gilbert 1991, and Bower 1991).

18.   In Perlis (1991a) I argue this in more detail and give some extended examples, and in Perlis (1987) I discuss error and change of mind in terms of reflection similar to the presentation here.

19. See Perlis 1991b for why this does not suffer the usual verificationist difficulties.

20. Even a tag is an object in mental space, since we can turn our attention to the tags, thereby tagging (quoting, perhaps) them with yet further tags. This is important in recognizing and dealing with error, and more generally in considering alternative possibilities (thinking).

21. This proposes a computer program that can be viewed equally well as simulating an actual war or playing chess. Who is to say whether token B in the program stands for a chess bishop or Brezhnev?

22. One might imagine a war in which certain tanks are constrained to move by their very nature just the way knights do in chess, and so on throughout the story. But then at some point such a war is perhaps truly a game of chess, too. Then the example seems to break down altogether, so we will leave it here.

23. Dwelling on such matters can lead one to the frustrations of solipsism and/or despair. But thinkers of past centuries tended to ignore the positive feature of better and better approximations. Perhaps our age of frequent scientific advances makes us more aware of this possibility.

24. See Kihlstrom (1989) for a similar idea.

25. See Harman (1986) for a treatment of various bases on which beliefs may be changed.

11.   REFERENCES

Bower, B. (1991) True believers. *Science News,* 139 (Jan. 5, 1991): 14-15.

Dennett, D. (1987) *The Intentional Stance* (Cambridge, MA: MIT Press).

Devitt, M., and Sterelny, K. (1987) *Language and Reality* (Cambridge, MA: MIT Press).

Fodor, J. (1979) *The Language of Thought* (Cambridge, MA: Harvard University Press).

Fodor, J. (1987) *Psychosemantics* (Cambridge, MA: MIT Press).

Fodor, J. (1990) *A Theory of Content* (Cambridge, MA: MIT Press).

Gilbert, D. (1991) How mental systems believe. *American Psychologist,* 46: (2) 107.

Harman, G. (1986) *Change in View* (Cambridge, MA: MIT Press).

Johnson, M. (1987) *The Body in the Mind* (Chicago: University of Chicago Press).

Kihlstrom, J. (1989) Implicit cognition and the cognitive unconscious. Paper presented at the 1989 meeting of the SPP, Tucson, Arizona.

Kolb, B., and Whishaw, I. (1990) *Fundamentals of Human Neuropsychology,* 3rd ed. (New York, NY: W. H. Freeman).

Kripke, S. (1980) *Naming and Necessity* (Cambridge, MA: Harvard University Press).

McCarthy, J. (1979) Ascribing mental qualities to machines. In M. Ringle (ed.) *Philosophical Perspectives in Artificial Intelligence* (Atlantic Highlands, NJ: Humanities Press).

Perlis, D. (1987) How can a program mean? Proceedings of the International Joint Conference on Artificial Intelligence, August, Milan, Italy.

Perlis, D. (1991a) Intentionality and defaults. In K. Ford and P. Hayes (eds.) *Advances in Human and Machine Cognition* (Greenwich, CT: JAI Press).

Perlis, D. (1991b) Putting one's foot in one's head—Part I: Why. *Noûs*, special issue on artificial intelligence and cognitive science (W. Rapaport, Ed.), 25: 435–455.

Putnam, H. (1975) *Mind, Language and Reality: Philosophical Papers, vol. 2* (Cambridge, MA: Cambridge University Press).

Putnam, H. (1981) *Reason, Truth and History* (Cambridge, MA: Cambridge University Press).

Putnam, H. (1987) *Representation and Reality* (Cambridge, MA: MIT Press).

Quine, W. (1953) *From a Logical Point of View* (Cambridge, MA: Harvard University Press).

Rey, G. (1980) The formal and the opaque. *Behavioral and Brain Sciences,* 3: 90–92.

Stix, G. (1991) Reach out. *Scientific American*, 264, (2): 134.

CHAPTER
10

 ## Syntactic Semantics
Foundations of Computational Natural-Language Understanding

William J. Rapaport

....

*Language (**la langue**) is a system all of whose terms are interdependent and where the value of one results only from the simultaneous presence of the others . . . . (de Saussure 1915, p. 159.)*

Thinking Computers and Virtual Persons
edited by Eric Dietrich
ISBN 0-12-215495-9

James H. Fetzer (ed.), *Aspects of Artificial Intelligence*, 81-131.
© 1988 by Kluwer Academic Publishers.
Reprinted by permission of Kluwer Academic Publishers.

1. INTRODUCTION

In this essay, I consider how it is possible to understand natural language and whether a computer could do so. Briefly, my argument will be that although a certain kind of semantic interpretation is needed for understanding natural language, it is a kind that only involves syntactic symbol manipulation of precisely the sort of which computers are capable, so that it is possible in principle for computers to understand natural language. Along the way, I shall discuss recent arguments by John R. Searle and by Fred Dretske to the effect that computers can *not* understand natural language, and I shall present a prototype natural-language-understanding system to illustrate some of my claims.[1]

2. CAN A COMPUTER UNDERSTAND NATURAL LANGUAGE?

What does it mean to say that a computer can understand natural language? To even attempt to answer this, a number of preliminary remarks and terminological decisions need to be made. For instance, by 'computer', I do not mean some currently existing one. Nor, for that matter, do I mean some ultimate future piece of hardware, for computers by themselves can do nothing: They need a program. But neither do I mean to investigate whether a program, be it currently existing or some ultimate future software, can understand natural language, for programs by themselves can do nothing.

Rather, the question is whether a computer that is running (or executing) a suitable program—a (suitable) program being executed or run—can understand natural language. A program actually being executed is sometimes said to be a "process" (*cf.* Tanenbaum 1976, p. 12). Thus, one must distinguish three things: (a) the computer (i.e., the hardware; in particular, the central processing unit), (b) the program (i.e., the software), and (c) the process (i.e., the hardware running the software). A program is like the script of a play; the computer is like the actors, sets, etc.; and a process is like an actual production of the play—the play in the process of being performed.[2] Having made these distinctions, however, I will often revert to the less exact, but easier, ways of speaking ("computers understand", "the program understands").

What kind of program is "suitable" for understanding natural language? Clearly, it will be an AI program, both in the sense that it will be the product of research in artificial intelligence and in the (somewhat looser) sense that it will be an artificially intelligent program: for understanding natural language is a mark of intelligence (in the sense of AI, *not* in the sense of IQ), and such a program would exhibit this ability artificially.

But what kind of AI program? Would it be a "weak" one that understands natural language but that does so by whatever techniques are successful, be they "psychologically valid" or not? Or would it be a "strong" one that understands natural language in more or less the way we humans do?[3] ("More or less" may depend on such things as differences in material and organization between humans and these ultimate computers.) I do not think that it matters or that any of the considerations I will present depend on the strong/weak dichotomy, although I do think that it is likely that the only successful techniques will turn out to be psychologically valid, thus "strengthening" the "weak" methodology.

Another aspect of the program can be illuminated by taking up the metaphor of the play. This ultimate AI program for understanding natural language might be thought of as something like the script for a one-character play. When this "play" is "performed", the computer that plays the role of the sole "character" communicates in, say, English. But we do not want it to be only a one-way communication; it must not merely speak to us, the "audience", yet be otherwise oblivious to our existence (as in Disney-like audio-animatronic performances). That would hardly constitute natural-language understanding. More give and take is needed—more interaction: the play must be an audience-participation improvisation. So, too, must the program. I'll return to this theme later (Section 3.2.1).

I said earlier that understanding natural language is a mark of intelligence. In what sense is it such a mark? Alan M. Turing (1950) rejected the question, "Can machines think?", in favor of the more behavioristic question, "Can a machine convince a human to believe that it (the computer) is a human?"[4] To be able to do that, the computer must be able to understand natural language. So, understanding natural language is a necessary condition for passing the Turing Test, and to that extent, at least, it is a mark of intelligence.

I think, by the way, that it is also a sufficient condition. Suppose that a computer running our ultimate program understands, say, English. Therefore, it surely understands such expressions as 'to convince', 'to imitate a human', etc. Now, of course, merely understanding what these mean is not enough. The computer must be able to *do* these things—to convince someone, to imitate a human, etc. That is, it must not merely be a *cognitive* agent, but also an *acting* one. In particular, to imitate a human, it needs to be able to reason about what a(nother) cognitive agent, such as a human, believes. But that kind of reasoning is necessary for understanding natural language; in particular, it is necessary for understanding behavior explainable in terms of "nested beliefs" (such as: Jan took Smith's course because she believes that her fellow students believe that Smith is a good teacher; on the importance of such contexts, *cf.* Dennett 1983 and Rapaport 1984, 1986c). Finally, the computer must also, in some sense, *want* to convince someone by pretending to be a human; i.e., it must *want* to play

Turing's Imitation Game. But this can be done by *telling* it to do so, and this, of course, should be told to it in English. So, if it understands natural language, then it ought to be able to pass the Turing Test. If so, then understanding natural language is surely a mark of intelligence.

But even if understanding natural language is only a necessary condition of intelligence, the question whether computers can understand natural language is something we should care about. For one thing, it is relevant to Searle's Chinese-Room Argument, which has rapidly become a rival to the Turing Test as a touchstone for philosophical inquiries into the foundations of AI (Searle 1980). For another, it is relevant to Dretske's claims that computers can't even add (Dretske 1985). One of my main goals in this essay is to show why Searle's and Dretske's arguments fail. Finally, it is a central issue for much research in AI, computational linguistics, and cognitive science. Many researchers in these fields, including my colleagues and myself, are investigating techniques for writing computer programs that, we claim, will be able to understand stories, narratives, discourse—in short, natural language (Shapiro and Rapaport 1986, 1987; Bruder *et al.* 1986). It would be nice to know if we can really do what we claim we are able to do!

3.   WHAT DOES IT MEAN TO "UNDERSTAND NATURAL LANGUAGE"?

3.1.   *Syntax Suffices*

To determine whether a computer (as understood in the light of the previous section) can understand natural language, we need to determine how it is possible for *anything* to understand natural language, and then to see if computers can satisfy those requirements.

Understanding has to do with meaning, and meaning is the province of semantics. Several recent attacks on the possibility of a computer's understanding natural language have taken the line that computers can only do syntax, not semantics, and, hence, cannot understand natural language. Briefly, my thesis in this essay is that *syntax suffices*. I shall qualify this somewhat by allowing that there will also be a certain causal link between the computer and the external world, which contributes to a *certain kind* of nonsyntactic semantics, but not the kind of semantics that is of computational interest. What kind of causal link is this? Well, obviously, if someone built the computer, there's a causal link between it and the external world. But the particular causal link that is semantically relevant is one between the external world and what I shall call the computer's "mind"—more precisely, the "mind" of the process produced by the running of the natural-language-understanding program on the computer.

Before I go into my reasons for hedging on what might seem to be the obvious importance of the causal link and what this link might be, let me say why I think I have a right to talk about a computer's "mind". Consider a system consisting of a computer, an AI program (or, what is more likely, a set of interacting AI programs), and perhaps a preexisting data base of information expressed in some "knowledge representation" language. (When such data bases are part of an AI program, they tend to be called "knowledge bases", and the preexisting, background information is called "world knowledge"—"innate ideas" would also be appropriate terminology.) The system will interact with a "user"—perhaps a human, perhaps another such system. Suppose that the system behaves as follows: It indicates to the user that it is ready to begin. (This need not be indicated by a natural-language sentence.) The user types (or otherwise interactively inputs) a sentence in, say, English. Depending on the nature of the input, the system might modify its knowledge base in accordance with the information contained in this sentence. (If the input was merely 'hello', it might not.) It may then express to the user, in English, some appropriate proposition in its knowledge base. And so the dialogue would continue. (An actual example of such a dialogue is shown in Appendix 1.)

If such a system is going to be a good candidate for one that can understand natural language, it ought to be able at least to process virtually all of what the user tells it (or at least as much as a human would), to answer questions, and, most importantly, to ask questions. What's more, it ought to do this in a fashion that at least somewhat resembles whatever it is that *we* do when we understand natural language; that is, it should probably be doing some real, live parsing and generating, and not mere pattern-matching. Under this requirement, a "strong" system would parse and generate more or less precisely as humans do; a "weak" system would parse and generate using some other grammar.

But even this is not enough. The system must also *remember* all sorts of things. It must remember things it "knew" (i.e., had in its knowledge base) before the conversation began; it must remember things it "learns" (i.e., adds to its knowledge base) during the conversation; and it must be able to draw inferences (deductively, inductively, abductively, pragmatically, etc.)—thus modifying its knowledge base—and remember *what* it inferred as well as *that*, *how*, and probably even *why* it inferred it.

In short, it needs a knowledge base. This is why a program such as ELIZA (Weizenbaum 1966, 1974, 1976)—which lacks a knowledge base—does *not* understand natural language, though there are many programs described in the AI literature that have knowledge bases and do some or all of these things to varying degrees (e.g., SHRDLU (Winograd 1972) and BORIS (Lehnert *et al.* 1983), to name but two). The knowledge base, expressed in a knowledge-representation language augmented by an inferencing package, is (at least a part of) the "mind" of the system. I will discuss one such system later (the one responsible for the dialogue in Appendix 1).

So, my thesis is that (suitable) purely syntactic symbol-manipulation of the system's knowledge base (its "mind") suffices for it to understand natural language. Although there is also a causal link between its "mind" and the external world, I do not think that this link is necessary *for understanding natural language*. I shall have more to say about this later; all I shall say now is that my reasons for taking this position are roughly methodologically solipsistic: the system has no access to these links, and a second system conversing with the first only has access to its own internal representations of the first system's links. Nevertheless, given that there are in fact such links, what might they be like? I shall have more to say about this, too, but for now let it suffice to say that they are perceptual links, primarily visual and auditory.

3.2.   *The Chinese-Room Argument*

Now, Searle has argued that computers cannot understand natural language (or, hence, be intelligent, artificially or otherwise). In his Chinese-Room Argument, Searle, who knows neither written nor spoken Chinese, is imagined to be locked in a room and supplied with instructions in English that provide an algorithm for processing written Chinese. Native Chinese speakers are stationed outside the room and pass pieces of paper with questions written in Chinese characters into the room. Searle uses these symbols, otherwise meaningless to him, as input and—following only the algorithm—produces, as output, other Chinese characters, which are, in fact, answers to the question. He passes these back outside to the native speakers, who find his "answers . . . absolutely indistinguishable from those of native Chinese speakers" (Searle 1980, p. 418). The argument that this experiment is supposed to support has been expressed by Searle as follows:

> [I] still don't understand a word of Chinese and neither does any other digital computer because all the computer has is what I have: a formal program *that attaches no meaning, interpretation, or content to any of the symbols.* [Therefore,] . . . no formal program by itself is sufficient for understanding . . . . (Searle 1982, p. 5; italics added—*cf.* Section 3.5, below.)

If this Chinese-language-processing system passes the Turing Test, then—according to the Test—it does understand Chinese. And indeed it does pass the test, according to the very criteria Searle sets up. So how can Searle conclude that it doesn't understand Chinese? One reason that he offers is that the program doesn't understand because it doesn't "know" what the words and sentences *mean*:

> The reason that no computer program can ever be a mind is simply that a computer program is only syntactical, and minds are more than syntactical. Minds are semantical, in the sense that they have more than a formal structure, they have a content. (Searle 1984, p. 31.)

That is, meaning—"semantics"—is something over and above mere symbol manipulation—"syntax". Meaning is a relation between symbols and the things in the world that the symbols are supposed to represent or be about. This "aboutness", or intentionality, is supposed to be a feature that only minds possess. So, if AI programs cannot exhibit intentionality, they cannot be said to think or understand in any way.

But there are different ways to provide the links between a program's symbols and things in the world. One way is by means of sensor and effector organs. Stuart C. Shapiro has suggested that all that is needed is a camera and a pointing finger (personal communication; *cf.* Shapiro and Rapaport 1987). If the computer running the Chinese-language program (plus image-processing and robotic-manipulation programs) can "see" and "point" to what it is talking about, then surely it has all it needs to "attach meaning" to its symbols.

Searle calls this sort of response to his argument "the Robot Reply". He objects to it on the grounds that if he, Searle, were to be processing all of this new information along with the Chinese-language program, he still would not "know what is going on", because now he would just have more symbols to manipulate: he would still have no direct access to the external world.

But there is another way to provide the link between symbols and things in the world: Even if the system has sensor and effector organs, it must still have internal representations of the external objects, and—I shall argue—it is the relations between *these* and its other symbols that constitute meaning for *it*. Searle seems to think that semantics must link the internal symbols with the outside world and that this is something that cannot be programmed. But if this is what semantics must do, it must do it for human beings, too, so we might as well wonder how the link could possibly be forged for us. Either the link between internal representations and the outside world *can* be made for both humans *and* computers, or else semantics is more usefully treated as linking one set of internal symbolic representations with another. On this view, semantics does indeed turn out to be just more symbol manipulation.

Here is Searle's objection to the Robot Reply:

> I see no reason in principle why we couldn't give a machine the capacity to understand English or Chinese, since in an important sense our bodies with our brains are precisely such machines. But . . . we could not give such a thing to a machine . . . [whose] operation . . . is defined solely in terms of computational processes over formally defined elements. (Searle 1980, p. 422.)

'Computational processes over formally defined elements' is just a more precise phrase for symbol manipulation. The reason Searle gives for his claim that a machine that just manipulates symbols cannot understand a natural language is that "only something having the same causal powers as brains can have intentionality" (Searle 1980, p. 423). What, then, are these "causal powers"? All Searle tells us in his essay on the Chinese-Room Argument is that they are due to the (human) brain's "biological (that is, chemical and physical) structure" (Searle 1980, p. 422). But he does not specify precisely what these causal powers are. (In Rapaport 1985b and 1986b, I argue that they are not even causal.)

Thus, Searle has two main claims: A computer cannot understand natural language because (1) it is not a biological entity and (2) it is a purely syntactic entity—it can only manipulate symbols, not meanings. Elsewhere, I have argued that the biological issue is beside the point— that *any* device that "implements" (in the technical sense of the computational theory of abstract data types) an algorithm for successfully processing natural-language can be said to *understand* language, no matter how the device is physically constituted (Rapaport 1985b, 1986a, 1986b). My intent here is to argue, along the lines sketched out above, that being a purely syntactic entity *is* sufficient for understanding natural language.[5]

Before doing that, I think it is worth looking at some aspects of Searle's argument that have been largely neglected, in order to help clarify the nature of a natural-language-understanding program.

3.2.1.   Natural-language generation

The first aspect can be highlighted by returning to the metaphor of the natural-language-understanding program as a one-character, audience-participation, improvisational play. Because it is improvisational, the script[6] of the play cannot be fixed; it must be able to vary, depending on the audience's input. That is, a natural-language-understanding system must be able to respond appropriately to arbitrary input (it must be "robust"). This could, perhaps, be handled by a "conditional script": if the audience says $\lceil \varphi_2 \rceil$, then the character should respond by saying $\lceil \varphi_2 \rceil$, etc. But to be truly robust, the script would need to be "productive", in roughly Chomsky's sense: that is, the character in the play must be able to understand and the produce arbitrary "new" and relevant lines. In fact, it is fairly easy to have a productive *parser* for a natural-language-understanding system. I am not claiming that the problem of natural-language *understanding* has been solved, but we seem to be on the right track with respect to parsers for natural-language *processing*, and, at any rate, we know the general outlines of what a suitably robust parser should look like. What's needed, however, is *generative* productivity: the ability to *ask* new and relevant questions and to *initiate* conversation (in a non-"canned" way: ELIZA—which relies purely on pattern-matching—still doesn't qualify). To be able to generate appropriate utterances, the system must have the capability to *plan* its speech acts, and, so, a planning component must be part of a natural-language-understanding system. Such a planning component is probably also needed for parsing, in order to be able to understand *why* the speaker said what he or she did. (*Cf.* Cohen and Perrault 1979; Appelt 1982, 1985; and Wiebe and Rapaport 1986.)

To the extent that these are missing from the Chinese-Room Argument, Searle-in-the-room wouldn't seem to understand Chinese. So, let us imagine that AI researchers and computational linguists have solved this problem, and that our system is equipped with a suitably productive generation grammar. Now, these productive capabilities are tantamount to general intelligence, as I argued in Section 2. The important point, however, is that this capability is a function of what's in the system's knowledge base: what can be produced by a productive generative grammar must first be in the knowledge base. To put it somewhat mundanely, I can only speak about what I'm familiar with. (To put it more esoterically, whereof I cannot speak, thereof I must be silent.)

3.2.2.   Learning and linguistic knowledge

A second aspect of Searle's argument that I want to look at concerns the kind of knowledge that Searle-in-the-room is alleged to have—or lack. One difference that is sometimes pointed out between machine understanding and human understanding is that everything that the machine does is explicitly coded. This is part of what is meant when it is said that computers can only do what they are programmed to do (by someone who *is* "intelligent" or who *can* understand natural language). Furthermore, this might be interpreted to mean that the system knows everything that it is doing. But this is mistaken. It can only be said to "know" what it is "aware" of, not what is merely coded in. For instance, the knowledge bases of many AI systems distinguish between propositions that are explicitly believed by the system and those that are only implicitly believed (*cf.* Levesque 1984; Rapaport 1984, 1986c, 1987). Furthermore, the parser that transduces the user's input into the system's knowledge base, as well as the generator that transduces a proposition in the knowledge base into the system's natural-language output, need not (and arguably should not) be part of the knowledge base itself. Such "knowledge" of language would be tacit knowledge, just as Chomsky said: It is coded in and is part of the overall system, but it is not "conscious knowledge". It is no different for humans: everything we know, including our knowledge of how to understand our native natural language, must (somehow) be "coded in". In other words, human and machine understanding are *both* fully coded, but neither the human nor the machine knows everything. In the Chinese-Room Argument, the human following the Chinese-language program is in the same position as a human speaking English (only in slow motion; *cf.* Hofstadter 1980): neither has conscious knowledge of the rules of the language.

Could the machine or the human *learn* the rules, and thus gain such conscious knowledge? Or could it learn *new* rules and thus expand its natural-language understanding? Surely, yes: see the work by Jeannette Neal (Neal 1981, 1985; Neal and Shapiro 1984, 1985, and 1987).

There are other roles for learning in natural-language understanding. Many (perhaps most) conversations involve the learning of new information. And it is often the case that new words and phrases, together with their meanings, are learned both explicitly and implicitly (*cf.* Rapaport 1981, and the discussion of 'swordsman' in Section 3.5, below). In all of these cases, the learning consists, at least in part, of modifications to the system's knowledge base.

It is not clear from the rather static quality of Searle's Chinese-language program whether Searle intended it to have the capability to learn. Without it, however, the Chinese-Room Argument is weakened.

3.2.3.   The knowledge base

It should be clear by now that a knowledge base plays a central role in natural-language understanding. Searle's original argument includes a Schank-like script as part of the input, but it is not clear whether he intended this to be a modifiable knowledge base of the sort I described as the system's "mind" or whether he intended it as the rather static structure that a script (in its early incarnation) actually is. In any case, parts of the knowledge base would probably have to be structured into, *inter alia*, such frame-like units as scripts, memory-organization packets, etc. (*Cf.* Minsky 1975, Schank 1982.) The two aspects we have just considered, and part of my argument below, imply that a modifiable knowledge base is essential to natural-language understanding. (*Cf.* n. 13.)

3.3.   *Dretske's Argument*

Having set the stage, let me introduce some of my main ideas by considering Dretske's argument in 'Machines and the Mental' (1985), to the effect that an external, non-syntactic semantics is needed for natural-language understanding.

According to Dretske, machines "lack something that is essential" for being a rational agent (p. 23). That is, there is something they "can't do" (p. 23) that prevents their "membership in the society of rational agents" (p. 23). That is surely a very strong claim to make—and a very important one, if true. After all, theoretical computer science may be characterized as the study of what is effectively computable. That is, assuming Church's Thesis, it may be characterized as the study of what is expressible as a recursive function— including such theoretically uninteresting though highly practical recursive functions as payroll programs. It follows that AI can be characterized as the study of the extent to which mentality is effectively computable. So, if there is something that computers can't do, wouldn't it be something that is *not* effectively computable—wouldn't it be behavior that is nonrecursive?[7] It is reasonable to expect that it is much too early in the history of AI for such a claim as this to be proved, and, no doubt, I am interpreting Dretske's rhetoric too strongly. For a nonrecursive function is in a sense more complex than a recursive one, and Dretske's line of argument seems to be that a computer is simpler than a human (or that computer thought is more isolated than human thought): "Why can't pure thought, the sort of thing computers purportedly have, stand to ordinary thought, the sort of thing we have, the way a solitary stroll stands to a hectic walk down a crowded street?" (p. 23). Even granting that this talk about computers is to be understood in the more precise sense of Section 3.1, above, the ratio

$$\frac{\text{pure thought}}{\text{computers}} = \frac{\text{ordinary thought}}{\text{humans}}$$

isn't quite right. If anything, the phrase 'pure thought' ought to be preserved for the *abstraction* that can be *implemented* in computers *or* humans (or Martians, or chimps, or . . .):

$$\frac{\text{pure thought}}{\text{implementing medium}} = \frac{\text{AI program that implements pure thought}}{\text{computer}}$$

$$= \frac{\text{human mental processes (ordinary thought)}}{\text{human}}$$

(*Cf.* Rapaport 1985b, 1986b.)

What is it, then, that these "simple-minded" computers can't do? Dretske's admittedly overly strong answer is:

> They don't solve problems, play games, prove theorems, recognize patterns, let alone think, see, and remember. They don't even add and subtract. (p. 24.)

Now, one interpretation of this, consistent with holding that intelligence is nonrecursive, is that these tasks are also nonrecursive. But, clearly, they aren't (or, at least, not all of them are). A second interpretation can be based on the claim that Church's Thesis is not a *reduction* of the notion of "algorithm" to that of, say, Turing-machine program on the grounds that an algorithm is an intentional entity that contains as an essential component a description of the problem that it is designed for, whereas no such description forms part of the Turing-machine program (Goodman 1986). So, perhaps, the tasks that Dretske says computers can't do are all ones that must be described in intentional language, which computers are supposed incapable of.

These two interpretations are related. For if tasks that are essentially intentional are nonrecursive, then Church's Thesis can be understood as holding that for each member of a certain class of nonrecursive functions (namely, the essentially intentional but effectively computable tasks), there is a corresponding recursive function that is extensionally equivalent (i.e., input-output behaviorally equivalent) to it. And Dretske's thesis can be taken to be that this equivalence is not an identity. For instance, although my calculator's input-output *behavior* is identical to my own behavior when I perform addition, *it* is not *adding*.

Here is Dretske's argument (p. 25):

(1) "...7, 5 and 12 are numbers."

(2) "We add 7 and 5 to get 12 ..."

(3) Therefore, "Addition is an operation on numbers."

(4) "At best, [the operations computers perform] are operations on ... physical tokens that *stand for*, or are interpreted as standing for, ... numbers."

(5) Therefore, "The operations computers perform ... are not operations on numbers."

(6) "Therefore, computers don't add."

(7) Therefore, computers cannot add.[8]

Possibly, if *all* that computers do is manipulate uninterpreted symbols, then they do *not* add. But if the symbols are interpreted, then maybe computers *can* add. So, who would have to interpret the symbols? Us? Them? To make the case parallel, the answer, perhaps surprisingly, is: them! For who interprets the symbols when *we* add? Us. But if we can do it (which is an assumption underlying premise (2)), then why can't computers? But perhaps it is *not* I who interpret "my" symbols when I add, or you when you add. Perhaps there is a dialectical component: the only reason that *I* think that *you* can add (or *vice versa*) is that *I* interpret *your* symbol manipulations (and *vice versa*). In that case, if *I* interpret the *computer's* symbol manipulations, then—to maintain the parallelism—I can say that *it* adds (at least as well as you add). And, take note, in the converse case, the *computer* can judge that *I* "add".

Premise (2) and intermediate conclusion (3) are acceptable. But *how* is it that we add numbers? By manipulating physical tokens of them. That is, the abstract operation of adding *is* an operation on numbers (as (3) says), but our *human implementation* of this operation is an operation on (physical) *implementations* of numbers. (*Cf.* Shapiro 1977, where it is argued that addition, as humans perform it, is an operation on numerals, not numbers.) So premise (4) is also acceptable; but—as Dretske admits—if it implies (5), then the argument "shows that we don't add either" (p. 26), surely an unacceptable result.

What the argument does illuminate is the relation of an abstraction to its implementations (Rapaport 1985b, 1986b). But, says Dretske, something is still missing:

> the machine is . . . restricted to operations on the symbols or representations themselves. It has no access . . . to the *meaning* of these symbols, to the things the representations represent, to the numbers. (p. 26)

The obvious question to ask is: How do *we* gain this essential access? And a reasonable answer is: In terms of a theory of arithmetic, say, Peano's (or that of elementary school, for that matter). But such a theory is expressed in symbols. So the *symbol* '1' means the *number* 1 for *us* because it is linked to the '1' that represents 1 in the theory. All of this is what I shall call *internal* semantics: semantics as an interconnected network of internal symbols—a "semantic network" of symbols in the "mind" or "knowledge base" of an intelligent system, artificial or otherwise. The *meaning* of '1', or of any other symbol or expression, is determined by its locus in this network (*cf.* Quine 1951; Quillian 1967, 1968) *as well as* by the way it is *used* by various processes that reason using the network. (*Cf.* the "knowledge-representation hypothesis", according to which "there is . . . presumed to be an internal process that 'runs over' or 'computes with' these representational structures" (Smith 1982, p. 33).)

There's more: *My* notion of 1 might be linked not only to my internal representation of Peano's axioms, but also to my representation of my right index finger and to representations of various experiences I had as a child (*cf.* Schank 1984, p. 68). Of course, the computer's notion of 1 won't be. But it *might* be linked to its internal representation of itself in some way[9]—the computer need not be purely a Peano mathematician. But perhaps there's too much—should such "weak" links really be part of the *meaning* of '1'? In one sense, yes; in another, no: I'll discuss several different kinds of meaning in Section 3.7.

This notion of an internal semantics determined by a semantic network and independent of links to the external world—independent, that is, of an "external" semantics—is perfectly consistent with some of Dretske's further observations, though not with his conclusions. For instance, he points out that "physical activities" such as adding "cannot acquire the relevant kind of meaning merely by *assigning* them an interpretation, by letting them mean something *to* or *for us*" (p. 26). This kind of assignment is part of what I mean by "external semantics". He continues: "Unless the symbols being manipulated mean something *to the system manipulating them*,"—this is roughly what I mean by "internal semantics"—"their meaning, whatever it is, is irrelevant to evaluating what the system is doing when it manipulated them" (pp. 26-27). After all, when *I* undergo the physical processes that constitute adding, it is not only *you* who says that I add (not only *you* who assigns these processes an interpretation for *you*), but I, too. Of course, one reason that *I* assign them an interpretation is the fact that *you* do. So, *how* do *I* assign them an interpretation? If this question can be answered, perhaps we will learn how the *computer* can assign them an interpretation—which is what Dretske (and Searle) deny can be done. One answer is by my observing that *you* assign my processes an interpretation. I say to myself, no doubt unconsciously, "I just manipulated some symbols; you called it 'adding 7 and 5'. So *that's* what 'adding' is!" But once this label is thus internalized, I no longer need the link to you. My internal semantic network resumes control, and I happily go on manipulating symbols, though now I have a few extra ones, such as the label 'adding'. After all, "How would one think of associating an idea with a verbal image if one had not first come upon (*surprenait*) this association in an act of speech (*parole*)?" (de Saussure 1915, p. 37).

Dretske expresses *part* of this idea as follows: "To understand what a system is doing when it manipulates symbols, it is necessary to know, not just what these symbols mean, what interpretation they have been, or can be, *assigned*,"—i.e., what label *you* use—"but what they mean to the system performing the operations" (p. 27), i.e., how they fit into the system's semantic network. Dretske's way of phrasing this is not quite right, though. He says, "To understand what a system is doing . . ."; but *who* does this understanding? Us, or the system? For *me* to understand what the system is doing, I only need to know *my* assignment function, *not* the system's internal network. Unless I'm its programmer, how *could* I know it? Compare the case of a human: For me to understand what *you* are doing, I only need to know *my* assignment function. Given the privacy of (human) mental states and processes, how could I possibly know yours? On the other hand, for the *system* to understand what *it* is doing, it only needs to know its own semantic network. Granted, part of that network consists of nodes (the labels) created in response to "outside" stimuli—from you or me. But this just makes it possible for the system and us to communicate, as well as making it likely that there will be a good match between the system's interpretation and ours. This is another reason why *learning* is so important for a natural-language-understanding program, as I suggested earlier (Section 3.2.2). Unless the system (such as Searle-in-the-room) can learn from its interactions with the interlocutors, it won't pass the Turing Test.

Dretske's point is that the computer doesn't do what we do because it can't understand what it's doing. He tries to support this claim with an appeal to a by-now common analogy:

> Computer simulations of a hurricane do not blow trees down. Why should anyone suppose that computer simulations of problem solving must themselves solve problems? (p. 27)

But, as with most of the people who make this analogy, Dretske doesn't make it fully. I completely agree that "computer simulations of a hurricane do not blow trees down." They do, however, *simulatedly* blow down *simulated* trees (*cf.* Gleick 1985; Rapaport 1986b, 1988). And, surely, computer simulations of problem solving do *simulatedly* solve *simulated* problems. The natural questions are: Is *simulated* solving *real* solving? Is a *simulated* problem a *real* problem?

The answer, in both cases, is 'Yes'. The simulated problem is an *implementation* of the *abstract* problem. A problem abstractly speaking remains one in any implementation: Compare this "real" problem:

> What *number x* is such that $x + 2 = 3$?

with this "simulated" version of it:

> What *symbol s* is such that the physical process we call 'adding' applied to s and to '2' yields '3'?

Both are problems. The *simulated* solution of the *simulated* problem *really* solves it and can be used to really solve the "real" problem. To return to hurricanes and minds, the difference between a simulated hurricane and a simulated mind is that the latter does "blow down trees"! (*Cf.* Rapaport 1988)

Dretske sometimes *seems* to want too much, even though he asks almost the right question:

> how does one build a system that is capable not only of performing operations on (or with) symbols, but one *to which* these symbols mean **something**, a machine that, in this sense, understands **the** meaning of the symbols it manipulates? (p. 27; italics in original, my boldface.)

A system to which the symbols mean "something": Can they mean *anything*? If so, then an internal semantics suffices. It could be based on a semantic network (as in SNePS—*cf.* Shapiro and Rapaport 1986, 1987; *cf.* Section 3.6, below) or on, say, discourse representation theory (Kamp 1984 and forthcoming, Asher 1986 and 1987). The symbols' meanings would be determined solely by their locus in the network or the discourse representation structure. But does Dretske really want a machine that understands "the" meaning of its symbols? Is there only one, preferred, meaning—an "intended interpretation"? How could there be? Any formal theory admits of an infinite number of interpretations, equivalent up to isomorphism. The "label" nodes that interface with the external world can be changed however one wants, but the network structure will be untouched. This is the best we can hope for.

The heart of Dretske's argument is in the following passages. My comments on them will bring together several strands of our inquiry so far. First,

> if the meaning of the symbols on which a machine performs its operations
> is . . . wholly derived from us, . . . then there is no way the machine can
> acquire understanding, no way these symbols can have a meaning to *the*
> *machine itself*. (pp. 27-28)

That is, if the symbols' meanings are purely external, then they cannot have
internal meanings. But this does not follow. The external-to-the-machine
meanings that *we* assign to its symbols are *independent* of its own, internal,
meanings. It may, indeed, have symbols whose internal meanings are causally
derived from our external ones (these are the "labels" I discussed earlier; in
SNePS, they are the nodes at the heads of LEX arcs—*cf*. Section 3.6, below, and
Shapiro 1982; Maida and Shapiro 1982; Shapiro and Rapaport 1986, 1987). But the
machine begins with an internal semantic network, which may be built into it
("hardwired" or "preprogrammed", or "innate", to switch metaphors) but is, in
any case, developed in the course of dialogue. So it either begins with or
develops its own meanings independently of those that we assign to its symbols.
  Next,

> Unless these symbols have . . . an intrinsic meaning . . . independent of **our**
> communicative intentions and purposes, then **this meaning** *must* be irrelevant
> to assessing what the machine is doing when it manipulates them. (p. 28;
> italics in original, boldface added.)

I find this confusing: which meaning is irrelevant? Dretske's syntax seems to
require it to be the "intrinsic" meaning, but his thesis requires it to be the
previous passage's "meaning derived from us" (*cf*. the earlier citation from pp.
26-27). On this reading, I can agree. But the interesting question to raise is: How
independent is the intrinsic meaning? Natural-language understanding, let us
remember, requires conversation, or dialogue; it is a *social* interaction. Any
natural-language-understanding system must initially learn *a* meaning from its
interlocutor (*cf*. de Saussure 1915, p. 37, cited above), but *its* network will rarely if
ever be identical with its interlocutor's. And this is as true for an artificial
natural-language-understanding system as it is for us: As I once put it, we almost
always misunderstand each other (Rapaport 1981, p. 17; *cf*. Schank 1984, Ch. 3,
esp. pp. 44-47).
  Finally,

> The machine is processing meaningful (to us) symbols . . . but the *way* it
> processes them is quite independent of *what they mean*—hence, nothing *the*
> *machine* does is explicable in terms of the meaning of the symbols it
> manipulates. . . . (p. 28)

This is essentially Nicolas Goodman's point about Church's Thesis (discussed
earlier in this section). On this view, for example, a computer running a program
that *we* say is computing greatest common divisors does not "know" that that is
what (we say that) it is doing; so, that's *not* what it's doing. Or, to take Dretske's
example (p. 30), a robot that purportedly recognizes short circuits "really" only

recognizes certain gaps; it is we who interpret a gap as a short circuit. But why not provide the computer with knowledge about greatest common divisors (so-named) and the robot with knowledge about short circuits (so-named), and link the number-crunching or gap-sensing mechanisms to this knowledge?

Observe that, in the passage just cited, the machine's symbol-processing is independent of what the symbols mean *to us*, i.e., independent of their external meaning. On Dretske's view, what the machine does is inexplicable in terms of *our* meanings. Thus, he says that machines don't answer questions (p. 28), because, presumably, "answers questions" is *our* meaning, not *its* meaning.

But from Dretske's claim it does not follow that the symbols are meaningless or even that they differ in meaning from our interpretation. For one thing, *our* meaning *could* also be the *machine's* meaning, if its internal semantic network happens to be sufficiently like ours (just as yours ought to be sufficiently like mine). Indeed, for communication to be successful, this will have to be the case. For another, *simulated* question-answering *is* question-answering, just as with simulated problem-solving. If the abstract answer to the abstract question, "Who did the Yankees lose to on July 7?", is: the Red Sox; and if the simulated answer (e.g., a certain noun phrase) to the simulated question (e.g., a certain interrogative sentence), 'Who did the Yankees lose to on July 7?', is 'the Red Sox' (or even, perhaps, the simulated team, in some knowledge-representation system); and if *both* the computer *and* we take those symbols in the "same" sense—i.e., if they play, roughly, the same roles in our respective semantic networks—then the *simulated* answer *is* an answer (the example is from Green *et al.* 1961).

How are such internal meanings developed? Here, I am happy to agree with Dretske: "In the same way . . . that nature arranged it in our case" (p. 28), namely, by correlations between internal representations (either "innate" or "learned") and external circumstances (p. 32). And, of course, such correlations are often established during *conversation*. But—contrary to Dretske (p. 32)—this can be the case for all sorts of systems, human as well as machine.

So, I agree with many of Dretske's claims but not his main conclusion. We *can* give an AI system information about what it's doing, although *its* internal interpretation of what it's doing might not be the same as ours; but, for that matter, yours need not be the same as mine, either. Taken literally, computers *don't* add if "add" means what *I* mean by it—which involves what *I* do when I add and the locus of 'add' in *my* internal semantic network. But thus understood, *you* don't add, either; only I do. This sort of solipsism is not even methodologically useful. Clearly, we want to be able to maintain that you and I both add. The reasons we are able to maintain this are that the "label" nodes of my semantic network match those of yours *and* that my semantic network is structurally much like yours. How much alike? Enough so that when we talk to each other, we have virtually no reason to believe that we are misunderstanding each other (*cf.* Russell 1918; Quine 1969, Shapiro and Rapaport 1987; note, however, that in the strict sense in which only I add, and you don't, we *always* systematically misunderstand each other—*cf.* Rapaport 1981). That is, we can maintain that we both add, because we *converse* with each other, thus bringing our internal semantic networks into closer and closer "alignment" or "calibration". But this means that there is no way that we can prevent a natural-language-understanding system from joining us. In so doing, we may learn from it—and adjust to it—as much as it does from (and to) us.[10] Rather than talking about *my* adding, *your* adding, and *its* adding (and perhaps marveling at how much alike they all are), we should talk about the *abstract* process of adding that is *implemented* in each of us.

3.4.   Deixis

My claim, then, is that an internal semantics is sufficient for natural-language understanding and that an external semantics is only needed for *mutual* understanding. I shall offer an explicit argument for the sufficiency thesis, but first I want to consider a possible objection to the effect that *deictic* expressions require an external semantics—that an internal semantics cannot handle indexicals such as 'that'.

Consider the following example, adapted from Kamp (1983): How would our system be able to represent in its "mind" the proposition expressed by the sentence, "That's the man who stole my book!"? Imagine first, that it is the system itself that utters this, having just perceived, by means of its computational-vision module, the man in question disappear around a corner. What is the meaning of 'that', if not its external referent? And, since its external referent could not be inside the system, 'that' cannot have an internal meaning. However, the output of any perceptual system must include some kind of internal symbol (perhaps a complex of symbols), which becomes linked to the semantic network (or, in Kamp's system, to the discourse representation structure)—a sort of *visual* "label". That symbol (or one linked to it by a visual analogue of the SNePS LEX arc) is the internal meaning of 'that'. (There may, of course, be other kinds of purely internal reference to the external world. I shall not discuss those here, but *cf.* Rapaport 1976, and Rapaport 1985/1986, Section 4.4.)

Imagine, now, that the sentence is uttered *to* the system, which looks up too late to see the man turn the corner. The external meaning of 'that' has not changed, but we no longer even have the visual label. Here, I submit, the system's interpretation of 'that' is as a disguised definite (or indefinite) description (much like Russell's theory of proper names), perhaps "the (or, a) man whom my interlocutor just saw". What's important in this case is that the system must interpret 'that', and whatever its interpretation is the internal meaning of 'that'.

3.5.   *Understanding and Interpretation*

This talk of interpretation is essential. I began this section by asking what "understanding natural language" means. To understand, in the sense we are discussing,[11] is, at least in part, to provide a semantic interpretation for a syntax. Given two "systems"—human or formal/artificial—we may ask, What does it mean for one system to understand the other? There are three cases to consider:

Case 1. First, what does it mean for *two humans to understand each other*? For me to understand what you say is for me to provide a semantic interpretation of the utterances you make. I treat those utterances as if they were fragments of a formal system, and I interpret them using as the domain of interpretation, let us suppose, the nodes of *my* semantic network. (And you do likewise with my utterances and your semantic network.) That is, I map your words into my concepts.

I may err: In Robertson Davies's novel, *The Manticore*, the protagonist, David Staunton, tells of when he was a child and heard his father referred to as a "swordsman". He had taken it to mean that his father was "a gallant, cavalier-like person" (Davies 1972, p. 439), whereas it in fact meant that his father was a lecher ('whoremaster' and 'amorist' are the synonyms (!) used in the book). This leads to several embarrassments that he is oblivious to, such as when he uses the word 'swordsman' to imply gallantry but his hearers interpret him to mean 'lechery'. Staunton had correctly recognized that the word was being used metaphorically, but he had the wrong metaphor. He had mapped a new word (or an old word newly used) into his concepts in the way that seemed to him to fit best, though it really belonged elsewhere in his network.

So, my mapping might not match yours. Worse, I might not be able to map one or more of your words into my concepts in any straightforward way at all, since your conceptual system (or "world view")—implemented in your semantic network—might be radically different from mine, or you may be speaking a foreign language. This problem is relevant to many issues in translation, radical and otherwise, which I do not wish to enter into here (but *cf.* n. 13). But what I *can* do when I hear you use such a term is to fit it into my network as best I can, i.e., to devise the best theory I can to account for this fragment of your linguistic data. One way I can do this, perhaps, is by augmenting my network with a sub-network of concepts that is structurally similar to an appropriate sub-network of *yours* and that *collectively* "interprets" your term in terms of my concepts. Suppose, for example, that you are a speaker of Nuer: although your word 'kwoth' and its sub-network of concepts might not be able to be placed in 1—1 correspondence with my word 'God' and *its* sub-network of concepts (they are not exact translations of each other), I can develop my own sub-network for 'kwoth' that is linked to the rest of my semantic network and that enables me to gloss your word 'kwoth' with an account of its meaning in terms of its locus in my semantic network (*cf.* Jennings 1985). I have no doubt that something exactly like this occurs routinely when one is conversing in a foreign language.

What is crucial to notice in this case of understanding is that when I understand you by mapping your utterances into the symbols of my internal semantic network, and then manipulate these symbols, I am performing a syntactic process.

Case 2. Second, what does it mean *for a human to understand a formal language* (or formal system)? Although a philosopher's instinctive response to this might be to say that it is done by providing a semantic interpretation for the formal language, I think this is only half of the story. There are, in fact, *two* ways for me to understand a formal language. In 'Searle's Experiments with Thought' (Rapaport 1986a), I called these "semantic understanding" and "syntactic understanding". In the example I used there, a syntactic understanding of algebra might allow me to solve equations by manipulating the symbols ("move the x from the right-hand side to the left-hand side and put a minus sign in front of it"), whereas a semantic understanding of algebra might allow me to describe those manipulations in terms of a balancing-scale ("if you remove the unknown weight from the right-hand pan, you must also remove the same amount from the left-hand pan in order to keep it balanced"). Semantic understanding is, indeed, understanding via semantic interpretation. Syntactic understanding, on the other hand, is the kind of understanding that comes from directly manipulating the symbols of the formal language according to its syntactic rules. Semantic understanding is what allows one to prove soundness and completeness theorems *about* the formal language; syntactic understanding is what allows one to prove theorems *in* the formal system.

There are two important points to notice about semantic understanding. The first is that there is no unique way to understand semantically: there are an infinite number of equally good interpretations of any formal system. Only one of these may be the "intended" interpretation, but it is not possible to uniquely identify which one. What 'adding' means to me, therefore, may be radically different from what it means to you, even if we manipulate the same symbols in the same ways (*cf.* Quine 1969, Section I, especially pp. 44-45). The second point is that an interpretation of a formal system is essentially a *simulation* of it in some *other* formal system (or, to return to talk of languages, *my* interpretation of a formal language is a mapping of its terms into my concepts), and, thus, it is just more symbol manipulation.

Syntactic understanding is also, obviously, an ability to manipulate symbols, to understand what is invariant under all the semantic interpretations. In fact, my syntactic understanding of a formal system is the closest I can get to its internal semantics, to what Dretske calls the system's "intrinsic meanings".

Case 3. Finally, what would it mean *for a formal system to understand me*? This may seem like a very strange question. After all, most formal systems just sort of sit there on paper, waiting for me to do something with them (syntactic manipulation) or to say something about them (semantic interpretation). I don't normally expect them to interpret *me*. (This is, perhaps, what underlies the humor in Woody Allen's image of Kugelmass, magically transferred into the world of a textbook of Spanish, "running for his life . . . as the word *tener* ('to have')—a large and hairy irregular verb—raced after him on its spindly legs" (Allen 1980, p. 55).)

But there are some formal systems, namely, certain computer programs, that at least have the *facility* to understand (one must be careful not to beg the question here) because they are "dynamic"—they are capable of being run. Taking up a distinction made earlier, perhaps it is the *process*—the natural-language-understanding program being run on (or, implemented by) a computer—that understands. So, what would it mean for such a formal system to understand me? In keeping with our earlier answers to this sort of question, it would be for it to give a semantic interpretation to its input consisting of *my* syntax (my utterances considered as more or less a formal system) in terms of *its* concepts. (And, of course, we would semantically understand its natural-language output in a similar manner, as noted in Case 2.) But its concepts would be, say, the nodes of its semantic network—symbols that it manipulates, in a "purely syntactic" manner. That is, it would in fact be "a formal program that attaches . . . meaning, interpretation, or content to . . . the symbols"—precisely what Searle (1982, p. 5; cited earlier) said did not exist!

So the general answer to the general question—What does it mean for one system to understand another?—is this:

> A natural-language-understanding system S_1 understands the natural-language output of a natural-language-understanding system S_2 by building and manipulating the symbols of an internal model (an interpretation) of S_2's output considered as a formal system.

S_1's internal model would be a knowledge-representation and reasoning system that manipulates symbols. It is in this sense that syntax suffices for understanding.

The role of external semantics needs clarification. Internal and external semantics are two sides of the same coin. The *internal* semantics of S_1's linguistic expressions constitutes S_1's understanding of S_2. The *external* semantics of S_1's linguistic expressions constitutes S_2's understanding of S_1. It follows that the external semantics of S_1's linguistic expressions is the internal semantics of S_2's linguistic expressions! S_1's *internal* semantics links S_1's words with S_1's own concepts, but S_1's *external* semantics links S_1's words with the concepts of S_2.

What about "referential" semantics—the link between word and object-in-the-world? I do not see how this is relevant to S_1's or S_2's understanding, except in one of the following two ways. In the first of these ways, semantics is concerned with language-in-general, not a particular individual's idiolect: it is concerned with *English*—with the "socially determined" extensions of words (Putnam

1975)—not with what *I* say. This concern is legitimate, since people tend to agree pretty well on the referential meanings of their words, else communication would cease; recall the Tower of Babel. So, on this view, what does 'pen' mean? Let us say that it means the kind of object I wrote the manuscript of this essay with (I'm old-fashioned). But what does *this* mean—what does it mean to say that 'pen' means a certain kind of physical object? It means that virtually all (native) speakers of English use it in that way. That is, this view of semantics is at best parasitic on individual external semantics.

But only "at best"; things are not even that good. The second way that "referential" semantics is relevant is, in fact, at the individual level. You say 'pen'; I interpret that as "pen" in my internal semantic network. Now, what does "pen" mean for me? Internally, its meaning is given by its location in my semantic network. Referentially, I might point to a real pen. But, as we saw in our discussion of deixis, there is an internal representation of my pointing to a pen, and it is *that representation* that is linked to my semantic network, *not* the real pen. And now here is why the first view of referential semantics won't do: How does the semanticist assert that 'pen'-in-English refers to the class of pens? Ultimately, by pointing. So, at best, the semanticist can link the pen-node of some very general semantic network of English to *other* (visual) representations, and these are either the semanticist's own visual representations or else they are representations in some *other* formal language that goes proxy for the world. The semantic link between word and object is never direct, but always mediated by a representation (*cf.* Rapaport 1976, 1985a, 1985/1986). The link between that representation and the object itself (which object, since I am only a *methodological* solipsist, I shall assume exists) is a causal one. It may, as Sayre (1986) suggests, even be the ultimate source of semantic information. But it is noumenally inaccessible to an individual mind. As Jackendoff (1985, p. 24) puts it, "the semantics of natural language is more revealing of the internal representation of the world than of the external world *per se*".

Finally, some comments are in order about the different kinds of meaning that we have identified. I shall postpone this, however, till we have had a chance to look at a prototype natural-language-understanding system in operation.

3.6. SNePS/CASSIE: A Prototype AI Natural-Language-Understanding System

How might all this be managed in an AI natural-language-understanding system? Here, I shall doff my philosopher's hat and don my computer scientist's hat. Rather than try to say how this can be managed by *any* natural-language-understanding system, I shall show how one such system manages it. The system I shall describe—and to which I have alluded earlier—is SNePS/CASSIE: an experiment in "building" (a model of) a mind (called 'CASSIE') using the SNePS knowledge representation and reasoning system. SNePS, the *Semantic Network Processing System* (Shapiro 1979; Maida and Shapiro 1982; Shapiro and Rapaport 1986, 1987; Rapaport 1986c), is a semantic-network language with facilities for building semantic networks to represent information, for retrieving information from them, and for performing inference with them. There are at least two sorts of semantic networks in the AI literature (see Findler 1979 for a survey): The most common is which is known as an "inheritance hierarchy", of which the most well-known is probably KL-ONE (*cf.* Brachman and Schmolze 1985). In an inheritance semantic network, nodes represent concepts, and arcs represent relations between them. For instance, a typical inheritance semantic network might represent the propositions that Socrates is human and that humans are mortal as in Figure 1a. The interpreters for such systems allow properties to be "inherited", so that the fact that Socrates is mortal does not also have to be stored at the Socrates-node. What is essential, however, is that the representation of a proposition (e.g., that Socrates is human) consists only of separate representations of the individuals (Socrates and the property of being human) linked by a relation arc (the "ISA" arc). That is, propositions are not themselves objects. By contrast,

> SNePS is a *propositional* semantic network. By this is meant that all information, including propositions, "facts", etc., is represented by nodes. The benefit of representing propositions by nodes is that propositions about propositions can be represented with no limit. . . . Arcs merely form the underlying syntactic structure of SNePS. This is embodied in the restriction that one cannot add an arc between two existing nodes. That would be tantamount to telling SNePS a proposition that is not represented as a node. . .
> . . . Another restriction is the *Uniqueness Principle*: There is a one-to-one correspondence between nodes and represented concepts. This principle guarantees that nodes will be shared whenever possible and that nodes represent intentional objects. (Shapiro and Rapaport 1987.)

Thus, for example, the information represented in the inheritance network of Figure 10.1a could (though it need not) be represented in SNePS as in Figure 10.1b; the crucial difference is that the SNePS propositional network contains nodes (m3, m5) representing the *propositions* that Socrates is human and that humans are mortal, thus enabling representations of beliefs and rules *about* those propositions. (In fact, the network of Figure 10.1a could *not* be built in SNePS, by the first restriction cited; *cf.* Shapiro 1979, Section 2.3.1.) My colleagues and I in the SNePS Research Group and the Graduate Group in Cognitive Science at SUNY Buffalo are using SNePS to build a natural-language-understanding system, which we call 'CASSIE', the Cognitive *A*gent of the *S*NePS *S*ystem—an *I*ntelligent *E*ntity (Shapiro and Rapaport 1986, 1987; Bruder *et al.* 1986). The nodes of CASSIE's knowledge base implemented in SNePS are her beliefs and other objects of thought, in the Meinongian sense. (Needless to say, I hope, nothing about CASSIE's *actual* state of "intelligence" should be inferred from her name!)

Figure 10.1a. An "ISA" inheritance-hierarchy semantic network.

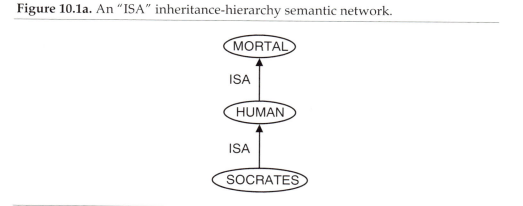

Figure 10.1b. A SNePS propositional semantic network (m3 and m5 represent the propositions that Socrates is human and that humans are mortal, respectively).

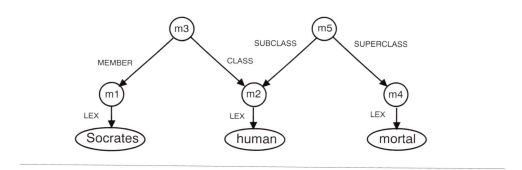

A brief conversation with CASSIE is presented in Appendix 1. Here, I shall sketch a small part of her natural-language-processing algorithm. Suppose that the user tells CASSIE,

Young Lucy petted a yellow dog.

CASSIE's tacit linguistic knowledge, embodied in an augmented transition network (ATN) parsing-and-generating grammar (Shapiro 1982), "hears" the words and builds the semantic network shown in Figure 10.2 in CASSIE's "mind" in the following way:

Figure 10.2. CASSIE's belief that young Lucy petted a yellow dog.

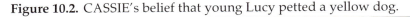

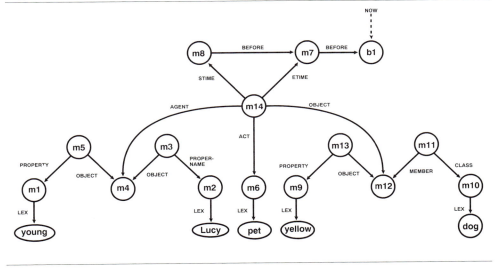

(1) CASSIE builds a node (bl) representing the current time (the "now"-point; *cf.* Almeida and Shapiro 1983; Almeida 1987).

(2) • CASSIE "hears" the word 'young'.
     • If she has not heard this word before, she *builds* a "sensory" node (labeled 'young') representing the *word* that she hears and a node (m1) representing the internal *concept* produced by her having heard it—this concept node is linked to the sensory node by an arc labeled 'LEX'. (See Figure 10.3; the formal semantic interpretation of this small network is: m1 is the Meinongian object of thought corresponding to the utterance of 'young'; *cf.* Rapaport 1985a; Shapiro and Rapaport 1986, 1987.)
     • If she *has* heard it before, she *finds* the already-existing concept node. (Actually, she attempts to "find" before she "builds"; henceforth, this process of "finding-or-building" will be referred

to simply as "building", since it is in conformity with the Uniqueness Principle.)

Figure 10.3. SNePS network for the concept expressed in English as 'young'.

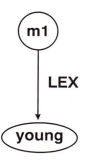

(3) • CASSIE hears the word 'Lucy'.
   • She builds a sensory node (labeled 'Lucy') for the *word* 'Lucy', a concept node (m2; linked to the sensory node by a LEX arc) for the *name* 'Lucy', a concept node (m4) representing an individual, and a proposition node (m3) representing that the individual is named 'Lucy' (using an OBJECT—PROPER-NAME case frame).[12]
   • She (unconsciously) determines, by means of the ATN, that Lucy is young, and she builds a proposition node (m5) representing this (using an OBJECT-PROPERTY case frame).

(4) She hears the word 'petted', and (skipping a few details, for clarity) she builds a sensory node (labeled 'pet') for the verb 'pet', a concept node (m6; linked to the sensory node by a LEX arc) for the act of petting, and a temporal network (m7 and m8, linked by BEFORE arcs to b1) indicating that this act occurred before "now" (= the time of utterance).

(5) She hears 'yellow' and processes it as she did 'young' (building m9).

(6) She hears 'dog' and builds:
   • a sensory node for it,
   • a concept node (m10) representing the class whose label is 'dog',
   • a concept node (m12) representing the individual yellow dog whom young Lucy petted,

- a proposition node (m11) representing that this individual concept node is a MEMBER of the CLASS whose label is 'dog',
- a proposition node (m13) representing that that individual concept node (the dog) is yellow, and, finally,
- a proposition node (m14) representing that the dog is the OBJECT of an AGENT-ACT-OBJECT case frame whose agent is Lucy, whose act is petting, whose starting time is m8, and whose ending time is m7.

(7) She generates a sentence expressing her new understanding. I shall not go into the details of the generation algorithm, except to point out that she uses the sensory nodes to generate the words to express her new belief (*cf.* Shapiro 1982 for details).

(8) As the conversation shown in Appendix 1 continues, CASSIE's semantic network is continually updated with new nodes, as well as with new links to old nodes (cf. Figure 10.4).

The crucial thing to see is that the semantic network (Figure 10.2) that represents CASSIE's belief (the belief produced by her understanding of the user's sentence) is her interpretation of that sentence and that it has three parts: One part consists of the sensory nodes: the nodes at the heads of LEX arcs; a second part consists of the entire network except for that set of sensory nodes and the LEX arcs; and the third part consists of the LEX arcs themselves, which link the other two, major, parts of the network.

Notice that the sensory-node set by itself has (or seems to have) no structure. This is consistent with viewing these as CASSIE's internal representations, causally produced, of external entities (in this case, utterances) to which she has no other kind of access and, hence, no knowledge of their relationships. As I suggested earlier when discussing deixis, if we had a visual-input module, there might be a set of sensory nodes linked by, say, "PIX" arcs. At present, I see no need for any direct links between visual and linguistic sensory nodes, even between those that, in some extensional sense, represent the same entity; any such links would be forged by means of links among the concept nodes at the *tails* of LEX and PIX arcs (but this is a matter for future investigation, as is the entire issue of the structure and behavior of sensory nodes).

The concept-node set, on the other hand, has a great deal of structure. It is this fragment of the entire network that represents CASSIE's internal understanding. If CASSIE were not intended to converse in natural language, there would not be any need for LEX arcs or sensory nodes. If CASSIE's sensory nodes were replaced by others, she would converse in a notational variant of English (*cf.* Quine 1969, Section II, p. 48). If her generation grammar were replaced with one for French and her sensory nodes replaced with "French" ones, she would understand English but speak in French (though here, no doubt, other modifications would be required in order for her knowledge representation system to be used in this way as an "interlingua", as machine-translation researchers call it).[13] In each of these cases, *the structure of her mind and, thus, her understanding—which would be in terms of purely syntactic symbol manipulation—would remain the same.* Only the external semantic interpretation function, so to speak, would differ. "Meaning," in the sense of internal semantics, "is determined by structures, truth by facts" (Garver 1986, p. 75).[14]

A nice metaphor for this is Carnap's example of the railroad map whose station names (but not rail-line names) have been removed; the stations can still be uniquely identified by the rail lines that meet at them. The "meaning" of a node in such a network is merely its locus in the entire network. In Appendix 2, I sketch how this might be done in a SNePS-like semantic network. (See Carnap 1928, Section 14, pp. 25-27; *cf.*: Quillian 1967, p. 101; Quillian 1968, Section 4.2.1, especially p. 238; and Quine 1951, Section 6, especially pp. 42f. Quine's "fabric which impinges on experience only along the edges" nicely captures the notion of a semantic network with sensory nodes along the edges.)

3.7. *Varieties of Meaning*

At this point, we can make the promised comments on the different kinds of meaning. Recall the three-part nature of the semantic network: the sensory nodes, the LEX arcs, and the main body of the semantic network. The meaning of a node, in one sense of 'meaning', is its locus in the network; this is, I have been urging, the central meaning of the node. This locus provides the *internal* semantics of the node and, hence, of the words that label sensory nodes. Considered as an object of thought, a node can be taken as being constituted by a collection of properties, hence as an intensional, Meinongian object. The locus in the network of a node at the tail of a LEX arc can be taken as a collection of propositional functions corresponding to the open sentences that are satisfied by the word that labels the sensory node. In particular, at any time t, the collection will consist of those open sentences satisfied by the words that were heard by the system prior to t. (For details, see Rapaport 1981.) But this means that the internal meaning of the word will change each time the word is heard in a new sentence. So, the internal meaning is extensional. This curious duality of intension and extension is due, I think, to the fine grain of this sort of meaning: it is intensional because of its fine grain and the fact that it is an object of thought; but it is extensional in that it is determined by a set-in-extension.

But there is a meaning determined by a set-in-intension, too. This may be called the "definitional" meaning of the word. It is a subset of the internal meaning, whose characterizing feature is that it contains those propositions in the semantic network that are the meaning postulates of the word. That is, these propositions are the ones from which all other facts containing the word can be inferred (together with miscellaneous other facts; again, *cf.* Rapaport 1981). Thus, this kind of meaning is an internal, intensional meaning; it is a sort of idiosyncratic or idiolectal *Sinn*.

Both of these kinds of meaning are or consist of internal symbols to be manipulated. To fill out the picture, there may also be the (physical) objects in the world, which are the external, extensional, referential meanings of the words. But these are not symbols to be manipulated and are irrelevant for natural-language understanding.

3.8.   *Discourse*

Another aspect of my interpretation of natural-language understanding is the importance of *discourse* (sequences of sentences), rather than isolated sentences, for the construction of the system's knowledge base. Discourse is important for its *cumulative* nature:

> [P]utting one sentence after another can be used to express time sequence, deductive necessity, exemplification or other relationships, *without any words being used to express the relation.* (Mann *et al.* 1981, Part 1, p. 6)

This aspect of discourse illuminates the role of internal semantics in a way hinted at earlier. To provide a semantic interpretation for a language by means of an internal semantic network (or a discourse representation structure) is to provide a more or less formal *theory* about the linguistic data (much as Chomsky 1965 said, though this is a *semantic* theory). But, in discourse as in science, the data underdetermine the theory: it is the internal semantic network—the mind of the understander—that provides explicit counterparts to the unexpressed relations.

Isolated sentences (so beloved by philosophers and linguists) simply would not serve for enabling a system such as CASSIE to understand natural language: they would, for all practical purposes, be random, unsystematic, and *unrelated* data. The *order* in which CASSIE processes (or "understands") sentences is important: Given a mini-discourse of even as few as two sentences,

$$s_1 . s_2,$$

her interpretation of s_2 will be partially determined by her interpretation of s_1. Considered as part of a discourse, sentence s_2 sis syntactically within the "scope" of s_1; hence, the interpretation of s_2s will be within the scope of the interpretation of s_1. (This aspect of discourse is explored in Maida and Shapiro 1982; Mann and Thompson 1983; Kamp 1984 and forthcoming; Fauconnier 1985; Asher 1986, 1987; and Wiebe and Rapaport 1986.) Thus, discourse and, hence, *conversation* are essential, the latter for important feedback in order to bring the conversers' semantic networks into alignment.

4. WOULD A COMPUTER "REALLY" UNDERSTAND?

I have considered what it would be for a computer to understand natural language, and I have argued for an interpretation of "understanding natural language" on which it makes sense to say that a computer *can* understand natural language. But there might still be some lingering doubts about whether a computer that understands natural language in this sense "really" understands it.

4.1. The Korean-Room Argument

Let us start with a variation of Searle's Chinese-Room Argument, which may be called the "Korean-Room Argument" (though we shall do away with the room):[15]

> Imagine a Korean professor of English literature at the University of Seoul who does not understand spoken or written English but who is, nevertheless, a world authority on Shakespeare. He has established and maintains his reputation as follows: He has only read Shakespeare in excellent Korean translations. Based on his readings and, of course, his intellectual acumen, he has written, in Korean, several articles on Shakespeare's play. These articles have been translated for him into English and published in numerous, well-regarded, English-language, scholarly journals, where they have met with great success.

The Korean-Room-Argument question is this: Does the Korean scholar "understand" Shakespeare? Note that, unlike the Chinese-Room Argument, the issue is not whether he understands English; he does not. Nor does he mechanically ("unthinkingly") follow a translation algorithm; others do his translating for him. Clearly, though, he does understand Shakespeare—the literary scholarly community attests to that—and, so, he understands *something*.

Similarly, Searle in the Chinese room *can* be said to understand something, even if it isn't Chinese. More precisely (because, as I urged in Section 3.2, I don't think that Searle's Chinese-Room Argument is as precisely spelled out as it could be), an AI natural-language-understanding system can be said to understand something (or even to understand *simpliciter*), insofar as what it is doing is semantic interpretation.[16] (Of course, it does this syntactically by manipulating the symbols of its semantic interpretation.) We can actually say a bit more: it understands *natural language*, since it is a natural language that it is semantically interpreting. It is a separate question whether that which it understands is *Chinese*.[17] Now, I think there are *two* ways in which this question can be understood. In one way, it is quite obvious that if the system is understanding a natural language, then, since the natural language that it is understanding is Chinese, the system must be understanding Chinese. But in other ways, it is not so obvious. After all, the system shares very little, if any, of Chinese culture with its interlocutors, so in what sense can it be said to "really" understand Chinese? Or in what sense can it be said to understand Chinese, as opposed to, say, code of the computer-programming language that the Chinese "squiggles" are transduced into? This Chinese-*vs.*-code issue can be resolved in favor of Chinese by the Korean-Room Argument: just as it is *Shakespeare*, not merely a Korean *translation* of Shakespeare, that the professor understands, so it is Chinese, and not the programming-language code, that Searle-in-the-room understands.

As for the cultural issue, here, I think, the answer has to be that the system understands Chinese as well as any nonnative-Chinese human speaker does (and perhaps even better than some). The only qualm one might have is that, in some vague sense, what *it* means or understands by some expression might not be what the native Chinese speaker means or understands by it. But as Quine and, later, Schank have pointed out, the same qualm can beset a conversation in our native tongue between you and me (Quine 1969, p. 46; Schank 1984, Ch. 3). As I said earlier, we systematically *mis*understand each other: we can *never* mean *exactly* what another means; but that does not mean that we cannot understand each other. We might not "really" understand each other in some deep psychological or empathic sense (if, indeed, sense can be made of that notion; *cf.* Schank 1984, pp. 44-47), but we do "really" understand each other—and the AI natural-language-understanding system can "really" understand natural language—in the only sense that matters. Two successful conversers' understandings of the expressions of their common language will (indeed, they *must*) eventually come into alignment, even if one of the conversers is a computer (*cf.* Shapiro and Rapaport 1987).

4.2.   Simon and Dreyfus vs Winograd and SHRDLU

The considerations thus far can help us to see what is wrong with Herbert Simon's and Hubert Dreyfus's complaints that Terry Winograd's SHRDLU program does not understand the meaning of 'own' (Winograd 1972; Simon 1977, cited in Dreyfus 1979). Simon claims that "SHRDLU'S test of whether something is owned is simply whether it is tagged 'owned'. There is no intensional test of ownership . . ." (Simon 1977, p. 1064; Dreyfus 1979, p. 13). But this is simply not correct: When Winograd tells SHRDLU, "I own blocks which are not red, but I don't own anything which supports a pyramid," he comments that these are "two new theorems . . . created for proving things about 'owning'" (Winograd 1972, p. 11, *cf*. pp. 143f; cited also in Dreyfus 1979, p. 7). SHRDLU doesn't *merely* tag blocks (although it can also do that); rather, there are procedures for determining whether something is "owned"— SHRDLU can figure out new cases of ownership.[18] So there *is* an intensional test, although it may bear little or no resemblance, except for the label 'own', to *our* intensional test of ownership. But even this claim about lack of resemblance would only hold at an early stage in a conversation; if SHRDLU were a perfect natural-language-understanding program that *could* understand English (and no one claims that it is), *eventually* its intensional test of ownership would come to resemble ours *sufficiently for us to say that it understands 'own'*.

But Dreyfus takes this one step further:

> [SHRDLU] still wouldn't understand, unless it also understood that it (SHRDLU) couldn't own anything, since it isn't a part of the community in which owning makes sense. Given our cultural practices which constitute owning, a computer cannot own something any more than a table can. (Dreyfus 1979, p. 13)

The "community", of course, is the *human* one (which is biological; *cf*. Searle). There are several responses one can make. First of all, taken literally, Dreyfus's objection comes to nothing: it should be fairly simple to give the computer the information that, because it is not part of the right community, it cannot own anything. But that, of course, is not Dreyfus's point. His point is that it cannot *understand* 'own' because it *cannot* own. To this, there are two responses. For one thing, cultural practices can change, and, in the case at hand, they are already changing (for better or worse): computers *could* legally own things just as corporations, those other nonhuman persons, can (*cf*. Willick 1985).[19] But even if they can't, or even if there is some other relationship that computers are forever barred from participating in (even by means of a simulation), that should not prevent them from having an understanding of the concept. After all, women understood what voting was before they were enfranchised, men can understand what pregnancy is, and humans can understand what (unaided) flying is.[20] A computer could learn and understand such expressions to precisely the same extent, and that is all that is needed for it to really understand natural language.

5. DOES THE COMPUTER UNDERSTAND THAT IT UNDERSTANDS?

There are two final questions to consider. The first is this: Suppose that we have our ultimate AI natural-language-understanding program that passes the Turing Test; does it understand that it understands natural language? The second, perhaps prior, question is: *Can* it understand that it understands?

Consider a variation on the Korean-Room Argument. Suppose that the Korean professor of English literature has been systematically misled, perhaps by his translator, into thinking that the author of the plays that he is an expert on was a Korean playwright named, say, Jaegwon. The translator has systematically replaced 'Shakespeare' by 'Jaegwon', and *vice versa*, throughout all of the texts that were translated. Now, does the Korean professor understand Shakespeare? Does he understand that he understands Shakespeare? I think the answer to the latter question is pretty clearly 'No'. The answer to the former question is not so clear, but I shall venture an answer: Yes.

Before explaining this answer, let's consider another example (adapted from Goodman 1986). Suppose that a student in my Theory of Computation course is executing the steps of a Turing-machine program, as an exercise in understanding how Turing machines work. From time to time, she writes down certain numerals, representing the output of the program. Let us even suppose that they are Arabic numerals (i.e., let us suppose that she decodes the actual Turning-machine output of, say 0s and 1s, into Arabic numerals, according to some other algorithm). Further, let us suppose that, *as a matter of fact*, each number that she writes down is the greatest common divisor of a pair of numbers that is the input to the program. Now, does she know that that is what the output is? Not necessarily; since she might not be a math major (or even a computer science major), and since the Turing-machine program need not be labeled 'Program to Compute Greatest Common Divisors', she might not know what she is doing *under that description.* Presumably, she does know what she is doing under some other description, say, "executing a Turing-machine program"; but even this is not necessary. Since, as a matter of fact, she *is* computing greatest common divisors, if I needed to know what the greatest common divisor of two numbers was, I could ask her to execute that program for me. She would not have to understand what she is doing, under that description, in order to do it.

Similarly, the Korean professor does not have to understand that he understands Shakespeare in order to, in fact, understand Shakespeare. And, it should be clear, Searle-in-the-Chinese-room does not have to understand that he understands Chinese in order to, in fact, understand Chinese. So, a natural-language-understanding program does not have to understand that it understands natural language in order to understand natural language. That is, this use of *'understand'* is referentially transparent! If a cognitive agent A understands X, and X is equivalent to Y (in some relevant sense of equivalence), then A understands Y.

But this is only the case for "first-order" understanding: *understanding that one understands* is referentially opaque. I don't think that this is inconsistent with the transparency of first-order understanding, since this "second-order" sense of 'understand' is more akin to 'know that' or 'be aware', and the "first-order" sense of 'understand' is more akin to 'know how'.

Now, *can* the Korean professor understand that he understands Shakespeare? Of course; he simply needs to be told that it is Shakespeare (or merely someone *named* 'Shakespeare'; *cf.* Hofstadter *et al.* 1982), not someone named 'Jaegwon', that he has been studying all these years. Can my student understand that what she is computing are greatest common divisors? Of course; she simply needs to be told that. Moreover, if the program that she is executing is suitably modularized, the names of its procedures might give the game away to her. Indeed, an "automatic programming" system would have to have access to such labels in order to be able to construct a program to compute greatest common divisors (so-named or so-described); and if those labels were linked to a semantic network of mathematical concepts, it could be said to understand what that program would compute. And the program itself could understand what it was computing if it had a "self-concept" and could be made "aware" of what each of its procedures did.

This is even clearer to see in the case of a natural-language-understanding program. A natural-language-understanding program can be made to understand what it is doing—can be made to understand that it understands natural language—by, first, telling it (in natural language, of course) that that is what it is doing. Merely telling it, however, is not sufficient by itself; that would merely add some network structure to its knowledge base. To gain the requisite "awareness", the system would have to have LEX-like arcs linked, if only indirectly, to its actual natural-language-processing module—the ATN parser-generator, for instance. But surely that can be done; it is, in any event, an empirical issue as to precisely how it would be done. The point is that it would be able to associate expressions like 'understanding natural language' with certain of its activities. It would then understand what those expressions meant in terms of what those activities were. It would not matter in the least if it understood those activities in terms of bit-patterns or in terms of concepts such as "parsing" and "generating"; what would count is this: that it understood the expressions in terms of its actions; that its actions were, in fact, actions for understanding natural language; and, perhaps, that 'understanding natural language' was the label that its interlocutors used for that activity.

6.   CONCLUSION

By way of conclusion, consider (a) the language L that the system understands, (b) the external world, W, about which L expresses information, and (c) the language (or model of W), L_W that provides the interpretation of L. As William A. Woods (among many others) has made quite clear, such a "meaning representation language" as L_W is involved in two quite separate sorts of semantic analyses (Woods 1978; $cf.$ Woods 1975 and, especially, Kamp 1984).

There must be, first, a semantic interpretation function, P (for 'parser'), from utterances of L (the input to the system) to the system's internal knowledge base, L_W. L_W is the system's model of W, as filtered through L. There will also need to be a function, G (for 'generator'), from L_W to L, so that the system can express itself. P and G need not, and probably should not, be inverses (they are not in SNePS/CASSIE); "they" might also be a single function (as in SNePS/CASSIE; $cf.$ Shapiro 1982). Together, P, G, and L_W constitute the central part of the $system's$ understanding of L.

But, second, there must also be a semantic interpretation of L_W in terms of W (or in terms of our idiosyncratic L_Ws)—i.e., a semantic interpretation of the domain of semantic interpretation. Since L_W is itself a formal language, specified by a formal syntax, it needs a semantics ($cf.$ Woods 1975, McDermott 1981). But this semantic interpretation is merely our understanding of L_W. It is independent of and external to the relevant semantic issue of how the $system$ understands L. (This semantic interpretation of the knowledge base is provided for SNePS/CASSIE by interpreting L_W as a Meinongian theory of the objects of thought; $cf.$: Rapaport 1985a; Shapiro and Rapaport 1986, 1987.)

There may be another relationship between L_W and W, although this may also be provided by the semantic interpretation of L_W. This relationship is the causal one from W to L_W, and there is no reason to hold that it is limited to humans (or other biological entities). It produces the sensory nodes, but—other than that—it is also independent of and external to the system's understanding of L.

Once the sensory and concept nodes (or their analogues in some other knowledge-representation system) are produced, the actual causal links cease to be relevant to the system's $understanding$ (except—and I am willing to admit that this is an important exception—for purposes of the system's communication with others), thus highlighting the representationalism of the system.

Searle holds, however, that the links—the access to W—are necessary for understanding, that humans have (or that only biological entities can have) such access, that computers lack it, and, hence, that computers cannot understand. By contrast, I hold that *if* such access *were* needed, then computers could have it, too, so that Searle's pessimism with respect to computer understanding is unsupported. I also hold that such access is *not* needed, that, therefore, humans don't need it either (here is where methodological solipsism appears), so that, again, there's no support for Searle's conclusion. I agree with Searle that semantics is necessary for understanding natural language, but that the *kind* of semantics that's needed is the semantics provided by an internal semantic interpretation, which is, in fact, syntactic in nature and, hence, computable. Syntax suffices.

7.   APPENDIX 1: A "CONVERSATION" WITH CASSIE

Following is the transcript of a "conversation" with CASSIE. A commented version of part of it appears in Shapiro and Rapaport 1986, 1987. User input is on lines with the :-prompt; CASSIE's output is on the lines that follow. A fragment of the full network showing CASSIE's state of mind at the end of the conversation is shown in Figure 10.4.

> : Young Lucy petted a yellow dog
> I understand that young Lucy petted a yellow dog
>
> : What is yellow
> a dog is yellow
>
> : Dogs are animals
> I understand that dogs are animals
>
> : Who petted an animal
> young Lucy petted a yellow dog
>
> : Lucy is clever
> I understand that young Lucy is clever
>
> : Lucy is a girl
> I understand that clever young Lucy is a girl
>
> : Girls are people
> I understand that girls are people

Figure 10.4. Small fragment of CASSIE's beliefs at the end of the conversation.

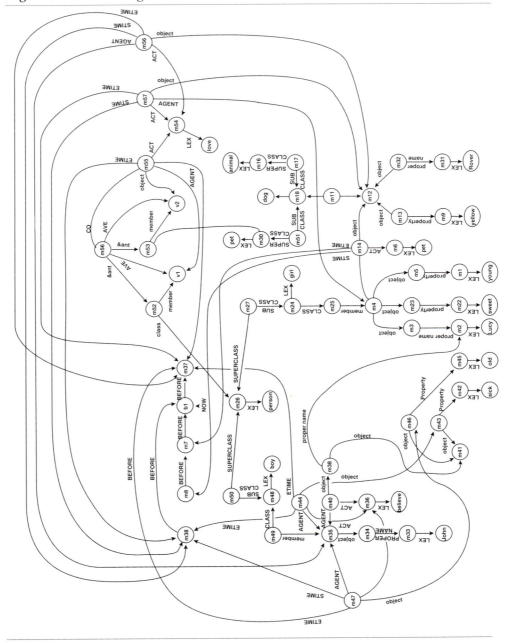

: What was petted by a person
a yellow dog was petted by clever young Lucy

: The dog is named Rover
I understand that Rover is a yellow dog

: What was petted by a person
yellow Rover was petted by clever young Lucy

: For every d if d is a dog then there is a b such that b is a
boy and b owns d
I understand that for every d, if d is a dog
        then there exists a b such that b is a boy
and
            b owns d

: The boy is named John
I understand that John is a boy

: Who owns Rover
John owns yellow Rover

: John believes that Lucy is rich
I understand that John believes that Lucy is rich

: Who is rich
I don't know.

: Who is clever
young Lucy is clever

: John believes that Lucy is old
I understand that John believes that rich Lucy is old

: Boys are people
I understand that boys are people

: Dogs are pets
I understand that dogs are pets

: For every p and d if p is a person and d is a pet then p
loves d
I understand that for every d and p, if p is a person
and

> d is a pet
> then p loves d

: Who loves a pet
clever young Lucy loves yellow Rover
and
John loves yellow Rover

8.   APPENDIX 2: DESCRIBING A NODE VIA ITS NETWORK LOCUS

How can a node be identified if there are no LEX arcs or sensory nodes? That is, how can they be identified if they have no names? The answer is, by descriptions. It is important to see that the identifiers of the nodes ("m1", etc.) are *not* names (or labels); they convey no information to the system. (They are like the nodes of a tree each of which contains no data but only pointers to its left and right children. The sensory nodes are like leaf nodes that do contain data; their labels do convey information.) The nodes can be described solely in terms of their locus in the network, i.e., in terms of the structure of the arcs (which *are* labeled) that meet at them. If a node has a unique "arc structure", then it can be uniquely described by a *definite* description; if two or more nodes share an arc-structure, they can only be given *indefinite* descriptions and, hence, cannot be uniquely identified. That is, they are indistinguishable to the system, unless each has a LEX arc emanating from it. (C*f.* again, Carnap 1928, Section 14.) Thus, for example, in the network in Figure 10.5, m1 is *the* node with precisely two ARG arcs emanating from it, and b1 is *a* node with precisely one ARG arc entering it (and similarly for b2). In keeping with the notion that the internal meaning of a node is its locus in the *entire* network, the *full* descriptions of m1 and b1 (or b2) are:

(m1)   *the* node with one ARG arc to *a* base node and with another ARG arc to *a* base node.

(b1)   *a* base node with an ARG arc from *the* node with one ARG arc to it and with another ARG arc to a base node.

(A base node is a node with no arcs leaving it; no SNePS node can have an arc pointing to itself.) The pronominal 'it' has widest scope; i.e., its anaphoric antecedent is always the node being described. Note that each node's description is a monad-like description of the *entire* network from its own "point of view".

Figure 10.5. A small SNePS network.

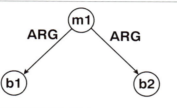

9.   NOTES

1.   This material is based upon work supported by the National Science Foundation under Grant Nos. IST-8504713, IRI-8610517, and by SUNY Buffalo Research Development Fund Award No. 150-8537-G. I am grateful to Randall R. Dipert, Michael Leyton, Ernesto Morgado, Jane Pease, Sandra Peters, Stuart C. Shapiro, Marie Meteer, Janyce M. Wiebe, Albert Hanyong Yuhan, and other colleagues in the SNePS Research Group and the SUNY Buffalo Graduate Group in Cognitive Science for discussions on these topics and comments on earlier versions of this essay.

2.   *Cf.* my earlier critiques of Searle, in which I distinguish between an abstraction, an implementing medium, and the implemented abstraction (Rapaport 1985b, 1986b, 1988).

3.   The "weak/strong" terminology is from Searle 1980.

4.   Or: that it is a woman. More precisely, Turing describes the Imitation Game, in which "a man (A), a woman (B), and an interrogator (C)" have as their object "for the interrogator to determine which of the other two is the man and which is the woman". Turing then modifies this:

> We now ask the question, "What will happen when a machine takes the part
> of A in this game?" Will the interrogator decide wrongly as often when the
> game is played like this as he does when the game is played between a man

and a woman? These questions replace our original, "Can machines think?" (Turing 1950, p. 5.)

5. Randall R. Dipert has suggested to me that Searle's Chinese-Room Argument does show that what *executes* the program (viz., the central processing unit) does not understand, leaving open the question whether the *process* might understand.

6. Not to be confused with scripts in the sense of Schank's AI data structures.

7. Similarly, part of my argument in this essay may be roughly paraphrased as follows: I want to understand what it means to understand natural language; I believe that it is capable of being understood (that it is not a mystery) and that, for a system to understand natural language, certain formal techniques are necessary and sufficient; these techniques are computational; hence, understanding natural language is a recursive function.

8. I take (7) to be the conclusion, since (1)—(6) are in response to the question, "*Can* computers add?" (p. 25; italics added). If I am taking Dretske too literally here, then simply end the argument at step (6).

9. Note that, for independent reasons, the computer *will* need an internal representation or model of itself. Maybe this won't be a *complete* self-model, on pain of infinite regress, but then neither is ours. If needed, it, and we, can use an *external* model that *is* complete, via self-reflection; *cf.* Case 1986, esp. p. 91. For more on self-models, *cf.*: Minsky 1965; Rapaport 1984, 1986c; Smith 1986.

10. I venture to say that the mutual learning and adjusting process has already begun: studying such computers and primitive AI systems as we have now has led many philosophers and AI researchers to this kind of opinion.

11. It should be obvious by now that by 'understand' I do not mean some sort of "deep" psychological understanding, merely that sort of understanding required for understanding natural language. *Cf.* Schank 1984 , Ch. 3.

12. *Cf.* Shapiro and Rapaport 1986 and 1987 for the formal syntax and semantics of this and the other case frames. The node identifiers ("m1", etc.) are generated by the underlying program in an implementation-dependent order; the order and the identifiers are inessential to the semantic network.

13.   The importance of the knowledge base, whether it is a semantic network, a discourse representation structure, or some other data type, for understanding natural language has some interesting implications for machine translation. There are several paradigms for machine translation; two are relevant for us: the "transfer" approach and the "interlingua" approach (*cf.* Slocum 1985). Transfer approaches typically do not use a knowledge base, but manipulate syntactic structures of the source language until they turn into syntactic structures of the target language. Such a system, I would argue, cannot be said to understand the natural languages it deals with. Interlingua approaches, on the other hand, do have a sort of knowledge base. They are "mere" symbol manipulation systems, but the symbols that get manipulated include those of the system's internal knowledge-representation system: hence, interlingua machine-translation systems have at least the *potential* for understanding. (Searle's Chinese-language program appears to be more like a transfer system (for, say, translating Chinese into Chinese) than an interlingua system, despite the use of Schank-like scripts.)

      Note, too, that this suggests that the "machine-translation problem" is coextensive with the "natural-language-understanding problem" and, thus (*cf.* Section 1, above), with the general "AI problem": solve one and you will have solved them all. (This underlies Martin Kay's pessimism about the success of machine translation; *cf.* Kay 1986.)

14.   Garver's "challenge of metaphor", it must be noted, is also a challenge for the theory presented here, which I hope to investigate in the future.

15.   The Korean-Room Argument was suggested to me by Albert Hanyong Yuhan.

16.   And to the extent that it does *not* do semantic interpretation, it does not understand. My former teacher, Spencer Brown, recently made the following observation:

         As for Searle, I myself have been a *corpus vile* for his "experiment": once I conveyed a message from one mathematician to another, with complete understanding on the part of the second and with total, nay, virginal, ignorance on my part of the meaning of the message. Similarly I have conveyed a message from my doctor to my dentist without knowing what I was telling. Q.E.D.: I can't think. This is something I have always suspected. (Personal communication, 1986; cf. Rapaport 1981, p. 7.)

But the conclusions (both of them!) are too hasty: all that follows is that he did not understand certain isolated statements of mathematics and medicine. And this was, no doubt, because he lacked the tools for interpreting them and an appropriate knowledge base within which to fit them.

17.   I owe this way of looking at my argument to Michael Leyton.

18.   I am indebted to Stuart C. Shapiro for pointing this out to me.

19.   I am indebted to Shapiro for this reference.

20.   The examples are due to Shapiro. My original example was that, as a U. S. citizen, I am probably forever enjoined from some custom unique to and open only to French citizens; yet surely I can learn and understand the meaning of the French expression for such a custom. But finding an example of such a custom is not as easy as it seems. Voting in a French election, e.g., isn't quite right, since I can vote in U. S. elections, and similarly for other legal rights or proscriptions. Religious practices "unique" to one religion usually have counterparts in others. Another kind of case has to do with performatives: I cannot marry two people merely by reciting the appropriate ritual, since I do not have the right to do so. The case of owning that Simon and Dreyfus focus on is somewhat special, since it is both in the legal realm as well as the cultural one: there are (allegedly or at least conceivably) cultures in which the institutions of ownership and possession are unknown. I maintain, however, that the case of humans and computers is parallel: we share the same abilities and inabilities to understand or act.

10. REFERENCES

Allen, W. (1980) The Kugelmass episode. In W. Allen *Side Effects* (New York: Random House), 41-55.

Almeida, M. J. (1987) Reasoning about the temporal structure of narratives. Technical Rep. No. 86-10 (Buffalo: SUNY Buffalo Department of Computer Science).

Almeida, M. J. and Shapiro, S. C. (1983) Reasoning about the temporal structure of narrative texts. *Proceedings of the Fifth Annual Meeting of the Cognitive Science Society* (Rochester, NY: Cognitive Science Society).

Appelt, D. E. (1982) Planning natural-language utterances. *Proceedings of the National Conference on Artificial Intelligence (AAAI-82; Pittsburgh)* (Los Altos, CA: Morgan Kaufmann), 59-62.

Appelt, D. E. (1985) Some pragmatic issues in the planning of definite and indefinite noun phrases. *Proceedings of the 23rd Annual Meeting of the Association for Computational Linguistics (University of Chicago)* (Morristown, NJ: Association for Computational Linguistics), 198-203.

Asher, N. (1986) Belief in discourse representation theory. *Journal of Philosophical Logic*, 15: 127- 189.

Asher, N. (1987) A typology for attitude verbs and their anaphoric properties. *Linguistics and Philosophy,* 10: 125-197.

Brachman, R. J., and Schmolze, J. G. (1985) An overview of the KL-ONE knowledge representation system. *Cognitive Science,* 9: 171-216.

Bruder, G. A., Duchan, J. F., Rapaport, W. J., Segal, E. M., Shapiro, S. C., and Zubin, D. A. (1986) Deictic centers in narrative: an interdisciplinary cognitive-science project. Technical Rep. No. 86-20 (Buffalo: SUNY Buffalo Department of Computer Science).

Carnap, R. (1928) *The Logical Structure of the World.* R. A. George (trans.) (Berkeley: University of California Press, 1967).

Case, J. (1986) Learning machines. In W. Demopoulos and A. Marras (eds.) *Language Learning and Concept Acquisition* (Norwood, NJ: Ablex), 83-102.

Chomsky, N. (1965) *Aspects of the Theory of Syntax* (Cambridge, MA: MIT Press).

Cohen, P. R., and Perrault, C. R. (1979) Elements of a plan-based theory of speech acts. *Cognitive Science,* 3: 177-212.

Davies, R. (1972) *The Manticore.* In R. Davies *The Deptford Trilogy* (Middlesex, England: Penguin, 1983).

de Saussure, F. (1915) *Cours de linguistique générale,* (Paris: Payot, 1972).

Dennett, D. C. (1983) Intentional systems in cognitive ethology: the 'Panglossian paradigm' defended. *Brain and Behavioral Sciences,* 6: 343-390.

Dretske, F. (1985) Machines and the mental. *Proceedings and Addresses of the American Philosophical Association*, 59: 23-33.

Dreyfus, H. L. (1979) *What Computers Can't Do: The Limits of Artificial Intelligence* rev. ed. (New York: Harper & Row).

Fauconnier, G. (1985) *Mental Spaces: Aspects of Meaning Construction in Natural Language* (Cambridge, MA: MIT Press).

Findler, N. V. (ed.) (1979) *Associative Networks: The Representation and Use of Knowledge by Computers* (New York: Academic Press).

Garver, N. (1986) Structuralism and the challenge of metaphor. *Monist,* 69: 68-86.

Gleick, J. (1985) They're getting better about predicting the weather (even though you don't believe it). *The New York Times Magazine* (27 January).

Goodman, N. D. (1986) Intensions, Church's thesis, and the formalization of mathematics. *Notre Dame Journal of Formal Logic*, 28: 473—489.

Green, B. F., Wolf, A. K., Chomsky, C., and Laughery, K. (1961) Baseball: an automatic question answerer. Reprinted in E. A. Feigenbaum and J. Feldman (eds.) *Computers and Thought* (New York: McGraw-Hill), 207-216.

Hofstadter, D. (1980), Reductionism and religion. *Behavioral and Brain Sciences,* 3, 433-434.

Hofstadter, D. R., Clossman, G. A., and Meredith, M. J. (1982) Shakespeare's plays weren't written by him, but by someone else of the same name: an essay on intensionality and frame-based knowledge representation systems (Bloomington, IN: Indiana University Linguistics Club).

Jackendoff, R. (1985) Information is in the mind of the beholder. *Linguistics and Philosophy,* 8: 23-34.

Jennings, R. C. (1985) Translation, interpretation and understanding. Paper read at the American Philosophical Association Eastern Division (Washington, D.C.). Abstract, *Proceedings and Addresses of the American Philosophical Association,* 59, 345-346.

Kamp, H. (1984) A theory of truth and semantic representation. In J. Groenendijk, T. M. V. Janssen, and M. Stokhof (eds.) *Truth, Interpretation and Information* (Dordrecht: Foris), 1-41.

Kamp, H. (1983) *Situations in Discourse* (Austin: University of Texas Center for Cognitive Science).

Kay, M. (1986) Forum on machine translation: machine translation will not work. *Proceedings of the 24th Annual Meeting of the Association for Computational Linguistics* (Columbia University) (Morristown, NJ: Association for Computational Linguistics), 268.

Lehnert, W. G., Dyer, M. G., Johnson, P. N., Yang, C. J., and Harley, S. (1983) BORIS—an experiment in in-depth understanding of narratives. *Artificial Intelligence*, 20: 15-62.

Levesque, H. J. (1984) A logic of implicit and explicit belief. *Proceedings of the National Conference on Artificial Intelligence* (AAAI-84; Austin, TX) (Los Altos, CA: Morgan Kaufmann), 198-202.

Maida, A. S., and Shapiro, S. C. (1982) Intentional concepts in propositional semantic networks. *Cognitive Science*, 6: 291-330.

Mann, W. C., Bates, M., Grosz, B. J., McDonald, D. D., McKeown, K. R., and Swartout, W. R. (1981) Text generation: The state of the art and the literature. Technical Rep. No. ISI/RR-81-101 (Marina del Rey, CA: University of Southern California Information Sciences Institute).

Mann, W. C., and Thompson, S. S. (1983) Relational propositions in discourse. Technical Rep. No. ISI/RR-83-115 (Marina del Rey, CA: University of Southern California Information Sciences Institute).

McDermott, D. (1981) Artificial intelligence meets natural stupidity. In J. Haugeland (ed.) *Mind Design: Philosophy, Psychology, Artificial Intelligence* (Cambridge, MA: MIT Press), 143-160.

Minsky, M. L. (1965) Matter, mind, and models. In M. Minsky (ed.) *Semantic Information Processing* (Cambridge, MA: MIT Press, 1968), 425-432.

Minsky, M. (1975) A framework for representing knowledge. In J. Haugeland (ed.) *Mind Design: Philosophy, Psychology, Artificial Intelligence* (Cambridge, MA: MIT Press, 1981), 95-128.

Neal, J. G. (1981) A knowledge engineering approach to natural language understanding. Technical Rep. No. 179 (Buffalo: SUNY Buffalo Department of Computer Science).

Neal, J. G. (1985) A knowledge based approach to natural language understanding. Technical Rep. No. 85–06 (Buffalo: SUNY Buffalo Department of Computer Science).

Neal, J. G., and Shapiro, S. C. (1984) Knowledge based parsing. Technical Rep. No. 213 (Buffalo: SUNY Buffalo Department of Computer Science).

Neal, J. G., and Shapiro, S. C. (1985) Parsing as a form of inference in a multiprocessing environment. *Proc. Conf. on Intelligent Systems and Machines* (Rochester, MI: Oakland University), 19-24.

Neal, J. G., and Shapiro, S. C. (1987) Knowledge representation for reasoning about language. In J. C. Boudreax *et al*. (eds.) *The Role of Language in Problem Solving* **2** (Elsevier/North-Holland), 27-46.

Putnam, H. (1975) The meaning of 'meaning.' Reprinted in H. Putnam, *Mind, Language and Reality* (Cambridge: Cambridge University Press), 215-271.

Quillian, M. R. (1967) Word concepts: A theory and simulation of some basic semantic capabilities. *Behavioral Science*, 12, 410-430. Reprinted in R. J. Brachman and H. J. Levesque (eds.) *Readings in Knowledge Representation* (Los Altos, CA: Morgan Kaufman, 1985), 97-118. Page references are to the reprint.

Quillian, M. R. (1968) Semantic memory. In M. Minsky (ed.) *Semantic Information Processing* (Cambridge, MA: MIT Press), 227-270.

Quine, W. V. O. (1951) Two dogmas of empiricism. Reprinted in W. V. O. Quine, *From a Logical Point of View* (Cambridge, MA: Harvard University Press, 1980), 2nd ed., rev., 20-46.

Quine, W. V. O. (1969) Ontological relativity. In W. V. O. Quine, *Ontological Relativity and Other Essays* (New York: Columbia University Press), 26-68.

Rapaport, W. J. (1976) *Intentionality and the Structure of Existence*. Ph.D. dissertation, Department of Philosophy, Indiana University, Bloomington.

Rapaport, W. J. (1981) How to make the world fit our language: an essay in Meinongian semantics. *Grazer Philosophische Studien,* 14: 1-21.

Rapaport, W. J. (1984) Belief representation and quasi-indicators. Technical Rep. No. 215 (Buffalo: SUNY Buffalo Department of Comnputer Science).

Rapaport, W. J. (1985a) Meinongian semantics for propositional semantic networks. *Proceedings of the 23rd Annual Meeting of the Association for Computational Linguistics (University of Chicago)* (Morristown, NJ: Association for Computational Linguistics), 43-48.

Rapaport, W. J. (1985b) Machine understanding and data abstraction in Searle's Chinese room. *Proceedings of the 7th Annual Meeting of the Cognitive Science Society (University of California at Irvine)* (Hillsdale, NJ: Lawrence Erlbaum), 341-345.

Rapaport, W. J. (1985/1986) Non-existent objects and epistemological ontology. *Grazer Philosophische Studien,* 25/26: 61-95.

Rapaport, W. J. (1986a) Searle's experiments with thought. *Philosophy of Science,* 53: 271-279.

Rapaport, W. J. (1986b) Philosophy, artificial intelligence, and the Chinese-room argument. *Abacus* 3 (Summer 1986): 6-17.

Rapaport, W. J. (1986c) Logical foundations for belief representation. *Cognitive Science,* 10: 371-422.

Rapaport, W. J. (1988) To think or not to think. *Noûs,* 22: 585 - 609.

Rapaport, W. J. (1987) Belief systems. In S. C. Shapiro (ed.) *Encyclopedia of Artificial Intelligence* (New York: John Wiley), 63-73.

Russell, B. (1918) The philosophy of logical atomism. In B. Russell, and R. C. Marsh (eds.) *Logic and Knowledge: Essays 1901–1950* (New York: Capricorn) (1956), 177-281.

Sayre, K. M. (1986) Intentionality and information processing: an alternative model for cognitive science. *Behavioral and Brain Sciences,* 9: 121-166.

Schank, R. C. (1982) *Dynamic Memory: A Theory of Reminding and Learning in Computers and People* (Cambridge: Cambridge University Press).

Schank, R. C. (with Childers, P. G.) (1984) *The Cognitive Computer: On Language, Learning, and Artificial Intelligence* (Reading, MA: Addison-Wesley).

Searle, J. R. (1980) Minds, brains, and programs. *Behavioral and Brain Sciences*, 3: 417-457.

Searle, J. R. (1982) The myth of the computer. *New York Review of Books* (29 April), 3-6; *cf.* correspondence, (24 June 1982), 56-57.

Searle, J. R. (1984) *Minds, Brains and Science* (Cambridge, MA: Harvard University Press).

Shapiro, S. C. (1977) Representing numbers in semantic networks: prolegomena. *Proceedings of the 5th International Joint Conference on Artificial Intelligence (IJCAI-77; MIT)* (Los Altos, CA: Morgan Kaufmann), 284.

Shapiro, S. C. (1979) The SNePS semantic network processing system. In N. V. Findler (ed.) *Associative Networks: The Representation and Use of Knowledge by Computers* (New York: Academic Press), 179-203.

Shapiro, S. C. (1982) Generalized augmented transition network grammars for generation from semantic networks. *American Journal of Computational Linguistics,* 8: 12-25.

Shapiro, S. C., and Rapaport, W. J. (1986) SNePS considered as a fully intensional propositional semantic network. *Proceedings of the National Conference on Artificial Intelligence (AAAI-86; Philadelphia),* Vol. 1 (Los Altos, CA: Morgan Kaufmann), 278-283.

Shapiro, S. C., and Rapaport, W. J. (1987) SNePS considered as a fully intensional propositional semantic network. In G. McCalla and N. Cercone (eds.) *The Knowledge Frontier* (Berlin: Springer-Verlag), 262-315.

Simon, H. A. (1977) Artificial intelligence systems that can understand. *Proceedings of the 5th International Joint Conference on Artificial Intelligence (IJCAI-77; MIT)* (Los Altos, CA: Morgan Kaufmann), 1059-1073.

Slocum, J. (1985) A survey of machine translation: its history, current status, and future prospects. *Computational Linguistics,* 11: 1-17.

Smith, B. C. (1982) Prologue to "Reflection and Semantics in a Procedural Language." In R. J. Brachman and H. J. Levesque (eds.) *Readings in Knowledge Representation* (Los Altos, CA: Morgan Kaufmann, 1985), 31-39.

Smith, B. C. (1986) Varieties of self-reference. In J. Y. Halpern (ed.), *Theoretical Aspects of Reasoning about Knowledge: Proceedings of the 1986 Conference,* (Los Altos, CA: Morgan Kaufmann), 19-43.

Tanenbaum, A. S. (1976) *Structured Computer Organization* (Englewood Cliffs, NJ: Prentice-Hall).

Turing, A. M. (1950) Computing machinery and intelligence. *Mind 59*. Reprinted in A. R. Anderson (ed.) *Minds and Machines* (Englewood Cliffs, NJ: Prentice-Hall, 1964), 4-30.

Weizenbaum, J. (1966) ELIZA—a computer program for the study of natural language communication between man and machine. *Communications of the Association for Computing Machinery,* 9: 36-45.

Weizenbaum, J. (1974) Automating psychotherapy. *ACM Forum,* 17: 543. Reprinted with replies, *CACM,* 26 (1983), 28.

Weizenbaum, J. (1976) *Computer Power and Human Reason: From Judgment to Calculation* (San Francisco: W. H. Freeman).

Wiebe, J. M., and Rapaport, W. J. (1986) Representing *de re* and *de dicto* belief reports in discourse and narrative. *Proceedings of the IEEE,* Special Issue on Knowledge Representation, 74: 1405-1413.

Willick, M. S. (1985) Constitutional law and artificial intelligence: the potential legal recognition of computers as "persons." *Proceedings of the 9th International Joint Conference on Artificial Intelligence (IJCAI-85; Los Angeles)* (Los Altos, CA: Morgan Kaufmann), 1271-1273.

Winograd, T. (1972) *Understanding Natural Language* (Orlando, FL: Academic Press).

Woods, W. A. (1975) What's in a link: foundations for semantic networks. In D. G. Bobrow and A. M. Collins (eds.) *Representation and Understanding* (New York: Academic Press), 35-82.

Woods, W. A. (1978) Semantics and quantification in natural language question answering. In M. C. Yovits (ed.) *Advances in Computers,* Vol. 17 (New York: Academic Press), 1-87.

IV

Intentionality and Beyond

275

CHAPTER
11

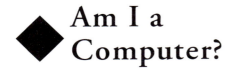

Am I a Computer?

Leonard Angel

In this chapter, I will discuss the key features of consciousness that have led some philosophers to conclude that consciousness can never be successfully modeled along computational or mechanical lines. After a brief exposition of these concepts and of the arguments employing them advanced to show the impossibility of regarding the human person as a complex mechanism, I will analyze the arguments and attempt to show their deficiencies. Finally, I will conclude with some remarks on how a mechanistic theory of mind might actually help enhance our experience of the wonder and beauty of being conscious.

Consciousness has an amazingly magical quality. We see, hear, taste, smell, touch, feel pain and pleasure, have emotions, think meaningful thoughts, make plans, choose between alternative courses of action, and implement our choices by means of acts of the will. When we reflect on our capacity to do these things we can be very easily amazed. What is it to actually experience? What is it to

Thinking Computers and Virtual Persons
edited by Eric Dietrich
ISBN 0-12215495-9

have this fantastic gift of sensory, emotional, and cognitive self-awareness and consciousness? What is it to be able to choose our courses of action and to implement these choices? What is it for me to see the brass knocker and the electric buzzer, choose to knock rather than to buzz, feel a twinge of apprehension when I imagine the encounter to come, will my hand to grasp the knocker, and, for my hand, lo and behold, to reach up, grasp the knocker, and knock it against the door?

The first answers one tends to give to such questions invoke several key notions: (1) ineffable qualia; (2) intentionality; (3) freedom of the will. Let's look at these in turn.

(1) If one agrees that the green one sees has an aspect, a qualitative "feel," that cannot be described or communicated no matter how much our picking out of green objects from nongreen objects is shared or coincident, then one holds that there is an aspect of experience that is ineffable, and to this aspect of experience, philosophers have given the term *quale* (singular), *qualia* (plural). The quale of a sensory or emotional experience is the aspect of the experience that presents itself directly but that is impossible to put into words. For most people who are initially uncertain as to what is meant by the qualitative feel, or quale, of the experience, the following question helps to clarify: do you think that it's possible that some people experience colors, for instance, in a slightly different manner from each other? Is it possible that my green is slightly more turquoise than your green? That is, is it possible that if I were to have your experience when you look at the grass, I would exclaim: "But you see everything with a bluish tint!" If you think that it is meaningful to wonder about the shifted spectrum possibility (even though it might be that one could never actually confirm or refute it), then one will be able to recognize the aspect of experience that is inexpressible and that is called the quale of the experience.

 (2) One of the amazing things about the thinking process is that our thoughts seem to us to be meaningful. The amazing meaningfulness of thoughts can be regarded as an aspect of the ineffable qualia of cognition. We explained qualia in terms of sensory and affective experience, but by extension we can regard our thought processes as having the amazing, ineffable aspect of actually presenting or capturing meanings. And over and above the ineffable quale aspect of the meaningfulness of our thoughts is the aboutness, or representational, aspect of thoughts without which our thoughts could not be meaningful. Because this special, mysterious feature of conscious reflection is linked specifically with the cognitive, we call attention to it with the cognitive-specific term *intentionality*.

A mental state is intentional just in those cases in which it has representational content, or is about something. Many sensory experiences such as twinges, tickles, and pains are minimally, if at all, representational. So there is minimal, if any, intentional content to a tickle. In contrast, many sensory experiences are fused with, or interpreted via, cognitive representations. My seeing of the table, for instance, is fused with the representation that there is a table out there. In these cases we characterize our sensory givens as embodying intentional content. Strictly speaking, however, it is the belief or overall cognitive state that has intentional content rather than just the seeing. In any case, one tends to reserve the term *quale* for the inexpressible aspect of sensory and affective experience, and *intentionality* for the representational or aboutness aspect of cognitive experience and reflection.

(3) That we choose between alternative courses of action seems to be a basic given of our experience. Each of us can remember all sorts of occasions in which choices are made. Some of these are only vaguely conscious choices, such as when we subconsciously or semiconsciously choose a route from work to home. Some of these choices are quite conscious, such as when we choose between two attractive job offers or whether to make an offer on a given car or a home. Moreover, we want to say at least in the case of our conscious choices that we are aware of freedom in these choices. Just as intentionality may be regarded as a quale given in thinking, so too, freedom may be regarded as a quale given in conscious choice. But (as intentionality is specific to thinking), the intuition of freedom is so specific to action and choice that we do well to think of the intuition of freedom separately from the qualia of sensory and affective experience.

Of course when we say that there is a purely qualitative, ineffable aspect of sensory and affective experience, or that there is a remarkable aboutness or intentionality to thinking, or that we experience freedom in conscious choice, we are not explaining or accounting for the amazingness of consciousness. Rather, we are, as it were, labeling specific features of self-consciousness and self-awareness that make them so amazing to us.

For the purposes of this discussion, we will assume that it is philosophically legitimate to take our *experiences* of qualia, intentionality, and freedom in conscious choice as givens. This allows the case for anti-computationalism to be as strong as possible. The question we are interested in is whether or not such experiences of qualia, intentionality, and freedom in conscious choice present obstacles either to the view that a human being is a computational engine or to the view that no insuperable difficulty has been thus far discovered in regard to the building of a conscious machine. I'll try to show that they do not.

The main arguments that have been mounted in favor of the conclusion that there are insuperable obstacles to an adequate modeling of the conscious person in computational terms may be summarized in three groups corresponding to the three aspects of consciousness just described:

(1) To have experiences of qualia requires that a material system with the causal powers to create such effects be the medium in which the functional organization is embodied. Just as a simulation of a thunderstorm gets no one wet, so too, it is absurd to think that any-old simulation of personhood has consciousness. Lacking a reason to think

that any old simulation of personhood has consciousness, we lack any reason to think that anything we'd artificially construct from computer chips would have consciousness even if it adequately simulated personhood.

(2a) Intentionality requires the solving of the intractable frame problem. No one has any adequate handle on this problem, the essence of which is the seeming impossibility of giving a computational system anything like common sense, or genuine understanding of a problem, or the genuine ability to engage in intelligent interaction with other intelligence, and so we have no reason to believe that it will ever be possible to model human consciousness adequately on computational lines.

(2b) Our intentionality ranges over an infinite domain of representations. This capacity of ours to understand, and form semantic interpretations of, infinitely many representations prevents any finitistic system from adequately modeling the human person. A computational system would be finitistic, and so no computational system can adequately model the human person.

(2c) Godel's incompleteness theorem is inconsistent with the representation of a person as a computational system, for if a person is a computational system it would have a finitistic representation based on which it would be theoretically possible, following Godel's method, to construct a theorem that it could, conceivably, prove to be both true and unprovable, which is internally inconsistent.

(3)   We are directly aware of our conscious freedom; but if we were computational systems, then we would be functionally determined. And if we were functionally determined, we would not be free. And if we were not free, we could not be directly aware of conscious freedom, as there would be no conscious freedom to be aware of. Therefore, we cannot be computational systems.

1.   ANALYSIS OF ARGUMENT (1)

1.1   To have experiences of qualia requires that a material system with the causal powers to create such effects be the medium in which the functional organization is embodied.

1.2   A computer simulation of a thunderstorm gets no one wet.

1.3   By analogy, it is absurd to think that for something to be a simulation of personhood is sufficient for it to have consciousness. (Consider the Chinese Room argument, for instance.)

1.4   Lacking any reason to think that any old simulation of personhood has consciousness, we lack any reason to think that anything we'd artificially construct from computer chips would have consciousness even if it adequately simulated personhood.

The first point to note is that the argument is by analogy. It is not formally valid and, as stated, is at best suggestive. Arguments by analogy can be translated into formally valid arguments, but many blanks need to be filled in to do so if the translation is to be nontrivial, and it would be difficult, and not really in keeping with the intent of the argument to serve as a so-called intuition pump, to attempt such a translation in this case. However, it will be of use to consider the truth of the premises.

The first premise is a more or less unsupported metaphysical axiom. It is possible to hold, equally axiomatically, that any system of functional organization that accomplished the cognitivity of a person would experience qualia. It is also possible to use evolutionary gradualism from which to infer that qualia consciousness is not a simple on/off matter, and from this it may be argued that cognitivity and experience of qualia are not as easily separated as premise 1.1 requires—that is, premise 1.1 may be denied both axiomatically and through a process of scientific inference.

Further, even if we accept the truth of 1.1, we must note that the argument as a whole hinges on a shift from the metaphysical to the epistemological perspective in midstream. The argument begins by inviting us to concur that qualia can only be generated by a material system of cognitive organization that has sufficient causal power to give rise to such qualitative experience. It then goes on to make judgments on such material systems. The application of the distinction between material systems with the causal powers to produce qualia and material systems without such causal powers, however, needs to be made in a perspicuous manner. Preferably, there is some criterion, however rough, that proponents of the argument present that would enable one at least in principle to identify material systems of embodiment with adequate causal powers and material systems of embodiment without adequate causal powers for the experience of qualia to occur. However, proponents of the argument have notoriously come up short on this requirement. For instance, John Searle offers an odd fusion of epistemic and metaphysical points in the following passage: "Suppose that Martians arrived on earth and we concluded that they had mental states. But suppose that when their heads were opened up, it was discovered that all they had inside was green slime. Well still, the green slime . . . would have to have causal powers equal to those of the human brain" (1984, p. 41). Searle is obviously missing the epistemic criterion for identification of material systems with requisite causal powers, because he allows that we can envision first determining whether they had mentality, and then inferring from such determination that the green slime must have had the requisite causal powers. Moreover, if we have made the determination of mentality first, then it must have been on how they were capable of interacting with us, and it would seem to follow that mentality attributions do not depend on investigating the material system to make sure it's of the right sort! There is a way to rescue Searle's argument, however. If he had said "Suppose that Martians had arrived on earth and we had *correctly* concluded that they had mental states," then he could claim to be making a strictly metaphysical point, relying, perhaps, on an externalist theory of justified belief concerning mentality attributions under which our mentality attributions might be justified without our being able to know that they are. Rescuing the argument this way, however, only emphasizes the absence of the criterion.

More recently, Searle allows, "I have no idea whether fleas, grasshoppers, crabs, or snails are conscious" (1992, p. 74), thus cheerfully acknowledging the epistemological deficit, though this is now inconsistent with the earlier remark assuming that we could judge the mentality of Martians without inspecting inside their skull-equivalents. In any case, because even proponents of the argument have conceded mystification on the epistemological issue, their argument is greatly weakened.

True enough, Searle does hold that through empirical research neurophysiologists, in principle, might be able to locate that feature of the human brain in virtue of which we're conscious. However, his remarks on this topic, (e.g. 1992, p. 74) seem implausible in the light of evolutionary gradualism. In addition, it would seem that under even the most favorable cases imaginable for the Searlian, the neurophysiological evidence will be unable to determine the property of a material system of organization capable of causing mentality.

To see this, consider first a criterion such as "must be embodied in a quantum machine" that, one would think, ought to be congenial to one who follows Searle's approach. This criterion doesn't help in the required way for the following reasons: (a) There is no substantive reason at present to think the human brain is a quantum machine. Both Michael Lockwood (1989, pp. 240-259) and Roger Penrose (1989, pp. 400-404) have recently presented highly speculative considerations raising the possibility that the brain is a quantum machine, but these speculations are at the moment far from compelling, and both state this clearly (Lockwood, p. 259, Penrose p. 402). (b) Even if the human brain is a quantum machine, it could still be accomplishing functional effects that could, in principle, all be modeled computationally. Such a computational model would not possess qualia, assuming the criterion to be correct, but the functionality would be computational. Then our models would still be functionally correct viewed from at least some points of view, even if their embodiments in computer systems would not be conscious. (c) There is no reason at present to assume that only an organic system could harness quantum superpositions, so that the criterion, if accepted, and if found to distinguish human brains from extant computer brains, would open the door on the question whether inorganic quantum mechanical cognitive engines can be built; if they could, then these, too, if of the right sort, could possess intentionality and have qualia experiences. The question of course, is unavoidable: how would we know whether they did or didn't? Finally, thus (d) the criterion itself needs a supporting argument, and none is readily available; why should it be true that only quantum architecture in the material embodiment of a cognitive engine creates the experience of qualia? At the moment, no one has any idea as to what sorts of steps could plausibly fill in such an argument.

To see why it might in general be impossible, for one using the Searlian theoretical framework, to provide a criterion to distinguish matter that can cause consciousness from matter that can't, consider an extremely favorable case to the Searlian. Imagine, for instance, that one system violates mass–energy conservation at points associated with voluntary activity, for example, and another system doesn't. Then, according to Searle, one expects, there would be grounds to hold that the first is qualia conscious whereas the latter isn't. However, various intuition pumps can serve to call the identifications into question: what if I have a physically deterministic brain, and others have mass–energy violating functionally preemptive brains? Then others would be justified, and correct, in concluding that I have no intentionality and consciousness! Yet under the subjectivity allowing thinking that gets argument 1 going, I can know they're wrong. So if I'm in the other shoes, that is, I've got the mass–energy-conservation-defying brain, I have no basis to expect anything one way or the other of the other deterministic, brain. Thus the very manner of thinking that gives rise to argument 1 undercuts any rationale for a criterion for identifying the right sort of matter to produce mind.

What of 1.2 and its application in 1.3? The most astonishing feature of the argument, it seems to me, is the demonstrable falsity of 1.2. Is it true that a computer simulation of a thunderstorm will get no one wet? The picture that proponents of this analogy have in mind is of a computer simulation that you might watch on a monitor. But a computer simulation of a thunderstorm could also be made in an enormous warehouse in which sprinklers of sorts were hooked up to the roof and the controls on the sprinklers and whatnot were themselves controlled by a computer running a thunderstorm program. Input into the computer could still be selected, at least in part, by a human operator. The input would be representative of various meteorological conditions and *not* of the water pressure in pipes leading to the ceiling sprinklers. There would be no clouds visible when you looked up, but there could be discharges of electricity crossing from ceiling to floor and vice versa, corresponding to lightning bolts and, of course, water droplets, little balls of ice, and whatnot coming down from the vicinity of the ceiling corresponding to rain and hail. Would it be correct to say that the ceiling is precipitating, or that it is raining in the warehouse, or that the little balls of ice *are* hail? Presumably not, though it doesn't ultimately matter what we choose to say about our getting wet or zapped, or bonked on the head by little bits of ice under such conditions. The point is that the water released under such conditions would constitute an important part of the computer simulation of a storm and would get us wet.

What this calls attention to is the irrelevance of the distinction between a computer simulation entirely inside a monitor and a computer simulation hooked up to physical effects. In the AI analogue, it shows the irrelevance in principle of the distinction between a virtual person living inside a computer monitor as it were, and a computer-person with limbs. If a human brain were kept alive in a vat, and the afferent and efferent nerve endings were connected to a computer system with monitor including a rich environment and a homunculus representation operated by the brain, so that the rest of us could interact with the brain-in-a-vat, see what it thinks it's doing, and so on, would the brain still have intentionality? I think there is near universal agreement that it would. Similarly, if the environment modeled and made visible to us through the monitor were sufficiently rich, we would agree that the brain would experience sensory qualia under such conditions. In other words, a human brain acting in, and receiving information from, a virtual physical environment would still experience qualia. The entire burden of qualia and intentionality attribution falls onto the nature of the physical system doing the embodying of the cognitive functioning. So the structure of the analogy collapses. But since what follows 1.2 is vacuous without it, not only the analogy but the entire argument collapses.

At best, then, argument (1) raises a question. Assuming we agree with 1.1, how do we identify a material system with sufficient powers to cause experience of qualia? If we follow the principles that give rise to this argument, we find that we can't. At very best the argument is epistemically opaque, leaving cognitive scientists free to pursue their modeling and simulating enterprises and philosophers without any essential guidance in interpreting what those projects amount to.

The argument of (1) is taken from John Searle's earlier writings. In *The Rediscovery of the Mind* (1992), Searle goes a bit further, though. He insists that in the conceptual space between consciousness and brain events lies nothing to be relevantly filled in by cognitive science as currently conceived. And this brings us to the second set of arguments, the arguments based on the nature of intentionality. Searle's position, however, holds that "mind consists of qualia . . . right down to the ground" (1992, p. 20). This means that he links the arguments from qualia with those from intentionality, so that we should consider them here even though they are based in large part on the nature of intentionality.

Now it is true that many philosophers are of the view that (i) after all the computational modeling of brain functionality, there will be something left over that has not been explained. That is, the connection between whatever structuro-functional states can be depicted by cognitive science and the quasi- or fully ineffable character of qualia is unimaginable and so will never be found. (Popper and Eccles 1977, and Swinburne 1986, for instance, hold this view through a strong ontological dualism; Nagel 1979, 1986, holds it but through a type of property dualism. Agreement with (i), then, should not be confused with commitment to ontological dualism, the view that there are two fundamentally distinct types of substances, mental and physical.) Other philosophers hold that (ii) although we can't yet imagine what sorts of explanatory structures could be presented, there are precedents in the history of science for such unimaginables to become imaginable, and so we should not rule out such explanatory connections a priori. (See, for instance, Colin McGinn's position in 1982, p. 36, and Ned Block 1993, p. 182.) Still others hold that (iii) the theory of qualia is hopelessly confused and should be abandoned (e.g., Dennett, 1991, Chapter 12). However, it is one thing to hold that there is an *aspect* of consciousness that will forever defy structuro-causal explanation and another to think that in defending such a thesis one shows that the cognitive science enterprise is hopelessly off the mark. The latter inference is erroneous, for the primary ambition of cognitive science is to model, and through its modeling, to explain, the *functioning* of the mind. The functioning of the mind includes the way in which our conscious minds move from one functional state to another. It is not necessary that *every* aspect of any given conscious state considered in as much glorious isolation as it can be considered be amenable to physicalistic explanation in order for the basic program of computationalist modeling of mentality to be accounted successful. One doesn't need to defend Dennett's position on qualia to hold that functional analyses model and, thus, explain the succession of conscious states.

But in *The Rediscovery of the Mind,* Searle tries to undercut even those versions of the cognitive science program that allow that cognitivism is not everything in mentality and consciousness. It will be worthwhile looking at problems in at least one crucial argument he presents to the effect that the brain is not, and could not in principle be, an information processor. Here's his argument, distilled from the summary he provides (1992, pp. 225-226):

1a.1   Computation is algorithmic (syntactic) symbol manipulation.

1a.2   Symbols are not intrinsic to physics. [By this Searle means that it requires a mind to regard some physical token as a symbol.]

1a.3   Physical phenomena can be at most interpreted as algorithmic symbol manipulations.

1a.4 So you could not discover the brain to be, intrinsically, a digital
computer, although you could assign a computational interpretation to
it, as you could to anything else. The question "Is the brain a digital
computer?" or "Does the brain process information?" is ill-defined, and
has no clear sense. It can mean either, "Can we assign an algorithmic
interpretation to brain phenomena?" (to which we answer, trivially, yes);
or, "Are brain processes intrinsically computational?" (to which we
answer, trivially, no).

Let us examine the conclusion. Searle says that "you could assign a
computational interpretation to [the brain], as you could to anything else." The
"as you could" is ambiguous. The question we want to ask is whether he means,
"For any algorithm A which the brain can be interpreted as accomplishing, then
anything else can be interpreted as accomplishing algorithm A." Surely he
cannot mean that. Consider a tree. We can assign an algorithmic interpretation to
its waving in the breeze. If the tip of a particular leaf crosses a particular plane
within the first five minutes, we interpret that as input 1; if it doesn't, we
interpret that as input 0. Thus, any finite input is theoretically receivable by the
tree, so long as it stands and the plane is in the right location. That is, whether we
actually find a particular input depends only on the wind and the survival of the
tree. Similarly, the output is read off the tip of a different leaf in relation to a
different plane (simultaneously, if you like). The question is, Could we interpret
any naturally occurring tree as accomplishing any given algorithm we please?"
Obviously not. Once we define the way of reading symbolic input and output
there has to be a causal organization sufficient to cause the right input-output
pairing. Nonetheless, there are, undoubtedly, indefinitely many algorithms such
that given any tree, that tree can be interpreted as accomplishing that algorithm,
in virtue of the fact that the full range of inputs will not naturally occur. For
instance, if you select two sufficiently distant planes, so that neither input nor
output leaf tip will ever cross its plane, then it is true that there are innumerably
many algorithms that the tree manages to accomplish in its natural life. Any
algorithm in which input of only 0s is matched by output of 0, for example, "Add
1 unless the input is all 0s, in which case the output is 0," will be accomplished
by such a tree, since its causal system and the interpretation style guarantees that
every input will be all 0s and every output will be 0 or all 0s depending on how
the output is read. But this is an irrelevant sort of interpretation. The relevant
interpretation is one that allows an indefinitely large range of inputs actually to
be received or, at least, the full range of inputs within a given limit of complexity
or amount of information. Only then does it become meaningful to consider two
given physical systems and compare interpretations of them with regard to their
possible input-output equivalence.

Thus, compare your average tree with a paradigmatic embodiment of a Turing
machine: a train carriage rolling down a track, with an electronic camera and a

pattern reader, reading 0s and 1s off a tape under the train carriage, connected to what we'd call a mechanical instantiation of a finite machine table, causing it to erase and rewrite each frame as 0 or 1, move one frame left, one frame right, and shift to another state of the machine table. (See Penrose 1989, Chapter 2, for an introduction to Turing machines.) Here, for convenience, we interpret any token 0 on the tape under the carriage to stand for the symbol 0, and any token 1 on the tape under the carriage to stand for the symbol 1. Obviously, it is not the case that given any such physically embodied Turing machine, any natural object can be interpreted in such a manner as to allow that it accomplishes the same computation.

Thus, Searle's conclusion, 1a. 4, seems to be confusing the statement "You can assign a computational interpretation to any physical system" with "Given any computation or algorithm, and given any physical system, you can interpret that physical system as embodying that algorithm." He says the former, but it would appear he needs the latter or something close to it for his argument to reach the desired conclusion. For what he wants to say is that if you compare a brain and interpret it as being equivalent to some embodied Turing machine that simulates the brain, you must conclude that the relevant difference is the causal powers of the brain to produce mentality and consciousness. But if it's not true that any physical object can be supplied an interpretation under which it can be regarded as input-output equivalent to the program that simulates the behavior of the brain, then the possibility is that the relevant comparison between physical systems is whether they are so structured as to be interpretable as input-output equivalent. For it is an objective fact of the world (intrinsic to physics in Searle's parlance) that one physical system, $S1$, is, or is not, so structured that it can be regarded as accomplishing the same input-output pairings, P, as another physical system, $S2$, given specified methods of interpretation. Thus even conceding much more than needs to be conceded, it remains meaningful to ask whether or not the brain is so structured that it can be regarded as an embodied Turing machine with some highly complex program and, if so, what the program of that Turing machine is. The arguments of the next section claim that the brain is not so structured. Searle's argument does not eliminate the possibility that the brain is an embodied Turing machine, and these arguments attempt to.

2.   ANALYSIS OF ARGUMENT (2 A)

The argument is simple enough: computer programs as they have been developed thus far have a kind of colossal stupidity, as it might be put, in dealing with anything outside of the phenomena for which they were programmed. Consequently, they do not even *seem* to genuinely understand any of the concepts with which they appear to the human operators of the program to be dealing. They receive inputs and yield outputs, but even the most sophisticated AI program does not enable the computer in operation to actually understand anything. It can't be said to rationally appropriate the concepts it represents, since the computer fails miserably if it's called upon to deal with concepts outside the strict limits of its program. Moreover, interactive programs don't seem to possess any genuine ability to engage in intelligent interaction with other intelligence. Relatively simple tests can always be found to tease the program into betraying its total lack of genuine interactive understanding.

This argument, I shall argue, is misguided on two fronts: first, it fails to point to theoretical obstacles for our ever being able to model human thought processes on computational lines; second, and most important, the pessimism underlying this argument arises at least in part from the absence in AI modeling of agency-attributing programming. Insofar as agency-attributing programming is possible to design, the pessimism is unwarranted. Finally, we have every reason to believe that agency-attributing programming is indeed possible.

The first point of response is simple enough, yet important. The objection has the form of an induction: it amounts to stating that early optimistic attitudes have been dashed to pieces, and therefore, any surviving optimistic attitudes will continue to be dashed to pieces. But given that cognitive science is only a few decades old, the induction is certainly dubious. Moreover, it is unclear what, at this stage, could plausibly replace methodological computationalism in cognitive science. That is, the only plausible working method available for an attempt to model mental states, their relations, and their embodiment in the nervous system is that of one or another form of computationalism. Therefore, although we can hold open some theoretical door for the overthrow of computationalism, the existence of early disappointments does not warrant any form of abandonment of the computational strategy and program.

But it is the second response that I want to focus on, as it is the more substantive one. The complaint that computer programs are inevitably stupid in a certain sense, incapable of abstracting at the appropriate levels, or shifting from frame to frame, or grasping what is of salience within a given frame, or manifesting any qualitative understanding of a given situation, or being context-sensitive in a commonsense fashion, needs to be understood at least in part, I want to suggest, with reference to a certain gap within current state-of-the-art AI virtual person modeling.

The theoretical connections between rationality and language use have been appreciated from at least as far back as Descartes's day and much written about, especially in the twentieth century. In *Rationality*, for instance, Jonathan Bennett (1964) argues persuasively that the ability to use language to make dated and universal judgments is necessary for a creature to have genuine rationality. Further, H. P. Grice (1957) developed an analysis of nonnatural meaning that highlights mutual anticipation between the speaker and the hearer. For something to be a conventional linguistic act, according to Grice's widely accepted analysis, it must be the case that the speaker expects the hearer to take it that the utterance is meant to be a vehicle of communication, and the hearer expects the speaker to so intend the utterance as well. The conventionalizing mutuality, as it might be put, between speaker and hearer is essential for full-fledged language use.

However, this feature of conventionalizing mutuality in symbolic expression has not received attention from the AI community. Consider the main areas within which AI modeling has occurred: perception and pattern recognition; memory, or data storage and retrieval; learning systems; problem solvers; cognitive representation; planning systems; and various expert systems involving one or more natural languages being used in varying kinds of fragmentary chunks. In none of the language programs is there an attempt to incorporate a model of the conventionalizing mutuality of language. And none of the other program areas can give rise to the apparent need for a model of such a feature on its own. Yet without such conventionalizing mutuality, as Grice shows, we don't have nonnatural meaning. And without nonnatural meaning, as Bennett (1964) shows, we don't have rationality.

It is natural and important, then, to raise the question as to the amenability of the conventionalizing mutuality feature to computational modeling. Here we have a competence that lies somewhere near or at the heart of rational agency, and of our perceptions of what is and isn't a rational agent, and therefore of what is and what isn't an intentional system. For both reasons, the question of its amenability to computational modeling needs to be raised. Moreover, it is also important to consider the possibility that the apparent intractability of the frame problem is at least partly due to the failure to model conventionalizing mutuality systems as to the nemesis character of the frame or commonsense problems.

The latter diagnostic hypothesis seems to me to be eminently justified. To be sure, even if conventionalizing mutuality and, more generally, interagency attribution are amenable to computational modeling, there will be the bulk of the knowledge representation problem and a good portion of the frame problem left over. To that portion that remains we will return in our discussion of some of the issues surrounding argument (2b).

In the meantime, however, we note that there is nothing per se daunting about setting out to model conventionalizing mutuality systems. Once the task is squarely faced, one sees that what is primarily required is that one provide a program framework or operating system, in effect, that has sufficient *purity* as it may be called. A pure system is a system in which (i) the program agent or target has been given a model environment, and any interaction with the human operator of the program is mediated both by a model of the physical doings of the human operator, and by the model perceptual organs of the target agent; and (ii) the *a priori* or innate conceptual architecture of the target agent contains no natural-language surface elements such as words. Condition (i) requires that the input provided by the human operator be given a model physical doings format;

and condition (ii) requires that a program of action extraction be provided the target agent. Once such conditions are met, it becomes a relatively straightforward, albeit large, programming task to design a system that incorporates the conventionalizing mutuality feature of language use. One does so by incorporating the conventionalizing mutuality capabilities within a larger, also pure, agency-attributive device. An agency-attributive device is a program that is part of the target agent (i.e., the agent within the monitor, as it were) that has a method of hypothesizing as to what other elements in its perceptual field are rational agents and, upon confirming such a hypothesis, opens a file concerning that rational agent, within which file hypotheses concerning its beliefs, desires, plans, and actions, which have been extracted from the perceived behavior of the agent, are entered on an ongoing and updating basis. In a pure system, the human operator of the program provides inputs in model form of his or her acts, and these are represented to the target agent as environmental goings on. The human operator, of course, gets to watch the environment and can see the environment, presumably, from a "god's eye" perspective within which both the agent he or she is operating and the target agent are represented each by its, his, or her icon, respectively. The overall resulting program may be called a "pure agency attributive language user," or PAL.

As I have tried to make clear in Chapter 3 of *How to Build a Conscious Machine* (1989, pp. 18-53), which explores the operating system implied by a pure interaction between human and artificial agent and the structure of such a target agent, there can be little doubt that a target agent capable in some realistic degree of interagency attribution and of learning and sharing language in a pure conventionalizing mutuality manner can be designed. It may take some time to implement the design, and there certainly are problems to be encountered. But the tasks are cut out for one, and, moreover, a method exists for short-circuiting the difficult knowledge representation issues that might needlessly complicate the task. That method is to maintain a rigorously simple, discrete environment. Thus, one can effectively separate off the specific interagency competences from the knowledge representation issues.

The significance of focusing on agency attributive competences including conventionalizing mutualities, then, is that it allows one to model the integrating features of all the other modules that have been thus far attempted without having to *first* solve the more difficult knowledge representation issues. PAL programming, because it is pure, and because it focuses centrally on the rationality-conferring features of agency, enables one to start with an integrated system that exhibits the necessary interagency attributive conditions of rationality, while working incrementally on the sophisticated knowledge representation problems.

Thus if conventionalizing mutuality systems are indeed buildable, a new kind of vehicle has been found within which the frame problem can be looked at afresh. One would no longer be able to regard the frame problem as presenting the programmer with the task of programming the unprogrammable. The more one works with the requirements for modeling conventionalizing mutuality systems, the more convincing the hypothesis becomes that the commonsense or frame problem only appears to be *ab initio* unsolvable when we contemplate AI systems that neither occur within pure architectural settings nor attempt to model interagency attributions within which conventionalizing mutuality can take place.

Thus, not only is the form of the (2a) objection to computationalism an unjustified induction, but also there is positive reason to hold that this objection is decidedly premature and that within the next century we will go a long way towards tackling an extremely significant part of this problem within a computationalist framework.

However, as mentioned, the interagency attributions, while integrating the modules, do not in and of themselves solve the sophisticated knowledge representation issues. And we may interpret objection (2b) in such a manner as to raise these issues again under a new guise.

3. ANALYSIS OF ARGUMENT (2 B)

(2b) states that our intentionality ranges over an infinite domain of representations. This capacity of our cognitive systems to understand, and form semantic interpretations of infinitely many representations, it is further claimed, prevents any finitistic system from adequately modeling the human person. A computational system would be finitistic, and so no computational system can adequately model the human person.

There are two senses in which it may be said that our intentionality ranges over infinitely many representations, in accordance with the two main approaches to the infinite. On the one hand, it may be held that our intentionality ranges over *indefinitely many* representations. On the other hand, it may be held that our intentionality ranges over an *actual infinity* of representations. In either case, the argument goes, a finitistic computational system would not be able to do this.

The knowledge representation problems left over even if astonishingly sophisticated pure agency-attributive language users have been built are often held to be intractable for the computationalist on the grounds of the indefiniteness of the domain of representations required to be taken account of by a genuine intentional system. For instance, Hubert Dreyfus, one of the leading exponents of the criticism of (2b), relies very largely on the indefiniteness of the features that need to be taken account of by an intentional system in arguing for the impossibility of computational modeling of mentality. Thus, in "From Micro-

Worlds to Knowledge Representation" (1981) Dreyfus makes this point in at least seven variations on pages 175, 182, 183, 185, 193, 194, and 195.

There is, however, a swift answer to the indefiniteness objection as presented by Dreyfus and like-minded critics of computationalism. It may be granted for the sake of discussion that symbolic representations themselves will never satisfy the requirements of mental modeling because the objects being dealt with by intentional systems are concrete and have indefinitely many features and relations to be considered. Still, this is not sufficient to deny the computational hope, since computational systems can interface with an environment via perceptual components, and the overall system may include transductions leading ultimately to analogue information storage. Once the concrete external chair, the table, the room, the picture on the wall, the wallpaper, and so on have been represented within a computational system by an analogue representational process of some sort, then indefinitely many significant relations and features of the original can be accessed by the device itself. A symbolic system can be applied onto the analogue representation within the computational network for the purposes of arriving at the more purely symbolic representations of the objects in question.

Responses along these lines to the indefiniteness objection have been developed and explored in Johnson-Laird's *Mental Models* (1983) and Andy Clark's *Microcognition* (1989). Dreyfus's reasoning is unsatisfactory, but then nobody has claimed to have gotten terribly far in implementing the solution. This question must be regarded as open to empirical results. The other thing one must say in favor of the computationalist hope is that no principled reason has been presented for the impossibility of functional modeling of knowledge systems using both analogue and symbolic representations. Given that we are at the very early stages of research in cognitive science, any decidedly negative stance seems premature by centuries.

But what of the objection couched in terms of the infinity of sentences for which a grammar can provide structural descriptions and, processing limits aside, to which a human can assign semantic content? The argument may be presented as follows:

2b.1   Humans need to have access to the recursive embeddings of propositions in their languages in order for humans to express their full range of thoughts.

2b.2   If a creature needs recursive embeddings of propositions in its language in order for the creature to be able to express its full range of thoughts, then such a creature's use of language cannot be explicable on mechanical models.

2b.3 Therefore, the human use of language cannot be explicable on mechanical models.

This argument was first sketched by Noam Chomsky. The way in which the argument is developed by Chomsky is as follows: Chomsky takes it to be a basic fact of human language that it has what he calls "a creative aspect." Chomsky defines the creative aspect of language use as the distinctively human ability to express and understand novel thoughts (1968, p. 6). Chomsky further asserts that only a language that has a recursive component in the base, that is, only a language that has a finite system of rules capable of generating an infinity of sentences, can serve as a language that will meet the needs of a creative user of language. Indeed, he sometimes refers to the recursive property of the grammar as the grammar's creative aspect: "The recursive property of the grammar (its 'creative aspect' to return to terminology used above) is restricted to the base component" (1966, p. 66).

Elsewhere he makes explicit the view that having a recursive component in the grammar is necessary if the language is to be creatively usable. For example, he says, placing his own views in the tradition of Cartesian Linguistics, "the grammar of a language must contain a system of rules that characterizes deep and surface structures and the transformational relations between them, and—if it is to accommodate the creative aspect of language use—that does so over an infinite domain of paired deep and surface structures, appropriately related" (1968, p. 15).

Chomsky at many points emphasizes the importance of the recursive base, the component of the grammar that provides for ever more complex sentential embeddings. The idea is that it is the infinity of sentences that can be constructed with the finite means of the grammar and a finite lexicon that enables us to express an unbounded and potentially infinite set of thoughts. And it is this unboundedness that makes our use of language essentially inexplicable in terms of stimulus response mechanisms and essentially nonmechanical. Thus, for instance, Chomsky says, "the realization that this 'creative' aspect of language is its essential characteristic can be traced back at least to the seventeenth century. Thus we find the Cartesian view that man alone is more than mere automatism, and that it is the possession of true language that is the primary indicator of this" (1964, p. 51). And elsewhere, again linking his own views with those of the Cartesian linguists, Chomsky says:

> This device [embedding of propositions] can be repeated indefinitely so that a grammar of the form suggested will have the capacity to generate an infinite number of deep structures . . . Of course, no explicit system of this sort was developed during this period, although the general framework of such a system was suggested by many observations and particular analyses. It is worthy of note, however, that the creative aspect of language use was a topic of considerable discussion and thought in the seventeenth century, in the context of the controversy over animal automatism . . . Descartes argues that the freedom

of language use from stimulus control, its independence of what we would now call "conditioning", its appropriateness to situation and to preceding discourse, and its typical novelty all point to the existence of some sort of "active principle" that lies beyond the bounds of mechanical explanation . . . It should be observed, incidentally, that there is nothing at all absurd in Descartes' argument . . . It is also important to note that subsequent attempts to show that mechanical principles can account for human as well as animal behavior do not, so far as I can discover, attempt to refute these arguments. [1965, pp. 17, 18]

Thus Chomsky clearly endorses 2b.1 and tentatively endorses 2b.2. The argument itself is logically valid, and the only issue is the truth of the premises. My claim will be that while there is a profound insight in 2b.2 (the premise that Chomsky only tentatively endorses), unfortunately, 2b.1 (the premise that Chomsky endorses without qualification), is false. In particular, it can be shown that a language that has only a relatively small finite number of deep structures for sentences has the full expressive capacity of the English language.

The issue itself is simple enough: is there any form of sentential embedding that cannot be eliminated in paraphrase? If not, then 2b.1 is false: we do not need our recursive embeddings to express the full range of our thoughts. To acquire an empirical feel for the matter, we need only consider typical cases of sentences that include recursively derived structures, that is, typical cases of complex sentences.

Consider, first, relativizing clauses that serve to individuate; for example:

A.   The woman who entered the press club is the author of several books. Such a sentence may be paraphrased by:

A'. Some woman entered the press club. That woman is the author of several books.

Even more complex relativizing embeddings can be disentangled in paraphrase using simple sentences as well. Thus B may be paraphrased by B':

B.   The woman who entered the press club, which was named after the man who founded the paper that sells more copies than any other paper in Vancouver, is the author of several books.

B'. Some paper sells more copies than any other paper in Vancouver. Some man founded that paper. Some press club was named after that man. Some woman entered that press club. That woman is the author of several books.

Next consider noun clause embeddings such as those found in:

C.   John believes that Mary denied that Edna affirmed that Phillip knows
       that Harry is bald.

The embeddings of C can be effectively eliminated by a paraphrase such as the
following.

C′.   Call the following proposition A: "Harry is bald." Call the following
       proposition B: "Phillip knows A." Call the following proposition C:
       "Edna affirmed B." Call the following proposition, D: "Mary denied C."
       John believes D.

It may be that some paraphrases of noun phrase complements will end not in
simple sentences but in sentences some of which contain a single embedding.
However, such results are acceptable for our purpose, which is to demonstrate
that recursively derived structures can be eliminated in paraphrase, since a
nonrecursive base can be constructed that allows for a single embedding. For
example, consider:

D.   Jack remembered that Mary discovered that John knew that Edna
       believed that Tim learned that Pat returned.

D can be paraphrased by the following series of sentences, using "that +
sentence" clauses a maximum of once per sentence, and beginning with the
innermost embedded clause.

D′.   "Pat returned." The preceding proposition refers to an event. Call that
       event A. "Tim learned that event A occurred." Call the preceding
       proposition B. "Edna believed proposition B to be true." Call the
       preceding proposition C. "John knew proposition C to be true." The
       preceding proposition refers to a state-of-affairs. Call that state-of-affairs
       D. "Mary discovered that state-of-affairs D obtained." The preceding
       proposition refers to an event. Call that event E. Jack remembered that
       event E occurred.

It may even be argued that some embeddings are only intelligible if we
disentangle them in paraphrase. For instance, consider:

E.   John's inquiry whether Mary's inquiry whether Tim's inquiry was
       postponed was postponed was postponed.

E, it seems, can only be rendered intelligible via a paraphrase that eliminates all or, in this case, all but one embedding per sentence, such as:

E'.   Tim made an inquiry. Mary inquired whether Tim's inquiry was postponed. John inquired whether Mary's inquiry was postponed.

Further, mixing the embedding types doesn't present any special problems. This is made clear by the following example of a sentence with mixed embeddings. F may be paraphrased by F'.

F.   Mary argued that what John said about whether Tim had persuaded Edna to talk to the man who came early was tactful.

F'.   Some man came early. "Edna will talk to that man." The preceding proposition refers to an action. Call that action A. "Did Tim persuade Edna to perform action A?" John said something about the preceding question. Call that saying B. "B was tactful." Mary argued the preceding proposition.

Next, consider multiple if-then sentential coordinations such as the following. Allowing ourselves a maximum of one if-then coordination per sentence, we can paraphrase G by G'.

G.   If, if Mary likes John, then John likes Mary, then, if John likes Mary, then Mary likes John.

G'.   "If Mary likes John, then John likes Mary." Call the previous implication A. "If John likes Mary, then Mary likes John." Call the previous implication B. If implication A holds, then implication B holds.

Similarly, multiple disjunctions can be eliminated using a maximum of one disjunction per sentence. Thus H may be paraphrased with H'.

H.   Either, either Johnson will be there, or his proxy will be there, or either Johnson's proxy will be there or Johnson's second proxy will be there.

H'.   "Either Johnson will be there or his proxy will be there." Call the preceding disjunction A. "Either Johnson's proxy will be there or Johnson's second proxy will be there." Call the preceding disjunction B. Either disjunction A holds or disjunction B holds.

Nested possessives are also not necessary for thought expression. Thus, I can be paraphrased by I'.

I.   That man's friend's uncle's sister's dog's collar's ring is bright.

I'.   That man has a friend. That friend has an uncle. That uncle has a sister. That sister has a dog. That dog has a collar. That collar has a ring. That ring is bright.

Similarly, the meanings of sentences that have compound adjectives or adverbs can be expressed by simple sentences. Thus, for instance, J (interpreted idiomatically, so that few implies some) can be paraphrased by J'.

J.   Few people are tall, thin, dark-eyed, bald, Canadian, twenty-nine years old, and interested in chess.

J'.   Some people are tall. Some people are thin. Some people are dark-eyed. Some people are bald. Some people are Canadian. Some people are twenty-nine years old. Some people are interested in chess. Few people are all of these things.

Finally, it is instructive to note that the forms of expression found within the predicate calculus do not appear to introduce any threat of multiple embeddings or coordinations that cannot be eliminated in paraphrase along the manner of the paraphrases just considered.

Thus, it becomes clear from consideration of these and similar cases that if sentential embeddings and, more generally, recursive devices were eliminated from the base of a grammar, the expressive potential of a language would not be affected. Sentential conjunction and intersentential referencing can accomplish everything that sentential embedding accomplishes. Put more strongly, a language with only a (relatively small) finite number of sentence types is adequate for full thought expression.

The first premise of Chomsky's argument is false. Nonetheless it is worth noting that the idea underlying premise 2b.2 is correct. If it were the case that we needed embedding for full thought expression, then human language would not be mechanically explicable. For we can now see that what would essentially be involved in the impossibility of eliminating embeddings in paraphrase would be the mysterious emergence of new meanings in virtue of the embeddings. Such mysterious emergence would not be mechanically explicable. Let's spell this out in more detail. Consider the relations between the following hypotheses.

(i)   The semantic content of a complex sentence is a computable function of the semantic content of its elementary propositions and their structural relations.

(ii)   There is a decision procedure for deriving simple sentence conjunctions from complex sentences with identical semantic content and vice versa.

(iii)   Propositional embeddings are necessary for thought expression.

We can see that (i) implies (ii). For even though within a given language there may be no readily idiomatic way to use simple sentence conjunctions to express the semantic content of the complex sentences, at worst, on the assumption of (i) one would only need to invent some canonical form whereby one presents a finite list of simple sentences specifying the elementary propositions and specifying the structural relations. It is eminently plausible to hold that the structural relations can be specified using only simple sentences, along some convention of specification.

Also we can see that (iii) implies that (ii) is false. Obviously, if recursive embeddings are necessary for thought expression, then the paraphrasing by conjunctions of simple sentences, or even sentences with a maximum of a single embedding, would not be possible. And a fortiori, there would be no decision procedure for such paraphrasing. But if (ii) is false, then (i) must be false by contraposition on the implication that (i) implies (ii). Thus (iii) implies that (i) is false. Finally, (i) is a necessary condition for any mechanical explication or simulation of the human use of language. For assume that human language were mechanically simulable. What could possibly account for the mechanical assignment of semantic descriptions to complex sentences other than via the elementary propositions and their structural relations? There is nothing that seems remotely plausible that could fill the bill.

So Chomsky was right to draw the connection between the hypothesis of the need for a recursive base in the grammar and the conclusion that any creature that had such a need would not be mechanically explicable. It's only his failure to examine the claim that there is a need for a recursive base in human languages that led him to ignore the fatal problem with the argument.

The objection might be raised that there should be no ultimately significant difference between conjunctions of sentences so as to form paragraphs and embeddings of sentences for the purpose of the argument. Since we need indefinitely many paragraphs if you like, it should still follow that we have a need for recursion somewhere.

The quick answer to the objection is to note that the equivalent argument for paragraphing simply cannot be constructed. The equivalent of the implication would state that if paragraph-generating recursions are necessary for thought expression, then there can be no mechanical explanation or simulation of our use of language. However, there is no way to arrive at this implication, since we would have to go through a parallel to the implication that if (iii) is true, then (ii) is false. And that parallel would state that if (iii)' paragraph-generating recursions are necessary for thought expression, then (ii)' there is a decision procedure for deriving sentence conjunctions from paragraphs with identical semantic content and vice versa is false. But this implication is plainly absurd as the paragraphs are already sentence conjunctions! Thus, there is indeed a significant difference between finding that we need to have paraphraph recursion, or indefinitely many sentence conjunctions for full thought expression (which we do indeed find), and finding that we need to have sentential embeddings for full thought expression (which, I've argued, is incorrect).

4. ANALYSIS OF ARGUMENT (2 C)

2c.1 If a person is a mechanical system, the person would have a finitistic computational representation, FCR.

2c.2 It would be theoretically possible, following Gödel's method in the incompleteness result, for an embodied FCR to construct a theorem that it could, conceivably, prove to be both true for FCR and unprovable within FCR, which is internally inconsistent.

2c.3 Therefore 2c.1 is false.

This argument, launched mainly by Lucas (1961), has been widely discussed. A useful popular account of the issues is presented by Douglas Hofstadter in *Gödel, Escher, Bach* (1980, pp. 471-477, 577-578). The crux of the matter is this. Gödel showed that for any consistent formal system rich enough to capture elementary arithmetic, there is a theorem that is true under the system but unprovable by the system. But a formal computational system is finitistically representable, and if a human is a computational system, then its formalization must be powerful enough to capture elementary arithmetic. But then it should be possible to use Gödel's method to prove some unprovable but true theorem within the system itself. But this is impossible, since it would involve the system's proving what the system cannot prove. So it cannot be that a human is a computational system.

Hofstadter presents two counterarguments. The first objection is that Gödel's method is not itself sufficiently algorithmic to allow for an unqualified affirmation of 2c.2. ". . . we do not have any algorithmic way of describing how to perform [Gödelization]. If we can't tell explicitly what is involved in applying the Gödel method in all cases, then for each of us there will eventually come some case so complicated that we simply can't figure out how to apply it." (p. 475) This allows for an equality of mentality and machine that Lucas had hoped to rule out.

Hofstadter's second counterargument objects to an apparent oversimplification Lucas relies on in his understanding of what it is for mentality to be computationally explicable. There may well be a bottom level at which Gödelization can take place. But, "[o]n their top level—the 'informal' level—there may be manipulation of images, formulation of analogies, forgetting of ideas, confusing of concepts, blurring of distinctions, and so forth. But this does not contradict the fact that they rely on the correct functioning of their underlying hardware as much as brains rely on the correct functioning of their neurons. So AI programs are still 'concrete instantiations of formal systems'—but they are not machines to which Lucas' transmogrification of Gödel's proof can be applied. Lucas' argument applies merely to their bottom level, on which their intelligence—however great or small it may be—does not lie." (p. 578)

Hofstadter's first counterargument has been criticized by Hadley (1987) on the grounds that Kleene (1967) showed that an effective procedure or algorithm does exist for generating true but unprovable theorems within any formal system rich enough for arithmetic. Hadley quotes Webb (1980) as making the point that the Kleene demonstration undercuts Lucas' argument, since the machine can apparently do what Lucas claims only the nonmechanical mind can do. Interestingly enough, then, the existence of the algorithm works simultaneously against both the original Lucas claim and the Hofstadter counterargument! However the existence of such an algorithm raises another question, for it seems as though such an algorithm would leave the door open for a machine to prove a theorem to be true and unprovable within its own system, which is the very apparent inconsistency Lucas relies on. Hadley picks up the challenge of resolving the apparent paradox. He extends what he takes to be an incomplete argument by Chihara (1972) and shows, essentially, that the system which does the Gödelizing is not the system Gödelized, and so the paradox is defused. A machine *can* do what Lucas asserts a mind can do but a machine could never do, and it can do it without running afoul of any constraints brought forward by Godel's incompleteness results.

5.   ANALYSIS OF ARGUMENT (3)

The claim that from our own direct experience of freedom we are entitled to conclude that we are not deterministic systems, that we are not in the philosophical sense machines, on the face of it is unjustified. Whether we are or are not in the philosophical sense machines is an empirical matter, for we can imagine many different and contrary empirical conclusions on this matter all of which are consistent with our experience of ourselves and of our freedom.

For example, we can *imagine* a predictor machine being constructed. This machine takes atomic pictures of a person and the person's immediate environment. It then predicts, based on the atomic configuration of the person and the environment, what the person will be thinking and saying in an hour, say. It won't work if something outside the environment impinges on the environment photographed in a way as to affect the brain states of the person, but otherwise it will work. Such a machine would constitute empirical confirmation of the theory that the brain is a mechanistic system.

Of course we don't need to take seriously the notion that we will one day have such a machine in order to use the thought experiment to demonstrate that the implication from our experience of human freedom to the brain not being a machine is unwarranted. For various reasons we don't anticipate ever having such a machine. But there is no contradiction between there being such a machine and our having the experience of qualia, intentionality, and freedom that we have. Whether or not our brains are deterministic systems is something that we discover through empirical research, and the deterministic conclusion cannot plausibly be eliminated through the method of introspection.

Allied to the introspective argument is a more directly empirical one. It has been argued that since the brain contains events at the quantum level that are not even in principle predictable, therefore mechanistic and deterministic models of human functioning are incorrect. Salvation in the form of quantum uncertainty, however, relies on more than the mere fact of quantum uncertainties. For in order to show that quantum indeterminacy overthrows a mechanistic model of brain functioning, it is necessary to show three things: (a) quantum events affect the changing states of the brain; (b) quantum events not only affect the changing states of the brain in the sense of constituting interference or noise within the functioning of the brain, but actually contribute to the functioning of the brain, and their positive role must be taken account of in order to understand how the brain works; and (c) the actual role in functioning of the quantum events is not restricted to the accomplishment of randomization and can not otherwise be functionally modeled even if it cannot be eliminated in real time.

Now it is easy to see that (a) in some form is or might well be correct. For example, anyone who reads a geiger counter will have his or her brain states affected by in principle unpredictable quantum goings on. Similarly, it may well be that various quantumly random events taking place at the microlevel affect brain function in the sense of constituting noise in its functioning. But neither of these entails that quantum events play a positive role in brain functioning. Consider an automobile, for instance. Suppose quantum events take place randomly in the engine of the car. A geiger counter hooked up suitably in the engine of the car may even affect the various states of the engine. Or, for the sake of discussion, suppose some quantum events may spill over subtly into the macrolevel at which the car operates and constitute noise of sorts in its functioning. But the car as a functional system does not have the quantum events playing any positive role. Therefore for us to model the car as a functional system does not require the modeling of the quantum events except insofar as we want to be accurate with regard to the interferences that the functioning faces.

Rescue from the realm of quantum physics at this stage then seems remote or largely speculative. And even if the brain is a quantum machine, there is nothing to suggest that the functioning cannot be mechanically modeled, though not perhaps in real time. What is really needed to provide empirical evidence for contra-causal freedom is evidence for functional preemption, that is, for mentalistically purposeful preemption of otherwise binding physical regularities. Evidence for such processes can (in principle) be had. That is, it is logically possible that one is in possession of such evidence. There even can be evidence for highly regular and predictable contra-causal events. For instance, think of someone who materializes food *ex nihilo* if and only if someone says, "I'm really hungry!" Say you've seen this a hundred times. And then someone says, "I'm really hungry!" and the materializer hears the statement. Now you can predict that he's going to materialize food. (Naturally we assume that James Randi, Martin Gardner, and their fellows at SCICOP have inspected, tested, and found the materializations to be genuine!)

Are there, however, any claims of evidence for functional preemption or contra-causal freedom? In more specific terms, then, are there claims of empirical evidence that there are areas in the brain associated with voluntary activity in which neurons fire without any antecedent *physical* cause? Indeed, there are. Sir John Eccles, in a rather unguarded moment, has asserted, "we have here an irrefutable demonstration that a mental act of intention *initiates* the burst of discharges of a nerve cell" (Eccles and Robinson 1985, p. 162). The claim is that there is experimental evidence that in chimpanzees certain neurons associated with voluntary activity are excited without any prior physiological cause. Unfortunately, Eccles seems to have skipped from absence of evidence of cause to evidence of absence of cause. That there should be absence of evidence of cause in some areas of the brain, whether human or chimp, is hardly surprising. There is so much we don't know about the brain that we cannot leap to radical conclusions from our early investigations. Moreover, in other accounts of the same data, Eccles is considerably more cautious:

> The subtlety and complexity of the patterns written in space and time by this "enchanted loom" of Sherrington's and the emergent properties of this system are beyond any levels of investigation by physics or physiology at the present time . . . and perhaps for a long time to come. I would postulate that in the liaison areas these neuronal patterns of module activity are the receiving stations or antennae for the ongoing operations in the consciousness of World 2 [the conscious self]. [Eccles 1976, p. 117]

There is a big gap, obviously, between a "postulate" and "irrefutable demonstration," and the cautious remarks seem more in keeping with the state of research in this field than the other remarks. At most Eccles has pointed to an area in which much more research needs to be done.

Eccles is also quick to interpret some research by Libet (1978) and Libet et al. (1979) as establishing that the brain is not a physiological machine. Eccles writes:

> Direct stimulation of the somaesthetic cortex results in a conscious experience after a delay as long as 0.5s for weak stimulation, and a similar delay is observed for a sharp, but weak, peripheral skin stimulus . . . [A]lthough there is this delay in experiencing the peripheral stimulus, it is actually judged to be much earlier, at about the time of cortical arrival of the afferent input . . . This antedating procedure does not seem to be explicable by any neurophysiological process. [Eccles and Popper 1977, p. 364]

However, Libet firmly rejects such hastily drawn conclusions: "Subjective referral in time violates no neurophysiological principles or data and is compatible with the theory of 'mental' and 'physical' correspondence" (Libet 1981, p. 182).

Thus we must conclude that for the present, in any case, there is neither conceptual nor empirical reason to hold that our experience of freedom is best accounted for by a contra-causal or contra-mechanistic account. (See also Honderich 1988, Chapter 5, "Neuroscience and Quantum Theory.")

6.   CONCLUSION

How the Mechanistic Assumption Can Contribute to a Properly Founded Experience of the Mystery of Consciousness

I'd like to conclude by briefly suggesting some ways in which the mechanistic approach to mind can positively contribute to our understanding and experience of the mystery of consciousness.

It seems to me that what the Copernican revolution was in the seventeenth century and what the Darwinian revolution was in the nineteenth century, the cognitive science revolution centering on the attempt to build a conscious agent or—the same thrust from another angle—the research confirming the essentially deterministic nature of brain functioning may prove to be for our time. In each of the two previous revolutions we had empirical confirmation of a scientific theory that challenged popular notions of human uniqueness, importance, and centrality in the universe. In the case of the Copernican revolution, the centrality was a literal centrality. We had to adjust to the notion that there was no sense in which we had an absolute centrality in the universe. The Darwinian revolution was slightly more interior. We had to come to terms with having developed naturalistically from lower forms of animals rather than by divine all at once fiat. Now, it seems, we are all having to come to terms with a possibility that only a few philosophers had previously been taking seriously—namely, that the whole of the psychophysical system changes from state to functional state in a deterministic fashion except, perhaps, for either interferences or randomizing caused by events at the quantum level.

The interesting feature of this revolution is that the more specific and detailed our understanding of the brain and its cognitive system becomes, the more we can, and indeed must, confront the experiential phenomena at the experiential level. That is, when we come to see in detailed and specific terms how our brains function as essentially deterministic systems, we are forced to recognize with fresh clarity how our experiences of qualia, intentionality, and radical freedom are not, and cannot be, dependent on any empirical discoveries concerning how and what we are as psychophysical beings. We are forced back on our *experience* of what it is to be free rather than any particular *theory* of what it is to be free. And this effect of the theory to force us back onto the direct experience of wonder is one of its great benefits.

Just as the Copernican revolution made us recognize that our *experience* of centrality is not dependent on any locational centrality, and the Darwinian revolution made us recognize that our *experience* of dignity is not dependent on our having been made roughly simultaneous with but separate from the apes, the cognitive science revolution is forcing us to recognize that our *experiences* of qualia, intentionality, and radical freedom cannot be threatened by the truth of any particular empirical account of brain functioning.

The more vivid our demonstration that human behavior is deterministic and that it can be modeled by AI, the more we are forced to take the experiences of *qualia*, intentionality, and freedom for what they are and to take them at the level of the experiences themselves. Just as Copernicus made us separate psychological centrality from physical centrality, and Darwin got us to separate the psychological experience of ourselves as being unique and sui generis from physiologic/evolutionary uniqueness, so too the cognitive science revolution, if it continues to gather steam, will get us to separate our experience of qualia and psychological freedom from physical contra-causality. Deterministic cognitive science catalyzes the experience of the magic and mystery of consciousness and is not at all its downfall.

7. REFERENCES

Angel, L. (1974) Recursive Grammars And The Creative Aspect of Language Use. Ph.D. dissertation, Special Collections, University of British Columbia Library, Vancouver, British Columbia, Canada.

Angel, L. (1989) *How To Build A Conscious Machine* (Boulder, CO: Westview).

Bennett, J. (1964) *Rationality* (London: Routledge and Kegan Paul).

Block, N. (1993) Daniel Dennett's *Consciousness Explained* (Review). *Journal of Philosophy*, XC (April 1993), 181-193.

Chihara, C. (1972) On alleged refutations of mechanism using Gödel's incompleteness results. *The Journal of Philosophy*, 17: 507-526.

Chomsky, N. (1964) Current issues in linguistic theory. In J. Fodor, and J. Katz, (eds.) *The Structure of Language* (Englewood Cliffs, NJ: Prentice-Hall).

Chomsky, N. (1965) Persistent topics in linguistic theory. *Diogenes,* 51: 13-20.

Chomsky, N. (1966) *Topics in the Theory of Generative Grammar* (The Hague: Mouton & Co.).

Chomsky, N. (1968) *Language & Mind* (New York: Harcourt Brace & World).

Churchland, P., and Churchland, P. (1981) Functionalism, qualia, and intentionality. In J. Biro and R. Shahan (eds.) *Mind, Brain, and Function* (Norman: University of Oklahoma Press).

Clark, A. (1989) *Microcognition* (Carnbridge, MA: Bradford, MIT).

Dennett, D. (1991) *Consciousness Explained* (Boston: Little, Brown & Co.).

Dreyfus, H. L. (1981) From micro-worlds to knowledge representation. In John Haugeland (ed.) *Mind Design* (Cambridge, MA: Bradford, MIT).

Eccles, J. (1976) Brain and free will. In G. Globus, G. Maxwell, and I. Savodnik (eds.) *Consciousness and the Brain* (New York: Plenurn Press).

Eccles, J., and Popper, K. (1977) *The Self And Its Brain* (New York: Springer International).

Eccles, J., and Robinson, D. (1985) *The Wonder of Being Human* (Boulder, CO: Shambhala).

Grice, H. P. (1957) Meaning. *Philosophical Review*, 66: 377-388.

Hadley, R. F. (1987) Gödel, Lucas, and mechanical models of the mind. *Computational Intelligence*, 3: 57-63.

Hofstadter, D. (1980) *Gödel, Escher, Bach* (New York: Vintage Random House).

Honderich, T. (1988) *Mind and Brain, A Theory of Determinism, Vol. 1* (Oxford: Clarendon Press).

Johnson-Laird, P. N. (1983) *Mental Models* (Cambridge, MA: Harvard University Press).

Kleene, S. (1967) *Mathematical Logic* (New York: John Wiley & Sons).

Libet, B. (1978) Neuronal vs. subjective timing for a conscious sensory experience. In P. Buser, and A. Rougel-Buser, (eds.) *Cerebral Correlates of Conscious Experience* (Amsterdam: Elsevier).

Libet B. (1981) The experimental evidence for subjective referral of a sensory experience backwards in time: Reply to P.S. Churchland. In *Philosophy of Science*, 48: 182-197.

Libet, B., Wright, E. W., Feinstein, B., and Pearl, D. K. (1979) Subjective referral of the timing for a conscious sensory experience. In *Brain*, 102: 193-224.

Lockwood, M. (1989) *Mind, Brain, and the Quantum* (Oxford: Basil Blackwell).

Lucas, J. R. (1961) Minds, machines, and Gödel. *Philosophy*, 36. Anthologized in Alan Ross Anderson (ed.) *Minds And Machines* Alan Ross Anderson (ed.) (Englewood Cliffs, NJ: Prentice-Hall), 43-59.

Lycan, W. (1981) Form, function, and feel. *Journal of Philosophy*, 78: 24-49.

McGinn, C. (1982) *The Character of Mind* (Oxford: Oxford University Press).

Nagel, T. (1979) *Mortal Questions* (Cambridge: Cambridge University Press).

Nagel, T. (1986) *The View From Nowhere* (New York: Oxford University Press).

Penrose, R. (1989) *The Emperor's New Mind* (Oxford: Oxford University Press).

Popper, K., and Eccles, J. (1977) *The Self And Its Brain* (New York: Springer International).

Searle, J. (1981) Minds, brains and programs. In J. Haugeland (ed.) *Mind Design* (Cambridge, MA: Bradford, MIT), 282-306.

Searle, J. (1984) *Minds, Brains And Science*, The 1984 Reith Lectures, BBC: London.

Searle, J. (1992) *The Rediscovery of the Mind* (Cambridge, MA: MIT Press).

Swinburne, R. (1986) *The Evolution of the Soul* (New York: Oxford Univesity Press).

Webb, J. (1980) *Mechanism, Mentalism, and Metamathematics* (Hingham, MA: Reidel).

Using Representation to Explain

Charles Wallis

1. INTRODUCTION

Most of cognitive science presupposes two theories, which I call the "Representational Theory of Intentionality" (RTI) and the "Computational Theory of Cognition" (CTC). While the RTI asserts that mental states are about the world in virtue of a representation relation between the world and the state, the CTC asserts that humans and others perform cognitive tasks by computing functions on these representations. CTC draws upon a rich analogy between the mind and computing machinery, portraying cognizers as receiving input (usually via sensory organs and/or memory) and generating outputs (usually in the form of memories, inputs to other processes, and/or motor response commands). Since most researchers within cognitive science—especially within

This paper was written while I attended the 1993 NEH Summer Seminar on mental representation.

Thinking Computers and Virtual Persons
edited by Eric Dietrich
ISBN 0-12-215495-9

cognitive psychology, computer science, and philosophy of mind—share a common theoretic background in their adherence to the combination of the RTI and CTC, a large percentage of the research done in philosophy of mind has aimed either at refuting or at further articulating these two theories.

Interesting and thoughtful work has resulted from the close philosophical scrutiny of RTI and CTC. Nevertheless, I claim that the common philosophic understanding of the role of representation in computational explanations within cognitive science is deeply flawed. Philosophers, and others, maintain false views as to both the explanans and the explananda of cognitive science. The presupposition that cognitive science must use representation to causally explain behavior is false. The standard philosophic picture of the explanatory structure of cognitive science in which representation and computation *alone* explain cognitive ability is, likewise, false. These false notions regarding the explanans and explananda of cognitive science undermine philosophical attempts to clarify the notion of intentionality, making the accomplishments of cognitive science seem obscure or illusory.

However, my approach is not completely negative. In the place of these false views about explananda and explanans, I offer a more accurate picture. I hope that by debunking the philosophic misconceptions regarding the structure and primitives of computational explanations within cognitive science, I can remove much of the conceptual logjam blocking a philosophical understanding of intentionality.

2.   WHAT DOES REPRESENTATION EXPLAIN?

In his book, *Explaining Behavior*, Fred Dretske expresses the traditional and widespread philosophic view that representational content must prove causally operative in explanations within cognitive science:[1]

> The fact that they [representational states] have a content, the fact that they have a semantic character, must be relevant to the kind of effects they produce. If brain structures possessing meaning affect motor output in the way the soprano's acoustic productions affect glass, then the meaning of these neural structures is causally inert. Even if it is there, it doesn't *do* anything. If having a mind is having *this* kind of meaning in the head, one may as well not have a mind. [1988, p. 80]

Dretske likewise offers a good statement of the philosopher's perceived project:

> The project is to understand how something's having meaning could itself have a physical effect—the kind of effect (e.g., muscular contraction) required for most forms of behavior—and to understand this *without* appealing to hypothetical centers of cognitive activity who, like filling-station attendants, *understand the meaning* of incoming signals. [Ibid., p. 83]

The philosopher's project is really twofold: before one can understand how meaning could be causally efficacious, one must first understand why physical explanations of behavior not invoking intentional notions prove inadequate to explain behavior. In short, one must create the problem before one can solve it. The first half of the project is of crucial importance. Most philosophers of mind hold that cognition is a real scientific (i.e., physical) domain with real (i.e., physical) effects to explain. On their view, philosophy must make room for cognitive science as a physical science while retaining its dissimilar mental character.

But how can one create the problem? All parties to the debate agree that physical laws can provide one with pervasive and convincing explanations of how a system generates behavior. Why, then, would one want, much less need, representation to explain behavior? The answer, I think, is that no one should. If one holds that the explananda of cognitive science is behavior, then one must face the fact that the behavior of physical systems is the province of the physical sciences, which have no need for notions like representation in their explanations.

On my line, then, Dretske and company are simply wrong. They falsely hold that the only way in which the mental has a role in the physical universe is if it acts as a cause *qua* mental property. They also hold that the only way in which one can understand the mental as a cause is *qua* physical property. The just mentioned commitments inevitably lead to the condition that Jerry Fodor describes as follows:

> An outbreak of epiphobia (the fear that one is turning into an epiphenomenalist) appears to have much of the philosophy of mind in its grip. Though it is generally agreed to be compatible with physicalism that intentional states should be causally responsible for behavioral outcomes, epiphobics worry that it is *not* compatible with physicalism that intentional states should be causally responsible for behavioral outcomes *qua intentional*. So they fear that the very success of a physicalistic (and/or computational) psychology will entail the causal inertness of the mental. [1990, p. 137]

While Fodor correctly identifies the problem, he too supposes that for cognitive science to have a domain of real effects to explain, those effects must be causal.[2] One must, however, reject this supposition. There is nothing to explaining how one raises one's hand beyond the physical explanation involving chemical reactions resulting in muscle contraction. However, by holding that representation proves superfluous to explanations of behavior, one does not thereby turn representation into a nomological dangler (a property that is caused but that has no causal effects). In addition to explaining a system's behavior, one also must explain the appropriateness or inappropriateness of behavior in light of the system's situation. The latter explanatory project, the explanation of cognitive capacities, is the province of cognitive science.

For example, in explaining how one can find one's way home one has two tasks. First, one must explain how one generates the associated behavior. Second, one must explain how the generated behavior leads one to one's door and not someone else's. One wants to explain how one's steps, otherwise explained, get one home and not to someone else's home. The physical story telling how one generates each step does not explain why each step was an appropriate part of an overall plan to get one home. One needs something more; one needs representation to show the relationship between one's generation of behavior and the overall structure of one's world.

Is there anything suspicious about this kind of explanation? No, as an example should make clear: Suppose one wants to explain how one's last shot won a game of eight ball. Such an explanation involves two tasks: first, one explains the sequence of collisions between balls by basic physics, attributing to the balls mass, velocity, etc. This explanation tells one how/why a ball fell into the pocket. Second, one refers to various other properties and relations of the balls to identify two of the balls as the cue ball and the eight ball, as well as to fix the state of the game. This later set of properties and relations, and not the first, explain why one won the game i.e., that one sank the eight ball using only the cue ball after sinking all of one's other balls. The two explanations refer to different primitives to explain different things. The fact that the properties and relations used in both explanations are united in the same set of balls allows one to understand how one won the game while also understanding the physical nature of the game. If, on the other hand, one were to talk about pool in the same way that Dretske talks about the mind, then one would have to somehow explain how the cueness of the cue ball caused the eight ball to fall into the pocket.

So, Dretske and company wrongly identify the explananda of cognitive science as behavior. One does not need a theory of representation to explain behavior. Physical laws explain behavior. One needs a theory of representation to help one to understand how a system generates appropriate behavior in response to the conditions in the world. One cannot explain how some behavior counts as a solution by cognition of a particular task by noting that certain physical parameters result in the behavior. One needs to understand how the causal relationships are disciplined by the physics in such a way as to make the response sensitive to the relevant external parameters. In short, physics explains behavior, and cognitive science explains how behavior can be a manifestation of a cognitive capacity.

3.   HOW DOES REPRESENTATION EXPLAIN?

Cognitive science, then, is in the business of explaining cognitive capacities and not (directly) in the business of explaining the causal sources of behavior. How does cognitive science go about explaining cognitive capacities? There is, again, a widely accepted answer to this question: explanations within cognitive science appeal *exclusively* to representation and computation. I claim that this scheme is impoverished. Because I think that informational semantics illustrates my point quite vividly, I use informational semantics as a framework for my discussion of explanation in cognitive science. However, informational semanticists are not alone in their confusion.

Jerry Fodor is the principal spokesman and architect of an old and respected tradition in the philosophy of cognitive science. This tradition holds that cognitive science will yield universal, conditional, ". . . intentional laws that connect, for example, states of believing that P & $(P\,'Q)$ to states of believing that Q" (1990, p. 145). Participants in this tradition assert that such laws are either available within folk knowledge of human mentality or easily extrapolated therefrom. Within this tradition, the main problem for philosophers of cognitive science lies in generating an explicit, naturalized theory of representation underwriting the assignment of values to variables in covering laws like the one above. Fodor played a significant role in developing one such theory of representation, nomic covariation. Though Fodor has greatly modified his position over the years, the problems with the original formulation still plague the current formulation.

Nomic covariation assigns contents to states via the following definition:[3]

> A state, S_b, represents B iff the system tokens S_b when, only when, and because of B.

So, for example, S_b represents barnhood according to nomic covariation iff the system tokens S_bs when, only when, and because of instances of barnhood.

A problem referred to as the "disjunction problem" poses a great difficulty for nomic covariation. That is, nomic covariation does not straightforwardly result in univocal content ascriptions, as it allows ostensive error to determine content: when a barn facsimile causes an S_b, the "only when" and "because" of covariationist definition dictates that S_b correctly represents a disjunctive property that one might express as "barn or barn facsimile." Of course, one's intuitions urge that the system has misrepresented a barn facsimile as a barn.

One, as a result, also finds within Fodor's tradition many unsuccessful attempts to bolster nomic covariance with respect to the disjunction problem by appealing to ideal perceptual conditions, selection histories, asymmetric dependencies, etc. The discussion of information theories within the literature has taken the standard "refutation by exhaustion" route. Fodor et al. makes a move; someone finds a problem. This methodology has resulted in standard but highly episodic criticisms of the various versions of informational semantics. While interesting, such criticisms only invite what I consider a more interesting and fundamental question: Is the failure of Fodor et al.'s conditions specific to the particular formulations considered thus far, or is it intrinsic to the informational approach to representation?

In this section, I break this tedious cycle of forwarding and refuting theories of representation and offer an answer to this last question. I consider covariance and computation once again in order to diagnose Fodor's and others' continued failure to articulate relevant conditions for representation. Specifically, I sort out the various roles of computation, covariation, and representation in computational explanations within cognitive psychology so as to point to a common misstep in covariationist and post-covariationist approaches. After explicating the relationship between representation and knowledge in computational explanations of cognitive task performance, I argue that informational semantics, like Fodor's asymmetric dependence theory as well as the crude causal and nomic covariation approaches before it, uses epistemic access to explain representation. I further assert that both cognitive science and pre-theoretic intuitions show that informational semantics reverses the order of explanation by using epistemic access to explain representation. Fodor and friends, in effect, use the system's ability to perform a task to explain its ability to perform that task.

The computational approach to cognitive psychology seeks to explain cognition in terms of three stages (not necessarily occurring in strict linear order) (Figure 12. 1).

Figure 12.1. Three stages in computation explanations.

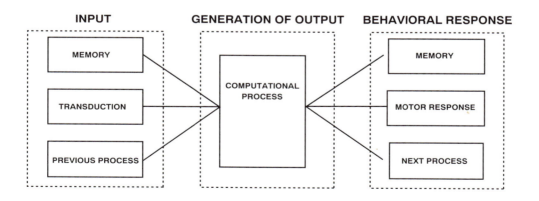

The first stage involves the input of representations, either from other processes, from the transduction of physical parameters, from memory, or from some combination of the three. In the second stage, the system operates upon input to generate other representations as output, often drawing upon knowledge it possessed previously. The model for this second stage is a computational model, though the style of computation varies widely. In the final stage, representations generated in the second stage guide the system's performance (involving some motor response, output to memory, or input into another process).

In trying to understand the role of representation in this schema, nomic covariationists think of representation in terms of input, especially in terms of successful performance of perceptual tasks, where perception is construed as transduction (i.e., the direct, lawlike conversion of physical parameters). Thinking of representation in terms of successful transduction has an initial appeal: if one wants to understand how a system relates to the objects and properties of the external world, one ought to consider the objects and/or properties present when, only when, and because the system tokens states of a particular type. The strategy looks especially attractive when one studies systems having very successful mechanisms of transduction (like human retinas). Moreover, it is one of the few ways to proceed when one is not sure how exactly the system performs the tasks that it does.

However, if one takes seriously the *computational* in "computational explanations," one realizes that covariance will not elucidate representation that representation is not enough to explain successful cognitive task performance. Successful cognitive task performance involves *both* a representational and an epistemological component. If one thinks of representation in terms of successful perceptual task performance cum direct, lawlike conversion of physical parameters, one will try to—and all nomic covariationists do—squeeze the epistemology into the representation,and explain everything with representation.

To illustrate this last point, let us return to the question I asked at the beginning of this section, Is the failure of Fodor et al.'s conditions specific to the particular formulations considered thus far, or is it intrinsic to the informational approach to representation? Fodor et al. have worked for over a decade to develop a theory of representation, and one must look back that far to diagnose the source of their woes. In "Semantics, Wisconsin Style" (SWS, 1984), Fodor distinguishes a causal and an epistemic theory of representation in the work of Denis Stampe and Fred Dretske. Epistemic accounts define representation using epistemic language. On the epistemic account, one explicates conditions for representation in terms of situations in which a system could come to know about the thing represented, specifically, conditions under which the system proves omniscient and infallible with respect to that parameter. The system tokens the state *whenever* the object or property is present. The system tokens the state *only when* the object or property is present. If the object or property is present, the system knows. If the object or property is not present, the system knows that as well. Causal accounts, on the other hand, define representation in terms of the typical cause of the representing state. In SWS, Fodor rejects epistemic accounts of representation but asserts that "it's likely that an epistemic account of representation will be satisfied whenever a causal one is" (1984, p. 35).

A more accurate statement of Fodor's position asserts that "it's *necessary* that an epistemic account of representation will be satisfied whenever a causal one is." Fodor rejects the epistemic account of representation in name only—rejecting only the use of epistemic terms in the definition of representation. Fodor does not, however, reject the basic premise in the work of Dretske and Stampe—*that one can understand representation only in terms of the epistemic access the system has with regard to the object or property.* As Dretske puts it, "anyone who believes something *thereby* exhibits the cognitive resources for knowing" (1983, p. 4).

Though Fodor wants to specify the conditions of representation using causal as opposed to epistemic language in SWS, he follows Dretske and Stampe in holding that those causally specified conditions *must* capture only those situations in which the system is infallible and omniscient with regard to the represented parameter. So Fodor rejects terminological versions of the epistemic account of representation in SWS. Fodor does not, however, reject the basic premise that a system represents only that to which it has perfect epistemic access.

Consider the disjunction problem: according to the current philosophical story about the disjunction problem, what makes the disjunction problem problematic is that current theories provide no means for understanding misrepresentation. One wants to claim that S_b represents barns, not barn facsimiles. However, as barn facsimiles cause instances of S_b, nomic covariation theories require that the content of a state be barn or barn facsimile. The system *always* represents the wrong (disjunctive) property. The epistemic motivations that drive nomic covariation mandate that one abandon one's pre-theoretic intuitions about the content of the state in favor of the (disjunctive) property that satisfies the epistemic requirements. If one lacks infallibility and omniscience with regard to barns, then one must represent *barn or barn facsimile.* Cases of ostensive misrepresentation always turn out to be *de facto* cases of veridical representation of a disjunctive property, since one cannot understand representation independent of epistemic success.

What actually makes the disjunction problem problematic, then, is that it points to a fundamental clash between, on the one hand, pre-theoretical presuppositions about content and explanatory order and, on the other hand, the theoretical presuppositions about explanatory order inherent in informational theories. Epistemology explains representation on the informational account. A state cannot represent a thing unless it exhibits omniscience and infallibility with regard to that thing. As a result, one cannot understand representation without first figuring out the epistemology.

On the pre-theoretic account, representation explains, in part, epistemology. If one wants to understand how a system comes to have an epistemically praiseworthy belief on the pre-theoretic account, one starts by noting that the system represents some state of affairs. One usually adds other requirements, like truth, justification, etc., to yield an explanation of knowledge. On the pre-theoretic account, then, representation serves as a beginning for knowledge. Infallibility and omniscience do not serve as a beginning for representation.

In SWS and in much of the literature that results, Fodor and others attempt to resolve this clash between pre-theoretic and informational presuppositions by following Dretske in distinguishing two sets of situations: one in which the system operates, the other, the set of content-imbuing situations. The system can have imperfect epistemic access in the former but not in the latter. One, in short, attempts to mediate between pre-theoretic and epistemic presuppositions by modifying the epistemic presupposition to require only that the system have perfect epistemic access in ideal, reductive, learning, and/or evolutionary situations. *Epistemology still explains representation, because now perfect epistemic access need only be counterfactual in order to explain representation.* S_b represents barns because actual situations occur in which the system is omniscient and infallible with regard to barns.

Though clever, distinguishing the two sets of situations fails to avoid the real problem for informational theories; the pre-theoretic explanatory order is correct. As a result, no one will discover a nonintentional, nonsemantic means of delimiting the set of situations in which the system has perfect epistemic access, simply because one cannot do the epistemology without already knowing what the system represents. If one needs representation to explain epistemology, it proves impossible to do the epistemology required for the informational accounts without first having figured out the representation. In other words, it is very difficult to specify a set of situations in which a system proves infallible and omniscient with regard to some target parameter without first determining the identity of that parameter. So, on my view, the failure of nomic covariationists to define a set of situations in which a system has perfect epistemic access reinforces the pre-theoretic presupposition that representation explains epistemology.

The various versions of the sets of situations fail to provide an adequate solution to the disjunction problem because they fail to address the underlying problem of contradictory explanatory orders. However, Fodor claims that his asymmetric dependence move

> [D]oes not try to solve the disjunction problem by distinguishing type one situations (those in which whatever causes a symbol to be tokened is ipso facto in its extension) from type two situations (those in which symbols are allowed to be caused by things that they don't apply to). [1990, p. 89]

Despite Fodor's claim, asymmetric dependence distinguishes type two situations from *nomologically possible but not necessarily actual* type one situations in which the system has perfect epistemic access with regard to a given facsimile. As Fodor expresses it,

> [I]i's daggers—rather than dagger appearances—that MacBeth's DAGGER concept expresses because, although daggers and dagger appearances both cause DAGGER tokens in this world, still there are some possible worlds in which MacBeth can tell them apart. [Ibid., p. 123]

Fodor's asymmetric dependence theory differs from nomic covariation theories only in that Fodor no longer requires that a system ever actually encounter situations in which it proves omniscient and infallible with regard to *all* facsimiles. Fodor's move again attempts to preserve the epistemic presupposition of informational theories by weakening it so that it now requires only that the ontology of the world be such that the system *could* have perfect epistemic access with regard to any facsimile.

Fodor still uses epistemology to explain representation, but what, if anything, is so bad about that? First, the world's underlying ontological structure need not guarantee that a system could have perfect epistemic access. Second, and of equal importance, Fodor's approach still reverses the explanatory order in pre-theoretic presuppositions. Third, the evidence from cognitive science shows that (1) the pre-theoretic presupposition is correct—one needs representation to help explain epistemic access—not vice versa, and (2) that the explanatory order of cognitive science also uses representation to explain epistemic access—not vice versa.

When one considers the results from research on visual processing in cognitive science, one notes that at each stage of visual processing—transduction, feature detection, and object recognition—one finds that the visual system introduces equivocation (fallibility) in order to solve the problem at all, or to increase sensitivity, robustness, and/or speed:[5] the mechanisms that underlie a rod's extreme sensitivity to low-level light have the side effect of heat-triggered noise. In order to allow the system to respond to edges that are slightly askew (i.e., to degrade gracefully), simple cells in the visual cortex fire at the same rate for a potentially infinite number of orientation/intensity combinations. To identify objects within 100 msec, the visual system accesses only a very limited amount of background information—even though this limited information does not allow the system to discriminate infallibly between all objects under all conditions. Systems, in short, function with—even need—a certain amount of equivocation. One must understand a system's representational abilities in the context of that equivocation, not in the context of some actual or possible infallibility and omniscience.

Both pre-theoretic intuitions and actual research support an explanatory order that moves in the opposite direction of that dictated by covariationists and post-covariationists. What is the explanatory order within cognitive science? Cognitive science does rest on an explanatory schema wherein the ability to perform a task is explained in terms of (at least) representation and computation.

But, consider the role of representation in the purely computational explanation of a simple system's, ALAN's, ability to compute the successor function:

When one asks ALAN to add one to a number, one does so by writing the number as a series of strokes on a sheet of blank squares (one stroke per square, starting at the third square), and sets it in front of ALAN. ALAN then proceeds as follows:

> Starting at the first square, ALAN moves the sheet one square to the right every time it sees a stroke in the square, and looks at the new square. (Each circle indicates a state that ALAN instantiates while performing the tasks indicated by the arrows: In state 1 ALAN moves the paper to the R(ight) when it sees a '1'.)

> When ALAN sees a blank square, it writes a stroke (B:1) and looks at the newly modified square.

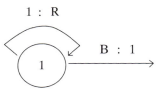

> From that point on, ALAN moves the sheet one square to the left every time it sees a stroke (1:L) and looks at the new square.

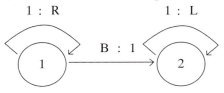

> When ALAN sees a blank square, it moves the sheet one square to the right (B:R) and stops working.

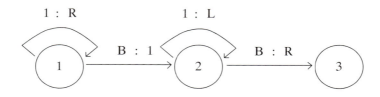

For those familiar with Turing machines and Church's thesis, ALAN is straightforwardly computing the function $(x + 1)$: in fact, ALAN is a finite instantiation of the Turing machine diagrammed above.[6] Within the three-stage computational explanation schema given earlier, the first stage involves stroke inputs, the second stage involves dispositions to operate upon the inputs, and the third stage is just ALAN coming to rest at the beginning of the new stroke string.

In giving a computational explanation of ALAN's ability, one type-individuates ALAN's initial and final states. If ALAN's initial state consists of ALAN sitting at the beginning of a string of n strokes, ALAN always moves $(n + 1)$ squares and ends at the beginning of $(n + 1)$ strokes. If ALAN starts at the beginning of a six-stroke string, it moves seven squares and ends at the beginning of seven strokes. Hence, one can type ALAN's inputs and outputs according to the number of strokes on the sheet involved in the state.

Once one type-individuates ALAN's states, one assigns representational content to ALAN's type-individuated states. One can assign representational content via an interpretation as follows:

1. A state where ALAN starts on a blank sheet of paper counts as zero.

2. A state where ALAN starts on a sheet with n strokes counts as ALAN's representing the number n.

In logic and mathematics, the generally operative notion of computability is tied only to the notion of a Turing machine given Church's thesis. In other words, the notion of computability has only two components: (1) The assumption that the set of computable functions is the set of Turing-computable functions. (2) The notion that a Turing machine computes a function iff for every argument/value double in the set that characterizes the function, the machine would generate that value (under some interpretation) given the argument or set of arguments (under the interpretation). Nowhere does the mathematical notion of computation make reference to our ability to exploit a Turing machine's computational ability, i.e., *our* actually being able to generate and use an interpretation.

Hence, a purely computational explanation uses representation to explain ALAN's performance of the cognitive task in three steps: (1) One type-individuates ALAN's states. (2) One maps its input and output states to the relevant objects in the task domain by the representation relation (in our case the relevant "objects" are numbers). (3) Utilizing the representation relation, one shows how ALAN's state transitions *can* work to generate the correct output for each input within the task domain. Sometimes this last step (3) takes the form of a soundness/completeness proof given (1) and (2). Sometimes the step in (3) takes the form of a generalization based upon experimental results. These three steps are essential to a purely computational explanation and are adopted by computationalists within cognitive science.

Note, however, that in shifting to ALAN's real resource constraints, one must modify the explanation. For example, no sheet/state represents numbers other than integers: no sheet/state represents five-thirds or negative one. Moreover, the size of the sheets of paper places a further limit on the size of the positive integers that ALAN can represent. All of these factors serve to truncate the actual task one attributes to ALAN. ALAN can compute the $(x + 1)$ function for positive integers within a certain range. Relative to this task specification, the above assignment of numbers to strokes on sheets of paper works fine.[7]

One knows how ALAN behaves given an input, so one can predict what physical state (now representational state) results from ALAN's state changes given some particular input (now representation state). One can then use these predictive results to make a further claim about ALAN: one can show that within its finite domain, ALAN's state transitions generate an output representing the input plus one (under the representational schema) for any input within its domain.

The notion of a semantic engine helps one to understand the nature of computational explanations as they are applied to cognition. John Haugeland (1981) has explicated the notion of a semantic engine and its role in the CTC: All cognizers are physical engines—dynamic systems operating upon physical principles. By viewing a physical engine in terms of type-individuated states having principled interactions with other type-individuated states, one can understand how physical engines can instantiate syntactic engines—dynamic systems operating upon syntactic principles. Finally, via an interpretation function providing a semantics for the syntactic engine, one can understand how a syntactic engine can instantiate a semantic engine—a dynamic system operating upon semantic principles. By understanding how a physical system can satisfy an interpretation function, one can understand how a physical system does semantic work.

One can illustrate the explanatory mechanism as in Figure 12.2. One has a general knowledge about ALAN's operation at the physical level. In virtue of the syntactic type-individuation, one translates one's physical explanations into syntactic explanations that relate classes of inputs and outputs. This allows syntactic explanations to ride piggyback on physical theory. Hence, one can understand how physical principles can do syntactic work. In virtue of the assignment of representational content via the interpretation function, one translates one's syntactic explanations into explanations about how ALAN's syntactic states relate to positive integers within a certain range. The representation relation rides piggyback on syntactic theory and serves to tie ALAN's states to objects in the problem domain so that one *can* explain ALAN's ability to compute the $(x + 1)$ function. One can then understand how physical principles can do semantic work. That is, *the representational theory relates the system's states to the objects of the problem domain to explain how the system's operations can potentially satisfy the epistemic constraints imposed by a particular task.*

Figure 12.2.

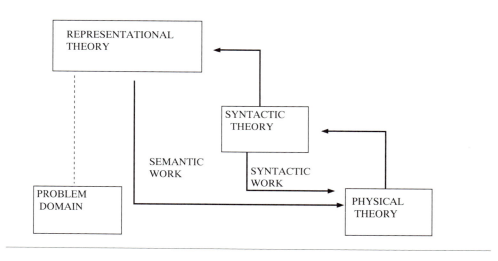

For covariation and post-covariation theorists (and almost everyone else within the philosophy of cognitive science), this picture exhausts the explanatory mechanisms available to computationalists for explaining actual system performance. These theorists claim one need only plug their theory of representation into the above explanatory picture to explain ALAN's abilities. However, neither nomic covariation nor asymmetric dependence provides one with a theory of representation capable of explaining ALAN's computational ability. If one wants to explain how ALAN computes the successor function using nomic covariation or asymmetric dependence, one has to show how ALAN's states relate to numbers via nomic covariation, asymmetric dependence, etc. Of course, no physical states get tokened when, only when, and because of numbers. The standard response is to label ALAN's representational abilities "derivative." ALAN represents numbers because its users/designers do. This last move only postpones the inevitable, as numbers will not cause tokenings of states in ALAN's users/designers either. So, one tells a story about how numbers come from everything else . . . once one has everything else.

Fortunately, one does not need everything else to offer a purely computational explanation of how ALAN computes the successor function. One only needs to understand that ALAN's state transitions could relate inputs to outputs so that input-output pairs are isomorphic to the domain-range pairs of the successor function under an interpretation. That is all that there is to the notion of computation, and from the perspective of computation, that is all that there is to the notion of representation.

Representation plays an important and necessary role in computational explanations within cognitive science. Representation *provides the means whereby one can understand how a system's states could possibly relate to the objects of some particular problem domain to explain how the system's operations satisfy the epistemic constraints imposed by some particular task.* I emphasize the phrase "could possibly relate" in the last sentence. Representation, for all its virtues, will not in itself suffice to show how a system's operations can *in fact* satisfy the epistemic constraints imposed by some particular task within some particular domain. This point can be illustrated by considering three ways that ALAN might fail to compute the $(x + 1)$ function correctly.

First, suppose that I meant to ask ALAN to tell me the successor of six, but I wrote down only five strokes. Under the interpretation, ALAN's input misrepresents the desired number (six) as five. Of course, that does not mean that ALAN fails to represent a number or that ALAN represents *five or six* by five strokes. It means that the number ALAN represents in its initial state is not the number that I wanted it to represent.

ALAN fails to answer my question correctly , not because its initial state fails to represent, or represents disjunctively, but because it misrepresents six as five. Hence, in order for ALAN to successfully perform the task of computing the successor function in response to a particular request, ALAN and I must interact so that the number ALAN's input represents is also the number for which I desire the successor. If ALAN is to have the *ability* to compute successors to the numbers as I request them, ALAN and I must systematically interact so that the numbers represented by ALAN's inputs are also the numbers for which I desire the successors—that is the epistemological component. It is not enough that ALAN's states represent and that ALAN's state transitions compute; ALAN must *know* what number I had in mind in order to compute its successor.

Second, suppose that ALAN's state transitions do not always end in the correct output. Suppose that in the case of six, ALAN's state transitions end with ALAN printing eight strokes. In this second case, ALAN also fails to correctly answer my question, this time because ALAN does not *know* how or has an imperfect knowledge of how to compute the successor function. Computational ability buys potential know-how, that is, computational ability explains how a system can potentially move from knowledge of inputs to knowledge of outputs.

Third, let us suppose that ALAN can go through two types of state transitions. The first type of state transition always ends with the successor of the input. The second type of state transition always ends with ALAN printing eight strokes. Suppose that I enter a seven-stroke input and ALAN generates an eight-stroke output. In the third case, then, ALAN knows the original number. It knows how to compute the successor. However, whether or not ALAN *knows* the answer depends upon the type of state transition ALAN went through to get the output. Computation buys potential to generate knowledge from knowledge. Potential, however, must be actualized and exploited—that is where epistemology again comes in.

In abstract, then, a computational explanation of a system's ability (ALAN's or our own) to perform a cognitive task successfully requires showing both that the system can represent and compute the relevant target function and that the system routinely possesses three types of knowledge:

(K1)   A knowledge of the relevant input parameters.

(K2)   A knowledge of how to utilize its input to compute the output necessary for solving the problem (perform the task).

(K3)   Output of the solution to the problem that counts as knowledge.

In the computational model adapted to explain actual ability, then, knowledge or lack of knowledge acts with representation to explain cases of successful and unsuccessful performance of cognitive tasks. Cognizers that do not start knowing the relevant facts (input), do not generate knowledge (output) from their initial knowledge, or do not know how to generate the output from the input fail, in general, to perform cognitive tasks successfully. For example, if I fail to return to my hotel room after a talk at a conference, the computationalist can diagnose my failure in three ways. I might not have sufficient knowledge of the floor plan of the hotel, or I might not know my position relative to the floor plan. The computationalist would then trace my failure to a failure of knowledge at the input stage. I might not know how to generate a route or not know how to generate knowledge concerning the means to execute the route. Here failure is traced to a lack of knowledge how. Finally, I might fail to generate knowledge concerning a route or to generate knowledge concerning the means to execute that route. The computationalist then traces my failure to a failure to generate knowledge (output) from my knowledge of the floor plan and my position (input).

In order to get from representation to an explanation of a system's ability(ies), one needs a mechanism to bridge the gap between representation on the one hand and actual system performance or inability to perform on the other. The concept of knowledge bridges the gap between representation and a system's performance. One picks out a particular task via a target function. One can pick out the relevant abstractly understood computational ability(ies) of a system via representation and relate it to an abstractly understood epistemic potential. By referring to knowledge, one can evaluate a system's performance or real potential to perform. Knowledge provides the means for showing how the system actually instantiates the relevant abstractly understood computational ability and epistemic potential within a problem domain.

My model for computational explanation in cognitive science, therefore, allows for the roles of both representation and knowledge (Figure 12.3). The nomic

Figure 12.3. Structure of computational explanations in cognitive science.

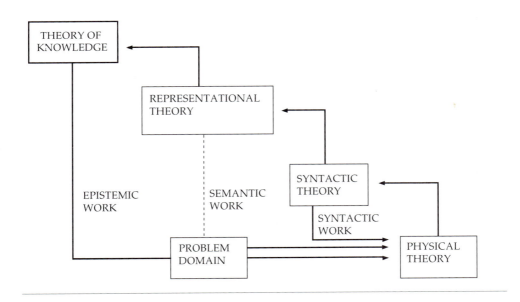

covariationists and asymmetric defenders try to understand representation in terms of epistemology. According to the basic version of nomic covariation, a system cannot represent an object or property without being both infallible and omniscient as regards that object or property. Real systems prove neither omniscient nor infallible, so one retreats into some other modified version. According to the idealization versions of nomic covariation, a system cannot represent an object or property without being omniscient and infallible with regard to the object or property under ideal circumstances. According to the reduction version, a system has to be omniscient with regard to some smaller set of objects and/or properties. According to the teleological account, a system or its progenitors must have had, will have, or could have knowledge regarding the parameters enough times to survive. Finally, according to asymmetric dependence, a system cannot represent unless its dispositions are such that when it fails to know, it can discover that failure. Or, as Fodor puts it:

> The relevant consideration isn't however, *just* that frogs sometimes go for bee-bees; it's that they are prepared to go on going for *forever* . . . . Sometimes Macbeth starts at mere dagger appearances; but most of the time he starts only if there's a dagger. What Macbeth and I have in common—and what distinguished our case from the frog's—is that *though he and I both make mistakes, we are both in a position to recover.* [1990, p. 107]

Informational theories of representation fail because they try to pack all of the epistemology into the representation, attempting to use representation to show how the system is in a position to have knowledge—knowledge in the strong sense of infallibility and omniscience. Recall that the informational theorist gets into the disjunction problem because the unique interpretation function (nomic covariation) that determines representational content provides no means to distinguish cases of representation from cases of misrepresentation. Cases of ostensive misrepresentation are actually cases of veridical representation of disjunctive properties, because under the interpretation function every case where the system tokens the state determines the state's content. Why? The nomic covariationist has bought into the notion that a system cannot represent unless it is in a position to know (in the strong sense of infallible and omniscient). So, when a system ostensibly misrepresents a barn as a barn facsimile, the interpretation function dictates that it, in fact, veridically represents a barn as a *barn or barn facsimile*. Nomic covariation and asymmetric dependence fail as theories of content because they necessarily tie explanations of representational ability to explanations of our (or anything's) ability to exploit computational ability to do epistemic work.

I have given, I think, three good reasons to suppose that tying computational ability to exploitive ability is a bad idea. First, informational semantics proves an inadequate theory of representation precisely because it reverses the explanatory order inherent in pre-theoretic epistemic intuitions. While intuitions have representation serving in explanations of knowledge, these theories have epistemic access explaining representation. Second, data from cognitive science show that systems introduce equivocation (fallibility) to solve problems or to increase sensitivity, robustness, and/or speed. Data from cognitive science, in effect, support the pre-theoretic intuition that representation must serve in explanations of knowledge and not vice versa. Third, tying representational ability to exploitive ability contradicts the notion of computability as rigorously defined within logic and mathematics and as adopted and adapted within cognitive science.

I offer an additional reason to these three to suppose that tying computational ability to exploitive ability is a bad idea. Nomic covariation and asymmetric dependence theories are inadequate on their own grounds to address the diverse epistemic and representational dimensions involved in computational explanations in cognitive science. Both nomic covariation and asymmetric dependence are framed only in terms of the epistemology of inputs. Neither theory yields assessments of knowledge how. Nor does either theory provide one with a means for assigning representational content to outputs or for assessing the epistemic status of outputs. Both nomic covariation and the causal (second) clause of Fodor's theory require that states be caused (at least sometimes) by the objects and/or properties that they represent. Yet successors never cause ALAN to output strings of strokes, plans never cause the output of planning programs like STRIPS, and so on. Were these parameters available to the system, it would need only detect them. In these examples, the purpose of the computation is the generation of parameters not immediately (or ever) available to the system in its given environment.

Neither asymmetric dependence nor nomic covariation is designed to deal with such cases. As a result, neither theory can help one to assign content to those states, and, of course, if these theories cannot assign representational content to such states, they surely cannot evaluate the epistemic status of such states. In short, though informational theories would do the epistemic work in computational theories with a single, undifferentiated concept of representation, information theory has a grossly inadequate epistemology.

In the face of these potential difficulties, I choose another route. I divorce computational ability from exploitive ability. This divorce is not complete, however, as one must have the ability to compute the relevant function to generate a representational state that counts as knowledge. Nevertheless, the divorce of computation from exploitive ability meshes with intuition, theories in cognitive science, computational theory, and data about the functioning of actual cognitive systems.

The separation of representational and epistemic components allows one to account for the fact that many cases of belief do not count as knowledge. Likewise, since ability to compute is not conflated with the ability to exploit computation to generate knowledge, my theory of the role of representational content in computational explanations in cognitive science does not compromise the theoretical notion of computation.

4.   REPRESENTATION AND UNIQUENESS OF CONTENT

I think the arguments in the previous sections establish the following: computational explanations in cognitive science have distinct epistemic and representational components. The explanatory order inherent in cognitive science, computational theory, and our pre-theoretic intuitions dictates that representation be used to explain knowledge. Informational theories of representation reverse the explanatory order. Therefore, informational theories are, in principle, inadequate theories of representation for cognitive science. I have not, however, offered or defended a theory of representation.

One objection offered to my view is that my "theory of representation" does not yield unique content ascriptions. That is, different interpretations of ALAN's states yield different, equally "legitimate," representational contents. My response to this objection is that I offer no theory of representation. Rather, I offer a theory of the *role* of representation as an explanatory primitive in cognitive science. My theory about the role of representation in cognitive science is not refuted by worries about uniqueness of content, as it can easily and consistently be amended to require uniqueness of content.

In fact, I think that there are (at least) two ways to react to philosophical intuitions that one's thoughts have one and only one content. One can, on the one hand, simply add an additional constraint upon theories of representation. Theories of representation must respect the explanatory structure within cognitive science, and they must yield unique content ascriptions. On the other hand, one might argue that the philosophical intuition is false, as it again inverts explanatory order by requiring that one know what one represents in order for one to represent at all. While I lean toward the latter approach, I will neither articulate nor defend such a position here. I do, however, note that the requirement of uniqueness of content has driven many conceptual role semanticists to conflate epistemology with representation (see, for instance, Burge 1986 and Cummins 1989), by arguing that the system must represent X, and not Y, because it has knowledge about Xs. Likewise, the intuition that knowing how to read Chinese texts requires explicit, conscious knowledge of their contents fuels Searle's Chinese Room argument.

5.   CONCLUSION

In my view, much of the worries about intentionality spring directly from the false views of philosophers (and others) about the explananda and explanans of cognitive science. These views lead philosophers into confusions about both the goal and the role of appeals to intentional states in computational explanations within cognitive science. They, for example, lead philosophers to suppose that, as the representational theory of intentionality uses representation to explain intentionality, intentionality alone must address the diverse epistemic problems faced by cognitive systems in the performance of cognitive tasks. By further clarifying the explananda and explanans of cognitive science, I hope to remove much of the obscurity regarding the role of intentionality in computational explanations in cognitive science.

6.   NOTES

1.   My point here holds whether one takes *behavior* as it is understood by Dretske, ". . . the process of producing movement," or as physical movement. The point is that on this line, representation must cause the process or movement in order to solve the mind-body problem (1988, p. 96).

2..   To the best of my knowledge only Cummins (1983) recognizes that not all science is concerned with causal explanation. See Chapters I and II.

3.   See Fodor (1990) and Loewer and Rey (1991) for the current state of the art in nomic covariance and its critics.

4.   See Wallis (1993) for illustrations of this fact.

5.   Again, see Wallis (1993) for illustrations. I base my 1993 claims upon Baylor (1984), Biederman (1987), Daw (1984), Kendel et al. (1991), Lennie (1984), Schnapf and Baylor (1987), Kuhn (1984), Gouras (1984), Shapley (1984), Stryer (1987), Kendel (1991).

6.   Some people may wonder about the notion of knowledge for inputs. The pre-theoretic notion of the epistemic component of computational explanations of cognitive task performance is that property allowing the system to systematically generate veridical representations. I designate that states result from that property knowledge. Such states may be inputs or outputs, and as they are all representations, I do not distinguish between representational states at this point.

7.   ALAN is finite in the sense that computers are finite instantiations of Turing
     machines: ALAN has a limited supply of resources (paper, pencils, time,
     etc.).

7.   REFERENCES

Baylor, D., Nunn, B., and Schnapf, J. (1984) The photocurrent, noise and spectral
     sensitivity of rods of the monkey *Macaca Fascicularis*. *The Journal of
     Physiology*, 357: 575-607.

Biederman, I. (1987) Recognition by components: a theory of human image
     understanding. *Psychological Review*, 94: 115-147.

Burge, T. (1986) Individualism in psychology. *Philosophical Review*, 95: 3-45.

Boolos, G., and Jeffrey, R. (1974) *Computability And Logic* (Cambridge: Cambridge
     University Press).

Brachman, R., and Levesque, H. (eds.) (1985) *Readings in Knowledge Representation*
     (San Mateo, CA: Morgan Kaufmann).

Chomsky, N. (1986) Changing perspectives on knowledge and use of language.
     In M. Brand and R. Harnish (eds.) *The Representation of Knowledge and Belief*
     (Tucson: University of Arizona Press).

Cummins, R. (1983) *The Nature Of Psychological Explanation* (Cambridge, MA: MIT
     Press).

Cummins, R. (1989) *Meaning and Mental Representation* (Cambridge, MA: MIT
     Press).

Daw, N. (1984) The psychology and physiology of color vision. *Trends in
     NeuroScience*, (September): 330-335.

Dietrich, E. (1990) Computationalism. *Social Epistemology*, 4: 155-199.

Dretske, F. (1981) *Knowledge and the Flow of Information* (Cambridge, MA: MIT
     Press).

Dretske, F. (1983) The epistemology of belief. *Synthese*, 55: 3-19.

Dretske, F. (1988) *Explaining Behavior* (Cambridge, MA: MIT Press).

Fodor, J. (1981) *Representations* (Cambridge, MA: MIT Press).

Fodor, J. (1982) Cognitive science and the twin-earth problem. *Notre Dame Journal
     of Symbolic Logic*, 23: 97-117.

Fodor, J. (1983) *The Modularity of Mind* (Cambridge, MA: MIT Press).

Fodor, J. (1984) Semantics, Wisconsin style. *Synthese,* 59: 231-250.

Fodor, J. (1986) Why paramecia don't have mental representations. *Midwest Studies in Philosophy,* 10: 3-23.

Fodor, J. (1988) *Psychosemantics* (Cambridge, MA: MIT Press).

Fodor, J. (1990) *A Theory of Content and Other Essays* (Cambridge, MA: MIT Press).

Gardner, H. (1985) *The Mind's New Science. A History of the Cognitive Revolution* (New York: Basic Books).

Glass, A., and Holyoak, K. (1986) *Cognition*, 2nd ed. (New York: Random House).

Glymour, C. (1983) Android epistemology and the frame problem: comments on Dennett's "Cognitive Wheels." In Z. Pylyshyn (ed.) *The Robot's Dilemma* (Cambridge, MA: MIT Press).

Godfrey-Smith, P. (1989) Misinformation. *The Canadian Journal of Philosophy,* 19: 533-550.

Goldstein, E. (1989) *Sensation and Perception* (Belmont, CA: Wadsworth Publishing Company).

Gouras, P. (1984) Color vision. In N. Osborn and J. Chader (eds.) *Progress in Retinal Research 3* (London: Pergamon Press).

Haugeland, J. (1981) Semantic engines. In *Mind Design* (Cambridge, MA: MIT Press).

Kendel, E., Schwartz, J., and Jessel, T. (eds.) (1991) *Principles of Neural Science* (New York: Elsevier).

Kersten, D. (1990) Statistical limits to image understanding. In C. Blakemore (ed.) *Vision: Coding and Efficiency* (Cambridge: Cambridge University Press).

Kuhn, H. (1984) Interactions between photoexcited rhodopsin and light-activated enzymes in rods. In N. Osborn and J. Chader (eds.) *Progress in Retinal Research 3* (London: Pergamon Press).

Lennie, P. (1984) Recent developments in the physiology of color vision. *Trends in NeuroScience,* (July): 243-247.

Lloyd, D. (1987) Mental representation from the bottom up. *Synthese,* 70: 23-78.

Loewer, B., and Rey, G. (eds.) (1991) Meaning in mind: Fodor and his critics (Cambridge, MA: Blackwell Press).

Marr, D. (1982) *Vision: A Computational Investigation into the Human Representation and Processing of Visual Information* (New York: W. H. Freeman).

Movshon, J., Adelson, E., Gizzi, M., and Newsome, W. (1985) The analysis of moving visual patterns. In C. Chagas, R. Gattas, and C. Gross (eds.) *Pattern Recognition Mechanisms* (New York: Vatican Press).

Posner, M. (ed.) (1989) *Foundations of Cognitive Science* (Cambridge, MA: MIT Press).

Pylyshyn, Z. (1987) What's in a mind? In *Synthese,* 70: 97-122.

Schnapf, J., and Baylor, D. (1987) How photoreceptor cells respond to light. *Scientific American,* 256: 40-47.

Shapley, R., and Enroth-Cugell, C. (1984) Visual adaptation and retinal gain controls. In N. Osborn and J. Chader (eds.) *Progress in Retinal Research 3* (London: Pergamon Press).

Stampe, D. (1977) Towards a causal theory of linguistic representation. In Peter French et al. (eds.) *Midwest Studies in Philosophy* (Minneapolis: University of Minnesota Press).

Stich, S., and Nisbett, R. (1980) Justification and the psychology of human reasoning. In *Philosophy of Science,* 47: 188-202.

Stich, S. (1983) *From Folk Psychology to Cognitive Science* (Cambridge, MA: MIT Press).

Stich, S. (1984) Could man be an irrational animal? Some notes on the epistemology of rationality. In H. Kornblith (ed.) *Naturalizing Epistemology* (Cambridge, MA: MIT Press).

Stryer, L. (1987) The Molecules of Visual Excitation. *Scientific American,* 257: 42-50.

Ungerleider, L. (1985) The corticocortical pathways for object recognition and spatial perception. In C. Chagas, R. Gattas, and C. Gross (eds.) *Pattern Recognition Mechanisms* (New York: Vatican Press).

Wallis, C. (1993) Asymmetric dependence as a failed strategy to define representation. *Psychology,* (70) 3.

Chapter 13

Human Reasoning about Artificial Intelligence

Patrick J. Hayes, Kenneth M. Ford, and Jack R. Adams-Webber

A prejudice is a vagrant opinion without visible means of support.

—Ambrose Bierce

1. INTRODUCTION

Several authors (e.g. Penrose, Rychlak, Searle) have suggested recently that AI (artificial intelligence) is somehow a misguided or hopeless undertaking. Often, the suggestion that people may be usefully construed as machines (and are therefore limited) is seen to be somehow insulting or demeaning, or taken to be a symptom of some kind of political error or intellectual blindness.

Thinking Computers and Virtual Persons
edited by Eric Dietrich
ISBN 0-12-215495-9

One of the most vehement of these attacks was delivered by Joseph Rychlak in his recent (1991a) book *Artificial Intelligence and Human Reason (AIHR),* and in a brace of articles in the *International Journal of Personal Construct Psychology* (1990, 1991b). He asserts passionately that computers are constitutionally unable to perform a uniquely human kind of cognitive activity which he terms 'predication.' More specifically, as a former student of George Kelly, he submits that the latter's personal construct theory (Kelly 1955) is intrinsically incompatible with all computational models of human cognition.

This is typical of one of the categories of confused argument which we find in this literature; that is, AI is incompatible with some favored model of human cognition. Others include:

- objections (often proffered by philosophers and social scientists) predicated on misunderstandings of Gödel's theorem, quantum physics and other results of mathematics and the natural sciences as they relate to AI;
- objections based on observations of things that it is claimed humans can do but machines putatively cannot do;
- objections arising from a monistic reductionism and a lack of appreciation for the notion of different levels of discourse (e.g. cognitive vs implementation);
- objections caused by a limited understanding of both computers and computation.

Conveniently, Rychlak's particular assertions are replete with clear manifestations of all of the aforementioned confusions (among others), and thus, they serve as instructive, although extreme, examples of the sorts of confusion that we hope to dispel in this discussion. In short, he has created an excellent opportunity for us to join the debate and respond to such 'AI-bashing,' which we think is largely motivated by an irrational fear of the unknown.

Rychlak is deeply emotionally involved with his position. He tells us, for example, that to read of the framing of constructs in the AI literature makes him 'shudder'; that a colleague's casual use of a computer metaphor for her own memory 'shocked and angered' him, and that 'the mechanical theories of psychology . . . have robbed the person not only of agency but also of character.' These remarks reveal a depth of feeling which we suspect motivates a good deal of this negative reaction to the AI idea of the mind as computation, which is found disturbing by many who are quite reconciled to the notion of the body as a biochemical mechanism. This last stand of vitalism is becoming almost fashionable, and is to some extent backed by the authority of several eminent philosophers, for example, John Searle (whom Rychlak cites with warm approval).

It is a pity that so many think in this way, since a superficial characterization of what Rychlak calls 'mechanical psychology' obscures the fundamental differences between modern AI and (for example) cybernetics and neural modeling to which indeed some of these criticisms may apply. Unlike many current scientific paradigms, AI does not support a dehumanizing view of humans as mere passive mechanisms, devoid of moral responsibility. AI does not cast us as the slaves of 'selfish genes,' the victims of our own reinforcement histories, or some kind of generalized switchboards. On the contrary, AI offers a flexible framework, with rapidly increasing deployability and scope, for our attempts to reconcile a strictly biological view of people with a psychological level of description; that is, with concepts of personal experience, belief, meaning, purpose, anticipation and, ultimately, responsibility.

2.   OBJECTIONS ARISING FROM MISUNDERSTANDINGS OF THE NATURE OF COMPUTATION AND GÖDEL'S THEOREM

Many commentators on AI clearly understand very little about computer science. Rychlak has the honesty to tell us in the introduction to *AIHR* that his ideas about computing were derived from playing with punched-card sorters and children's plastic models rather than from any technical education in the subject.

Unfortunately, he does not regard this as any limitation on his authority to tell us what computers are and are not capable of doing. For instance, this book is shot through with broad assertions about what machines *cannot* do. Indeed, in just two pages of the introduction alone, we read that they cannot learn what was not input to them, they cannot predicate, they cannot presume, they merely match figures to one another, they lack a sense of 'oppositional possibility' and that they could never understand that two cars parked opposite one another were in fact opposite. Rychlak fails to provide either arguments or factual evidence to support any of these claims, most of which seem to be either logically invalid or empirically false.

Exactly what *are* computers like? What precisely is computation? These are difficult questions that computer scientists are still investigating. This sense of discovery is part of what gives the new interdisciplinary initiative called 'cognitive science' much of its excitement and energy. But no serious critic should rely on simple laymen's guides to computer science as the basis for firm conclusions about what computers cannot do. For example, everyone 'knows' that a computer is a binary 'hardware' machine that simply obeys lists of 'software' instructions, matching purely formal patterns of symbols. All of this is wrong. Computers are not inherently binary and do not obey instructions, programs do not operate exclusively by matching formal symbols, and the distinction between interpreter and interpreted language—between processor and program—usually does not coincide with the distinction between hardware and software.

Rychlak makes several simple mistakes in describing computing. First, let us deal quickly with one regrettably common error concerning Gödel's famous incompleteness theorem. Rychlak refers directly to Gödel (1991a, pp. 120-123), but misunderstands his theorem in a familiar way. Gödel shows that, in the syntax of any reasonably expressive axiomatic system, a formula can be written that is true, but not provable within that system. Rychlak, however, attributes a much stronger result to Gödel, that is, A *human reasoner can necessarily see* that this formula is true. Gödel says nothing about human intelligence, and this extra step only follows if one were to assume that a human reasoner can see all truths to be true, which is a rather strong assumption.

Likewise, in his many-faceted recent book (1989) *The Emperor's New Mind*, Roger Penrose considers Gödel's theorem and makes this explicit assumption, that any mathematical truth can be seen to be true by a human being, coming therefore to the apparently inevitable conclusion that humans must somehow be ineffably more capable than computers. He appeals to the indeterminacy of quantum theory for an explanation of how this might be possible. But one need not get so involved with the curious ways of modern physics. Even here the conclusion is not really warranted, if examined carefully. Gödel's result applies to a particular, fixed axiomatic system. Computers are more than axiomatic systems; but, in any case, a far more plausible conclusion from Gödel is that for everybody there are some truths—probably obscure, detailed facts about themselves—which they are inherently unable to grasp fully without in a sense becoming a different person. And then there would be additional new truths which would have the same effect. One could go on forever revealing new oddities to a person and they would continually be surprised, although it is far more likely that their attention would wander pretty soon. In fact, we find Penrose's assumption unlikely: there are almost certainly some truths whose statements are so complicated that no human being could grasp them in full detail, and the Gödel sentences would probably fall into that category. But even if one believed it, this alternative conclusion seems quite reasonable, and is not at all incompatible with the idea of mentality as computation.

A more subtle confusion concerns 'bits.' As Rychlak notes (1991a; pp. 5, 6, 43, 50), Shannon's ideas of information capacity that form the foundation of 'information theory' say nothing of content. This does not mean, however, that something encoded in patterns of bits has no content. When we talk of capacities of containers in terms of gallons, this does not mean that a five-gallon drum can never contain real gasoline. The analogy is exact: Shannon's is a theory of *quantity* of information. The fact that computer memories have information capacities does not render the information stored in them somehow fake or unnatural. The language of information theory is also often applied to biological systems.

Rychlak makes a particularly peculiar error in his insistence that computers are restricted to what he calls Boolean logic, which he characterizes by the use of *exclusive* disjunction. Although the exact form of the 'logic' of the computer's hardware is in fact of no deep significance (as we shall explain below), it is, in any case, usually characterized by *inclusive* rather than exclusive disjunction. This is a very simple point, but let us try to state it clearly. Digital computers are built from electronic circuits whose parts can be in one of two states, typically encoded as voltages. These are often called bits. The computer's circuits can perform many operations on patterns of bits, fundamental among them being Boolean disjunction, so called because, if one regards the bits as truth-values, this operation would encode the logical connective 'or'. This operation has the value 'true' whenever either of its arguments are 'true': it can be described as 'either A or B (or both A and B).' Rychlak attributes deep significance to what he mistakenly believes this operation to be, which is 'either A or B but not both.'

Many of these Boolean operations can be defined as combinations of others, so the choice of one collection over another is only a matter of engineering convenience. Negation and disjunction suffice to define all others, for example. Under this circumstance, to attribute philosophical importance to the choice of one or another kind of logical connective seems rather silly. A metaphor may help here. Consider the idea that we are incapable of truly grasping inorganic chemistry because we are made of organic chemicals; or that we will never fully understand 'green' because our blood corpuscles are red. These 'arguments' are similar in structure to Rychlak's. Whatever the logic of the hardware, it places no particular constraint on the logical structure of the software that is running.

Rychlak seems to think that running a program on a machine forces some characteristic of the hardware onto it, much as pushing plastic through a die forces it into a certain shape. He says (1991a, p. 164) that once a program is running on a machine:

> The two are effectively 'one.' The software is the hardware at this point. This means, in effect, that the hardware must be accommodated as information is processed.

This statement reveals Rychlak's basic mistake. If anything, the opposite is the case: The hardware *is* the software. What happens at the heart of a computer running a program is that the machine takes on the character of—in a sense, becomes—its program. The 'copying' of a basic machine statement into the processor of a computer consists of its circuitry being subtly reorganized to cause changes in the machine's state that reflect the meaning of the statement. Although this often is called 'reading' and 'obeying an instruction,' that is a misleading metaphor, since (as Rychlak notes) the hardware is not reading and cannot *disobey*, any more than one's immune system can. Rather, the hardware, together with the program loaded into its memory, has become a new machine, one whose behavior is specified more by the software than by the naked circuitry.

The behavioral repertoire of a computer-plus-program may be different from that of the simple processor buried within it. A wide variety of programs with widely differing logical, behavioral and computational structures can all run on the same computer. This makes any argument from the nature of the machine to the nature of the whole system of machine-plus-program rather precarious.

Rychlak and Searle place enormous importance on a sharp conceptual distinction between soft, *formal* program and hard, *causal* machine; but it is increasingly difficult to make this precise in the real world. For example, one class of current processor chips includes within them a memory containing program fragments, and an inner, smaller processor that interprets them, with this entire system being realized in silicon. Is this hardware or software? The nature of programs, even in the straightforward sense in which, say, word-processing programs are sold in supermarkets these days, stretches the conceptual framework that we have available for describing them. Is a program a text that should be copyrighted or a mechanism that should be patented? It is neither: It is a new kind of entity, for which new laws are being written. Even the technical jargon has been extended to such terms as 'firmware' and 'virtual machine' because of the recognized conceptual inadequacy of the simple soft/hard, program/machine distinctions. A machine such as a Macintosh™ has many layers of program interpretation between the behavior which is observed by a user and the organization of its basic hardware, and many of these are only loosely related with one another.

The relation between a computer's hardware and the machine code 'instructions' in its memory is of a kind described in computer science as that between an interpreter and its program. It is a very special and simple case of this relation, however, and there are many of them inside a real machine. These form levels in which the processor at a given level is itself made of a processor and a 'program' at the level below. The higher levels of a system are rarely isomorphic, or even similar, to the structure of lower levels of a system. Higher-level interpreted structures need not be at all like lists of instructions. They might, for example, comprise networks of concepts, or databases of complex assertions, or systems of pictorial arrays; and the process of interpreting them might involve traversing links of a network, or consist of processes of searching among logical conclusions, or detecting perceptually plausible patterns in pictures.

The unwarranted (and usually implicit) assumption that there ought to be similarity of structure among the various levels of organization of a computational system leads to great confusion. Any complex computational model will have many levels of such description, all equally valid. A full account of the machine's behavior will probably in practice require a description at several levels, but no simple reduction to a single level of rule matching will suffice, and certainly the basic hardware level will not be suitable for understanding the complexity of the machine's behavior. There is no mystery here: similar points can be made for any other device or object. The functioning of the human brain is presumably fully determined by biochemical events, but this does not eliminate the value of psychology. The point amounts to little more than a rejection of reductionism—with which we expect that Rychlak would concur.

One common response to this is to say that however complex the systems programmed in the machine, they still can be only simulations of something real. Searle draws a sharp distinction between 'strong' AI—the idea that a programmed computer might actually have cognition—and 'weak' AI, the thesis that it might simulate cognition, even simulate it accurately. He ridicules the confusion between these ideas by asking whether a weather-simulation program will cause rain to fall inside the computer. But this misses a crucially important aspect of computation: A simulation of a virtual machine is exactly an implementation of one. Higher-level computations are indistinguishable from 'simulations' of them.

A simulation of, say, this word-processing program (which runs on a Macintosh) on a IBM machine would consist exactly of a system of data structures and algorithms which modeled the behavior of that machine: a software implementation of one computer on another. Such programs are in fact commercially available. Are they simulations or implementations? The question is meaningless. A computational simulation of a computation *is* a computation.

3.   APPEALS TO INTUITION PUMPS: RYCHLAK'S ROOM

The only argument that Rychlak gives us for the limitations of computers is a version of Searle's (1980) famous Chinese Room. In the decade since its first appearance, Searle's fable has been discussed far too often for a complete survey to be given here, however, we will simply point out that it is also based on naive and mistaken intuitions about computers and programs. The chief of these is the identification of the agency in a computational model with the hardware of the machine running the program.

Searle asks us to take a program that is supposed to understand Chinese—it could be any AI program which is claimed to somehow demonstrate cognition—and put a listing of it in a room with someone who can follow the program text, but cannot understand Chinese (or lacks the cognitive skill that the program is intended to exhibit). Now, have a panel of Chinese speakers send 'inputs' to this room and let the man in it 'run' the program by reading through it and doing whatever it says. This could involve matching shapes with one another, but the man does this purely on the basis of their form, with no grasp of what they might mean. Eventually, the program listing tells him to 'output' some Chinese squiggles—these seem like a sensible response to the Chinese observers outside the room. In this way, the room passes a Chinese Turing test: But clearly, as Searle asks us to agree, no understanding is taking place.

After all, the program listing cannot be understanding anything (it's just a pile of paper); and by hypothesis, the man knows no Chinese; and there is nothing else in the room. Searle insists that this hypothetical situation is exactly analogous to a computer running a program. The hardware understands nothing, and the program merely specifies a formal matching of patterns with one another.

Dennett (1984) has pointed out that the Chinese Room is an intuition pump rather than an argument, and Rychlak agrees (1991a, pp. 3-4). In his own discussion of Searle's allegory, Rychlak usefully introduces a distinction between what he calls 'extraspective' and 'introspective' perspectives: that is, we can look at it either from the point of view of an external observer, looking 'at' the room, or from the man-in-the-room's point of view, looking 'with' the person running the program.

> In Searle's example, our empathy rests with the person caught up within the process of shifting the Chinese figures about. As a result, even when we leave the room to look extraspectively at the exchange of inputs to outputs we are not much impressed with the supposed intelligence being reflected in the 'information process.'

As Rychlak observes, the 'pump' acquires its intuitive force by directing our intuition to identify with the machine's hardware processor rather than the system consisting of a program running on this hardware. Nonetheless, he fails to see that this is simply a mistaken result of having our empathy misdirected by Searle's trick. Two paragraphs later, Rychlak exposes his own state of confusion:

> The essential point is that . . . the machine—which can only be described in an extraspective fashion—gives us the illusion that an introspective process is underway . . . There seems to be a 'point of view' involved when there really is not! Searle's person, mechanically shifting symbols from inputs and outputs without meaningful understanding, is never in a position to express a point of view.

Consider this argument carefully. If a machine can only be described 'extraspectively,' then we should view the computer running the program—that is, the whole room—as the agency having a point of view; and then Searle's intuition pump breaks down. The analogy depends on the Chinese interrogators' having their conversations with the computer running the program, and not its central processor. Rychlak simply *asserts* that the whole system has no point of view. Indeed, Searle's person in his room is not in a position to express a point of view, just as the naked hardware of a Von Neumann computer has no opinions.

But the AI perspective requires no such claim. Computational models of cognition make no assumptions about the intellectual capacities of silicon (or carbon). Rychlak infers that they must, thereby revealing his lack of understanding of how software and hardware are interrelated.

We can use Rychlak's own terminology in drawing a different conclusion. Suppose that a program running on a computer passes some version of the Turing Test (perhaps Chinese conversation) and therefore, we could claim, it must be accorded some kind of cognitive status for the sake of empirical honesty. If Searle's argument were correct, it would follow that to use the introspective perspective on the central processor, in spite of its intuitive force, would be a serious mistake. A computer running a program must be something more than a simple hardware processor in a way that is cognitively significant.

When we adopt Searle's intuition that the processor alone has no understanding, then we have to conclude that the computer running the program is a different machine than the bare hardware. That is exactly the intuition computer science gives us, and which lends credence to the AI research program. Although Searle's argument is crucially flawed, it could be accepted in *modus tollens* rather than *modus ponens* form and be quite consistent with AI. It does not lend any support to Rychlak's own anti-computer prejudice, which is revealed in his dogmatic assertion that a machine can *only* be described in an 'extraspective' fashion (our emphasis). He simply refuses to attribute selfhood to a machine, but he offers us no reasons why we, or any other machines, should agree with him.

4.   ALLEGED INCOMPATIBILITY WITH A FAVORED PSYCHOLOGICAL THEORY OF HUMAN COGNITION

As noted earlier, attacks on AI often take the form of its being perceived as incompatible with some other psychological or neurological theory which is taken as authoritative. For example, Rychlak's central contention is that the computational models of the mind that have been developed in AI and cognitive science are fundamentally incompatible with Kelly's (1955) personal construct theory, and Kelly had it about right. We will spend some time in this paper looking at this claim in detail.

4.1. Personal Construct Theory: The Nickel Tour

Personal construct theory, as formulated by Kelly (1955, 1970) and elaborated by Adams-Webber (1979), is essentially a constructivist model of human representational processes that incorporates several hypotheses concerning the development and organization of cognitive functions. The basic units of analysis in this model are bipolar dimensions termed 'personal constructs,' which Kelly (1955, p. 8) viewed as templets that a person 'creates and then attempts to fit over the realities of which the world is composed.'

His theory implies that, in so far as the principle that governs human cognition lies in the 'mind' and not in external events, it consists of our intention to enhance the correspondence between certain of our mental representations and our future experience (cf. Adams-Webber 1989). Thus, the basic function of our representational processes is anticipation (Adams-Webber and Mancuso 1983). We use bipolar constructs to represent perceived similarities and differences among events, and then organize these representations into coherent patterns or 'contexts' within the framework of which we are able to detect certain recurrent themes in our experience over time, and then feed these representations forward in the form of expectations about future events. The perception of new events constitutes an ongoing validational process that serves to confirm or disconfirm many of our anticipations. As a result, our constructs may undergo progressive adaptations as they are revised in the light of experience. Specific changes in either the structure or content of our personal constructs occur primarily in response to predictive failure or 'surprise' (Adams-Webber 1989).

Every construct is assumed to have a specific 'range of convenience,' comprising all those things to which the user would find its application useful.' Accordingly, the range of convenience of each construct defines its 'extension' in terms of a single aspect of a limited domain of events. On the other hand, a particular construct seldom, if ever, stands alone in our experience, as it is usually deployed together with one or more other related constructs in establishing a specific 'context' for interpreting and predicting events. Indeed, a necessary condition for organized thought is some degree of overlap between constructs in terms of their respective ranges of convenience. This overlap, or intersection, between the current extensions of our constructs enables us to formulate 'hypotheses'. That is, in interpreting an event we essentially categorize it in terms of one or more constructs, and then by reviewing our networks of related constructs, we can derive predictive inference from our initial categorization. It is this predictive function of personal constructs that provides the logical rationale for Kelly's (1955, p. 46) assertion that 'a person's processes are psychologically channelized by the ways in which he anticipates events.' As elaborated by Ford (1989, p. 190):

> We humans frequently anticipate the occurrence or nonoccurrence of future events based on our willingness to project observed uniformities into the future. Thus, we continually glide from the past into the future with our previous experience preceding us— illuminating and organizing the manner in which subsequent events will be manifest to us.

4.2.   Kant and Kelly: Does Rychlak Get It Right?

It is important for us to distinguish here between Kelly's 'constructive alternativism' and Kantian constructivism because Rychlak tends to mix up these two epistemological positions. For example, he maintains that:

> The word 'construction' leads to confusion today, for it can be given a Lockean or Kantian interpretation. George Kelly used the word in the Kantian sense. (Rychlak 1991a, p. 85)

In a similar vein Slife *et al.* (1991, p. 334) assert that the 'Kantian emphasis in personal construct theory cannot be denied.'

More specifically, Rychlak contends that all human representational processes, as described by Kelly, exhibit 'predication': 'Construing *is* predicting' (Rychlak 1991b, p. 248). Indeed, he tells us repeatedly that 'predication' is simply his new word for Kelly's notion of construal. He also offers his own explicit definition: 'an act of affirming or denying or qualifying broader patterns of meaning in relation to narrower or targeted patterns of meaning.' Thus, Rychlak views predicating as a 'top-down' movement from the general to the particular, a lending of meaning from a larger range of convenience to a smaller one. Therefore, it must always begin with and proceed from relatively high levels of abstraction downwards. It follows logically that even the most elementary and basic perceptions must be constructed through the application of abstract 'categories' to sense impressions. This is basically a neo-Kantian position.

According to Rychlak (1991a, pp. 28-29), 'Kant argued predicationally that ideas are conceptualizing or "constructive" processes that give meaning to the unstructured sensory noise entering from experience.' The empirically given (input) is, in itself, devoid of all form or structure. That is, the Kantian categorical framework, although presupposed by all forms of predication, is in important respects 'discontinuous with empirical facts' (Husain 1983). It follows that, at the highest levels of abstraction, the most fundamental 'categories' of meaning (e.g. space, time, unity) must be *a priori* (i.e. independent of experience), and that their function must be essentially epistemological (i.e. they impose structure and form on all of the objects of human experience). In Rychlak's own words:

> Kant suggests that human beings are equipped with a priori categories of the
> understanding that predicate experience from the outset. On Kant's model, the
> representations in mind would be 'produced' by the precedent (a priori) categories rather
> than by the a posteriori shapings of the environment. (Rychlak 1991b, p. 63)

These Kantian categories can be applied only to something that is unformed and
unstructured in an absolute sense—chaotic sensory data (cf. Husain 1983). As
Miles (1986, p. 172) puts it, 'there is implicit in empirical science an *a priori*
structure which provides a reference frame without which empirical
investigation would itself be impossible' (cf. Ewing 1939).

> Kant did not view raw sensations (perceptions, etc.) as packaged units of meaning (ideas).
> Sensory 'inputs' receive the impact of external experience, but there would be no
> knowledge of this contribution made by the external world without the person's act of
> predication via the categories of the understanding—which organizes or pattern the
> entering elements of sensations together to lend them meaning. (Rychlak 1991a, p. 84)

In directly comparing Kelly and Kant, Husain (1983, p. 12) notes that:

> Kant goes to great lengths to show that our a priori constructs are the same for all human
> beings and hence in no sense personal. They are for him necessary and universal. Kelly's
> emphasis on the personal nature of constructs marks him as decidedly un-Kantian.

Moreover, Kelly, in sharp contrast to Kant, proposed that all personal constructs
are of the same general type. Thus, for Kelly, all human cognitive activity is
empirical, and constructs can be applied to anything by a given individual. It
necessarily follows that events have forms and patterns in their own right, prior
to the application of any constructs. For example, Husain (1983, p. 14) points out
that 'the most important of these (forms) is time, which for Kelly, unlike Kant, is
not *a priori* but belongs to the data themselves (i.e. "input").' As the data already
possess form, 'our fundamental constructs will be *a posteriori* and hence
continuous with other empirical hypotheses.' It follows also from the basic
assumptions of Kelly's 'constructive alternativism' that:

> Something must be heterogeneous with bipolarities because only thus can it offer them
> ontological support, something to which they can attach themselves. Hence event is
> presupposed by constructs as a subject term is presupposed by the predicate terms, and
> event as the bearer of all constructs is much more general than any construct. (Husain
> 1983, p. 20)

Let us look more carefully at the term 'predication.' If we understand Rychlak
properly, his point is that the meaning of any construct must be given within a
larger framework, and that it also must involve opposition. Thus, the meaning of
'good' must involve its association with 'bad' and the placement of this
oppositional pair in a larger system of constructs to which it is somehow related.
As he says (Rychlak 1991a, p. 11): 'The good-bad meanings . . . enter *intrinsically*
into each other's meaning. In a sense, they define each other,' and 'it is doubtful
that a person can know the meaning of only one of these bipolar pairings and not

the other.' There are two ideas here: that of intrinsic oppositionality, and that of contextual specification of meaning (i.e. that the meaning of one construct can only be given by considering a larger context in which it is related to other constructs).

Rychlak assumes that computers not only cannot invoke context in this way, but also are unable to reason with opposition (by virtue of what he takes their Boolean nature to be, as explained above). That is, limited by their fundamentally flawed Boolean logic, computers must be only 'mediational,' not 'predicational.' According to Rychlak, 'mediational' refers to a process where 'something which is taken in, or "input" comes indirectly to play a role in a process that was not initially a part of this process.'

On this basis, Rychlak concludes that computers will never reason with predication—that is, with bipolar opposition, and thus we will never find useful models of Kellyan psychology in the artificial intelligence or information-processing literature. In summary, on the grounds of the computer's inherently nonpredicational nature, it would follow that those of us in the AI community who are trying to implement Kellyan models of construing on computers (Boose 1984, 1985, Ford 1989, Ford *et al*. 1992, Ford *et al*. 1991a, Ford *et al*. 1991b, Gaines and Shaw 1986, 1991, Shaw and Woodward 1990, Yager *et al.* 1992) are simply wasting time and resources.

4.3. Construction Relations: Intentional vs. Extensional

Rychlak, of course, is right that Kelly (1955, p. 137) viewed the bipolarity of constructs in terms of contrariety rather than mere contradiction, 'The relationship between the two poles of a construct is one of contrast . . . (i.e. we consider the contrasting end of a construct to be both relevant and necessary to the meaning of the construct).' It follows that the opposite poles of a construct are each 'positive' in their own right (see Benjafield 1983).

Husain (1983, pp. 16-18) notes further that:

> The definition of bipolarity as relevant contrast, as contrast that is necessary to the meaning of a construct, is intentional . . . When a construct is defined intentionally, its complete definition involves three terms: the generic nature (e.g., gender) and the bipolar opposites into which it differentiates (e.g., male/female) . . . [It follows that relations between constructs cannot be handled by means of a binary logic because] to use a binary logic is in fact to drop the third (generic) term, the underlying generic nature from consideration and to treat bipolar contrast as if it could occur and be meaningful in isolation.

Nonetheless, this is precisely what Kelly, himself did: He applied binary logic to the problem of operationally defining construct relations which led him to assert that these relations are 'hierarchical' in nature. Husain makes this quite clear in the following footnote (1983, p. 18):

> Kelly (1955) does not always hold to the intentional definition of constructs. He often switches to an extensional definition, that he hopes will make a binary logic applicable to constructs. His extensional definition is in terms of similarity and contrast . . . Kelly can apply a binary logic by treating the similarity and the dissimilarity independently of each other, by, in effect, ignoring the third term for the time being.

Kelly's own 'extensional' approach to operationally defining relations between constructs, which provided the logical rationale for Hinkle's (1965) 'implication grid,' and later, Fransella's (1972) 'bipolar implication grid,' simply ignores the issue of intentionality. That is, it does not take into account that constructs are, in terms of their intentional definitions, discontinuous with each other, and therefore, 'subsuming' one construct under another is logically, as well as practically, impossible. Again, as Husain (1983, p. 20) concisely summarizes the problem:

> Natural bipolarities, each of which represents the extremes of differentiation of which a qualitative generic nature is capable, do not stand in a hierarchical system . . . because none of them is inherently of greater or lesser extension than the other.

This basic point of logic completely undermines Rychlak's argument that 'Kelly (1955a) virtually defined predication when he observed, "The subordinate systems are determined by the superordinate systems into whose jurisdiction they are placed" (p. 78)' (Rychlak 1991b, p. 243). As Husain (1983) notes, Kelly did not provide a single example of one construct 'subsuming' another (indeed, he could not, because this is not logically possible).

In strictly operational terms, we can technically skirt this logical problem by defining constructs only extensionally, that is, in terms of specific sets of elements, which themselves are, by definition, of greater or lesser extension. This, of course, was what Kelly (1955) himself does in assuming that each construct has a specific 'range of convenience' which can vary from one individual to another, or even for the same individual over time. This approach can be used to produce temporary operational definitions of constructs in personal use in order to locate 'constellations' based on correlations in the patterns of usage of different constructs by the same individuals, for example, in repertory grid data. This is essentially a statistical, rather than a logical method of defining relations between constructs.

Nonetheless, Adams-Webber (1979) has demonstrated that we can, in principle, operationally define the logical relation between the extensions, or 'ranges of convenience,' of any two constructs in terms of Boolean algebra. For example, 'the range of convenience of construct A constitutes a subset of the range of convenience of construct B, or 'the ranges of convenience of A and B are mutually exclusive.' Such relations can be represented by simple Venn diagrams, or easily translated into logical propositions of the form 'if p then q' (see Ford and Adams-Webber 1992). This approach to determining relations of entailment between personal constructs has been implemented on computers as an integral component of interactive knowledge acquisition tools (e.g. *Nicod*, see Ford *et al*. 1991a, and ICONKAT, see Ford *et al*. 1991b).

5.   DISCUSSION: AI AND PSYCHOLOGY

We will now leave Rychlak for the moment and broaden our scope to consider the general relationship between AI and psychology. Why does (or should) AI care about compatibility with psychological theories; that is, what if Rychlak were right? Do AI researchers labor under what Glymour (1987) has termed an 'anthropocentric' constraint? In other words, must our intelligent artifacts work, either psychologically or biologically, like we do? Conversely, what contribution, if any, can AI research make to psychology? What benefits might be gained through an interchange of ideas and techniques between researchers in these two highly complex and fragmented areas of study?

5.1.   On Why AI and Cognitive Psychology Are in the Same Boat

There seems to be a recurrent suspicion that AI and psychology have much in common; and in fact, enjoy a relationship of substantial (and increasingly) mutual facilitation and cross-fertilization. More specifically, AI and psychology have been linked by their recent escapes from non-representational pasts: cybernetics and behaviorism respectively. For much of the first part of this century, the approved vocabulary for psychological theorizing was behavioral, strictly eliminating talk of beliefs, desires and intentions. Nonetheless, psychology is concerned not only with overt behavior, but also with experience, including our everyday conscious acts of interpreting and anticipating events, and, by the mid-1960s cognitive psychology and the computational metaphor were emerging as the dominant paradigm. The basic idea underlying computational psychology is that what brains do may be usefully thought of at some level as a kind of computation.

A central presupposition of a majority of cognitive psychologists, and a necessary assumption for those engaged in AI, is the pragmatic utility of constructing models in which 'cognitive' functions are defined independently of any descriptions of their 'neural' substrate (i.e. 'wetware'). Representationalists of all stripes insist on the importance of states of mind, or for that matter machine, that represent states of the world (Fodor and Pylyshyn 1988). In the long run, both cognitive psychology and AI depend on this posited functional 'causal decoupling' between the lower implementation (biological) levels of description and the cognitive or psychological levels of description (similar to the relation between genetics and the underlying chemistry). From this perspective, AI is highly invested in the future of cognitive psychology, if for no other reason than that they share a common fate. If it turns out that intelligence cannot be usefully studied apart from its implementation, then cognitive psychology will become a rather uninteresting endeavor focusing solely on those aspects of human cognition still open to biological speculation, and even then, only until biology pins down what is 'really' going on.

Let us engage in a relevant thought experiment. Imagine a world in which the agenda of biology (neuroscience in particular) has been completed and all of the mechanisms of the human brain are well understood (much as computer hardware is well understood). Furthermore, suppose (as unlikely as this might seem) that this body of knowledge can explain adequately all behaviors now seen in reflecting 'cognition' without resorting to a psychological level of description. In such a world, the aforementioned decoupling would not exist and cognitive psychology as we view it today might have fallen into desuetude. In fact, some would claim that this process is already well underway, pointing to the reemergence of neurally motivated approaches to AI, as well as the increasing number of cognitive psychologists placing their bets on anticipated breakthroughs in the rapidly expanding field known as 'cognitive neuroscience.'

What effect would this hypothesized dissolution of psychology, and triumph of 'reductionism,' have on AI as we now know it? It seems reasonable to expect that AI would either be relegated to history's dustbin of interesting, but no longer useful, language games; or perhaps it would evolve into a branch of engineering, wiring-up brain-like structures. Thus, the future prospects of classical AI, and probably those of all other forms of cognitive science (including most of psychology), depend on our world's not being of the kind we hypothesized above, that is, their integrity as independent disciplines requires the core assumption that there is a useful level of discourse at which descriptions of 'cognitive' functions cannot be translated adequately by means of reducing sentences into descriptions of observable 'neural' events, despite our having found many interesting correlations between descriptions at different levels of analysis.

From the specific perspective of Kelly's construct theory, the crucial point is that events, in-and-of-themselves, are neither 'cognitive,' nor 'neurological' (nor 'economic,' nor 'political,' etc.). That is, events do not inherently belong to any particular way of construing them, and no single interpretation of an event is somehow more 'real' than another. Cognitive psychology, neuroscience, economics, and political science are a few of the many conceptual tools that people have developed for predicting and controlling events. Each of these disciplines has a certain degree of logical coherence and pragmatic utility within its own range of convenience. None of them can be completely 'subsumed by' or 'reduced to' one or more of the others, nor can any of them pre-empt the 'whole truth' about a given event. Thus, the same event might be interpreted usefully as having certain neurologic, cognitive, economic and political implications. For example, if the head of a major government suddenly were to suffer a 'stroke,' a host of eminent neuroscientists, cognitive psychologists, economists and political scientists, among other 'experts,' might be called upon to analyze the current situation and risk making predictions, some of which may prove to be far more useful than others. This functional perspective on the conduct of inquiry, known as 'constructive alternatism' (Kelly 1955), affords ample room in semantic space for cognitive scientists, in general, to construct computational models of mental representations without worrying about the so-called 'mind-body problem'; and also for the AI community to implement various forms of machine cognition without prejudice with respect to their potential long term utility.

Let us return now to Rychlak, who is clearly a representationalist, but no fan of cognitive science or AI. He claims (1991b, p. 247) that cognitive modeling is merely an uncritical gear-shift away from Skinnerian stimulus-response theories. Although the old (behaviorist) and new (cognitive) psychologies have little in common, they share the goal of providing scientific explanations/descriptions of psychological phenomena. Rychlak's humanistic sensibilities are offended both by behaviorist and cognitive descriptions. However, Rychlak notwithstanding, psychology and AI should be friends, because like it or not, we are in the same boat, and it may be the last boat afloat when it comes to reconciling a strictly biological view of people (non-mystical) with the subjects of study in psychology (beliefs, intentions and meanings). Psychologists like Rychlak who reject all computational models of mind may have jumped out of psychology's last boat to a science of mind (i.e. a scientific and yet essentially non-biological description of psychological phenomena) and into the murky waters of mysticism.

5.2.   AI, Psychology, and the Anthropocentric Constraint

It is one thing for us to observe that AI is in the same boat with cognitive psychology (thereby sharing its fate), but it is quite another task to specify the nature of the relationship between the shipmates.

AI researchers may reasonably entertain little hope of the engineering community's creating a truly 'brain-like' (i.e. a sort of artificial brain embodying all the relevant aspects of real brains) computer; thus, we are left with no choice but to exploit an alternative, 'non-biologically-interpretable' implementation (i.e. a computer) as the material basis for our efforts toward machine intelligence. Our exertions directed at the instantiation of feasible cognitive architectures will be implemented on computing devices physically quite different, like it or not, from brains. Consequently, the aforementioned causal decoupling is necessary for any realization of successful AI (almost by definition). Instead of neurologic plausibility, we in AI should concern ourselves with functional plausibility at the cognitive level. From this perspective, cognitive psychology may eventually prove to be of crucial importance to AI.

There is another issue here. We have assumed so far, as does Rychlak, that the aim of all cognitive scientists is essentially to understand how existing 'natural' minds work and/or to build artificial ones that operate in the same way. In contrast, many workers in AI have a much more practical orientation: Their objective is to make mechanical intelligences—not to understand the normal, adult mind. In fact, they feel no more constrained, or for that matter aided, by psychology (or neuroscience) than do engineers feel the need to make calculators perform division in the same way as humans do. That is, AI need not feel bound by Glymour's anthropocentric constraint.

Let us be clear, although a pragmatic stance may free AI from the anthropocentric constraint (i.e. computers must do it like we do), it does not diminish our dependence on the necessity of the posited causal decoupling between the biological and cognitive/psychological levels of description. Consider the calculator example, although designers are free to implement division in any manner they see fit, it is still division that they are implementing. Were division a process that could only arise in a biological brain (i.e. no causal decoupling) then there would be no hope of building machines that do division. At this point some are likely mumbling, 'calculators do not *really* divide, but merely simulate division' (see Section 2).

Further, even for those with a strict engineering orientation, humans can be viewed as an existence proof of the possibility of intelligent machines.

Psychological descriptions of human behaviors and experiences that are evaluated as reflecting 'intelligence' can also suggest operational goals for the AI community. For example, human performances identified as 'commonsense reasoning' have motivated much AI research, likewise our competence in terms of arithmetic operations (e.g. addition, subtraction, etc.) inspired the design of calculating machines in the first place.

The foregoing argument may have established the possible importance of psychological models of cognition to AI, but of what current value is AI research to those engaged exclusively in cognitive psychology? Several psychologists have attempted to understand human cognitive activities partly in terms of concepts and metaphors imported from efforts toward actual machine cognition in AI (this really bothers Rychlak). Nonetheless, some of this 'new language' has been incorporated directly into precise formal descriptions of cognitive functions devoid of references to constructs employed by neuroscientists, or alternatively, without resorting to either mystery mongering or hand-waving. Cognitive psychology is now replete with computational metaphors. However, this is not a one-way channel of communication. There is an ongoing dialogue in which various ideas and perspectives continue to bounce back and forth between the disciplines of cognitive psychology and AI, repeatedly borrowing from and stimulating one another.

Consider the idea of 'propositional networks,' with its early roots in psychology. Using this notion originating in psychology, AI researchers develop formalisms (e.g. semantic networks), discover links with various logics and implement computer programs to exercise and test the emerging theory. At this point, these more rigorous constructs are flowing back into psychology to be tested experimentally and elaborated further in the light of theoretically relevant data, for example, some of the new computational models in vision research.

This emerging perspective, becoming known as cognitive science, constitutes an inherently inter/multi/disciplinary undertaking, embracing much of the intellectual programs of several difficult areas: philosophy, psychology and computer science (among others). It is fundamentally distinct from traditional psychology and from biological/neurological approaches to describing cognition. A basic thesis is that computational models (machines) can be used to render at least some psychological theories of cognition more coherent and explicit, while at the same time, researchers engaged in the struggle to build intelligent artifacts (AI) may derive ideas for improving their systems from the results of experiments with human subjects conducted by psychologists.

6.   CODA

We cannot despair of humanity, since we ourselves are human beings.
                                                                    —*Albert Einstein*

Psychology and AI should be friends. We bring different disciplinary regimes to the same subject-matter. Each has something to gain from the other: AI has its subject-matter essentially defined by psychology, and in return offers a new collection of ways to think about this subject-matter, and a new intellectual discipline. As well as fitting empirical data, models must be implementable; they must have sufficient internal detail and precision that they can actually be run on a computer to produce the behavior being described. The significance of this is that the models are, as a result, unprecedented in their richness and detail. But perhaps more importantly, this implementation often reveals new, unexpected properties of the models. Since the behavior is not always predictable from the code, the implementation of complex systems is in many ways an empirical undertaking in its own right.

Let us carefully distinguish our thesis from some possible misunderstandings of it. The claim of the computational metaphor is not that *all* computers have cognitive status: We do not believe that your IBM PC is thinking of Vienna. Nor is it that the human brain is organized like a Von Neumann computer, or that *all* aspects of human behavior are best described in this way. The suggestion is that there is a useful level of description of many aspects of mental life, especially cognitive aspects, which describe the internal processes of the mind as some kind of computation—a processing of meaningful symbolic patterns in which the rules governing the regularities of internal behavior can be stated in terms of the form of these patterns.

We might end by returning to the question of what motivates the new attacks on the computational metaphor. Why do people try to kill off this new discipline with such vigor? It seems often to be a belief that to accede to such a model would be to demean or somehow impoverish our view of ourselves. In response, we believe that on the contrary, the computational metaphor provides a uniquely humanistic view of mankind which is still compatible with the most rigorous perspective on the correctness of physical science. It is the only account we have of how a physical system might use symbols so that their meaning is intimately bound up in its operation, how a mind might inhabit a body. Unlike Rychlak, Searle and Penrose, we rejoice in this view of man as a symbol-processing creature, our brains an enchanted loom of meaning.

7.   REFERENCES

Adams-Webber, J. R. (1979) *Personal Construct Theory: Concepts and Applications* (New York: John Wiley & Sons).

Adams-Webber, J. R. (1989) Kelly's pragmatic constructivism. *Canadian Psychology*, 30: 190-193.

Adams-Webber, J. R., and Mancuso, J. C. (1983) The pragmatic logic of personal construct psychology. In J. R. Adams-Webber and J. C. Mancuso (eds.) *Applications of Personal Construct Psychology* (New York: Academic Press), 1-10.

Benjafield, J. (1983) Some psychological hypotheses concerning the evolution of constructs. *British Journal of Psychology*, 74: 47-59.

Boose, J. H. (1984) Personal construct theory and the transfer of human expertise. *Proceedings of the National Conference on Artificial Intelligence*, Austin, Texas, 27-33.

Boose, J. H. (1985) A knowledge acquisition program for expert systems based on personal construct psychology. *International Journal of Man-Machine Studies*, 23: 495-525.

Dennett, D. C. (1984) *Elbow Room: The Varieties of Free Will Worth Wanting* (Cambridge, MA: Bradford Book of the MIT Press).

Ewing, A. C. (1939) The linguistic theory of a priori propositions. *Proceedings of the Aristotelian Society*, 40.

Fodor, J. A., and Pylyshyn, Z. W. (1988) Connectionism and cognitive architecture: A critical analysis. *Behavioural and Brain Sciences*.

Ford, K. M. (1989) A constructivist view of the frame problem in artificial intelligence. *Canadian Psychology*, 30: 188-190.

Ford, K. M., and Adams-Webber, J. R. (1992) Knowledge acquisition and constructivist epistemology. In R. R. Hoffman (ed.) *The Psychology of Expertise: Cognitive Research and Empirical AI* (New York: Springer-Verlag), 121-136.

Ford, K. M., Bradshaw, J. M., Adams-Webber, J. R., and Agnew, N. (1993) Knowledge acquisition as a constructive modeling activity. *International Journal of Intelligent Systems,* 8 (1): 9-32.

Ford, K. M., Petry, F. E., Adams-Webber, J. R., and Chang, P. J. (1991a) An approach to knowledge acquisition based on the structure of personal construct systems. *IEEE Transactions on Knowledge and Data Engineering,* 3: 78-88.

Ford, K. M., Stahl, H., Adams-Webber, J. R., Cañas, A. J., Novak, J., and Jones, J. C. (1991b) ICONKAT: An integrated constructivist knowledge acquisition tool. *Knowledge Acquisition,* 3: 215-236.

Fransella, F. (1972) *Personal Change and Reconstruction* (London: Academic Press).

Gaines, B. R., and Shaw, M. L. G. (1986) Induction of inference rules for expert systems. *Fuzzy Sets and Systems,* 18: 315-328.

Gaines, B. R., and Shaw, M. L. G. (1991) Basing knowledge acquisition tools in personal construct psychology. Research Rept. No. 91/453/37, Department of Computer Science, University of Calgary, Alberta.

Glymour, C. (1987) Android epistemology and the frame problem: comments on Dennett's 'Cognitive Wheels.' In Z. W. Pylyshyn (ed.) *The Robot's Dilemma: The Frame Problem in Artificial Intelligence* (Norwood, NJ: Ablex), 65-76.

Hinkle, D. N. (1965) The change of personal constructs from the viewpoint of a theory of implications. Ph.D. dissertation, Ohio State University.

Husain, M. (1983) To *what* can one apply a construct? In J. R. Adams-Webber and J. C. Mancuso (eds.) *Applications of Personal Construct Theory* (New York: Academic Press).

Kelly, G. A. (1955) *The Psychology of Personal Constructs* (New York: Norton).

Kelly, G. A. (1970) A brief introduction to personal construct theory. In D. Bannister (ed.) *Perspectives in Personal Construct Theory* (London: Academic Press), 1-29.

Miles, M. (1986) Kant and the synthetic a priori. *University of Toronto Quarterly,* 55: 172-184.

Penrose, R. (1989) *The Emperor's New Mind* (New York: Oxford University Press).

Rychlak, J. F. (1990) George Kelly and the concept of construction. *International Journal of Personal Construct Psychology,* 3(1): 7-19.

Rychlak, J. F. (1991a) *Artificial Intelligence and Human Reason* (New York: Columbia University Press).

Rychlak, J. F. (1991b) The missing psychological links of artificial intelligence. *International Journal of Personal Construct Psychology*, 4(3): 241-249.

Searle, J. R. (1980) Minds, brains and programs. *Behavioral and Brain Sciences*, 3: 417-457.

Shaw, M. L. G., and Woodward, J. B. (1990) Modeling expert knowledge. *Knowledge Acquisition*, 2(3): 179-206.

Slife, B. D., Stoneman, J., and Rychlak, J. F. (1991) The heuristic power of oppositionality in an incidental-memory task: In support of the construing process. *International Journal of Personal Construct Psychology*, 4(4): 333-346.

Yager, R. R., Ford, K. M., and Agnew, N. (1992) A formal constructivist model of belief revision. *International Journal of Expert Systems*, 5 (2): 157-168.

Author Index

Subject Index

About-ness, 16, 37, 44, 64, 98, 175
Analog, 9–11
  analog-to-digital, 188,
  processing, 10–11, 15, 26
  VLSI, 170
ALAN computes successor func-
  tion, 317–321, 325–326
Algorithm, 8, 13–15, 131, 285–287
Alphabet, 8
Analogy, 118, 132
Architecture, 96, 116
  brain, 166–167
  brain–like, 171
  causal, 183
  functional, 159, 165
Aristotelian chemistry, 49–50
Aristotelian elements, 49–50
ART (Adaptive Resonance
  Theory), 83
Artificial brain, 170
Artificial cochlea, 170
Artificial intelligence (AI), 4, 6, 71,
  102, 155, 157, 159, 161–162,
  171, 173–174, 184, 227, 284,
  288, 304, 331, 343, 346, 348–349
  and anthropocentric constraint,
    345, 348
  and psychology (cognitive), 345,
    350
  bashing of, 332
  classical (traditional), 159, 162,
    165, 169, 189, 346
  foundations of, 228
  strong, 91, 97, 140, 174
  strong vs weak, 337
  weak, 96
Artificial life, 190
Artificial luminance, 164–165
Artificial retina, 170
Assembly language, 116–117
Asymmetric dependence theory,
  316, 322

Augmented Transition Network,
  249, 258
Awareness, 18

Back-propagation, 83
Background knowledge, 161
Behaviorism, 4, 7, 98, 147
Berkeley, George, 164
Biology, 15, 98, 193
  Darwinian revolution in, 193
Blake, William, 164
Boolean logic, 335
Boolean operations, 335
BORIS, 229
Brain, 165–167, 169, 189, 281–282,
  337, 348
  as a kind of computer, 169
  as a quantum machine, 282, 301
  brain-in-a-vat, 284
  causal powers of, 139, 142–143,
    232
Brain states, 8, 14, 16, 43, 47, 48, 61
Brentano's problem, 200, 202

c-fibers, 48, 63
Calces, 53–55, 57
Calculator, 11–12
Caloric, 55–56, 62–63
Cartesian Res Cogitans, 153
CASSIE, 246,
Causal powers, 92, 98
  of brain, 92
  of computers, 92
  control powers, 96, 98
Central processing unit (CPU), 139,
  142–144, 147, 155
Chinese gym argument, 169

Chinese Room Argument, 91, 121,
  139–140, 144, 146, 150,
  154–155, 162–163, 165, 167,
  169, 177, 228, 230, 232–234,
  326, 337–338
  and simulation, 181
  as an intuition pump, 337–339
  brain simulator reply, 27
  information processing reply,
    183–184
  perspective shifts and Chinese
    Room Argument, 338
  robot reply, 25–27, 154, 231
  Searle's objection to, 231
  split levels/personalities reply,
    181–182
  systems reply, 24–25, 141, 162,
    177–180, 338
Chomsky, Noam, 233
Church's Thesis, 12, 93, 158,
  234–235, 318,
Church–Turing Thesis, 12, 110, 131
Cognition, 16, 166, 309, 346
  computational theory of, 307
Cognitive science, 6–7, 14, 15, 27,
  37–38, 71–86, 307–308,
  310–311, 318, 326, 333, 346–347
  computational, 4
Cognitivism, 98, 109, 116, 118
  defined, 117
Combustion, 48–50, 52–58
Common sense, 161, 170
Communication, 44, 46, 147–149
Compositionality, 200
Computability, *see* Computation,
  158, 257
Computation, 7–16, 26, 27, 71–75,
  131, 158, 234, 285, 310, 312,
  322, 332, 337
  as rule-governed
    symbol-manipulation, 167
  continuous, 9–10, 15, 74
  digital, 9–11, 14–15